THE
WORKING
WRITER

THE
WORKING
WRITER

TOBY FULWILER
UNIVERSITY OF VERMONT

A BLAIR PRESS BOOK

Prentice Hall, Englewood Cliffs, New Jersey 07632

Library of Congress Cataloguing-in-Publication Data

Fulwiler, Toby
The Working Writer / Toby Fulwiler
Includes Index.
ISBN 0-13-307372-6
1. English language — Rhetoric.   I. Title
PE1408. F82   1994   94-23915
808′.042 — dc20   CIP

Interior design: Anna George
Cover design: Wendy Alling Judy
Cover photo: Jan Riley, Tony Stone Images, Inc.
Buyer: Robert Anderson
Editorial, production, and design supervision: John Svatek

A BLAIR PRESS BOOK

 ©1995 by Prentice-Hall, Inc.
A Simon & Schuster Company
Englewood Cliffs, New Jersey 07632

Printed in the United States of America
10 9 8 7 6 5 4 3 2 1

ISBN: 0-13-307372-6

Prentice Hall International, (UK) Limited, *London*
Prentice-Hall of Australia Pty., Limited, *Sydney*
Prentice-Hall Canada Inc., *Toronto*
Prentice-Hall Hispanoamericana, S.A., *Mexico*
Prentice-Hall of India Private Limited, *New Delhi*
Prentice-Hall of Japan, Inc., *Tokyo*
Simon & Schuster Asia Pte., Ltd., *Singapore*
Editora Prentice-Hall do Brasil, Ltda., *Rio de Janeiro*

This is dedicated to
the one I love.

Preface

This is the best book I've ever written. It's based on the opening rhetorical chapters of *The Blair Handbook*, a 1994 work I coauthored with Alan Hayakawa. The four years it took to write the *Handbook* forced me to articulate clearly—sometimes for the first time—what I most believed about teaching writing. When that collaborative book was done, however, I realized that, in spite of its merits as a comprehensive reference work, it was not a book for everyone. Many instructors, myself included, prefer briefer rhetorics for classroom instruction because briefer works are more portable, personal, and, perhaps, less intimidating to first-year college writers.

So I rethought, rewrote, retitled, and rearranged the rhetorical chapters from *The Blair Handbook* and then reshaped them into the briefer 27-chapter rhetoric now in your hands. And, as you might expect, this reworking has pushed these chapters toward still further clarity. *The Working Writer* includes personal elements not appropriate to a coauthored handbook: more of my own voice, more student voices, more sample papers, more unusual assignments, more encouragement to experiment.

At the same time, this book isn't for all teachers. It is a composing-process book that includes numerous student samples in every chapter, that treats research—including field research—as a regular part of the composing process, that features collaborative and expressive writing assignments, and that emphasizes revision as the secret to better writing. In other words, *The Working Writer* is aimed at instructors who believe student writers profit from a generous amount of ungraded writing; who believe writing is an unpredictable, messy process that can be brought under control by thoughtful revision; who believe that students need to take risks with form, style, and convention in order to grow and develop as writers. Many of the ideas that inform this book come from the current practices of fiction and nonfiction writers alike, whose prose contains careful research on the one hand and lively voices and provocative formats on the other.

In sum, you may find *The Working Writer* especially useful if you ask students to keep journals and to work in collaborative groups; if you teach writing as rewriting, encourage field as well as library research, center your class around student writing, assess the results with portfolios, and have some sense of humor. That, at least, is how I teach and how I have structured this book.

Finally, I would like to acknowledge those who helped make *The Working Writer* work: first, of course, Nancy Perry, my tough-love editor at Blair Press. Next those who reviewed the manuscript with careful and critical eyes: Gay Lynn Crossley, Kansas State University; Ernest H. Johansson, Ohio State University; Fred Kemp, Texas Technical University; and Ronald Shook, Utah State University. And, as always, Laura, Megan, and Annie for their encouragement, patience, and support.

Toby Fulwiler
Essex Junction, Vermont

Brief Contents

Contents

WRITING AND LEARNING

Chapter 1

College Writing

I am the absolute worst writer. I will never forget when I had to write my college essay. I thought it was good and then I brought it downstairs to have my parents read it and they tore it apart. By the time they were finished with it, I had to rewrite it five times. I was so mad, but the weird part was, the final copy was exactly what I wanted to say. They had to tear it out of me.

— JESSICA

I like to write. Writers are nothing more than observant, perceptive, descriptive people.

— PAT

ONE THING YOU CAN COUNT ON — attending college means writing papers. Whether you enroll in a first-year writing class or other courses in the arts and sciences, you'll be asked to write critical essays, research reports, position papers, book reviews, lab reports, essay exams, and sometimes journals. You may have been asked to write similar assignments in high school, so you've had some practice. The quality of writing expected in college will soon put that practice to a test.

This chapter will introduce you, first, to some of the concerns that students customarily have about writing in college and then, second, to some of the reasons why writing is valued so highly in colleges and universities — as well as virtually everywhere else in the modern world.

Recently I asked a group of first-year students to talk about themselves as writers. Several described where they wrote. Amy, for example, said she did most of her writing "listening to classical music and, if it is a nice day, under trees," while Jennifer felt "most comfortable writing on [her] bed and being alone." Others described their attitudes. John said he wrote best "under pressure." Becky, however, preferred writing when she "felt strongly or was angry about something," while Kevin "hated deadlines." In fact, there proved to be as many different ways of being writers as there were students in the class. To continue the conversation about writing, I asked more-specific questions.

WHAT IS SO DIFFICULT ABOUT WRITING?

Even professional authors admit that writing is not easy. In writing this book, I encountered numerous problems, from organizing material to writing clearly to finding time and meeting publication deadlines. What, I wondered, did first-year college writers find difficult about writing? Were their problems similar to or different from mine? Here is what they told me:

JENNIFER: "I don't like being told what to write about."

AMY: "I never could fulfill the page requirements. My essays were always several pages shorter than they were supposed to be."

JILL: "I *always* have trouble starting off a paper . . . and I hate it when I think I've written a great paper and I get a bad grade. It's so discouraging and I don't understand what I wrote wrong."

JOLENE: "I get so bent out of shape because I'm sometimes unsure if I need a comma."

OMAR: "Teachers are always nitpicking about little things, but I think writing is for communication, not nitpicking. I mean, if you can read it and it makes sense, what else do you want?"

MIKE: "If I'm in a bad mood or don't have the right beginning, I find myself stumbling and not giving a hoot about whether it's right or not."

JARED: "I worry about spelling words correctly, and if I don't know how, I will sit and think of some other way to say it so I don't have to look up the word in a dictionary."

KENNON: "Putting the thoughts down on paper *as they are in your mind* is the hardest thing to do. It is like in music — to make the guitar make the sound you imagine in your head, to make the words on the page paint the picture in your head."

I wasn't surprised by these answers, since I, too, remembered writing in college and wondering, What *did* teachers want? How long was *enough*? Where *did* the commas go?

WRITING 1

What do you find difficult about writing? Is it a problem with whom you're writing to? Or being motivated to do it? Or something about the act of writing itself? Explain in your own words by writing fast for five minutes. (This writing is for yourself; you won't have to hand it in.)

WHAT DO YOU ENJOY ABOUT WRITING?

In addition to difficulties with writing, I remembered interesting and exciting times as well, so I asked the first-year students whether there was anything about writing that they enjoyed. Here is what they said:

JOLENE: "If I have a strong opinion on a topic it makes it so much easier to write a paper."

REBECCA: "On occasion I'm inspired by a wonderful idea. Once I get going, I actually enjoy writing a lot."

CASEY: "I enjoy most to write about my experiences, both good and bad. I like to write about things when I'm upset — it makes me feel better."

JOHN: "Letters are the type of writing I enjoy most because it's my own feelings written in my own way to someone who cares nothing about the way the grammar looks."

DARREN: "I guess my favorite kind of writing is letters. I get to be myself and just talk in them."

Here again, I wasn't too surprised. I also prefer to write about topics that inspire or interest me, and I find writing letters especially easy, interesting, and enjoyable.

WRITING 2

What do you most enjoy about writing? Is it what you're writing about? Is it the chance to communicate with somebody? Is there something about the process of doing it that you like?

WHAT SURPRISES ARE IN STORE?

After talking with first-year writers about writing, I asked a class of advanced writers about their experiences with writing. To catch their attention, I asked, "What has surprised you the most about writing in college?" Here is what they said:

SCOTT: "Papers aren't as hellish as I was told they would be before coming to college. In fact, I've actually enjoyed writing a lot of them — especially *after* they were done."

AARON: "I have gone through many changes, and rather than becoming more complex, my style has become more simple."

KERRY: "The most surprising, frustrating, and annoying things have been the different reactions I've received from different professors who read my papers. One professor tells me to write one way, but the next one says, no, write another way. After awhile you just have to learn to trust yourself."

ROB: "I'm always being told to be more concrete, that my writing is superficial, that I come up with good ideas but don't develop them."

JOHN: "The tutor at our writing lab took out a pair of scissors and said I would have to work on organization. Then she cut up my paper and taped it back together a different way. This really made a difference, and I've been using this method ever since."

CHRISSIE: "Sharing papers with other students is oh so very awkward for me, but it's extremely beneficial halfway through the semester when I trust and like my group — it is at this point that I relax enough to talk honestly about one another's papers."

Any surprises here? I was pleased that most of these advanced writers found ways to cope with and even enjoy college writing, that some learned to simplify rather than complicate their writing, and that others reported satisfying and profitable experiences sharing writing with each other. At the same time, I was sorry that some students, even in their last year, could not figure out what some instructors wanted — which, of course, reflects the reality that different audiences will always have different expectations, and it's our job as writers to figure those out.

WHY IS WRITING SO IMPORTANT?

I also asked the advanced writers why they had chosen to enroll in still another writing class when it was not required. In other words, "Why is writing so important to you?"

KIM: "I have an easier time expressing myself through writing. When I'm speaking, my words get jumbled — writing gives me more time, and my voice doesn't quiver and I don't blush."

RICK: "Writing allows me to hold up a mirror to my life and see what clear or distorted images stare back at me."

GLENN: "The more I write, the better I become. In terms of finding a job after I graduate, strong writing skills will give me an edge over those who are just mediocre writers."

AMY: "I'm still searching for meaning. When I write, I feel I can do anything, go anywhere, search and explore."

AARON: "I'm fascinated with the power of words."

ANGEL: "I feel I have something to say."

I found myself agreeing with virtually all of these reasons. At times writing is therapeutic, at other times it helps clarify our ideas, and at still other times it helps us get and keep jobs.

WRITING 3

Look over the various answers given by the advanced writers, and select one with which you especially agree. Explain why this aspect of writing is important to you, too.

WHAT CAN YOU LEARN FROM THE
ADVANCED WRITERS?

Since the advanced writers seemed to enjoy talking about writing, I asked them to be consultants and to offer advice to first-year college students. Here are their suggestions:

AARON: "Get something down!! The hardest part of writing is starting. Forget the introduction, skip the outline, don't worry yet about a thesis — just blast your ideas down, see what you've got, then go back and work on them."

CHRISTA: "Plan ahead. Although it sounds very dry, planning can make a writing assignment easier than doing laundry."

VICTOR: "Follow the requirements of the assignment to a T. Hand in a draft for the professor to mark up, then go and rewrite it. Do exactly what is asked, and remember to speak simply — the simpler the better."

ROB: "Never take anything for granted. Hand in everything on time. Proofread, check your spelling."

ALLYSON: "Don't think every piece you write has to be a masterpiece. Sometimes the writing you think is the worst turns out to be the best. Don't worry so much about what the professor says, just worry about how you feel about what you said."

CHRISSIE: "Imagine and create, never be content with just retelling something. And never be content with your first telling. Dive into the experience deeply and give the reader something to dream about."

RICK: "When someone trashes your writing, thank them and listen to their criticism. It stings, but it helps you become a better writer."

JASON: "Say what you are going to say as clearly and as straightforwardly as possible. Don't try to pad it with big words and fancy phrasing."

ANGEL: "Read for pleasure from time to time. The more you read, the better you write — it just happens."

KIM: "When choosing topics, choose something that has a place in your heart. It will be enjoyable to read because it came from within you and wasn't just translated through you."

These are pretty good suggestions to any writers: start fast, plan ahead, plan to revise and edit, listen to critical advice, consider your audience, be clear, read a lot. I hope, however, that instructors respond to your writing in critically helpful ways and don't "trash" it or put it down. At the same time, whether or not you take some of the advice will depend on what you want from your writing: Good grades? Self-knowledge? Personal satisfaction? Clear communication? A response by your audience? When I shared these suggestions with first-year students, they nodded their heads, took some notes, and laughed — often with relief.

WHAT ELSE DO YOU WANT TO LEARN
ABOUT WRITING?

Realizing that the first-year college writers already had twelve years and more of "good advice" about learning to write, I asked them one more question: "What do you want to learn about writing that you don't already know?" Here are their questions:

JOLENE: "How do I develop a faster way of writing?" (See Chapter 7, "Inventing and Discovering.")

AMY: "Is there a trick to making a paper longer without adding useless information? (See especially Chapter 22, "Limiting and Adding.")

SAM: "How do I learn to express my ideas so they make sense to common intelligent readers and not just to myself?" (See Chapters 5, "The Writer's Audience," and 21, "How Writers Revise.")

MIKE: "I want to learn to talk to people comfortably with pen and paper." (See especially Chapters 4, "The Writer's Purpose," and 5, "The Writer's Audience.")

SCOTT: "How can I make my writing flow better and make smooth transitions from one idea to the next?" (See Chapter 26, "Editing and Publishing.")

KENNON: "The more I write, the more I expect to learn about myself — will college assignments let me do that?" (See Chapters 8, "Keeping a Journal," and 10, "Recounting Experience.")

TERRY: "How can I learn to like to write, so I won't put off assignments until the last minute?" (See Chapter 3, "How Writers Write," and the rest of the chapters in Part II.)

JENNIFER: "I have problems making sentences *sound* good. Can I learn to do that?" (See Chapter 26, "Editing and Publishing.")

BRETT: "I hope to learn to write on and on without stopping, always making it better." (See Chapter 21, "How Writers Revise.")

JOHN P.: "I would like to develop some sort of personal style so when I write people know it's me." (See Chapter 6, "The Writer's Voice.")

JOHN K.: "How can I become more confident about what I write down on paper? I don't want to have to worry about whether my documentation is correct or references are right." (See Chapter 19, "Writing with Sources.")

WOODY: "Now that I'm in college, I would like to be challenged when I read and write to think, to ask good questions, and to find good answers." (See Chapter 2, "College Reading.")

PAT: "I don't want to learn nose-to-the-grindstone, straight-from-the-textbook, hard-assed rules. I want to learn to get my mind into motion and pencil in gear." (See Chapters 3, "How Writers Write," and 7, "Inventing and Discovering.")

HEIDI: "I would love to increase my vocabulary. If I had a wider range of vocabulary, I would be able to express my thoughts more clearly." (See Chapters 2, "College Reading," and 26, "Editing and Publishing.")

JESS: "I'm always afraid that people will laugh at my writing. Can I ever learn to get over that and get more confident about my writing?" (See Chapters 3, "How Writers Write," and 9, "Sharing and Responding," and be sure that you write what you believe and know.)

I can't, of course, guarantee that by reading and studying *The Working Writer*, your writing will get easier, faster, longer, clearer, or more correct. Or, for that matter, that your style will become more personal and varied, or that you as a writer will become more confident and comfortable. No textbook can do that for you. Learning to be a better writer will depend on your own interest, attention, and self-discipline. It will also depend on the college you attend, the classes you take, and the teachers with whom you study. Actually, whether you read *The Working Writer* for class or on your own, if you read it carefully and practice its suggestions, you will find possible answers to all the questions posed by my first-year students — and many more.

I admit that there was at least one concern for which I really had no good response. Jessika wrote, "My biggest fear is that I'll end up one semester with four or five courses that all involve writing and I'll die." Or maybe I do have a response: if you become fast, clear, comfortable, and competent as a writer, you'll be able to handle all the writing assignments all your instructors throw your way. Even if you can't, Jessika, you won't die. It's just college.

SUGGESTIONS FOR WRITING AND RESEARCH

Individual

1. Interview a classmate about his or her writing experiences, habits, beliefs, and practices. Include questions such as those asked in this chapter as well as others you think may be important. Write a brief essay profiling your classmate as a writer. Share these profiles with classmates. (For additional help in writing profiles, see Chapter 11.)
2. Over a two-week period, keep a record of every use you make of written language. Record your entries daily in a journal or class notebook. At the end of two weeks, list all the specific uses as well as how often you did each. What activities dominate your list? Write an essay based on this personal research in which you argue for or against the centrality of writing in everyday life.

Collaborative

As a class or small group project, design a questionnaire about people's writing habits and attitudes. Distribute it to both students and faculty in introductory and advanced writing classes as well as classes in other disciplines. Compile the results to compare and contrast the ideas of writers at different levels and disciplines. Write a feature article for your student newspaper or faculty newsletter reporting what you found.

Chapter 2

College Reading

*Now that I'm in college, I would like to be challenged when I read
and write, to think, and ask good questions, and find good answers.*
— WOODY

To READ AND WRITE WELL IN COLLEGE means to read and write critically. In
fact, a major goal of most college curricula is to train students to be critical
readers, writers, and thinkers so they can carry those habits of mind into the
larger culture beyond college. What, you may ask, does it mean to be critical?
How does being a critical reader, writer, and thinker differ from being a plain,
ordinary, everyday reader, writer, and thinker?

Being critical in writing means making distinctions, developing interpretations, and drawing conclusions that stand up to thoughtful scrutiny by others. Being critical in reading means knowing how to analyze these distinctions,
interpretations, and conclusions. Becoming a critical thinker, then, means
learning to exercise reason and judgment whenever you encounter the language of others or generate language yourself.

Most of *The Working Writer* explores strategies for helping you become
an accomplished critical writer. This chapter, however, explores strategies for
helping you become a more accomplished critical reader and emphasizes as
well the close relationship between critical reading and critical writing.

WRITING 1

Describe yourself as a reader, answering some of these questions
along the way: How often do you read on your own? What kinds of
reading do you do when the choice of reading material is up to you?
Where and when do you most commonly do your reading? What is
the last book you read on your own? Who is your favorite author?
Why?

READING TO UNDERSTAND

Before you can read critically, you need to understand what you're reading. To understand a text, you need to know something about it already. It's virtually impossible to read and understand material that is entirely new. You need to understand enough of the text and its ideas to fit them into a place in your own mind where they make sense and connect with other information you already know. The following example will explain what I mean.

Reading Field Hockey

Have you ever watched a game for which you did not know the rules? Not long ago I saw a field hockey game for the first time, and for much of the game I was fairly confused. Players ran up and down a field swinging bent sticks at a little rubber ball. I guessed — because I knew something of other field games like soccer — that the objective was to drive the ball down the field with a stick and hit it into the opponent's net. But I didn't understand why the referee blew her whistle so often, or why the team lined up different way at different times, or what the offensive and defensive strategies were.

In other words, I saw the same game as many fans around me, but I understood less of it. I was unable to "read" it because I had do little prior knowledge. However, the more I watched, the more I began to learn. Even though field hockey was new to me, I began to make associations with what I knew about similar games, including ice hockey and soccer. Soon I found myself making predictions based on this associational knowledge, and many of these proved to be correct. I predicted, for instance, that when a player hit the ball in the air instead of along the ground, a whistle would blow, for this was a foul. I learned later that this foul was called "high sticking." The more games I saw, the more I predicted, learned, and understood — about "high sticking," "strikers," "corners," "long and short hits," and the like.

By midseason, I found myself correctly anticipating the referee's calls, second-guessing various offensive and defensive strategies, and understanding the scores. When I was puzzled by something, I also learned who among the other fans to ask for help. I learned to read this strange text, field hockey, by watching the game closely, by comparing it to what I already knew, by asking questions, by making trial-and-error guesses, and by consulting expert sources.

By season's end, I cheered good plays and shook my head at bad ones. I applauded certain coaching strategies but questioned (quietly) other ones. In fact, I began to feel knowledgeable enough about the game to answer other people's questions about what was happening, which reinforced my own sense of expertise and gave me confidence that I had become an expert of a sort. In the end, I actually learned enough not only to comprehend what I saw but to analyze, interpret, and evaluate it as well. I moved, in other words, from a mere watcher to a critical observer of field hockey.

Understanding Field Hockey

Let's look again at the strategies I employed to understand the game of field hockey.

First, I watched the game closely and *identified* what I saw. I looked at the number of players; their uniforms and equipment; the size, shape, and markings on the field; the action as the players ran up and down the field hitting the little rubber ball with their bent sticks; and the pauses, interruptions, cheers, and whistles. I noticed that the field resembled, in size, shape, and surface, a football or soccer field and that at each end was a net-like cage defended by a well-padded player who looked a bit like a goalie in ice hockey.

Second, I *questioned* what I saw. Why did the players line up in certain ways? What infractions caused the whistle to blow? How did they keep score? How long did a game last? Some of these I answered through further observation, and some were answered by other fans.

Third, I *predicted* (hypothesized) about what would happen in the game if my assumptions were correct. I guessed, for instance, that field hockey operated something like ice hockey. I then predicted that whenever the little rubber ball was driven into the opponent's net a score would be recorded.

Fourth, I *tested* my predictions and found that, yes, a score was recorded whenever the ball was driven into the opposing team's net — with some exceptions.

Finally, I *confirmed* my hunches by consulting expert sources and to find out more about the game. For instance, one time when I saw a ball driven into a opponent's net, a score was *not* recorded; I asked why and was told that a penalty had nullified the score. That made sense since the same thing occurs in football, soccer, and ice hockey, but I had not yet learned to recognize what constitutes a penalty in field hockey.

In other words, the more I observed and studied, the more I understood. The more I understood, the more I could assess what I saw, discuss it, and make critical judgments about it.

Reading Written Texts

The same strategies that taught me to "read" field hockey games apply to reading written texts. To understand a text, you need some context for the new ideas you encounter, some knowledge of the text's terms and ideas and of the rules that govern the kind of writing you're reading.

It would be difficult to read Mark Twain's novel *The Adventures of Huckleberry Finn* with no knowledge of American geography, the Mississippi River, or the institution of slavery. It would also be difficult to read a biology textbook chapter about photosynthesis but know nothing of plants, cell structure, or chemical reactions. The more you know, the more you learn; the more you learn, the more careful and critical your reading, writing, and thinking will be.

Many college instructors will ask you to read about subjects that are new to you; you won't be able to spend much time reading about what you already know. To graduate, you've got to keep studying new subjects that require, first, that you understand what you read and, second, that you can critically assess and write about this new understanding. As you move through the college curriculum, you will find yourself an expert reader in some disciplines, a novice reader in others, and neither expert nor novice in the rest — often during the same semester.

If getting a college degree requires that you read one unfamiliar text after another, how can you ever learn to read successfully? How do you create a context, learn a background, and find the rules to help you read unfamiliar texts in unfamiliar subject areas? What strategies or shortcuts can speed up the learning process? Let's consider some strategies for doing this.

Understanding Written Texts

As an experiment, read the following short opening paragraph from an eight-paragraph *New York Times* story entitled "Nagasaki, August 9, 1945." When you have finished, pause for a few moments, and think about (1) what you learned from it, (2) how you learned what you learned, and (3) what the rest of the story will be about.

> In August 1945, I was a freshman at Nagasaki Medical College. The ninth of August was a clear, hot, beautiful summer day. I left my lodging house, which was one and one half miles from the hypocenter, at eight in the morning, as usual, to catch a tram car. When I got to the tram stop, I found that it had been derailed in an accident. I decided to return home. I was lucky. I never made it to school that day.
>
> — MICHAITO ICHIMARU

How did you do? It is possible that your reasoning went something like mine, which I reconstructed here. Note, however, that although the following sequence presents ideas one after the other, that's not how it seemed to happen when I read the passage for the first time. Instead, meaning seemed to occur in flashes, simultaneously and unmeasurably. Even as I read a sentence for the first time, I found myself reading backward as much as forward to check my understanding. Here are the experiences that seemed to be happening.

1. I read the first sentence carefully, noticing the year 1945 and the name of the medical college, "Nagasaki." My prior historical knowledge kicked in, as I *identified* Nagasaki, Japan, as the city on which the United States dropped an atomic bomb at the end of World War II — though I did not remember the precise date.

2. I noticed the city and the date, August 9, and wondered if that was when the bomb was dropped. I *asked* (silently), Is this a story about the bomb?

3. Still looking at the first sentence, a reference to the writer's younger self ("I was a freshman"), I guessed that the author was present at the dropping of this bomb. I *predicted* that this would be a survivor's account of the bombing of Nagasaki.

4. The word *hypocenter* in the third sentence made me pause again; the language seemed oddly out of place next to the "beautiful summer day" described in the second sentence. I *questioned* what the word meant. Though I didn't know exactly, it sounded like a technical term for the place where the bomb went off. Evidence was mounting that the narrator may have lived one and a half miles from the exact place where the atomic bomb detonated.

5. In the next to the last sentence of the paragraph, the author says that he was "lucky" to miss the tram. Why, unless something unfortunate happened to the tram, would he consider missing it "lucky"? I *predicted* that had the author gone to school "as usual" he would have been closer to the hypocenter, which I now surmise was at Nagasaki Medical College.

6. I then *tested* my several predictions by reading the rest of the story — which you, of course, could not do. My predictions proved correct: Michaito Ichimaru's story is a firsthand account of witnessing and surviving the dropping of the bomb, which in fact killed all who attended the medical college, a quarter of a mile from the hypocenter.

7. Finally, out of curiosity, I looked up Nagasaki in the *Columbia Desk Encyclopedia* and *confirmed* that 75,000 people were killed by this second dropping of an atomic bomb, on August 9, 1945; the first bomb had been exploded just three days earlier, on August 6, at Hiroshima.

You'll notice that in my seven-step example some parts of the pattern of identifying/questioning/predicting/testing/confirming occur more than once, perhaps simultaneously, and not in a predictable order. This is a slow-motion description — not a prescription or formula — of the activities that occur in split seconds in the minds of active, curious readers. No two readers would — or could — read this passage in exactly the same way, because no two readers are ever situated identically in time and space, with identical training, knowledge, or experience to enable them to do so. However, my reading process may be similar enough to yours that the comparison will hold up: reading is a messy, trial-and-error process that depends as much on prior knowledge as on new information to lead to understanding.

Whether you read new stories or watch unfamiliar events, you commonly make meaning by following a procedure something like mine, trying to identify what you see, question what you don't understand, make and test predictions about meaning, and consult authorities for confirmation or information. Once you know how to read successfully for basic comprehension, you are ready to read critically.

WRITING 2

In a book you have been assigned to read for one of your courses, find a chapter that has not yet been covered in class. Read the first page of this chapter and then stop. Write out any predictions you have about where the rest of the chapter is going. (Ask yourself, for example, What is its main theme or argument? How will it conclude?) Finish reading the chapter and check its conclusion against your predictions. If your predictions were close, you are reading for understanding.

READING CRITICALLY

How people read depends on what they're reading; people read different materials in different ways. When they read popular stories and magazine articles for pleasure, they usually read not to be critical but to understand and enjoy. In fact, while pleasure readers commonly go through a process similar to the one described in the last section — identifying, questioning, predicting, and testing — they usually do so rapidly and unconsciously. Since such reading is seldom assigned in college courses, whether they go further to confirm and expand their knowledge depends solely on their time, energy, and interest.

When people read college textbooks, professional articles, technical reports, and serious literature, they read more slowly and carefully to assess the worth or validity of an author's ideas, information, argument, or evidence. The rest of this chapter describes the strategies that lead readers from *understanding* texts to *critically* interpreting and evaluating them, paying special attention to the strategies of *previewing, responding,* and *reviewing.*

Although critical reading is described here as a three-stage process, it should be clear that these activities seldom happen in a simple one-two-three order. For example, one of the best ways to preview a text is to respond to it briefly as you read it the first time; as you respond, you may find yourself previewing and reviewing, and so on. But if you're not engaging in all three activities at some time, you're not getting as much from your reading as you could.

Previewing Texts

To be a critical reader, you need to be more than a good predictor. In addition to following the thread of an argument, you need to evaluate its logic, weigh its evidence, and accept or reject its conclusion. You read actively, searching for information and ideas that you both understand and can make use of — to further your own thinking, speaking, or writing. To move from understanding to critical awareness, you plan to read a text more than once and more than one way — which is why critical readers *preview* texts before reading them from start to finish.

To understand a text critically, plan to preview before you read, and make previewing the first of several steps needed to fully appraise the value of the text.

First Questions

Ask questions of a text (a book, an article, a report) from the moment you pick it up. Ask first questions to find general, quickly gleaned information, such as that provided by skimming the title, subtitle, subheads, table of contents, or preface.

- What does the title suggest?
- What is the subject?
- What does the table of contents promise?
- What is emphasized in chapter titles or subheads?
- Who is the author? (Have I heard of him or her?)
- What makes the author an expert or authority?
- How current is the information in this text?
- How might this information help me?

You may not ask these first questions methodically, in this order, or write down all your answers, but if you're a critical reader you'll ask these types of questions before you commit too much time to reading the whole text. If your answers to these first questions suggest that the text is worth further study, you can continue with the preview process.

Second Questions

Once you've determined that a book or article warrants further critical attention, it's very helpful to read rapidly selected parts of it to see what they promise. Skim reading leads to still more questions, the answers to which you will want to capture on note cards or in a journal.

- Read the prefatory material: What can I learn from the book jacket, foreword, or preface?
- Read the introduction, abstract, or first page: What theme or thesis is promised?
- Read a sample chapter or subsection: Is the material about what I expect?
- Scan the index or chapter notes: What sources have informed this text? What names do I recognize?
- Note unfamiliar words or ideas: Do I have the background to understand this text?
- Consider: Will I have to consult other sources to obtain a critical understanding of this one?

In skim reading, you make predictions about coverage, scope, and treatment and about whether the information seems pertinent or useful for your purpose.

Previewing *Iron John*

One of my students has just given me a book called *Iron John*. To find out more about the book, I previewed it by asking first questions and second questions, the answers to which I've reproduced here for illustration.

ANSWERS TO FIRST QUESTIONS

- The title *Iron John* is intriguing and suggests something strong and unbreakable.
- I already know and admire the author, Robert Bly, for his insightful poetry, but I've never read his prose.
- The table of contents raises interesting questions, but doesn't tell me much about where the book is going:

  1. The Pillow and the Key
  2. When One Hair Turns Gold
  3. The Road of Ashes, Descent, and Grief
  4. The Hunger for the King in Time with No Father
  5. The Meeting with the God-Woman in the Garden

ANSWERS TO SECOND QUESTIONS

- The jacket says, "*Iron John* is Robert Bly's long-awaited book on male initiation and the role of the mentor, the result of ten years' work with men to discover truths about masculinity that get beyond the stereotypes of our popular culture."
- There is no introduction or index, but the chapter notes in the back of the book (260–67) contain the names of people Bly used as sources in writing the book. I recognize novelist D. H. Lawrence, anthropologist Mircea Eliade, poet William Blake, historian/critic Joseph Campbell, and a whole bunch of psychologists — but many others I've never heard of. An intriguing mix.

This preview, which took maybe ten minutes, confirmed that *Iron John* is a book about men and male myths in modern American culture by a well-known poet writing a serious prose book in friendly style. Apparently, Bly not only will examine current male mythology but will make some recommendations about which myths are destructive, which constructive.

Previewing is only a first step in a process that now slows down and becomes more time-consuming and critical. As readers begin to seriously preview a text, they often make notes in the text's margin or in a journal or notebook to mark places for later review. In other words, before the preview stage of critical reading has ended, the *responding* stage has probably begun.

Responding to Texts

Once you understand, through a quick critical preview, what a text promises, you need to examine it more slowly, evaluating its assumptions, arguments, evidence, logic, and conclusion. The best way to do this is to *respond*, or "talk back," to the text in writing.

Talking back can take many forms, from making margin notes to composing extensive notebook entries. Respond to passages that cause you to pause for a moment to reflect, to question, and read again, or to say Ah! or Ah ha! At all points of high interest, take notes.

If the text is informational, try to capture the statements that pull together or summarize ideas or are repeated. If the text is argumentative (and many of the texts you'll be reading in college will be), examine the claims the text makes about the topic and each piece of supporting evidence. If the text is literary (a novel, play, or poem), pay extra attention to language features such as images, metaphors, and crisp dialogue. In any text, notice words the author puts in boldface or italics — they have been marked for special attention.

Note what's happening to you as you read. Ask about the effect of the text on you: How am I reacting? What am I thinking and feeling? What do I like? What do I distrust? Do I know why yet? But don't worry too much now about answering all your questions. (That's where reviewing comes in.)

The more you write about something, the more you will understand it. Using a reading journal is a good way to keep your responses together in one place that you can return to when writing an essay or research paper. Write each response on a fresh page and include the day's date, the title, and author. Write any and all reactions you have to the text including summaries, notes on key passages, speculations, questions, answers, ideas for further research, and connections to other books or events in your life. Note especially ideas with which you agreed or disagreed. Explore ideas that are personally appealing. Record memorable quotations (with page numbers) as well as the reasons they strike you as memorable.

The following brief passage from Bly's *Iron John* is an example of a text to respond to.

> The dark side of men is clear. Their mad exploitation of earth resources, devaluation and humiliation of women, and obsession with tribal warfare are undeniable. Genetic inheritance contributes to their obsessions, but also culture and environment. We have defective mythologies that ignore masculine depth of feeling, assign men a place in the sky instead of earth, teach

obedience to the wrong powers, work to keep men boys, and entangle both men and women in systems of industrial domination that exclude both matriarchy and patriarchy. . . .

I speak of the Wild Man in this book, and the distinction between the savage man and the Wild Man is crucial throughout. The savage soul does great damage to soul, earth, and humankind; we can say that though the savage man is wounded he prefers not to examine it. The Wild Man, who has examined his wound, resembles a Zen priest, a shaman, or a woodsman more than a savage.

When you want to critically read a text such as this, do so with pen or pencil in hand. Mark places to examine further, but be aware that mere marking (underlining, checking, highlighting) does not yet engage you in a conversation with the text. To converse with the text, you need to actively engage in one or more of the following activities: probing, annotating, cross-referencing, and outlining. The following sections illustrate full responses for each activity; in reality, however, a reader would use no more than one or two of these techniques to critically examine a single text.

Probing

You probe a text when you raise critical questions and see if you can answer them. *Probing* is, in essence, asking deeper questions than those asked in previewing. What you ask will depend, of course, on your reason for reading in the first place. Here, for example, are the questions I raised about the *Iron John* passage:

- Bly refers to the dark side of men; does he ever talk about the dark side of women? How would women's darkness differ from men's? What evidence for either does he provide?
- Bly suggests that part of men's dark behavior is genetic, part cultural; where does he get this information? Does he think it's a 50/50 split?
- What "defective mythologies" is Bly talking about? Does he mean things like religion and politics, or is her referring to nursery rhymes and folktales?
- Bly generalizes in his opening sentence, "The dark side of men is clear" — in most sentences actually. Will subsequent chapters support these statements or are we asked to accept them on faith?
- I like the dimension Bly makes between "Wild" and "savage" men. Did he coin the terms or are they used pervasively in mythology in the same way? I wonder how sharp the line really is between the two.

Those are five good questions to ask about the passage; however, any other reader could easily think of five or more. These questions are "critical" in the sense that they not only request further information from the book — which all readers need to request — but also challenge the text's terms, statements, and sources to see if they will stand up under sharp scrutiny.

The questions are written in my own language. Using your own words helps in at least three ways: it forces you to articulate precisely; it makes the question *your* question; and it helps you remember the question for future use.

Annotating and Cross-Referencing

Annotating, or talking back to the author in the margins of the text, is an excellent way to make that text your own, a necessary step in understanding it fully. Annotating is easier if you have your own copy of the text — otherwise you can make your annotations on Post-It notes or in a notebook with page numbers marked. As a critical reader, you can annotate the following:

- Points of agreement and disagreement
- Exceptions and counterexamples
- Extensions and further possibilities
- Implications and consequences
- Personal associations and memories
- Connections to other texts, ideas, and courses
- Recurring images and symbols

To move beyond annotating (commenting on single passages) to *cross-referencing* (finding relationships among your annotations), devise a coding system to note when one annotation is related to another and thus identify and locate different patterns in the text. Some students write comments in different colored ink — red for questions, green for nature images, blue for speculations, and so on. Other students use numbers — 1 for questions, 2 for images, and so on.

In *Iron John*, for example, the term "Wild Man" occurs on pages 6, 8–12, 14, and 26–27, in other chapters, and in the title of the book's epilogue. A critical reader would mark all of these. In addition, the related term "Hairy Man" occurs on pages 5, 6, and 11, and so on. In cross-referencing, I noted in the margins when the two terms occurred together.

Outlining

Another way of talking back to a text is *outlining*. This involves simply writing out a condensed version of the opening sentence or topic sentence of each paragraph, capturing its essence, as I did for the two paragraphs from *Iron John*:

1. The dark side of men
2. The Savage Man versus the Wild Man

Of course, two paragraphs are simply a start; outlining ten or more paragraphs provides a real clue to the author's organizational pattern. Once you have outlined an article or chapter, you will remember that text better, be able to find key passages more quickly, and see larger patterns more easily.

WRITING 4

Keep a reading journal for one article, chapter, or book that you are assigned to read this semester. Be sure to write something in the journal after every reading session. In addition, annotate and cross-reference the text as you go along to see what patterns you can discover. Finally, make a paragraph outline of the text. Write about the result of these response methods in your journal. Did they help? Which ones worked best?

To *review* you need both to reread and to "re-see" a text, reconsidering its meaning and the ideas you have about it. You need to be sure that you grasp the important points within the text, but you also need to move beyond that to a critical understanding of the text as a whole. In responding, you started a conversation with the text so you could put yourself into its framework and context; in reviewing, you should consider how the book can fit into your own framework and context. Review any text you have previewed and responded to as well as anything you've written in response — journal entries, freewriting, annotations, outlines. Keep responding, talking back to the text, even as you review, writing new journal entries to capture your latest insights.

Reviewing can take different forms depending on how you intend to use the text — whether or not you are using it to write a paper, for example. In general, when reviewing a text you have to understand what it means, to interpret its meaning, to evaluate its soundness or significance, and to determine how to use it in your own writing.

Reviewing to Understand

Reviewing to understand means identifying and explaining in your own words the text's main ideas. This task can be simplified if you have outlined the text while responding or have cross-referenced your annotations to highlight relationships among ideas. In reviewing to understand, you can reread portions of articles that you previewed, considering especially abstracts, if there are any; first and last paragraphs; and sections entitled "Summary," "Observations," or "Conclusions." In a book, you can reconsider the table of contents, the introductory and concluding chapters, and central chapters that you recognize as important to the author's argument or theme.

Reviewing to Interpret

Reviewing to interpret means moving beyond an appreciation of what the text *says* and building your own theory of what the text *means*. An interpretation is an assertion of what you as a reader think the text is about.

In reviewing to interpret, look over any of your journal entries that articulate overall reactions to the text's main ideas. What did you see in the text?

Do you still have the same interpretation? Also reread key passages in the text, making sure that your interpretation is reasonable and is based on the text and is not a product of your imagination.

If you plan to write a critical paper about a text, it's a good idea to confirm your interpretation by consulting what others have said about that text. The interpretations of other critics will help put your own view in perspective as well as raise questions that may not have occurred to you. Try to read more than one perspective on a text. It is better to consult such sources in this reviewing stage, after you have established some views of your own, so that you do not simply adopt the view of the first expert you read.

Reviewing to Evaluate

Reviewing to evaluate means deciding whether you think the text accomplishes its own goals. In other words, is the text any good? Different types of texts should be judged on different grounds.

ARGUMENTS.   Many texts you read in college make arguments about ideas, advancing certain *claims* and supporting those claims with *evidence*. A claim is a statement that something is true or should be done. Every claim in an argument should be supported by reliable and sufficient evidence.

At the responding stage, you probably started to identify and comment on the text's claims and evidence. In reviewing, you can ask the following questions to examine and evaluate each part of the argument to see whether it is sound:

- Is the claim based on facts? A *fact* is something that can be verified and that most readers will accept without question. (Fact: The title of the book is *Iron John*; the author is Robert Bly; it was published in 1990; the myth of Iron John is found in several ancient folktales that have been written down and can be found in libraries and so on.)
- Is the claim based on a credible inference? An *inference* is a conclusion drawn from an accumulation of facts. (Bly's inferences in *Iron John* about the warrior in modern man are based on his extensive study of ancient mythology. His inferences have a basis in the facts, but other readers might draw other inferences.)
- Is the claim based on opinion? An *opinion* reflects an author's personal beliefs and may be based on faith, emotion, or myth. Claims based on opinion are considered weak in academic writing. (Bly's "dark side of men" is metaphorical and not factual. Some readers would consider it a fair inference based on the savage history of humankind; others would dismiss it as Bly's opinion, based on emotion rather than on facts and careful reasoning.)

All three types of evidence — facts, inference, and opinions — have their place in argumentative writing, but the strongest arguments are those that are based on accurate facts and reasonably drawn inferences. Look out for opinions that are masquerading as facts and for inferences that are based on insufficient facts.

INFORMATIONAL TEXTS.   In reviewing informational texts, like reviewing argumentative texts, you need to make sure that the facts are true, that inferences rely on facts, and that opinions presented as evidence are based on expertise, not emotion. Informational texts don't make arguments, but they do draw conclusions from the facts they present. You must decide whether there are enough reliable facts to justify these conclusions. Consider also whether you think the author is reliable and reasonable: Is the tone objective? Has all the relevant information been presented? Is this person an expert?

LITERATURE.   Literary texts (short stories, poems, and plays) don't generally make arguments, but they do strive to be believable, to be enjoyable, and to be effective in conveying their themes. One way to evaluate literature is to reread journal entries in which you responded to the author's images, themes, or overall approach. Then look through the text again — guided by any annotations you've made — and ask whether you think the author's choices were good ones. Look in particular for repeated terms, ideas, or images that will help you see the pattern of the text as a whole. Evaluating literature is often very personal, relying on individual associations and responses, but the strongest critical evaluations are based on textual evidence.

Reviewing to Write

Reviewing a text to use in writing your own paper means locating specific passages to quote, paraphrase, or summarize in support of your own assertions about the text. When you quote, you use the exact language of the text; when you paraphrase, you restate the text in your own words; when you summarize, you reduce the text to a brief statement in your own words. When you identify a note card that contains a passage to quote, paraphrase, or summarize, make sure that you have recorded the page on which the passage occurs in the text so you can find it again and so you can prepare correct documentation. (See Chapter 19 for advice about using textual sources in your papers.)

READING AND WRITING

Reading and writing, like production and consumption, are two sides of the same coin. When you study one, you inevitably learn more about the other at the same time. The more you attend to the language of published writers, the more you will learn about your own language. The more you attend to your own written language, the more you will learn about the texts you read.

In fact, many of the reading strategies you use to understand and evaluate published texts work equally well when reading your own writing. You can preview, respond to, and review your own or your classmates' writing to gain a critical understanding of your writing and to discover strategies for effective revision.

SUGGESTIONS FOR WRITING AND RESEARCH

Individual

Select a short text. First read it quickly for understanding. Second, read it critically as described in this chapter. Finally, write a short (two-page) critical review of the text, recommending or not recommending it to other readers. (For more detailed information about writing critically about texts, see Chapter 14.)

Collaborative

As a class or in small groups, agree on a short text to read and write about according to the preceding directions. Share your reviews in small groups, paying particular attention to the claims and evidence each writer uses in his or her review. Rewrite the reviews based on the responses in the groups. (For more information about responding to others' texts, see Chapter 9.)

THE WORK OF WRITERS

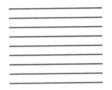

Chapter 3

How Writers Write

Is writing a matter of learning and practice, or are good writers born that way?

– Ross

THIS CHAPTER EXAMINES how writers go about writing, from the time they select something to write about, through their efforts at drafting, revising, and editing, until they send their writing out into the world. It also examines strategies to help writers move more quickly and efficiently through these different stages, commonly called the writing process. Writing, however, is a highly individual activity, so the ideas presented here will not necessarily work in the same way for all writers.

DESCRIBING WRITING AS A PROCESS

Have you ever thought about how you write? What do you do, for example, when you are assigned to write a paper due in one week? Do you sit down that day and start writing the introduction? Or do you sit down but do something else instead? If you don't work on the assignment right away, do you begin two days before the deadline, or is your favorite time the night before the paper is due? Do you write a few pages a day, every day, and let your paper emerge gradually? Or do you prefer to draft it one day, revise it the next, and proofread it just before handing it in?

What writing conditions do you seek? Do you prefer your own room? Do you like to listen to certain kinds of music? Do you deliberately go somewhere quiet, such as the library? Or do you prefer a coffee shop, a café, or a booth at McDonald's?

With what do you write? Your own computer with WordPerfect or MacWrite, or the school's computer with whatever software is available? Your old Smith Corona portable typewriter, or a pencil on pads of lined paper? Or do you write first with a favorite pen and then copy the result onto a computer?

Which of the habits or methods described here is the right one? Which technique yields the best results? There is no right method, no single best way to write. Different people prefer, insist on, and tolerate wildly different conditions and still manage to get good writing done.

While there is no one way to write, there are some ways of writing that seem to work for more people on more occasions than others. On the one hand, writing is and will always remain a complex, variable, many-faceted process that refuses to be reduced to a step-by-step procedure or foolproof formula. On the other hand, people have been writing since the dawn of recorded history, for thousands of years, and during that time some habits and strategies have proved more helpful than others. Learning what these are may save you some time, grief, or energy — perhaps all three.

WRITING 1

Answer the questions posed on the opening pages of this chapter: Where, when, and how do you usually write? What are the usual results?

INVENTION AND DISCOVERY

Sometimes it's hard to separate inventing, drafting, researching, revising, and editing. Many times in writing *The Working Writer*, I sat down to explore a possible idea in a notebook and found myself drafting part of a chapter instead; at other times, when I was trying to advance an idea in a clear and linear way, I kept returning instead to revise a section just completed. While it's useful to separate these several phases of writing when you can, don't worry too much if they refuse to stay separate. In most serious writing, the writing process is recursive — that is, it moves back and forth almost simultaneously and maybe even haphazardly from invention to revision to editing to drafting, back to invention, and so on.

The first phases of writing involve creating, discovering, locating, developing, organizing, and trying out ideas that might become papers, essays, and reports. Writers invent and discover topics and approaches to topics when they make notes, turn casual lists into organized outlines, write journal entries, compose rough drafts, and consult with others. They also invent and discover less deliberately when they walk, jog, eat, read, browse in libraries, converse with friends, or wake up in the middle of the night thinking.

At its beginning, a writing task has an almost unlimited number of ways of being accomplished, so getting started often involves articulating the possibilities, sorting through them, trying some while discarding others. Starting to write also involves limiting those many options, locating the best strategy for the occasion at hand, and focusing energy in the most productive direction.

The invention and discovery phase comes first in the writing process. It also comes second and third. No matter how carefully you develop your first ideas, the act of writing usually necessitates that you keep generating new ideas throughout the writing process as you think about why you are writing, what you are writing, and for whom. For example, when the purpose for writing is not your own, such as when a supervisor requests a report or an instructor makes an assignment, a writer will write to clarify their purpose. When writers want to communicate to someone else but are not sure how their ideas will be received, they often write to themselves first, testing their ideas on a friendly audience.

If you plan to spend time with invention strategies before you start writing, in the long run your writing will be more directed, purposeful, and efficient. Finding ideas is a back and forth process — it starts one place but ends up another; it goes on all the time, as long as writers write, even at the end, when they just want to be proofreading their final draft, but a new idea pops up because they're re-reading and need to use it. This whole messy process can be both wonderful and exhausting. Remember, though, that in the preliminary stages of any writing task, finding and exploring ideas counts more than the neatness or correctness of the language.

While no single invention strategy works all the time or for everybody, you should be able to find some useful techniques in Part III of *The Working Writer*.

Strategies for Invention and Discovery

1. Make invention and discovery writing a first, separate stage in your writing process. You will feel freer to explore ideas and directions for your writing if you compose tentative outlines, take notes, and write journal entries before attending to matters of neatness, correctness, and final form.
2. Plan to play with ideas while you draft, research, revise, and edit. Just as it's important for invention and discovery to be a first, discrete stage, it's also important to continue inventing and discovering as your draft moves toward its final shape.
3. When you begin writing, write out crazy as well as sane ideas. While the wild ones may not in themselves prove useful, they may suggest others that do.
4. When stuck for ideas, try to articulate — in writing or speech — how you are stuck, where you are stuck, and why you think you are stuck. Doing so may help you get unstuck.
5. When searching for direction, *read* to find new information, *talk* to find out how your ideas sound to others, *listen* to the responses you receive, and *keep writing* to test the directions you find.

WRITING 2

Describe the invention strategies you commonly use when you plan a paper or a report. How much do your strategies vary from time to time or assignment to assignment? Now use your favorite strategy for twenty minutes to generate ideas for a paper you have been assigned.

DRAFTING

At some point all writers need to move beyond thinking, talking, inventing, and discovering and actually start writing. Many writers like to schedule a block of time — an hour or more — to draft their ideas, give them shape, see what they look like. One of the real secrets to good and productive writing is learning to *sit down* and stay seated long enough to do this.

You begin drafting when you actually start to write your paper. First drafts are concerned with ideas, with getting the direction and concept of the piece of writing clear. Subsequent drafting — stages called *revising* and *editing* — is concerned with making the initial ideas ever sharper, clearer, and more precise.

While most writers hope their first draft will be their final draft, it seldom happens. Still, try to make early drafts as complete as possible, to compose in complete sentences, to break into paragraphs where necessary, and to aim at a form that might prove final. At the same time, all experienced writers, even those who write good first drafts, allow time for second and third drafts and maybe more.

Strategies for Drafting

1. Sit down and turn on your computer, or place paper in your typewriter, or open your writing notebook and pick up a pen. Once you have done any of these initial acts, your chances of starting your paper increase dramatically. Plan to sit still and write for one hour.
2. Start writing by writing. Do not sit and stare at the blinking cursor or the blank page. Instead, put words and sentences in front of you and see where they lead. Do this for at least fifteen minutes and then pause and see what you've got.
3. Plan to throw away your first page. This simple resolution will take off a lot of pressure, help you relax, and let the momentum of the writing take over. Later, you may even decide to keep some of this page — a clear bonus.
4. Compose in chunks. It's hard to write a whole term paper; it's fairly easy to write a section of it; it's easier still to write a paragraph; it's

a breeze to write a sentence or two. In other words, even large projects start with single words, sentences, and paragraphs.

5. Allow time to revise and edit. Start drafting any writing assignment as soon as you can, not the night before it's due.

WRITING 3

Describe the process you most commonly use to draft a paper. Is your way of starting consistent from paper to paper? Now write the first draft for the paper you planned in Writing 2, using the following basic method: Sit down and for one hour compose as much of the paper as you can, noting in brackets as you go along where you need to return with more information or ideas.

RESEARCHING

Writers need something to write about. Unless they are writing completely from memory, they need to locate ideas and information. Writers conduct research as a natural part of the writing process whenever they pose questions and then go looking for answers. Even personal essays can benefit from additional factual information that substantiates and intensifies what the writer remembers.

As a college student, you do a form of research every time you write an analysis or an interpretation of a text — reading and rereading the text is the research. You do research when you compare one text to another to write a report. You do research to track down the dates of historical events. You do research when you conduct laboratory experiments for geology, visit museums for art history, or interview people in the college community for the school newspaper. Some of this research takes place in libraries and some is conducted in other settings, including where students live.

Whenever you write about unfamiliar subjects, you have two choices: to research and find things out or to bluff with unsupported generalizations. Which kind of paper would you prefer to read? Which kind of writing will help educate you as a learner, writer, and thinker?

Strategies for Writing with Research

1. Consider incorporating research information into every paper you write. For interpretive papers, revisit your texts; for argument and position papers, visit the library. For experiential papers, revisit places and people.

2. Research in the library. Visit the library, look around, hang around, ask questions, and take a tour. The library is the informational cen-

ter of the university; using it well will make all of your writing and learning more substantial.

3. Research people. Interview experts to add a lively and local dimension to your papers. Consider who in your college community can provide current information, ideas, or insider stories to enhance your paper.

4. Research places. Visit settings in which you can find real, concrete, current information. Where appropriate, visit local sites — stores, institutions, streets, neighborhoods, farms, factories, and lakes — to connect local people with your topic.

5. Learn to document sources. Whenever you do research, write down who (the author) said what (an idea or quote), where (publication), and when (date). Then, as needed, look up the specific forms required in specific disciplines.

WRITING 4

Describe the kind of research you have conducted for writing assignments in the past. Now locate additional research information to add to the paper you began drafting in Writing 3, using any research process with which you are familiar.

REVISING

Somewhere in the middle to later stages of writing, writers revise their drafts. Revising involves rewriting to make the purpose clearer, the argument stronger, the details sharper, the evidence more convincing, the organization more logical, the opening more inviting, the conclusion more satisfying.

This book treats revising as separate from editing, yet the two tasks may not always be distinctly separable. Essentially, revising occurs at the level of ideas; editing occurs at the level of the sentence and word. Revising means re-seeing the drafted paper and thinking again about its direction, focus, arguments, and evidence. Editing involves sharpening, tightening, and clarifying the language, making sure that paragraphs and sentences express exactly what you intend.

In writing *The Working Writer*, I revised ceaselessly to get the chapters in the best order and to get each chapter just right. For instance, this is the third complete rewrite of "How Writers Write," which at different times was to appear either first or fourth in this book; as you can see, it has finally, after considerable revision, become Chapter 3. At the same time, nearly every paragraph was rewritten — revised and edited — from start to finish even though I had already revised and edited each one for the previous draft.

While it's tempting to edit individual words and sentences as you revise, it makes more sense to revise *before* you edit, simply because it saves time and energy. Revising to refocus or redirect your paper often requires that you delete paragraphs, pages, and whole sections of your initial draft — which is painful if you have already carefully edited them.

Strategies for Revising

1. Plan to revise from the beginning. Allow time to examine early drafts for main points, supporting evidence, and logical direction from first to last. (In addition, allow time later to edit and proof-read.)
2. Revise by limiting your focus. Many first drafts bite off more than they can chew. When you revise, make sure your topic is narrow enough for you to do it justice, given the time and space you have available. Often, this means omitting points that aren't really relevant to your main focus.
3. Revise by adding new material. An excellent time to do additional research, regardless of the kind of paper you are writing, is *after* you've written one draft and now see exactly where you need more information.
4. Revise by reconsidering how you tell your story. Consider the effect other points of view may have on your subject. Consider the effect of past tense versus present tense.
5. Revise for order, sequence, and form. Have you told your story the only way you can, or are there alternative structures that would improve how you tell it?

WRITING 5

Does your usual process for revising a paper include any of the ideas discussed in this section? Describe how your process is similar or different. Now revise the paper to which you added research information in Writing 4, using any revision techniques you are comfortable with.

EDITING

Most writers refer to the final stages of writing as editing, the part of the process for rechecking the paper to see that everything works as intended: the clarity of ideas, the arrangement and logic of paragraphs, the directness and vitality of sentences, the precision and aptness of words, and the correctness and accuracy of facts and references, spelling and punctuation.

Whether writers have written three, five, or ten drafts, they want the last one to be perfect — or as nearly perfect as possible. Many writers edit to please themselves, so that their language sounds right to their own ears, and at the same time with readers in mind, hoping their writing will please their readers' ears as well.

In editing, writers continually ask questions such as: Is this the best way to phrase this idea? Would another term be more appropriate or powerful? Have I said what I mean as directly as I want to? When I read this sentence or passage aloud, does it sound good to my ear? If not, what word or words are out of tune? Can I add an example to clarify an abstract point? Do my sentences end emphatically, with the strongest point at the end? Am I overusing the verb *to be*? Have I carefully qualified debatable or controversial statements? And so on.

At the very end, just before manuscripts are put in the mail or handed over to their intended audience, most writers *proofread* the revised and edited pages to make sure there are no errors in spelling, punctuation (especially commas), noun/verb agreement, paragraphing, typing, formatting, and the like. In addition, they check to see if the writing is laid out well on the page, and whether the manuscript has a title, author, and a date. At this stage, most writers do not want to make any more changes and, often, if they find one or two small errors, they may simply correct them in pencil and, finally, send the manuscript on its way.

Keep in mind at all times that the goal of editing is to improve communication, to make the paper as sharp and pointed and persuasive as possible, to share your ideas so that both you, the writer, and the ideas are well received. It would be a shame for good ideas to be dismissed by the reader because the whole of the writing does not seem careful or serious — which can happen for a variety of reasons, including vague, undefined, or inappropriate terminology, misspellings, and typos.

In finishing *The Working Writer*, I went over every word and phrase to make each one do exactly the work I wanted it to do. Then my editors did the same. They then sent the manuscript to other experts on writing, who also went over the whole manuscript looking for both large and small matters that might be troublesome. Then I revised and edited once again.

Strategies for Editing

1. Read your draft out loud. Does it sound right? Your ear is often a trustworthy guide, alerting you to sentences that are clear or confused, formal or informal, grammatically correct or incorrect.
2. "Simplify. Simplify. Simplify." Henry David Thoreau offers this advice about both life and writing in his book *Walden*. I agree. When you edit, simplify words, sentences, paragraphs, the whole paper so that you make your point clearly and directly.
3. Delete unnecessary words. The easiest of all editing actions is to omit words that do not carry their own weight. Cut to improve clarity, simplicity, directness, as well as sentence rhythm.
4. Proofread by reading line by line with a ruler to mask out the following sentences. This forces your eyes to read word by word and allows you to find mistakes you might otherwise miss. This is important advice even if you use a spell checker on a computer, for it will not catch all mistakes.

WRITING 6

Do you edit your papers using any of the ideas mentioned in this section? Describe your usual techniques for editing. Now edit the paper you revised in Writing 5, using the techniques that usually produce the best results.

A STRATEGY FOR THINKING ABOUT WRITING: WASPS

The number of choices writers must make in composing even short papers is sometimes daunting. In truth, any act of writing, whether assigned or self-initiated, does involve an infinite number of choices — about topics, approaches, order, tone, style, and so on. Writers can simplify this choice-making process by breaking it down into five main dimensions: the Writer, the Audience, the Subject, the Purpose, and the Situation — WASPS for short.

1. As a *writer*, you must choose how to present yourself to your readers. Do you call attention to yourself by writing in the first person (*I*) or recede into the background by selecting an objective, third-person voice (*he, she, it, they*)? Do you include or avoid personal stories that identify your values, beliefs, or opinions? Do you use strongly opinioned or neutral language? When you receive an assignment, consider carefully how visible you want to be in the paper. (For more information about the writer's presence, see Chapter 6.)

2. You need to know something about the *audience* who will read your writing. What do your readers already know? What will they be looking for? What are their biases, values, and assumptions? Although you may sometimes write for yourself or your classmates, instructors are the most common audience for college writing — those who make the assignments and who will read and evaluate the results and who are usually experts in their field. (For more information about audience, see Chapter 5.)

3. Every piece of writing has a *subject*, the idea or information being communicated to the audience. The subject of a college paper could be a concept, event, text, experiment, period, or person that you need to identify, define, explain, illustrate, or argue about. In most college papers, you are asked to emphasize the subject and downplay your writer's presence.

4. Your *purpose* for writing is what you intend to accomplish by the act of communication. Purpose is usually specified by the assignment: to explain, to analyze, to interpret, to evaluate, to compare and contrast, and so on. Most papers include secondary purposes as well; for example, in an effective argument paper you may also need to explain, describe, narrate, and so on to help advance your point. (For more information on purpose, see Chapter 4.)

5. The *situation* is the circumstance or environment in which the writing takes place. Most college writing is done in an academic and evaluative environment defined by the expectations of the discipline. As a writer you must be aware of what the academic ground rules are at your institution, in your field of study, and make choices in subject, purpose, approach, and style accordingly. Remember that, in your absence, your writing speaks for you.

SUGGESTIONS FOR WRITING AND RESEARCH

Individual

1. Add one more suggestion to each list of suggestions at the end of each phase of the writing process (invention and discovery, drafting, researching, revising, and editing) as described in this chapter. Compare your suggestions with your classmates' and find out how many other good ideas you have among you.
2. Study your own writing process as you work on one paper from beginning to end, taking notes in your journal to document your habits and practices. Write an analytic sketch describing the way you write and speculating about the origins of your current habits.

Collaborative

With your classmates, form interview pairs and identify local professional writers or professors who publish frequently in your college community. Each interview pair should make an appointment with one of these practicing writers, interview him or her about the writing process he or she practices, and report back to the class. Write a collaborative report about writers in your community; make it available to other writing classes or to your writing across the curriculum director.

Chapter 4

The Writer's Purpose

Why do teachers always make you write about what they
want you to and never what you want to?
What is the writing for anyway?
– ERIC

WRITING DOESN'T HAPPEN ACCIDENTALLY, but on purpose. When you initiate your own writing, you know why you are doing it. However, when you write in response to an assignment, an instructor determines why. To produce good writing, regardless of who initiated it, you need to take control of your purpose. The question for college writers, then, is how to control the purpose when writing is assigned.

Think first about the range of purposes that writing can serve. People write for a wide variety of reasons: to discover what's on their minds, to solve problems, to vent frustrations, to keep records, and to remember things. They write to communicate information, ideas, feelings, experiences, concerns, and questions. And they sometimes write for the sheer pleasure of creating new forms, imaginary concepts, and vicarious experiences. This chapter examines these three broad purposes of writing — *discovering, communicating,* and *creating* — and discusses the various strategies for accomplishing each one successfully.

Although these purposes are treated here as separate entities to make each one especially clear, in actuality, they overlap all the time. When drafting a paper, you may at the same time be figuring out what you want to say (discovering), saying it (communicating), and taking pleasure in saying it with a certain flair or style (creating). Once you know how each purpose functions, you shouldn't worry about trying to keep each one separate. Simply keep in mind that whenever you try to discover, communicate, or create, you shape your writing toward one purpose or another.

WRITING TO DISCOVER

Writing helps people discover ideas, connections, and patterns about their lives and the world. In college, writing can help you discover and develop topics, expand and explain ideas, and connect seemingly unrelated material into coherent patterns. Even the act of writing essay examinations can help you retrieve information that you once knew and may have temporarily forgotten. In this sense, writing is one of your most powerful learning tools.

Writing, unlike talking, makes language — and therefore thought — visible and permanent. It allows you to examine your ideas from a distance, holding them still long enough to be understood, critiqued, rearranged, and corrected. You can generate and modify these thoughts as you write them, or you can save them to be scrutinized and revised later.

Christopher Fry, a playwright, once said, "My trouble is I'm the sort of writer who only finds out what he is getting at by the time he's got to the end of it." In other words, when Fry writes, whether he works from an outline or not, his purpose and plan become clear only *after* he's written a whole draft; he knows that the act of writing will help him find his way. While he calls this *his* trouble, in truth it's a trouble that many well-known writers share: essayist Joan Didion says, "I write entirely to find out what I'm thinking, what I'm looking at, what I see and what it means. What I want and what I fear." Playwright Arthur Miller says, "I'm discovering it, making up my own story. I think at the typewriter." And psychologist Lev Vygotsky explains, "Thought is not merely expressed in words, it comes into existence through them."

These writers are all talking about the inventive power of writing that helps them construct their finished plays, stories, essays, and poems. But rather than considering this inventive power of writing as a *problem* — to use Fry's word — consider it as a *solution* to many other problems. Once you know that writing can generate ideas, advance concepts, and forge connections, then you can use it deliberately and strategically to help you write college papers.

Discovery writing helps you, the writer, first and foremost. Since the audience is yourself, it doesn't matter what form or shape your language takes — you can use abbreviations and shortcuts, settle for fragments, not worry about spelling or punctuation, let run-on sentences go, and realize that it's impossible to generate and organize material at the same time.

Anytime you write, you may find new or lost ideas, implications, and directions; however, sometimes it pays to write with the specific intention of discovering, leaving communication with readers for later. Following are two specific reasons for using discovery writing in college:

Finding Topics

College assignments typically invite you to choose a topic from a limited number of possibilities, often specifying your general purpose: to argue for or against something, to research a current issue, to recount a personal experience, and so on. In these assignments, your general purpose is fixed by your need to argue, research, or recount; however, your specific topic remains your own: Which position to argue? What issue to investigate? What experience to recount? To control an assignment, first write to discover a topic within the purpose of the assignment and second to limit, focus, and advance that topic. In the following example, Jim writes a journal entry to discover a topic.

> 10/12 We're supposed to find a topic to argue about, but I can't think of anything. The election campaign is still dragging on and I suppose I could take sides, but by now I don't really care who wins--it seems like they've been attacking each other forever. Maybe I could write about the election itself, but not take sides. Instead, I could argue that the election season is too long, that there should be rules to limit when money can be raised, not allow speeches or debates until a month before the election--maybe that's too short.

In the middle of expressing his doubts about finding a topic, Jim finds one; once he wrote about the election, his language led him to the campaign itself as a possible topic, something he didn't *see* until he began to write.

Advancing the Paper

Once you've started your paper, discovery writing can help move it along. Whether you are methodically logging your thoughts about your paper in a journal or are stuck in the middle of a draft wondering where to go next, pausing to examine where you are and where you want to go can advance your work. In the following example, Jill writes about the failure of her fourth draft and produces some ideas for her fifth.

> Well, I thought my fourth draft would be so much better, but it isn't. Now I have a story, but no detail. This is so frustrating--Whoops, I'm supposed to <u>show</u> not tell what frustration is! Right now I feel like I'm looping in circles. I could show what my co-workers, boss, and customers look like. I was so intent on getting my story straight that I omitted the description. I'll also describe the shop, the colors, the floor layout, & the display window.

This example finds Jill having a good time ("Whoops") and taking a few shortcuts ("&"), freedoms associated with writing for yourself and not for others. But, more importantly, the process of writing about the failure of draft four suggests the solutions for draft five.

SUGGESTIONS FOR WRITING TO DISCOVER

1. Think with a pencil or keyboard. Whether reading texts, writing papers, or taking examinations, you will both advance your thought and remember it better if you write it down; you will not simply by staring at the ceiling, closing your eyes, or chewing on your pencil.

2. Forget about an audience. You're writing this for yourself, nobody else need see it. Relax, explore, experiment, and have a good time while you write.
3. Write like you talk. Write in your most natural easy-going voice so that you direct all of your attention on your content. You can always make your writing more formal and careful later on in the writing process.

WRITING 1

Describe one time you used writing for discovery. Did you set out to use writing this way or did it happen accidentally? Have you used it deliberately since then? With what results?

WRITING TO COMMUNICATE

The most common purpose for writing in college is to communicate to an audience: comments on papers to friends, essays and exams to instructors, and applications and résumés to potential employers. Also, most acts of communication are acts of persuasion: a comment persuades a friend that your suggestion is reasonable; an essay persuades your instructor that you know the material; a résumé persuades someone to hire you. To communicate, your writing needs to be *clear* so that others understand you and *effective* and *correct* so that they believe you.

In college writing, there are several common specific purposes within the general purpose of communication.

Recounting Experience

The purpose of recounting your experience is to share something about yourself, make it intelligible and interesting to others, and in the process teach readers something they don't already know. Common assignments in writing classes ask you to explore personal experiences that were especially meaningful to you. Your purpose in such cases is to put your readers in your shoes and make them experience how you were thinking and feeling at the time. Such writing often takes the shape of autobiographical sketches or personal and reflective essays.

Reporting Information

The purpose of reporting information is to share the knowledge you have of a particular topic with your readers. You do this by observing carefully, noting important details, and using words that appeal to the senses to reproduce the object or event for readers who have not witnessed it themselves. It's usually best to keep the subject in the foreground, yourself and your opinions in the background.

Explaining Ideas

The purpose of explaining ideas is to make them clear to somebody who knows less about them than you do. You do this best by stating the ideas as simply as possible and providing plenty of details and examples. When you explain an idea or concept, pay special attention to the sequence of your explanation — let your readers absorb the idea a little at a time. Examples can illustrate abstractions, and sources can explain where the ideas came from.

Arguing Positions

The purpose of arguing a position in writing is the same as in speaking — to persuade your readers that your position is the best one. College assignments frequently ask you to explore both sides of ideas, issues, policies, and

---

WRITING 2

List all of the communicative writing you have done in the past two weeks. Who were your audiences? Were all of your acts of communication successful? If not, why not?

SUGGESTIONS FOR WRITING TO COMMUNICATE

1. Identify the audience. The purpose of writing to communicate is to transmit ideas, information, or feelings as clearly as possible to another audience; if you understand what the audience knows and believes, you can shape your message more precisely.
2. Be clear. To this end, prefer simple words and make direct statements, avoiding jargon and unnecessary complexity where possible, organize according to logical principles.
3. Be specific. Document, illustrate, and provide evidence for all your ideas, interpretations, and arguments. In research papers, use formal documentation techniques as appropriate to your discipline; in informal essays, cite your sources within your text — but be sure to cite them.

WRITING TO CREATE

When you write to create, you pay special attention to the way your language looks and sounds, to its form, shape, rhythm, images, and texture.

Though the term *creative writing* is most often associated with poetry, fiction, and drama, any act of writing, from a personal narrative to a research essay, is potentially creative.

When you write to create, you pay less immediate attention to either an audience or the idea itself and more to the form of your expression. Writing with creative intention puts you into the role of spectator, looking at experience or ideas from a distance. In this role you do not attempt to influence the world so much as reflect on it, see what it means, and, ultimately, portray it in a unique light for both you and your readers. The creative purpose, in other words, is embedded in language as much as in content.

In most college papers, your primary purpose is clear communication of your ideas; however, an important secondary purpose is often to make your readers pause, see something from a different angle, perhaps reflect on what it means, or experience a special pleasure from the way your communication was accomplished.

Intensifying Experience

When Amanda recounted her experience picking potatoes on board a mechanical harvester on her father's farm, she decided that the best way to explain the job was to make her readers *feel* the experience as she did. She wrote her account in the present tense, crafting her language to duplicate the sense of hard, monotonous work.

> Potatoes, mud, potatoes, mud, potatoes, that was all I saw in front of me. They moved from my right side to my left, at hip level. A conveyor belt never stopping. On and on and on.
>
> I bounced and stumbled around as the potato harvester moved over the rough earth, digging the newly grown potatoes out of the ground, transporting them up a conveyor belt and pushing them out in front of me and three other ladies, two on either side of the belt.
>
> The potatoes passed fast, a constant stream. My hands worked deftly, pulling out clods of dirt, rotten potatoes, old shaws, and anything else I found that wasn't a potato. They were sore, rubbed raw with the constant pressure of holding dirt. They were numb, partly from the work and partly from the cold. It was October, the ground was nearly frozen, the mud was hard and solid. Cold. Dirt had gotten into my yellow and yet brown rubber gloves, had wedged under my nails increasing my discomfort.

For more examples from Amanda's essay, see Chapter 10.

Experimenting with Form

Keith created a special language effect for an otherwise traditional and straightforward academic assignment by writing a poetic prologue in a research essay about homeless people in New York City. The full essay includes factual information derived from social workers, agency documents, and library research. Here is the experimental poetic form:

```
The cold cement
     no pillow
The steel grate
     no mattress
But the hot air
     of the midnight subway
Lets me sleep.
```

Keith's poem was written not to stand alone as a poem but instead to suggest to readers what it might be like to sleep on the street. Using the poetic form creates a brief emotional involvement with the research subject, allowing readers to fill in missing information with their imagination. Note, however, that the details of the poem (cold cement, steel grate, subway) do not spring from the writer's fanciful imagination, but from his research notes and observations.

Be especially careful if you write for emotional effect in an otherwise traditional paper, as Keith did, that your creative language serves a purpose and that the traditional part of the essay is full of accurate, informative data. The creative language should enhance, not camouflage, your ideas.

WRITING 3

Describe one time when your primary purpose in writing was to create rather than to discover or communicate. Were you pleased with the result? Did you share this writing with anyone else? What was that person's reaction?

SUGGESTIONS FOR WRITING TO CREATE

1. Observe well. Take notes about what you see and develop a store of images, impressions, and scenes from the world to use in your writing for illustrative and comparative purposes.
2. Play with form. The look, shape, and structure of a piece of writing carry information and represent ideas in different ways. You may surprise your readers, causing them to take special notice when, for instance, you write a letter or memo in the form of a poem to convey not only information but a sense of joy or play as well.
3. Read your writing out loud. Listen for the sounds, harmonies, and rhythms of the language. Reading out loud will also tell you where your images are sharp, your cadences just right, your voice strong.
4. Know your audience. Be sure that the instructor for whom you are writing creatively is receptive. If you are not sure, ask.

APPROACHING COLLEGE WRITING ASSIGNMENTS

When you receive a writing assignment, purpose is involved in two ways. First is the larger intention of the assignment, normally to write-to-communicate, coupled with the instructor's specific purpose — to recount an experience, make an argument, interpret a text, and so on. Second is the purpose you impart to the assignment by your choice of topic. ("OK, so I'm supposed to communicate something by interpreting a text, but what text do I want to work with and why?") Good papers are written only when writers make all purposes their own.

How can you ensure that your writing serves both your instructor's purpose and your own? Let's look at two typical writing assignments taken from a first-year writing class and see what they ask for.

ASSIGNMENT 1

Write a personal essay in which you explore a recent personal experience of some significance to you or that marked a turning point in your life. Write the paper in such a way that your audience understands this event's importance and what you learned from it. After reading your paper, the audience should know more about both you and the experience you describe.

ASSIGNMENT 2

Write a research essay in which you investigate and report on one of the following: (a) an issue or problem recently reported in the news media that has some local impact, or (b) a local institution, including what it does, how it works, who works there, and what issues concern it. In completing this report, please include information derived from library research, site visitations, and expert interviews.

Would you know what to do if you were given these writing assignments? Would you know how to find and state the instructor's general purpose? Your own?

Following are four steps to help you gain an understanding of any writing assignment: (1) find and state the instructor's general purpose, (2) find a specific topic that interests you, (3) find your approach to the topic, and (4) make the topic — and hence the assignment — your own.

Finding the Instructor's Purpose

Look at the assignment for key words. First, find the direction words, verbs that tell what action you are expected to perform. Next find the subject words, nouns that specify the general subject of the assignment.

In Assignment 1, the direction word is *explore*, which suggests an open approach allowing the writer to investigate an experience and examine different dimensions of it; *explore* is a direction word that usually allows latitude for the writer. The key subject words are *personal experience*, *significance*, and *turning point*, words that define what the writer is to explore. The experience also needs to be *recent*. How recent? This is a good question to ask the instructor.

In Assignment 2, the direction words are *investigate* and *report*. Additional words of nearly equal importance are *research*, *visitation*, and *interviews* because they specify the nature of the investigation. The word *report* suggests that communicating information is the main goal. The key subject words are *issue* and *institution*. It would be a good idea to explore with the instructor the definition of *institution* — would it include Woolworth's, the airport, an elmentary school?

Finding a Topic

The subject words in an assignment are usually quite broad; they define a set of possible subjects without prescribing which one to write about. For example, *a recent personal experience,* the subject words from Assignment 1, could describe a wide variety of things that happened to you.

You must first find a subject you care about and then narrow it to a topic that will specify what you want to say about the subject. Subjects are large and inclusive, such as *sports* or *soccer.* Within each subject are many possible topics: *competition versus community in high school sports* or *what I learned playing soccer my senior year.* A good topic should serve both your instructor's purpose (it fulfills the assignment) and your own. Try to select a topic that actually holds your interest rather than one that seems merely easy or handy, especially if the assignment will last several weeks or more. An interesting subject will cause you to ask more and better questions and result in more, not less, involvement in later drafts.

In Assignment 1, you might choose as a subject your experience playing high school sports and then narrow that to a topic: one important year rather than four, one crucial game, one theme such as competition or losing with grace.

In Assignment 2, if pollution is your issue, you could narrow the topic to one kind of pollution, to a specific incident such as the closing of a public beach or to a particular place or time where an incident occurred.

Determining Your Approach

Specific purposes imply specific approaches, which means determining what information and ideas you need and how you are going to get them. Most college writing assignments need to be supported by material that will make readers believe that what the paper says is true. In personal experience writing, you create belief by recording the inner details from your long-term memory; in most other writing, you create belief by using knowledge you've gained from sources outside yourself — books, lectures, and so on.

Assignment 1 requires remembered knowledge, putting memories on paper where you can look at them in more detail and organize them in a meaningful way. Though your memory may contain most of what you need, you might also consider revisiting the site of the experience or talking with others involved to retrieve more useful details.

Assignment 2 requires knowledge of recent issues or of the institution you have chosen. For the first part of the assignment, you might spend some time reading newspapers and listening to the news. For the second part, you could visit the institution and talk to people there.

WRITING 4

Identify the key words and the necessary sources of information for a current writing assignment. What do you need to know to develop your topic and complete your paper?

Owning the Assignment

To understand and take seriously assignments given by other people, you need to do more than merely react to them. You need to make them your own. One way of owning an assignment is to figure out how doing the assignment benefits you in some way — answers a nagging question, is fun or challenging, helps somebody you care about. Another way of owning an assignment is to break it down to a manageable size so you can handle it with the information and time available. In addition, you may also find a way of doing the assignment that's original and creative — an approach more likely than not to spark interest in your reader.

A good way to own any assignment is to write about it, using your own words to help find an angle or approach that is comfortable, sensible, or interesting. You can do this in a journal, log, or notebook, keeping a methodical record of thoughts about the assignment. Can you restate the assignment in your own words? Can you break it into component parts? Can you limit the scope or size?

In Assignment 1, find an experience that you want to explore and learn from. Then ask whether it might be of interest to others either because it's common and they could identify with it or because it's unusual and they could learn from it. You've got to want to learn from the experience yourself and at the same time make others want the same thing. For example, in writing about a sport, the time you sat on the bench may have taught you lessons as important as those you learned scoring the winning field goal. Your experience of a typical day on the job may provide just as interesting insights as the day the store caught fire. You can own your topic by writing about your insider knowledge, including unfamiliar details that make the experience come alive for your readers.

In Assignment 2, you can make your prospective topic more interesting to both you and your readers by digging up little-known details of a current event or the operation of an institution. Or you could identify something as an institution that one might not normally think of (the pretzel man at the mall?), finding a creative way to make your readers interested in your topic.

SUGGESTIONS FOR APPROACHING ASSIGNMENTS

1. Identify and analyze the direction and subject words that determine the purpose of the assignment. If the assignment asks for analysis, be sure your writing stresses the analytical rather than the personal or persuasive. If the assignment specifies a general subject, attend to the words that narrow it further.
2. Narrow the topic to one that is both interesting and manageable. Think first of as many possibilities as you can; think second about those that truly interest you; think third about the one you can best manage in the time available.
3. Write from what you know. Plan to research what you don't know. List both the information with which you are readily familiar and that which you will need to look up.
4. Own the assignment by adopting an original approach, slant or perspective that will separate your paper from less imaginative ones. If you invent an unusual way of handling an assignment, (a) check with your instructor to see how open he or she is to such an approach, and (b) be sure you include all the necessary information demanded of a more traditional approach.

SUGGESTIONS FOR WRITING AND RESEARCH

Individual

1. Select a topic that interests you — a hobby, a sport, a person, a current issue — and write about it in each of the three modes described in this chapter. First, begin with *discovery writing*, perhaps in a journal. Second, write a letter to *communicate* with somebody — another student in class, a friend, your teacher — about your interest. Third, write *creatively* about your topic in a short poem, story, or play. Finally, describe your experience writing in these different modes, perhaps answering some of these questions: What changed as you switched from one kind of writing to the other? Which gave you the most pleasure? When were you most conscious of your audience? Which was hardest to write? Did you learn anything new about your topic?
2. Write a letter to your writing teacher in which you explain what makes a good writing assignment and why. Plan to use some of the

insights from your own experience. Make a proposal for a writing assignment you would want to do for his or her course. Request a response.

Collaborative

1. Select a topic the whole writing group is interested in writing about. Divide your writing labors so that some of you do extensive discovery writing, some do more deliberate communicative writing, and some write creatively. As a group, with scissors and tape, combine your efforts into a single coherent, creative piece of collage writing, making sure that every member's writing is included in the finished product. Perform a reading of this collage, individually and chorally, for the other groups; listen to theirs in return.
2. As a class, research the history of writing assignments given in high school. Each person can examine old notebooks and papers for evidence of the teacher's instructions and look at the resulting papers if they are available. Write a collaborative research report on the topic "American School Assignments: The Good, the Bad, and the Ugly" in which you describe and analyze what is typical, explain what separates the good from the bad, and make a recommendation for improving assignments.

Chapter 5

The Writer's Audience

I find it very confusing moving from one professor to another.
They all expect different things. I still haven't learned yet
what makes a "good" paper as opposed to a "bad" paper.
— JENNIFER

EVERY PIECE OF WRITING IS READ BY SOMEBODY. And whether a piece of writing is "good" is largely a question of how effectively it communicates with those who read it, the audience. To write effectively, you need a good sense of who your audience is. You need to know not only that it is "Professor Watkins" or "the readers of the school paper," but also what your readers are like: what they know and don't know, what they find interesting or boring, what they expect from writing in general or this paper in particular. In other words, you need to figure out the best way to address this specific audience.

Writers and speakers share similar concerns. Both want to explain their ideas fully in language their audience understands, but they don't want to overexplain and risk boring their audience. They want to use a tone that seems appropriate for the occasion and to present ideas in the best possible order. Speakers have one advantage over writers: they can see their audience's reactions from moment to moment. They know exactly when something needs to be explained more carefully or when a humorous story isn't going well. Writers write alone and can only imagine the reactions of the people reading their work. To overcome this disadvantage, writers must carefully consider in advance the best way to address their readers.

This chapter focuses on the audiences you will address most often in writing classes: yourself, when you write in your journal; your peers, when you share drafts with one another; your instructor, who is the primary reader of your final draft; and possibly a more distant public, when you share your writing with others outside the classroom. While these audiences all need clarity and coherence, honesty and insight, exactly what constitutes clarity or honesty differs from audience to audience.

UNDERSTANDING COLLEGE AUDIENCES

You need to answer many questions about every audience you address in college — but you already know quite a bit about some of your audiences. It might help to think of different audiences as existing along a continuum, with those best known to you at one end and those least known to you at the other end. Try this: draw a horizontal line across a blank page. At the left end, place yourself, the person you know best; toward the middle, place the classmates whom you've come to know and trust; to the right of middle, place your instructor, whom you know but whose role and authority may cause uncertainty; at the far right, place the anonymous public. Your continuum should look something like this:

Self —— Peers ——Instructor —— Public

Now fill in some of the other audiences to whom you write: friends, parents, relatives, the college dean, employers, government agencies, newspaper editors, and so on. While your particular continuum will always differ from somebody else's, the principle — that you know some audiences better than others — is the same.

The better you know your readers, the more you know about their likes, dislikes, interests, politics, and so on. For example, every semester you go through the process of learning more and more about your instructors. At the beginning, you may be unsure of what your instructors expect from your papers. By the end, though, you know what topics or approaches each one appreciates, what sort of thinking each expects you to demonstrate, even what sort of humor each one prefers — or whether some of them would rather not see humor in your papers at all. Similarly, the closer your readers are to you, the more likely you will have beliefs and opinions in common. For example, you can assume that another student, even one you don't know well, would probably share your feelings about writing long research essays or about getting good grades.

This doesn't mean there is no chance of writing effectively to unknown readers or to readers who are unlike you. It only means that you need to take a little more time figuring out what they will respond to best. For any piece of writing you do, take some time early in the process to identify your readers and to think about what they're like. You may want to do some discovery writing and organize your thoughts about these people. (See Chapter 7.)

WRITING 1

Think back over the past several weeks and list all the audiences to whom you have written. To whom did you write most often? Why? Which audiences were easy for you to address? Which were difficult? Which of the elements of your writing did you consciously adjust as your audiences changed? Why?

WRITING TO DIFFERENT AUDIENCES

Thoughtful college papers are written to at least two audiences: the writer and the instructor. In addition, some college papers are also written for classmates. And some college writing is published for an even wider public in a student newspaper or literary magazine. This section examines the general characteristics of each of these possible college audiences and provides suggestions for writing effectively to each.

Shaping Your Writing for Different Audiences

To shape your writing for a particular audience, you need to think about the qualities of your writing that can change according to audience. Your purpose for writing, the context you need to provide, and the structure, tone, and style you use can all be affected by your audience. (Structure, tone, and style are important elements of voice. See Chapter 6.)

Purpose

The explicit purpose of your writing — to communicate, to persuade, to explain — depends more on you and your assignment than on your audience. For example, you might write to ask questions when writing to yourself in a journal, but you are more likely to try to answer these questions — and communicate the answers — when writing a paper for an instructor. Also, there are unstated purposes in any piece of writing, and these will vary depending on whom you're addressing. For example, is it important to you that your readers like you? Or that they respect you? Or that they give you good grades? Always ask yourself what you want a piece of writing to do for — or to — your audience and what you want your audience to do in response to your writing.

Context

Audiences need a context, different background information, in order to understand what you've written. Find out whether your audience already knows about the topic or whether it's totally new to them. Consider which terms or ideas need explaining. For example, other students in your writing group might know exactly whom you mean if your refer to a favorite singer, but you might need to identify the singer further in a paper for your instructor.

Structure

Every piece of writing is put together in a certain way — some ideas are discussed early, others late; transitions between ideas are marked in a certain way; similar ideas are either grouped together or treated separately. How you structure or organize a paper depends in large part on what you think will work best with your particular audience. For example, if you were writing an argument for someone who disagrees with your position, you might want to lead with the evidence that you both agree on and later introduce more controversial evidence. If you were explaining an idea new to your readers, you might take special care to break it into several smaller subtopics or to mark the beginning of each new idea with a clear transitional phrase.

Tone

The tone of a piece of writing conveys the writer's attitude toward the subject matter and audience. How do you want to sound to your readers? Do you want them to hear you as friendly? Businesslike? Angry? Serious? Humorous? Puzzled? You may, of course, have a different attitude toward each audience you address. In addition, you may want audiences to hear you in different ways. For example, when writing to yourself, you won't mind sounding puzzled or confused. When writing to instructors, though, you may want to sound confident and authoritative.

Style

In writing, style is largely a matter of the formality of your language. Writing ranges from the chatty and casual — full of frequent contractions and deliberate sentence fragments — to the formal and precise. You need to determine what style your readers will expect, what style will be most effective for your subject. Fellow students might be offended if you write in anything other than a friendly, down-to-earth style, but instructors might interpret the same style as too informal for your purpose.

Writing to Yourself

People write to themselves for many purposes, from simple reminders to deliberate acts of discovery to the therapeutic venting of frustration. They do so in notebooks and journals as well as on computers.

When you write to yourself to explore a topic or idea, you don't need to worry about context, since you are the audience and you know what you know. However, if you make a journal entry that you think you might want to refer to later, it's a good idea to provide more background and explanation than you need at the time. Including specific details will help you remember the event or the idea.

Similarly, you don't need to worry about structure or organization when you write for yourself. In fact, the structure that will occur most naturally will be free association, in which writing down one idea triggers another in your memory, and you write that, which triggers another, and so on. Structure may matter, however, if you are writing to discover the best organization for a paper.

In writing to yourself, neither style nor tone matters much. When you are the reader of your own writing, choose words, sentences, rhythms, images, and punctuation that come easiest and most naturally to you. Your style will probably resemble the style you use in writing letters to good friends. If you want to capture a particular mood or event accurately, however, you may need to make your tone reflect your feeling at the time of the event.

WRITING 2

Describe when and why you write to yourself. Does the discussion of writing to yourself in this section match your experience?

Writing to Peers

Your peers are your equals — people of similar age, background, or situation. Your peers in an academic situation are other students. Some of your assignments will ask you to consider the other students in the class to be your audience. Even though your instructor will still read and evaluate your paper, remember that you are writing to and for your classmates. In fact, part of your instructor's evaluation will probably be based on how well you anticipate and meet the needs of your classmates. Other writing addressed to peers includes written responses to papers shared in writing groups.

The primary difference between writing to yourself and writing to peers is the amount of context you need to provide to make sure your readers understand you. If your paper is about a personal experience, you need to provide the explanations and details that would allow your readers — who were not in your place for the experience — a full understanding. If your paper is about a subject that requires research, you need to determine how much information about the subject your readers already know, and how much needs explaining.

The structure of writing for your peers depends on whether you are narrating a personal experience, describing a research project, making an argument, explaining an idea, being reflective, or writing fiction. In general, you will want to write from the familiar to the unfamiliar, building on ideas as you write.

In writing to peers, your most likely tone will be one of candor and mutual respect. Your style will most likely be somewhat informal.

WRITING 3

To which of your peers do you write most often? How would you characterize your writing in terms of purpose, context, structure, tone, and style?

Writing to Instructors

Instructors are among the most difficult audiences for whom to write. First, they usually make the assignments, which means they know what they want and it's your job to figure out what that is. Second, they often know more about your subject than you do. Third, different instructors may have quite different criteria for what constitutes good writing. And fourth, each instructor may simultaneously play several different roles: a helpful resource, a critic, an editor, a coach, and, finally, a judge.

It is often difficult to know how much context to provide in a paper written for an instructor, unless the assignment specifies it. For example, in writing about a Shakespearean play to an English professor, should you provide a summary of the play when you know that he or she already knows it? Or should you skip the summary information and write only about your own original ideas? The safest approach is to provide full background, explain all ideas, support all assertions, and cite authorities in the field. You should write as if your instructor needs all this information and it is your job to educate him or her.

When writing papers to instructors, use a structure that is conventional for the type of paper you are writing. For example, personal experience papers generally are arranged chronologically or use flashbacks. (The chapters in Part IV describe conventional structures for the paper discussed there.)

In a writing class, you may encounter some confusion about the proper tone and style to use. Because your instructor is also your coach, you might feel it's appropriate to write in a friendly tone and a casual style. But even the friendliest, most casual instructor may want you to write more conventionally as training for other academic writing. Use a fair, respectful, and authoritative tone and a somewhat formal and sophisticated style.

One of your instructor's roles is to help you learn to write effective papers. But another role is to evaluate whether you have done so and, from a broader perspective, whether you are becoming a literate member of the college community. So your implicit purpose when you write to instructors is to demonstrate your understanding of conventions, your knowledge, your reasoning, and your originality.

Demonstrating Your Understanding of Conventions

The first thing your instructor may notice about your writing is what it looks like: Is it printed or handwritten? Does it have a title page? A title? A name? How long is it? How neat is it? How legible is the handwriting, how accurate the typing? How clear and correct are the first few sentences? Did the paper meet the deadline? Instructors make these observations rapidly — sometimes unconsciously — before they have finished reading the paper. Such observations, although superficial, often determine the instructor's attitude toward the whole paper. He or she is more likely to look favorably on a paper that is neat and free of spelling and grammatical errors than on one that is wrinkled and full of mechanical mistakes.

Of course, academic conventions require more than a neat appearance and correct spelling and grammar. They also affect your decisions about context, structure, tone, and style. Early in the term, your safest stance is to cover all the traditional bases of good academic writing, demonstrating that you can write about teacher-assigned subjects using a conventional structure and style, providing full explanations, supporting assertions with authority, using specialized terms carefully, and documenting all borrowed information. Later in the term, once you have established your academic legitimacy, your experiments with form, style, theme, and voice may be more readily accepted by your instructor. In truth, many instructors get tired of reading safe prose, written to satisfy requirements; they usually welcome creativity.

Demonstrating Knowledge

Your paper must also have substance. Even a good-looking paper must demonstrate what you know and how well you know it. If, for instance, you argue for the reintroduction of wolves into Yellowstone National Park, your instructor will look to see how much you know about wolves and parks. Your instructor will ask: Are the definitions, details, and explanations clear? Are they believable? Where did the information come from? How up-to-date is it? What sources were consulted? How reputable do they seem? Any paper must contain solid information.

You also must demonstrate the knowledge that you've gained in your writing class about the writing process itself — your understanding of planning, drafting, researching, revising, and editing, as shown in your paper.

Demonstrating Reasoning

Your papers should show your ability to reason logically, support assertions, and be persuasive whether you are writing a personal essay or an argument. In arguing for the reintroduction of wolves into Yellowstone, you would need to demonstrate that there are good reasons for doing so and refute opposing arguments. Your reasoning would show not only in your convincing details but also in the logic that holds your argument together.

Demonstrating Originality

No matter what the writing assignment, you can find creative ways of doing it. When assignments are open-ended, do not choose the first topic that comes to mind or that seems easiest. Let your mind roam over more unusual ideas. When topics are limited, allow yourself to consider some risky or new approach. When you provide support for your assertions, dig for information more unexpected than what's most commonly known. In your opening or conclusion, try to surprise your reader.

Writing to Public Audiences

Writing to a public audience is difficult for all writers because the audience is usually both diverse and unknown. The public audience can include people who know both more and less than you; it can contain experts who will notice the slightest mistake and novices who need even simple terms explained; it can contain opponents looking for reasons to argue with you and supporters looking for reasons to continue support. And you are unlikely to know many of these people personally.

You usually have some idea of who these anonymous readers are, however, or you wouldn't be writing to them in the first place. Still, it is important to learn as much as you can about their beliefs and characteristics that may be relevant to the point you intend to make. What is their educational level? What are their political, philosophical, or religious beliefs? Their interests?

When you don't know who your audience is, you need to provide context for everything you say. If you are referring to even well-known groups such as the NCAA (National Collegiate Athletic Association) or NAACP (National Association for the Advancement of Colored People), write out the full names the first time you refer to them; if you refer to an idea as "postmodern," define or illustrate what the term means. Your writing should be able to stand by itself and make complete sense to people you do not know.

The structure of public writing should be logical and clear; your opening paragraph should get rapidly to the point; your conclusion should be emphatic, perhaps making your strongest point. Your tone will depend on your purpose, but generally it should be fair and reasonable. Your style will depend on the publication you are writing for.

Your explicit purpose for writing to public audiences is usually to communicate — to inform them about something they do not already know or persuade them to see something from your point of view. However, your implicit purpose is to demonstrate that you are literate and well educated, which means you must be sure your ideas are clear and your language correct.

WRITING 4

How accurate do you find the discussion in this section of different college audiences? Describe circumstances that confirm or contradict the description here. If instructors are not your most difficult audience, explain who is.

SUGGESTIONS FOR WRITING AND RESEARCH

Individual

Select a paper written recently for an instructor. Rewrite the paper for a publication, choosing either a student newspaper or local magazine.

Before you start writing, make notes about what elements need to be changed: context, structure, tone, style, or purpose. When you finish recasting the paper to this larger, more public audience, send it to the publication.

Collaborative

In a group of five students, select a topic of common interest. Write about the topic (either as homework or in class for fifteen minutes) to one of the following audiences: yourself, a friend who is not here, your instructor, an appropriate magazine or newspaper. Share your writing with other members of the group and together list the choices you needed to make for each audience.

Chapter 6

The Writer's Voice

I would like to develop some sort of personal
style so when I write people know it's me.

— JOHN

ACH INDIVIDUAL SPEAKS with a distinctive voice. Some people speak loudly, some softly, others with quiet authority. Some sound assertive or aggressive, while others sound cautious, tentative, or insecure. Some voices are clear and easy to follow, while others are garbled, convoluted, and meandering. Some create belief and inspire trust, while others do not.

To some extent writers' voices, like their personalities, may be determined by factors beyond their control, such as their ethnic identity, social class, family, or religion. In addition, some elements of voice evolve as writers mature, such as their mode of thought (logical, intuitive) and political or philosophical stance (liberal, conservative). But writers also exert a great deal of control over the language they produce in their quest to make their ideas known and believed. They shape the style (colloquial, academic) and tone (serious, sarcastic) as well as its diction (simple, complex). The point is to control those elements of voice you can and be aware of those you can't.

DEFINING VOICE

The word *voice* means at least two distinctly different things. First, it is the audible sound of a person speaking. (*He has a high-pitched voice.*) Applied to writing, this meaning is primarily metaphoric — unless writers read their work aloud, readers don't actually *hear* writers' voices. Speaking voices distinguish themselves by physical auditory qualities such as pitch (high, low, nasal), pace (fast, slow), tone (angry, assertive, tentative), rhythm (regular, smooth, erratic), register (soft, loud), and accent (Southern, British, Boston).

Writing voices do much the same when the language on the page re-creates the sound of the writer talking. Careful writers control, as much as they can, the sound of their words in their readers' heads.

Second, voice is a person's beliefs and values. (*Her voice needs to be heard.*) Every writer's text conveys something of the person behind the words. The self that is conveyed often goes well beyond personality to include the writer's political, philosophical, and social values as well as his or her commitment to certain causes (civil rights, gun control, the environment). In addition, what writers stand for may be revealed in the way they reason about things — in an orderly, scientific manner or more intuitively and emotionally.

WRITING 1

In your own words, describe the concept of voice. Do you think writers have one voice or many? Explain what you mean.

ANALYZING THE ELEMENTS OF VOICE

Readers experience a writer's voice as a whole expression, not a set of component parts. However, to understand and gain control of your own voice, it helps to examine the individual elements that combine to make a whole expression.

Tone

Tone is your attitude toward the subject and audience: angry, joyous, sarcastic, puzzled, contemptuous, anxious, respectful, friendly, and so on. Writers control their tone just as speakers do — by adopting a particular perspective or point of view selecting words carefully, emphasizing some words and ideas over others, choosing certain patterns of inflection, controlling the pace with pauses and other punctuation.

To gain control of your tone, read drafts of your paper aloud and listen carefully to the attitudes you convey. Try to hear your own words as if you were the audience: How does this writer feel about the subject matter? How does this writer feel about the people being addressed? Decide whether the overall tone is the one you intended, and reread carefully to make sure every word and sentence contributes to this tone.

Style

Style is the distinctive way you express yourself. It can change from day to day and from situation to situation, but it is somehow always *you*.

The style you choose for a particular paper will largely depend on your subject, purpose, and audience for that paper. Style in writing is affected by the level of formality (formal, informal, colloquial) and by the simplicity or complexity of your words, sentences, and paragraphs.

To gain control of the style of your writing, learn to analyze the purpose and audience of your writing (see Chapters 4 and 5). Decide how you wish to present yourself, and examine your writing carefully to see that your style suits the occasion.

Structure

Structure is the organization of and relationships among the parts of your text: where you start, where you conclude, the order of sections in between, which ideas are grouped together, how explicit transitions between ideas are. Some pattern or logic — structure — holds together all thoughtful writing so that it makes sense. When you write, the structure of your sentences, paragraphs, and your text as a whole not only helps convey your meaning but also reveals how you think. A linear, logical structure presents you as a linear, logical thinker; a circular, intuitive structure shows you to be more creative and intuitive.

To gain control of the structure of your writing, outline both before and after you draft and revise so that your outline accurately reflects your reasoning patterns. Also consider the structure of your paragraphs and sentences. (For more on outlining see Chapters 7 and 19.)

Values

Your values include your political, social, religious, and philosophical beliefs. Your background, opinions, and beliefs will be part of everything you write, but you must learn when and where to express them directly and when and where not to. For example, including your values would enhance a personal essay or other autobiographical writing, but they would detract attention from the subject of a research or interpretive essay.

To gain control of the values in your writing, consider whether the purpose of the assignment calls for an implicit or explicit statement of your values. Examine your drafts for opinion and judgment words that reveal your values, and keep them or take them out as appropriate for the assignment.

Authority

In writing, authority comes from knowledge and is projected through self-confidence and control. You can exert and project real authority only if you know your material well, whether it's the facts of your personal life or carefully researched information. The more you know about your subject, the more sure of yourself you will sound, and the more readers will hear authority in your voice.

To gain control over the authority in your writing, do your homework, conduct thorough research, and read your sources of information carefully and critically. (See Chapter 2.)

WRITING 2

Describe your own writing voice in terms of each of the elements described in this section (tone, style, structure, values, authority). Then compare your descriptions with the voice you perceive in a recent paper you have written. In what ways does the paper substantiate your description? In what ways does it differ from your description? How do you account for the differences?

HEARING A RANGE OF VOICES

Looking closely at a few distinct voices focused on a common subject may be instructive. As you read the writing in this section, ask yourself what effect each voice creates and how it achieves that effect.

The following three passages have been taken from texts written by experts about trees. In that sense, they are all explanatory writing, meant to inform readers about the characteristics of certain trees. (The labels given these voices are meant to describe their effect rather than categorize them in any absolute way.)

Scientific/Technical

WHITE OAK (*Quercus alba*) leaves are deciduous, 5 to 9 inches long and 2 to 4 inches wide, with 7 to 9 rounded lobes divided by narrow, variable sinuses often extending nearly to midrib. The oblong acorns are set in a bowl-like cup covered with warty scales. The gray bark is in narrow, vertical blocks of scaly plates. Grows 80 to 100 feet tall and 3 to 4 feet in diameter, with a wide-spreading crown.

— C. FRANK BROCKMAN, *Trees of North America*

In this passage from a paperback guidebook, Brockman did not want readers to hear his individual voice at all. He wanted to provide straight, unbiased information about a particular kind of tree, omitting any language that would have led readers away from his purpose: to identify the white oak tree. All the language — including the numbers, the adjectives (*oblong, vertical, warty*), and the absence of words that make value judgments — contributes to an objective or neutral style typical of scientific and technical writing. At the same time, Brockman presents his description as beyond debate, totally believable, so there can be no doubt with authority here. In other words, there really is a voice in this passage, imparted through mathematical terms, Latin names, and technical terminology (*deciduous, lobes, sinuses*) — the voice of scientific certainty.

Familiar/Informal

White oak is the best known oak of all. Common throughout New England, its beauty attracted the attention of early colonists. In open places White Oak develops a broad symmetrical crown and majestic appearance. The light gray scaly bark is characteristic; so are the leaves with five to nine rounded lobes. . . .White Oak prefers rich soil but grows slowly. The large painted acorns in shallow cups were eaten by Indians. It is an outstanding lumber tree, used for furniture, boats, and barrels.

— HERBERT S. ZIM AND ALEXANDER C. MARTIN,
A Guide to Familiar American Trees

In another guidebook, the writers project a voice that is informed but also informal and friendly. They provide identifying information about the oak itself (the two middle sentences) but also comment on its beauty, majesty, history, and usefulness. Unlike the scientific voice, this friendly and engaging voice makes value judgments freely, calling the tree *beautiful* and *majestic*, the lumber *outstanding*. The informal and simple style and the friendly tone suggest that this guide was written to a young audience.

Creative/Poetic

There are two spiritual dangers in not owning a farm. One is the danger of supposing that breakfast comes from the grocery, and the other that the heat comes from the furnace.

To avoid the first danger, one should plant a garden, preferably where there is no grocer to confuse the issue.

To avoid the second, he should lay a split of good oak on the andirons, preferably where there is no furnace, and let it warm his shins while a February blizzard tosses the trees outside. If one has cut, split, hauled, and piled his own good oak, and let his mind work the while, he will remember much about where heat comes from, and with a wealth of detail denied to those who spend the week in town astride a radiator.

— ALDO LEOPOLD, *Sand County Almanac*

The voice in this passage is quite different from the voices in the first two. The writer's purpose here is not so much to teach readers to identify oak trees as to reflect on the role of nature in the lives of overcitified people. To do so, the writer creates a strongly creative and poetic voice, leading first with a teasing riddle — what are *two spiritual dangers in not owning a farm?* He follows with folksy yet carefully crafted parallel answers. (*To avoid the first . . .*

To avoid the second.) He writes all the while in simple, direct language, with only a few words of more than one syllable and many action verbs (*plant, cut, split, hauled, piled*) and colloquial terms (*lay a split*).

This more creative voice suggests that Leopold wants his readers to understand trees emotionally as well as rationally. His voice speaks with an authority not of the laboratory but of a personal life long lived and reflected on.

WRITING 3

List the nonfiction writers whose voices you remember best. After each writer, list the qualities that seem to make his or her voice distinctive.

HEARING THE RANGE OF ONE VOICE

All writing has a voice, even when it strives for apparent objectivity, as the first excerpt in the previous section does. In college writing, you will need different voices to address different purposes, audiences, and situations. To illustrate this range, we have selected five samples of writing, each with a different voice, from the portfolio written by Julie during her first semester in a college writing class.

Private

The first example comes from Julie's journal. In these entries she writes to herself about her first assignment, to recount a personal experience.

> October 8. I'm really struggling with my personal experience paper--I can't seem to get a good balance of description, dialogue, and depth--I get carried away with one and forget the others! I'm so frustrated--I'm going to give it one more attempt--I've written more of these drafts than any other paper and I'm getting so sick of it--it seems to be getting worse instead of better. . . .

> October 11. I just finished my final draft on my personal experience. It feels so good to be done with it--I think it's pretty good--not terrific, but much better. . . .

Julie's journal-writing voice was never meant for publication. These entries are not carefully crafted or revised like the other examples in this chapter. In fact, there's a raw, partially finished effect with all the dashes and repetitions. Her entries read the way personal journals read — unedited, private, off the record, a bit vulnerable, but believably honest.

Personal

The following is Julie's opening paragraph of a five-page personal essay recounting her experience playing varsity tennis in high school.

> Bounce. Bounce. Bounce. The sound is driving me insane, but I just can't get the nerve to toss the ball and serve. Am I scared? Yes. Of what, this girl or this match? This girl, this girl scares me. She is a natural talent. How many times is that cross-court forehand shot going to rip past me? Nuts! I am going to lose plain and simple. I'll just have to deal with it.

Julie invites her readers into the inner and usually hidden reaches of her mind with this personal — but not private — voice. Her clipped, internal voice sounds authentic and believable. (*Am I scared? Yes.*) She invites her audience to identify with her feelings of self-doubt. Hers is the individual voice of a good tennis player at a vulnerable moment.

Informative

This example is taken from the early pages of Julie's ten-page research essay focusing on a center for emotionally disturbed children.

> The Huron Center provides residential treatment for a limited number of emotionally disturbed children in the upper Midwest. The Center contains forty-five beds: thirty-five are reserved for long-term care, generally six months to a year; ten are assessment beds, reserved for stays of up to two months; and five are crisis beds, reserved for stays of ten days or less. The children live together, supervised by twelve staff members. They sleep two to a bedroom, share recreational areas, and eat all of their meals in the large common dining room.

Julie's voice here is that of a reporter presenting and explaining information; it provides numerical facts in a methodical manner and makes no value judgments. By adopting this neutral voice she put herself in the background but revealed nevertheless her careful attention to detail and organization.

Committed

The following is Julie's concluding paragraph from the Huron Center paper.

> The Huron Center is a haven for needy people who have run out of options for helping their own children. The facilities are modern, the services professional, and the setting rural and peaceful. However, the small, dedicated staff is stressed to the limit. They often work sixty-hour weeks, with children whose troubles they do not always under-

stand. Emotionally disturbed children need more, not less, help, but federal funds have dried up. Where will future resources come from? For now, the Center's best chance for survival depends upon public awareness. Wake up and help the children!

Julie here is an advocate for the plight of the understaffed center; she now uses judgment words (*haven, needy, stressed*) and ends with an emotional plea (*Wake up and help the children!*). Her voice is committed, but at the same time it remains precise, controlled, and faithful to the facts.

Reflective

Julie's final paper was an examination of her own voice as a writer. The following passage appears on the last page of her reflective essay.

> During the semester my real growth has been in thinking rather than writing. In my first paper, I had to rewrite and rewrite until readers could actually see me playing tennis. In my research paper I found statistics, interviewed staff members, and gathered evidence to show that the Huron Center was in trouble. In writing these papers, I've learned to slow down my thinking, to review it, to return to it, and make it clearer and clearer and clearer. That's what good writing is really about, isn't it, being clear?

Here Julie leads off with what seems to be a surprising discovery on her part — that she has grown more as a thinker than as a writer. She mulls over her experiences and concludes whimsically with a rhetorical question aimed as much at herself as at the reader. In the end, her voice is reflective, quite different from either the neutral voice or the committed voice from her research essay, but sharing some traits with both her journal and her personal essay.

Notice how Julie used her different voices to respond to different assignments. She was personal when recounting her own experience; she was neutral when reporting information; she was committed when arguing for the children. Just as her portfolio reveals five different Julies, it also reveals traits of a consistent Julie, found in more than one of her voices: her penchant for presenting information and ideas in an orderly manner, her lively language, her awareness of the power of repetition to create emphasis, a willingness to go out on a limb and admit limitations, an assertive nature, and a sense of honesty.

WRITING 4

How would you describe your own writing voice? How many voices do you have? Explain.

SUGGESTIONS FOR WRITING AND RESEARCH

Individual

1. Read a book or a substantial number of articles by one of your favorite writers of nonfiction. Make notes about the features of voice
   that you notice; describe them in terms of tone, style, structure,
   values, and authority. Write a report in which you explain and analyze the writer's voice.
2. Collect and examine as many samples of your past writing as you
   have saved. Also look closely at the writing you have done so far
   this semester. Write a paper in which you describe and explain the
   history and evolution of your voice and the features that most
   characterize your current writing voice.

Collaborative

Divide your writing group into pairs and exchange recently written
papers with a partner. Examine your partner's paper for the elements
of voice. In a letter, each of you describe what you find. How does
your partner's perception of your voice match or differ from your
own? Now do individual assignment number 2 including your partner's assessment as part of your analysis.

PART THREE

GETTING STARTED, GETTING HELP

Chapter 7

Inventing and Discovering

Get something down! The hardest part of writing is starting.
Forget the introduction, skip the outline, don't worry yet
about a thesis — just blast your ideas down, see what
you've got, then go back more slowly and work on them.

— AARON

WRITERS INVENT WHEN THEY CREATE NEW IDEAS. Writers discover when they relocate their own forgotten ideas or learn by reading or listening to others' ideas. Invention and discovery work together by helping writers recognize the huge amount of information stored in long-term memory, generate new ideas, and make connections among ideas.

Writers invent and discover in virtually all phases of the writing process: when they limit and focus assignments; when they find topics and approaches to topics; when they develop answers to questions and solutions to problems; and when they figure out openings and conclusions, arrange arguments, and place supporting examples. While the writing techniques that are discussed in this chapter can be used at any point during the writing process, this chapter focuses on strategies that help you get started at the very beginning of a project.

Invention and discovery writing is often the best antidote to "writer's block." It lets you start writing by writing, even when you think you have nothing to say. All writers have had the experience of written language generating or modifying thought. It happens whenever they find themselves writing something they hadn't thought about before they started writing. This occurs because writing lets people *see* their own ideas — perhaps for the first time — and then react to and even change those ideas. When you realize that writing has this potential, then you can use it as a tool for invention and discovery. You won't use all of the techniques that are discussed in this chapter in a single project, but they provide a good range of ways to begin any writing project.

WRITING 1

Describe the procedures you usually use to start writing a paper. Where do you get the ideas — from speaking? listening? reading? writing? Do you do anything special to help them come? What do you do when ideas don't come?

BRAINSTORMING

Brainstorming is systematic list making. You ask yourself a question and then list a variety of answers. The point is to get down on paper as many ideas or pieces of information as you can. Sometimes you can do this best by setting goals for yourself: *What are seven possible topics I could write about for my paper on pollution?* Sometimes you can do it by leaving the question open-ended: *What are all the sources of lake pollution that I've heard about?* Each item in your list becomes a possible direction for your paper.

By making a list, you let one idea lead to the next. For example, while making a grocery list you may write "eggs" on a piece of paper, which reminds you of "bacon," "bread," and "orange juice." By challenging yourself to generate as long a list as possible, you force yourself to find and record even vague, half-formed ideas in concrete language, where you can examine them and decide whether they're worth pursuing.

Following is one exercise to push a vague subject into a shaped topic:

- List as many topics as you can in three minutes. Circle the three topics that interest you most and write a paragraph about each.
- List two or more things in each paragraph that still puzzle you. Then list two solutions to your questions.
- List three ideas to open (or conclude) the paper.

As you can see, writers often brainstorm to help them decide where to go next. Some writers routinely make lists of possible topics to write about. Other writers think through their whole essays or reports by making quick lists of possible approaches, options, and directions.

WRITING 2

Brainstorm a topic for the next paper you need to write by following any of the list-making suggestions in this section.

FREEWRITING

When I freewrite, I tend to think faster and my thoughts come quicker and I digress more often and find all sorts of new stuff. If I didn't write, I wouldn't find that stuff.

– *BILL*

Freewriting is writing quickly without rules. You depend simply on one word to trigger the next, one idea to lead to another. It is an attempt to find a focus by writing intensely, nonstop, without censoring the words on your mind before you have a chance to look at them, giving these words a chance to suggest or discover ideas that could be useful.

Try the following suggestions for freewriting:

1. Write as fast as you can for a fixed period of time, say five or ten minutes, about whatever is on your mind.
2. Do not allow your pen to stop moving until the time is up.
3. Don't worry about what your writing looks like or how it's organized — the only audience for this writing is yourself.
4. If at some point you cannot think of what else to write, write about being stuck — something better will come soon.

If you digress in your freewriting, fine. If you misspell a word or write something silly, fine. If you catch a fleeting thought that's especially interesting, good. If you think of something you never thought of before, wonderful. And if nothing interesting comes out — well, maybe next time. The following five-minute freewrite by John, a first-year business major, shows his attempt to find a topic for a local research project.

> I can't think of anything special just now, nothing really comes to mind that I'm exactly burning to do, well maybe something about the downtown mall would be good because I wouldn't mind spending time down there. Jody suggested the airport, but who wants to go way out there? Anyway something about the mall . . . maybe the street vendors, the hot dog guy or the pretzel guy or that woman selling T and sweatshirts, they're always there, even in lousy weather--do they like it that much? Actually, all winter. Do they need the money that bad? Why do people become street vendors--like maybe they graduated from college and couldn't get jobs? Or were these the guys who never wanted anything to do with college? Actually, it could be kind of a free lifestyle, pushing your own cart, being responsible just to yourself.

John's freewrite is typical: he starts with no ideas, rejects the airport, but finds the mall appealing. Notice that his writing is unstructured; in freewriting a writer covers a lot of mental ground by jumping wherever his or her thoughts lead. This turned out to be an especially useful freewriting exercise — John found himself raising questions about the street vendors and ended up doing a paper on the life of a hot dog vendor at the mall.

WRITING 3

Freewrite for ten minutes to find your next topic for a paper or to advance one you're now working on. Do this for ten minutes a day each day for a week. Did it help? In what particular way?

INVISIBLE WRITING

An interesting way to do freewriting on a computer is to turn down the brightness level of the monitor until you cannot see the letters being generated as you type. Then begin writing rapidly, concentrating on the ideas in your head. The advantage of not seeing your writing is that your own words will not distract you. If you are among the many writers who find it easier to return to a draft than to start fresh, with invisible writing you can fool yourself into thinking that you have, in fact, already started your paper; after five or ten minutes of freewriting, when you turn the monitor back on, you have a text to return to.

WRITING 4

Turn your monitor's brightness level down and write invisibly for five minutes. Do this for five minutes each day for a week to help you find or advance an idea in a paper you are working on. After doing invisible writing for a week, do you think you will continue? Why or why not?

LOOPING

Looping or loop writing is a variation of freewriting in which you do a series of freewrites, each one focusing closer on the issue most current in your mind. To loop, follow this procedure:

1. Freewrite for ten minutes to discover a topic or advance the one you are working on.
2. Review your freewrite and select one sentence that seems closest to the idea you want to continue developing. Copy this sentence, and take off from it, freewriting for another ten minutes. (John might have selected the sentence *Why do people become street vendors?* for further freewriting.)
3. Repeat step 2 for each successive freewrite to keep inventing, discovering, or focusing.

Looping focuses freewriting to develop a paper's ideas and direction. In the following example, John loops back to his first freewrite and now focuses more closely on street vending as a possible topic:

> I've been thinking of questions to ask the guy who sells pretzels from his cart downtown--he does this all winter, maybe especially in winter, that's when people especially want pretzels: So how did he get started? Did he go to college? What did he major in? How long has he been doing it? How long does he plan to continue? What's the best thing about the job? The worst thing? Where's the best location? What was his

best day? Lots of questions to base a paper on, then I need to see what the library might have about cart vendors.

WRITING 5

Practice loop writing on a current topic that you need to develop more deeply. After several loops, record the results in your journal. Did it work? Did you enjoy it? Will you use it again?

ASKING A REPORTER'S QUESTIONS

Writers who train themselves to ask questions are also training themselves to find information. Reporters train themselves to ask six basic questions: *Who? What? Where? When? Why?* and *How?* Using this regular repertoire of questions will help you discover much information related to your topic.

Who was involved?

What happened?

Where did this happen?

When did it happen?

Why did it happen?

How did it happen?

WRITING 6

Once you have chosen a topic, apply the reporter's questions to find information about your topic.

MAKING OUTLINES

Outlines are, essentially, organized lists. In fact, outlines grow out of lists, as writers determine which ideas go first and which later, which have equal weight with others and which need to be subordinated to others. Formal outlines use a system of Roman numerals, capital letters, Arabic numerals, and lowercase letters to create a hierarchy of ideas. Some writers prefer informal outlines, using indentations to indicate relationships between ideas. In either case, outlines can help you understand and control the scope, direction, emphasis, and logic of a paper.

When Carol set out to write a research report on the effect of acid rain on the environment in New England, she first brainstormed a quick list of areas that such a report might cover:

What is acid rain?

What are its effects on the environment?

What causes it?

How can it be stopped?

After some preliminary research, Carol produced an initial outline:

I. Definition of acid rain
II. The causes of acid rain
    A. Coal-burning power plants
    B. Automobile pollution
III. The effects of acid rain
    A. Deforestation in New England
        1. The White Mountain study
        2. Maple trees dying in Vermont
    B. Dead lakes
IV. Solutions to the acid rain problem

Note how Carol rearranged the second and third items in her original list because she realized that it is more logical to talk about causes before effects. The very act of making the outline encouraged her to invent a structure for her ideas: What comes first? What next? Why? Moving entries around is especially easy if you are using a computer because you can see many combinations before committing yourself to any one of them. The rules of formal outlining also cause you to search for ideas. If you have a Roman numeral *I* you need a *II*; if you have a capital letter *A* you need a *B*. Carol immediately thought of coal-burning power plants as a cause, and then she brainstormed for several minutes to come up with an idea to pair with it.

Outlines are most useful if you let them grow and develop as you write and do not stick stubbornly to what you first jotted down. Use outlines and make them work for you, but change them when new arrangements occur to you.

WRITING 7

Once you have decided on a topic, make an outline of how the sections of your paper might be put together. Share your outline with a classmate and see where he or she has questions. Was your outline perfectly clear? What changes will clarify it? Does your paper now seem easier to start?

CLUSTERING

Clustering is a method of listing ideas in a nonlinear way to reveal the relationships among them. One idea begets another, and you find ideas you didn't realize you had. Clustering is useful for inventing and discovering a topic and for exploring a topic once you have done preliminary research.

To use clustering, follow this procedure:

1. Write a word or phrase that seems to be the focus of what you want to write about. (For her research paper about the environment, Carol wrote *acid rain*.)
2. Write as many ideas related to your focus as you can think of. Write the ideas in a circle radiating from the central idea. If one of the new ideas suggests others, write those in a circle around that idea. (Carol did this with her idea *Solutions*.)

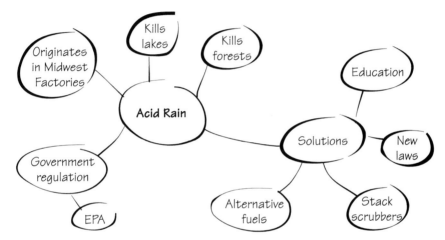

3. If one idea (like *Solutions*) begins to accumulate related ideas, start a second cluster with the new term in the center of the page. (When Carol did this, she changed the general idea *Solutions* to the more specific *Preventing acid rain* for her new cluster.)

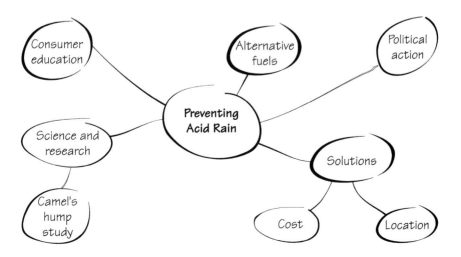

<hr>
WRITING 8

Make a cluster to find your next paper topic or to help you advance a topic you've already chosen.

COLLABORATING

Working with other writers to find and develop ideas can be a powerful invention and discovery strategy. Most commonly, four to six writers form a group to share their ideas and their writing. Group members use focused conversation to help individual writers develop ideas, focus a topic, critique a draft, and so on.

Any of the techniques discussed earlier in this chapter can be used in writing groups. At the beginning of a writing assignment, writers in a group may share lists of possible topics or journal entries exploring what to write about. At later stages, group members can critique one another's drafts, listing strengths as well as sources of confusion.

<hr>
WRITING 9

Describe one time, in high school or elsewhere, when you collaborated with others on an assignment or project. Explain how you worked together to invent and discover how the project should be done. Did the collaboration continue throughout the whole project?

<hr>
SUGGESTIONS FOR WRITING AND RESEARCH

Individual

Invent a technique for finding ideas that is not included in this chapter. Write a short section for this chapter in which you explain the technique, provide samples of it, and give clear directions to teach other writers how to use it. (If everyone in the class does this, you can publish a pamphlet including each writer's technique.)

Collaborative

Find a common writing topic by having each person in the group or class select one of the invention and discovery techniques described in this chapter and practice using it for ten minutes. Make a list on the board or on the overhead projector of the topic ideas generated this way. Then ask each student to select one topic, not his or her own, and write for another five minutes about that topic. Again make a list of topics and the important ideas generated about them. Discuss the ideas together and try to arrive at a consensus on a common writing topic.

$\equiv$

Keeping a Journal

Journal writing forces me to think about the problems I'm having
with a paper. It's almost a relief, like talking to a friend. I have
a conversation with myself and end up answering my own questions.

— PETER

JOURNALS ALLOW PEOPLE TO TALK to themselves without feeling silly. Writing in a journal helps college students think about what is happening in their personal and academic lives — an especially important activity for first-year students coping with a new, often bewildering and exciting environment. Sometimes students focus their journal writing narrowly, on the subject matter of a single discipline; at other times they speculate broadly, on the whole range of academic experience; at still other times they write personally, exploring their private thoughts and feelings.

College instructors often require or recommend that students keep journals to monitor what and how they are learning. Just as often, however, students require journals of themselves, realizing that journals are useful and easy to keep whether they're handed in or not.

CHARACTERISTICS OF JOURNALS

In simplest terms, journals are daily records of people's lives (*jour* is French for "day"). Journals are sometimes called *diaries, daybooks, logs, learning logs,* or *commonplace books.* No matter what you call them, the entries written in them are likely to include whatever thoughts, feelings, activities, or plans are on your mind when you sit down to write. In this sense, a journal can be whatever you want it to be, recording whatever snippets of life you find interesting and potentially useful. Certain characteristics, however, remain true for most journals.

Sequence

You use a journal to capture your thoughts sequentially, from one day to the next, though you may not write in it every day. Over time the entries form a cumulative record of what's on your mind.

Dating each entry allows you to compare ideas to later and earlier ones and provides an ongoing record of your constancy, change, or growth. You thus end up documenting your learning over the course of a semester or a project.

Audience

Journals are written to help writers rather than readers. A journal is a place for you to explore what's important to you, not to communicate information or ideas to someone else. While you may choose to share entries with readers whom you trust, that is not the reason you keep a journal. A journal assigned by an instructor who intends to read it may initiate an informal conversation between you and the instructor. As such, it has much in common with notes, letters, and other informal means of communication. Some instructors ask to see sample entries rather than read the whole journal. In most cases, required journals receive credit but not a specific grade.

Language

Journal writing is whatever writers want it to be. There usually are no rules — you choose your own language and your own subjects. (The exception may be an assigned journal.) Your focus should be on *ideas* rather than on style, spelling, or punctuation. In journal writing, simply concentrate on *what* you want to say and use the word, spelling, or punctuation that comes most readily to mind.

Freedom

Students usually are free to practice, discover, rehearse, and even get things wrong in journals without being penalized. Used in this way, journals are practice and discovery books — you can put new concepts into your own language, try out new lines of reasoning or logic, and not worry about completing every thought. If something doesn't work the first time, you can just try it again in subsequent entries — or abandon it entirely. In a journal, you always have the freedom to try again.

WRITING 1

Describe your experiences or associations with journals. Have you ever kept one for school before? In which class? With what result? Have you ever kept one on your own? With what result? Do you still keep one? What is it like?

USING JOURNALS IN COLLEGE

Academic journals differ from diaries, daybooks, and private journals in important ways. Whereas diaries and the like may record any and all events of the writer's day, academic journals focus more consistently on ideas under study in college.

Academic journals also differ in important ways from class notebooks, which record the instructor's words rather than the writer's. Academic journals might be called "learning logs" because they record the writer's own perceptions about the business of learning, including reactions to readings, impressions of class, and ideas for writing papers.

Academic journals might be described as a cross between private diaries and class notebooks. Like diaries, journals are written in the first person about ideas important to the writer; like class notebooks, they focus on a subject under study in a college course. We might diagram academic journals like this:

Diary ————→ Academic journal ————→ Class notebook

Academic journals are most often associated with writing classes, but they can be worthwhile in other classes, too, because they help students become better thinkers and writers.

Journals in the Writing Class

Journals are often assigned in writing classes both to help students discover, explore, advance, and critique their specific writing projects and to help instructors monitor and informally assess students' development as writers.

You can use your journal to find topics to write about, to try out introductions and arguments to use in a paper, to record relevant research and observations, to assess how a paper is turning out, and to make plans for what to do next. In the following journal entry, John tells himself what to do in the next draft of a paper describing his coaching of an eighth-grade girls' soccer team:

> 9/16 I'm going to try to use more dialogue in my paper. That is what I really think I was missing. The second draft is very dull. As I read it, it has no life. I should have used more detail.
>
> I'll try more dialogue, lots more, in draft #3. I'll have it take place at one of my practices, giving a vivid description of what kids were like.
>
> I have SO MUCH MATERIAL. But I have a hard time deciding what seems more interesting.

John's entry is an excellent example of a writer critically evaluating himself and, on the basis of that evaluation, making plans to change something.

Use your journal to record regularly what you are learning in class as you read the textbook, participate in class discussion, read other student papers and models of good professional writing, and review your own writing.

Near the end of John's writing course, he reflected in his journal about what he'd learned so far:

> 11/29 I've learned to be very critical of my own work, to look at it again and again, looking for big and little problems. I've also learned from my writing group that other people's comments can be extremely helpful--so now I make sure I show my early drafts to Kelly or Karen before I write the final draft. I guess I've always known this, but now I actually do it.

WRITING 2

Keep a journal for the duration of a writing project, recording in it all of your starts, stops, insights, and ideas related to the project. At the end, consider whether the journal presents a fair portrait of your own writing process.

Journals Across the Curriculum

Journals are good tools for learning any subject better. They are especially useful in helping you clarify the purposes of a course, pose and solve problems, keep track of readings, raise questions to ask in class, practice for exams, and find topics for paper assignments.

In science or mathematics, when you switch from numbers to words, you often see the problem differently. In addition, putting someone else's problem into your own words makes it your problem and so leads you one step further toward a solution. Ross made the following entry in a journal for a first-year biology course. He was trying to connect what he was learning in the class to what he knew from fishing.

> 10/7 I noticed that saltwater barracudas resemble freshwater pike, pickerel, and muskies. As a matter of curiosity, are these different species analogous--that is, equally successful forms but of different evolution, which converged toward similitude? Or are they of common heritage, homologous?

One of the best uses of a journal is to make connections between college knowledge and personal knowledge — each reinforces the other and the connections often lead to greater total understanding. Once Ross finds the answer to his questions, he will be more likely to remember this information than information about which he cannot make personal connections.

When you record personal reflections in a literature or history journal, you may begin to identify with and perhaps make sense of the otherwise distant and confusing past. When you write out trial hypotheses in a social science journal, you may discover good ideas for research topics, designs, or experiments. Whether or not an instructor assigns a journal, keeping one will help you raise, reflect on, and answer your own questions in almost any course.

WRITING 3

Think of a course you are taking that does not require a journal. Could you find a use for a journal in that class? What topics would you explore? Write about something in the course that you have not fully figured out. Or keep a journal for a week or two and see if it helps your understanding of the course. After doing so, consider how it worked. Did you find out something interesting? Explain.

Double-entry Journals

A double-entry journal can help you separate initial observations from later, more reflective observations. To make such a journal, divide each page in a notebook with a vertical line down the middle. On the left side of the page, record initial impressions or data observations; on the right side, return as often as necessary to reflect on the meaning of what you first recorded.

While the idea of a double-entry journal originated in the sciences as a way for lab scientists to collect data at one time and to speculate about them later, these notebooks also serve well in other courses. In a literature class, for example, you can make initial observations about the plot of a story on the left, while raising questions and noting personal reflections on the right.

The example on the next page is a sample journal entry by Susan, a first-year college student, who read Alice Walker's novel *The Color Purple* for the first time. In the left column, she recorded the plot; in the right column, she noted her personal reaction to what she was reading.

The reason Susan took such careful notes in a double-entry journal is that she intended to write an interpretive paper about the novel. You can see the value of a reader monitoring his or her reactions with such care, even noting which pages raise which questions. When Susan began to write her paper, these journal entries helped her to find a thesis and to locate particular passages in the novel to support her thesis.

WRITING 4

Keep a double-entry journal for two weeks. On one side of the page include notes from books you are reading or lectures you are attending. On the other side, write you own thoughts or reactions to those notes. At the end of two weeks, assess the value of this technique for your own understanding of the course material.

Personal Journals

Personal journal writing also has many powerful benefits for students and other writers. In personal journals writers can explore their feelings about any aspect of their lives — being in college, prospective majors, getting along

Summary	What I think
pp. 3 — 12. Celie's mother is dying so her father starts having sex with her. She got pregnant by him twice, and he sold both of her babies. Celie's mother died and he got married again to a very young girl. Mr. is a man whose wife died and he has a lot of children. He wants to marry Celie's sister Nettie. Their father won't let him. He says Nettie has too much going for her so he let him have Celie.	Why did Celie's father sell her kids? How could Mr. take Celie if he wanted Nettie so much? I think Celie's father is lowdown and selfish. A very cruel man.
pp. 13 — 23. Celie got married to Mr., and his kids don't like her. While Celie was in town she met the lady who has her kids. She was a preacher's wife. Nettie ran away and came to stay with Celie. Mr. still likes her and puts her out because she shows no interest in him. Celie tells her to go to the preacher's wife's house and stay with them because she was the only woman she saw with money.	I think it's wrong to marry someone to take care of your children and to keep your home clean. I think Celie was at least glad to know one of her children was in good hands. I am glad Neetie was able to get away from her Dad and Mr., hopefully the preacher & wife will take her in.
pp. 24 — 32. Shug Avery, Mr.'s old friend and also an entertainer, came to town. Mr. got all dressed up so he can go see her, he stayed gone all weekend. Celie was very excited about her.	How could he go and stay out with another woman all weekend? Why didn't he marry Shug? Why was Celie so fascinated with Shug?

with a roommate, the frustration of receiving a low grade on a paper, the weekend party, or a new date. Anne, a student in a first-year writing class, put it this way:

> Writing is a release, a way of expressing myself, and a way for me to be introspective. It helps me find meaning in my thoughts and gets me through hard times.

When you keep a journal in a writing class, it's a good idea to mark off a section for personal entries. Whether you share these with your instructor should be your choice. In the following example, Amy was writing more about herself than her writing class; however, she chose to share the entry with her instructor anyway.

> 11/12 I think I should quit complaining about being misunderstood . . . since I don't try very hard to be understandable, it's no wonder people don't. I just get ticked because more people don't even seem to try to understand others. So many people talk instead of listening. (I think I'm scared of the ones who listen.)

WRITING 5

Keep a personal journal for two weeks, writing faithfully for at least ten minutes each day. Write about your friends, family, future, work, money, frustrations, successes, failures, plans, dates, movies — whatever is on your mind. After two weeks, reread all of your entries and assess the value of such a journal to you.

EXPERIMENTING WITH JOURNALS

If you are keeping a journal for the first time, write often and regularly on a wide variety of topics, and take risks with form, style, and voice. Notice how writing in the early morning differs from writing late at night. Notice the results of writing at the same time every day, regardless of inclination or mood. Try to develop the habit of using your journal even when you are not in an academic environment. Good ideas, questions, and answers don't always wait for convenient times. Above all, write in your journal in your most comfortable voice, freely, and don't worry about someone evaluating you. The following selection of journal entries illustrates some of the ways journals can be especially helpful.

Inventing

Journals can help you plan and start any project by providing a place to talk it over with yourself. Whether it's a research paper, a personal essay, or a take-home exam, you can make journal notes about how to approach a project, where to start, or whom to consult before beginning a draft. Here are two entries from Peter's journal in which he tried to discover a research paper topic for his first-year writing class.

> 10/8 The first draft of this research paper is really difficult: how can you write about something you aren't even interested in? It was not a good idea to pick the "legalization of marijuana" just because the issue came up in class discussion. I'm afraid my paper will be all opinion and no facts, because I really don't feel like digging for these facts--if there are any.

> 10/12 Well, I switched my research topic to something I'm actually interested in, a handicapped children's rehabilitation program right here on campus. My younger brother was born deaf and our whole family has pitched in to help him--but I've never really studied what a college program could do to help. The basis of my research will be interviews with people who run the program--I have my first appointment tomorrow with Professor Stanford.

Sometimes planning means venting frustration about what's going wrong; at other times it means trying a new direction or topic. Peter does both. Journal writing is ultimately unpredictable: it doesn't come out neat and orderly, and sometimes it doesn't solve your problem — but it provides a place where you can keep trying to solve it.

Learning to Write

Part of the content of a writing course is the business of learning to write. In other courses, part of the content is learning to write papers about specific topics. You can use a journal to document how your writing is going and what you need to do to improve it. In the following example, Bruce reflects on his experience of writing a report.

> 10/3 I'm making this report a lot harder than it should be. I think my problem is I try to edit as I write. I think what I need to do is just write whatever I want. After I'm through, then edit and organize. It's hard for me though.

Bruce chastises himself for making his writing harder than need be but at the same time reminds himself about the process he learned in class that would help his report writing. Journals are good places to monitor your own writing process and document what helps you the most.

Writing to Learn

Journal writing can help you discover what you think. The act of regular writing certifies thoughts and even causes new ones to develop. In that sense, journal writing is an invention and discovery technique. (See Chapter 7.) In the following example, Julie, who kept a journal about all the authors she studied in her American literature course, noticed a disturbing pattern and wrote in her journal to make some sense of it.

> 5/4 So far, the first two authors we have to read have led tragic, un-happy lives. I wonder if this is just a coincidence or if it has something to do with the personality of successful writers. Actually, of all people, writers need a lot of time alone, by themselves, thinking and writing, away from other people, including, probably, close family members. The more I think about it, writers would be very difficult people to live with, that's it--writers spend so much time alone and become hard to live with . . .

Julie used the act of regular journal writing to discover and develop ideas, make interpretations, and test hypotheses. Writing to learn requires you to trust that as you write, ideas will come — some right, some wrong; some good, some bad.

Questioning and Answering

A journal is a place to raise questions about ideas or issues that don't make sense. Raising questions is a fundamental part of all learning: the more you ask, the more you learn as you seek answers. In the following example, Jim wrote in his journal to figure out a quotation written on the blackboard in his technical writing class:

> 9/23 "All Writing Is Persuasive"--It's hard to write on my understand-ing of this quote because I don't think that all writing is persuasive. What about assemblies for models and cookbook recipes? I realize that for stories, newspaper articles, novels, and so forth that they are per-suasive. But is all writing persuasive? I imagine that for assemblies and so forth that they are persuading a person to do something a par-ticular way. But is this really persuasive writing?

While Jim began by writing "I don't think that all writing *is* persuasive," he concluded that even assembly instructions "are persuading a person to do something a particular way." The writing sharpened the focus of Jim's questioning and made him critically examine his own ideas, leading him to reconsider his first response to the quotation.

Becoming Political

College is a good place to develop a wider awareness of the world, and a journal can help you examine the social and political climate you grew up in and perhaps took for granted. Jennifer used her journal to reflect on sexist language, recording both her awareness of sexist language in society as well as her own difficulty in avoiding it.

> 3/8 Sexist language is everywhere. So much so that people don't even realize what they are saying is sexist. My teacher last year told all the "mothers-to-be" to be sure to read to their children. What about the fathers? Sexist language is dangerous because it so easily under-mines women's morale and self-image. I try my hardest not to use sexist language, but even I find myself falling into old stereotypes.

Evaluating Classes

Journals can be used to capture and record feelings about how a class is going, about what you are learning and not learning. In the following entry, Brian seemed surprised that writing can be fun.

> 9/28 English now is more fun. When I write, the words come out more easily and it's not like homework. All my drafts help me put to-gether my thoughts and retrieve memories that were hidden some-where in the dungeons of my mind. Usually I wouldn't like English, like in high school, but I pretty much enjoy it here. I like how you get to hear people's reactions to your papers and discuss them with each other.

Entries like this can help you monitor your own learning process. Instructors also learn from candid and freely given comments about the effects of their teaching. Your journal is one place where you can let your instructor know what is happening in class from your point of view.

Clarifying Values

Your journal can be a record of evolving insight as well as the tool to gain that insight. You might ask yourself questions that force you to examine life closely: "If my house were on fire and I could save only one object, what would it be?" or "If I had only two more days to live, how would I spend them?" I used my journal to wrestle with the next direction my life would take:

> 3/12 Do I really want to switch jobs and move to North Carolina? The climate is warmer--a lot longer motorcycle season--and maybe this time we'd look for a farm. But Laura would have to start all over with her job, finding new contacts in the public school system, and we'd both have to find new friends, new doctors, dentists, auto mechanics, get new driver's licenses.

> In truth, we really like Vermont, the size, the scale, the beauty, our
> house, and Annie is just starting college. Money and sunshine aren't
> everything. . . .

What you read here is only one entry from nearly a month's worth of writing
as I tried to figure out what to do with an attractive job offer. In the end, and
with the clarifying help of my journal, I stayed put.

Letting Off Steam

Journals are good places to vent frustration over personal or academic
difficulties. College instructors don't assign journals to improve student's mental health, but they know that journals can help. Kenyon wrote about the
value of the journal experience:

> 10/14 This journal has saved my sanity. It got me started at
> writing. . . . I can't keep all my problems locked up inside me, but I
> hate telling others, burdening them with my problems--like what I'm go-
> ing to do with my major or with the rest of my life.

In many ways, writing in a journal is like talking to a sympathetic audience;
the difference, as Kenyon noted, is that the journal is always there, no matter
what's on your mind, and it never gives you grief.

Finding Patterns

The very nature of the journal — sequential, chronological, personal —
lends it to synthesizing activities, such as finding patterns or larger structures
in your learning over time. Rereading journal entries after a few weeks or
months can provide specific material from which you can make generalizations and hypotheses. Each individual act of summary becomes a potential
thread for weaving new patterns of meaning. Near the end of an American literature course, Maureen summarized the journal's cumulative power this way:

> 5/2 I feel that through the use of this journal over the weeks I have
> been able to understand certain aspects of each story by actually writ-
> ing down what I like, and what I don't. . . . Many times I didn't even
> realize that something bothered me about a story until I put down my
> feelings in words. I wasn't even sure how I even felt about The Sun
> Also Rises until I kicked a few ideas around on paper. Now I plan to
> write my take-home exam about it. In short, this journal has really
> helped me understand this class.

Recording Growth

Sometimes it's hard to see how a journal functions overall until you
reread it at the end of a term and notice where you began and where you

ended. All along your writing may have been casual and fast, your thought tentative, your assessments or conclusions uncertain. But the journal gives you a record of who you were, what you thought, and how you changed. Rereading a term's entries may be a pleasant surprise, as Jeff found out:

> 11/21 The journal to me has been like a one-man debate, where I could write thoughts down and then later read them. This seemed to help clarify many of my ideas. To be honest there is probably fifty percent of the journal that is nothing but B.S. and ramblings to fulfill assignments, but that still leaves fifty percent that I think is of importance. The journal is also a time capsule. I want to put it away and not look at it for ten or twenty years and let it recall for me this period of my life.

WRITING 6

Look over the examples in this section and see if you can think up half a dozen other uses for journals that the section does not cover. Can you provide any concrete examples from your own journal?

SUGGESTIONS FOR WRITING AND RESEARCH

Individual

1. Select a writer in your intended major who is known for having written a journal (for example, Mary Shelley, Ralph Waldo Emerson, Virginia Woolf, or Anaïs Nin in literature; Leonardo da Vinci, Georgia O'Keeffe, or Edward Weston in the arts; B. F. Skinner or Margaret Mead in the social sciences; Charles Darwin or Marie Curie in the sciences). Study the writer's journals to identify the features that characterize them and the purpose they served. Write a report on what you find and share it with your class.

2. At the end of the semester, review your journal and do the following: (a) put in page numbers, (b) write a title for each entry, (c) make a table of contents, and (d) write an introduction to the journal explaining how it might be read by a stranger (or your instructor).

3. Review your journal entries for the past five weeks, select one entry that seems especially interesting, and write a reflective essay of several pages on it. How are they different? Which is better? Is that a fair question?

Collaborative

Have each student bring to class typed copies of one journal entry written during the term. Exchange entries in writing groups or in the whole class and discuss interesting features of the entries.

Chapter 9

Sharing and Responding

*Listening to other people's criticism is really helpful, especially when they
stop being too nice and really tell you what they think about your paper.*

— *KELLY*

ALL WRITING PROFITS FROM HELP. Most published writing has been shared, explored, talked over, revised, and edited somewhere along the way to make it as readable, precise, and interesting as it is. The published writing you read in books, magazines, and newspapers that is signed by individual authors is seldom the result of either one-draft writing or one-person work. This is not to say that authors do not write their own work, for of course they do. But even the best of writers begin, draft, and revise better when they receive suggestions from friends, editors, reviewers, teachers, and critics. This chapter explores specific ways to ask for help with your own writing as well as to provide it to others.

SHARING YOUR WRITING

Writers can ask for help at virtually all stages of the writing process. Sometimes they try out ideas on friends and colleagues while they are still planning or drafting. More often, however, writers ask for help while they are revising, as they try to make their ideas coherent and convincing, and while they are editing, as they try to make their language clear and precise. In addition, when a draft is nearly final, many writers ask for proofreading help since most writers are their own worst proofreaders. Here are some suggestions for getting good help as you revise your writing.

SPECIFY WHAT YOU WANT. When you share a draft with a reader, be sure to specify what kind of help you are looking for. If you consider your draft nearly finished and want only a quick proofreading, it can be very frustrating if your reader suggests major changes that you do not have time for or interest in. Likewise, if you share an early draft and want help organizing and clarifying ideas because you intend to do major rewriting, it is annoying to have your paper returned with every sentence edited for wordiness, misspellings, and typographical errors. You can usually head off such undesirable responses by being very clear about exactly what kind of help you want. If you do want a general reaction, say so — but be prepared to hear about everything and anything.

ASK SPECIFIC QUESTIONS.   Tell your reader exactly what kinds of comments will help you most. If you wonder whether you've provided enough examples, ask about that. If you want to know whether your argument is airtight, ask about that. If you are concerned about style or tone, ask about that. Also mark in the margins your specific concerns about an idea, a phrase, a sentence, a conclusion, or even a title.

ASK GLOBAL QUESTIONS.   If you are concerned about larger matters, make sure you identify what these are. Ask if the reader understands and can identify your thesis. Ask if the larger purpose is clear. Ask if the paper seems right for its intended audience. Ask for general reactions about readability, style, evidence, and completeness. Ask if your reader can anticipate any objections or problems other readers may have.

DON'T BE DEFENSIVE.   Whether you receive the responses about your paper orally or in writing, pay close attention to them. You have asked somebody to spend time with your writing, so you should trust that that person is trying to be helpful, that he or she is commenting on your paper, not on you personally. While receiving oral comments, stay quiet, listen, and take notes about what you hear, interrupting only to ask for clarity, not to defend what your reader is commenting on. Remember, a first draft may contain information and ideas that are clear to you; what you want to hear is where they are less clear to someone else.

MAINTAIN OWNERSHIP.   If you receive responses that you do not agree with or that you consider unhelpful, do not feel obliged to heed them. It is your paper; you are the ultimate judge of whether the ideas in it represent you. You will have to live with the results; you may, in fact, be judged by the results. Never include someone else's idea in your paper if you do not understand it or believe it.

WRITING 1

Describe the best response to a piece of your writing that you remember. How old were you? What were the circumstances? Who was the respondent? Explain whether you think the response was deserved or not.

GIVING HELPFUL RESPONSES

When you are asked to respond to other writers' work, keep these basic ideas in mind.

FOLLOW THE GOLDEN RULE.   The very best advice is to give the kind of response to others' writing that you would like to receive on your own. Remember how you feel being praised, criticized, or questioned. Remember what comments help advance your own papers as well as comments that only make you defensive. Keeping those in mind will help you help others.

ATTEND TO THE TEXT, NOT THE PERSON.   Word your comments so that the writer knows you are commenting on his or her writing and not his or her person. The writer is vulnerable, since he or she is sharing with you a product of individual thinking and reasoning. Writers, like all people, have egos that can be bruised easily with careless or cruel comments. Attending to the text itself helps you avoid these problems. Point out language constructions that create pleasure as well as those that create confusion, but avoid commenting on the personality or intelligence of the writer.

PRAISE WHAT DESERVES PRAISE.   Tell the writer what is good about the paper as well as what is not good. *All* writers will more easily accept critical help with weaknesses if you also acknowledge strengths. But avoid praising language or ideas that do not, in your opinion, deserve it. Writers can usually sense praise that is not genuine.

ASK QUESTIONS RATHER THAN GIVE ADVICE.   Ask questions more often than you give answers. You need to respect that the writing is the writer's. If you ask questions, you give the writer room to solve problems on his or her own. Of course, sometimes it is very helpful to give advice and answers or to suggest alternatives when they occur to you. Use your judgment about when to ask questions and when to give advice.

FOCUS ON MAJOR PROBLEMS FIRST.   If you find a lot of problems with a draft, try to focus first on the major problems (which are usually conceptual), and let the minor ones (which are usually linguistic and stylistic) go until sometime later. Drafts that are too marked up with suggestions can overwhelm writers, making them reluctant to return to the job of rewriting.

WRITING 2

What kind of response do you usually give to a writer when you read his or her paper? How do you know what to comment on? How have your comments been received?

RESPONDING IN WRITING

The most common written responses that college students receive to their writing are those that instructors make in the margins or at the end of a paper, usually explaining how they graded the paper. Many of these comments — except the grade — are similar to those made by professional editors on manuscripts. In writing classes you will commonly be asked by classmates to read and write comments on their papers. Here are some suggestions to help you do that.

USE A PENCIL.   Many writers have developed negative associations from teachers covering their writing in red ink, primarily to correct what's wrong rather than to praise what's right. If you comment with pencil, the message to the writer is more gentle — if fact, erasable — and suggests the comments of a colleague rather than the judgments of a grader.

USE CLEAR SYMBOLS.   If you like, you can use professional editing symbols to comment on a classmate's paper. Or you can use other symbols that any writer can figure out. For example, underline words or sentences that puzzle you and put a question mark next to them. Put brackets where a missing word or phrase belongs or around a word or phrase that could be deleted. Circle misspellings.

There are many advantages to written responses. First, writing your comments takes less time and is therefore more efficient than discussing your ideas orally. Second, written comments are usually very specific, identifying particular sentences, paragraphs, or examples that need further thought. Third, written comments leave a record to which the writer can refer later — after days, weeks, and even months — when he or she gets around to revising.

There are also disadvantages to writing comments directly on papers. First, written comments may invite misunderstandings that the respondent is not present to help clarify. Second, written comments that are too blunt may damage a writer's ego — and it's easier to make such comments in writing than face to face. Third, written comments do not allow the writer and reader to clear up simple questions quickly and so risk allowing misinterpretations to persist.

WRITING 3

Describe your most recent experience in receiving written comments from a reader. Were the comments helpful? Did the respondent use an approach similar to that detailed in this section or some other approach? In either case, were the reader's comments helpful?

RESPONDING THROUGH CONFERENCES

Most writers and writing teachers believe that one-to-one conferences provide the best and most immediate help that writers can get. Sitting together, a reader and a writer can look at a paper together, read passages aloud, and ask both general and specific questions about the writing: "What do you want to leave me with at the end?" or "Read that again, there's something about that rhythm that's especially strong." or "Stop. Right there I could really use an example to see what you mean." Often an oral conference helps as a follow-up to written comments.

The suggestions for making effective written responses in the previous section also apply to oral conferences. In addition, here are a few other things to keep in mind.

BE RELAXED AND INFORMAL.   Having your conference in a comfortable place can go a long way toward creating a friendly, satisfying discussion. Don't be afraid of digressions. Very often a discussion about a piece of writing branches into a discussion about the subject of the paper instead of the paper itself. When that happens, both writer and reader learn new things about the subject and about each other, some of which will certainly help the writer. Of course, if the paper is not discussed specifically at all, the writer may not be helped at all.

ASK QUESTIONS.   If you are the reader, ask follow-up questions to help the writer move farther faster in his or her revising. If you have written your responses first, the conference can be a series of follow-up questions, and together you can search for solutions.

LISTEN.   If you are the writer, remember that the more you listen and the less you talk, the more you will learn about your writing. Listen attentively. When puzzled, ask questions; when uncertain, clarify misunderstanding. But keep in mind that your reader is not your enemy and that you and your work are not under attack, so you do not need to be defensive. If you prefer the battle metaphor, look at it this way: Good work will defend itself.

One advantage of one-to-one conferences is that they promote community, friendship, and understanding between writer and reader. Also, conferences can address both global and specific writing concerns at the same time. In addition, conferences allow both writer and reader to ask questions as they occur and to pursue any line of thought until both parties are satisfied with it. And finally, writer and reader can use their facial expression, body language, and oral intonation to clarify misunderstandings as soon as they arise.

There are, however, a few disadvantages to one-on-one conferences. First, it is harder to make tough, critical comments face to face, so readers are often less candid than when they write comments. Second, conferring together in any depth about a piece of writing takes more time than communicating through written responses.

WRITING 4

Confer with a writer about his or her paper, using some of the techniques suggested in this section. Describe in a journal entry how they worked.

RESPONDING IN WRITING GROUPS

Writing groups provide a way for writers to both give and receive help. When the group considers a particular writer's work, that writer receives multiple responses; and the writer is also one respondent among several when another writer's work is considered.

All of the suggestions in previous sections about responding to writing apply, with appropriate modifications, to responding in writing groups. But writing groups involve more people, require more coordination, take more time, and, for many people, are less familiar. Here are some guidelines for organizing writing groups.

FORM A GROUP ALONG COMMON INTERESTS.   Most commonly, writing groups are formed among classmates, often with the instructor's help, and everyone is working on the same or similar class assignments. Membership in a group may remain fixed over a semester, and members may meet every week or two. Or membership may change with every new assignment. Writing groups can also be created outside of class by interested people getting together regularly to share their writing.

FOCUS ON THE WRITING.   The general idea for all writing groups is much the same: to improve one another's writing and encourage one another to do more of it. Writers pass out copies of their writing in advance or read it aloud during the group meeting. After members have read or heard the paper, they share, usually orally but sometimes in writing, their reactions to it.

MAKE YOUR GROUP THE RIGHT SIZE FOR YOUR PURPOSE.   Writing groups can be as small as three or as large as a dozen. If all members are to participate, smaller groups need less time than larger groups and provide more attention to each member. Groups that meet outside of classroom constraints have more freedom to set size and time limits, but more than a dozen members will make it hard for each member to receive individual attention and will require several hours, which may be too long to sustain constructive group efforts.

PLAN HOW TO USE YOUR TIME.   Sometimes group meetings are organized so that each member reads a paper or a portion of a paper. At other times a group meeting focuses on the work of only one member, and members thus take turns receiving responses. If papers are to be read aloud, keep in mind that it generally takes two minutes to read a typed, double-spaced page out loud. Discussion time should at least match the oral reading time for each paper. If group members are able to read the papers before the meeting, length is not as critical an issue because group time can be devoted strictly to discussion. Independently formed groups can experiment to determine how much they can read and discuss at each session, perhaps varying the schedule from meeting to meeting.

There are many advantages to discussing writing in groups. First, writing groups allow a single writer to hear multiple perspectives on his or her writing. Second, writing groups allow an interpretation or consensus to develop through the interplay of those perspectives; the result can be a cumulative response that existed in no single reader's mind before the session. Third, writing groups can give both writers and readers more confidence by providing each with a varied and supportive audience. Fourth, writing groups can develop friendships and a sense of community among writers that act as a healthy stimulus for continuing writing.

The disadvantages are that groups meeting outside of class can be difficult to coordinate, set up, and operate, as they involve people with varied schedules. Also, at the outset, the multiple audiences provided by groups may be more intimidating and threatening to a writer than is a single person responding.

WRITING 5

Imagine a writing group you would like to belong to. What subjects would you write about? Whom would you invite to join your group? How often and where would you like to meet? Explain in a journal entry why you would or would not voluntarily join a writing group.

SUGGESTIONS FOR WRITING AND RESEARCH

Individual

Recently there has developed a large body of literature on the nature, types, and benefits of peer responses in writing. Go to the library and see what you can find about writing groups or peer response groups. Check, in particular, for work by Kenneth Bruffee, Peter Elbow, Anne Ruggles Gere, Thom Hawkins, and Tori Haring-Smith. Write a report to inform your classmates about your discoveries.

Collaborative

Form interview pairs and interview local published writers about the way in which response by friends, family, editors, or critics affects their writing. Share results orally or by publishing a short pamphlet.

WRITING ESSAYS

Chapter 10

Recounting Experience

Writing allows me to hold up a mirror to my life and
see what clear or distorted images stare back at me.
– RICK

People write about their personal experiences for a variety of reasons: to
know and understand themselves better, to inform and entertain others, and
to leave permanent records or their lives. Sometimes people recount their experiences casually, in forms never intended for wide circulation, such as journals, diaries, and letters. Sometimes they write in forms meant to be shared
with others, such as memoirs, autobiographies, or personal essays. In college,
the most common form for such writing is the personal experience essay.

This chapter examines how you can shape your personal experience into
meaningful narratives or stories. It describes the narrative elements that are
most useful in telling personal stories and recommends strategies that can help
you shape those elements to suit your purpose.

TELLING PERSONAL STORIES

What makes a story worth telling in the first place? Is it the *subject*, so
that big subjects such as earthquakes make better stories than small subjects
such as a pet cat? Is it the *character*, so that lively or quirky personalities are
worth hearing about while quiet and normal ones are not? Or is it not the
story itself that matters, but the *perspective* from which it is told, so that first
person, present tense is superior to third person, past tense? Is it the *setting*, so
that exotic locales with lots of palm trees, bamboo huts, and snakes make better stories than small towns in the Midwest? Is it the *sequence of events*, so that
stories with flashbacks are superior to stories told chronologically? Or is it the
theme, the meaning embedded in the story, so that themes of high drama need
be told while common ones do not?

These questions should make it clear that good stories can be told about virtually anything. Otherwise the best tale would be a tragic adventure taking place during an earthquake on a South Pacific island told through flashbacks by an idiot. Not only can good stories be about any subject, they can be quite simple and can take place in your own backyard. And you can tell them.

Potential stories happen all the time — in fact, daily. What makes them actual is recounting them, orally or in writing, so that they become verbal structures that convey some meaning. Your purpose as a writer is to select events from your life and craft them into a narrative that is informative, lively, and believable, a narrative that will mean something to you and your readers. This is what separates a good story from a simple string of facts.

All narratives, whether fictional stories, news reports, or accounts of personal experience, are made up of the same elements. News reporters refer to these as the five *W*'s and an *H*: *Who? What? Where? When? Why?* and *How?* Personal experience essays or fiction are described in terms of character, subject, setting, perspective, theme, and plot or sequence of events. To write a personal experience paper, you must make decisions about each of these elements and then weave them together to create a coherent whole.

WRITING 1

Think about the best stories you have read or listened to. What makes them memorable? What makes them believable?

FINDING A SUBJECT (WHAT?)

Subjects for good stories know no limits. You already have a lifetime of experiences to choose from, and each experience is a potential story to help explain who you are, what you believe, and how you act today. Here are some of the topics selected by a single first-year writing class:

- Playing oboe in Saturday orchestra rehearsals
- Counseling disturbed children at summer camp
- Picking strawberries on a farm
- Winning a championship tennis match
- Ballet dancing before a live audience
- Clerking at a drugstore
- Finishing second in a sailboat race
- Attending a Grateful Dead concert
- Trying out for the college volleyball team
- Touring Graceland in Memphis
- Painting houses during the summer

When you write a paper based on personal experience, your first questions should be Which experience do I want to write about? Will anybody else want to read about it? Following are three suggestions for areas to write about and one suggestion about an area to avoid.

Winning and Losing

Winning something — a race, a contest, a lottery — can be a good subject since it features you in a unique position and allows you to explore or celebrate a special talent. At the same time, the obviously dramatic subjects such as scoring the winning goal in a championship game or placing first in a creative writing contest may actually be difficult to write well about because they've been used so often before — readers have very high expectations.

The sad truth is that in most parts of life there are more losers than winners. While one team wins a championship, dozens do not. This means that there's a large, empathetic audience out there who will understand and identify with a narrative about losing. Although more common than winning, losing is less often explored in writing because it is more painful to recall. So there are fresher, deeper, more original stories to tell about losing. When you write about either winning or losing, describe what happened, explain what it meant to you, but refrain from making harsh judgments about your younger self.

Milestones

Perhaps the most interesting but also the most difficult experience to write about is one that you recognize as a turning point in your life, whether it's ballet dancing before a live audience for the first time or being a camp counselor. People who explore such topics in writing often come to a better understanding of them; their very significance challenges writers to make them equally significant for an audience that did not experience them. Because milestones are such big events in your life, it's tempting to skip the small details; when you write about milestones, pay special attention to the physical details of the scene that make it come alive for your readers.

Daily Life

Commonplace experiences make fertile subjects for personal narratives. Describe practicing for, rather than winning, the big game, or cleaning up after, rather than attending, the prom. Such subjects have been routinely ignored by professionals and amateurs alike and may offer special opportunities for unique stories. In fact, if you are accurate, honest, and observant in exploring a subject from which readers expect little, you are apt to pleasantly surprise them and draw them into your story. Work experiences are especially fruitful subjects, since you know the inside details and routines that the rest of your readers can only guess about.

A Caution About Love, Death, and Divorce

Several subjects that are good to write about extensively in journals are to be avoided in formal papers that will be revised, edited, and scrutinized by classmates and instructors. You are probably too involved in a love relationship to see or portray it with detailed objectivity; probably too close to the recent death of a person you care about to undertake a painful and faithful rendering of the details of dying; probably too angry, confused, or miserable to write well of your parents' divorce. Writing about these and other close or painful experiences can be immensely cathartic, but there is no need to share these with others unless you have good reason to.

WRITING 2

Make a list of a dozen subjects that you might tell stories about. Think of milestones and moments of special insight. But also think about commonplace events that were instructive or caused change, but in less dramatic ways. Share your list with classmates and find out which they would most like to hear about.

DELINEATING CHARACTER (WHO?)

The characters in a good story are believable and interesting; they come alive for readers. In personal experience writing, your main character is usually yourself, so you must give your readers a good sense of who you are. You accomplish this through the voice in which you speak, the actions you portray, the insights you share, and the vulnerability you display.

Voice

When you recount an experience, your language reveals the kind of person you are — playful, serious, rigid, loose, stuffy, warm, or whatever. In the following excerpt, Beth relates her experience playing oboe during a two-hour Saturday morning orchestra rehearsal.

> I love that section. It sounds so cool when Sarah and I play together like that. Now I can put my reed back in the water and sit back and listen. I probably should be counting the rests. Counting would mean I'd have to pay attention and that's no fun. I'd rather look around and watch everyone else sweat.

The self Beth shows here is serious about music — after all, she's rehearsing a difficult instrument on a Saturday morning — but also fun-loving, impish, and just a little bit lazy ("I'd rather look around and watch everyone else sweat.") (For more information on voice, see Chapter 6.)

Actions

Readers learn something about the kind of person you are from the actions you take in the course of your story. While the word *action* usually suggests movement of some kind, it can also be very quiet, as Mary demonstrates in relating her experience as a summer camp counselor for emotionally disturbed children.

> Josh looked so peaceful and sweet asleep that it was hard to imagine how difficult he had been all afternoon. He asked me to rub his head so he could fall asleep. I remember that first night hoping that he liked me--at least a little bit. I was so happy that I could give him a week of the love and happiness he couldn't get at home.

Mary's bedside observation shows readers that she enjoys working with children — with Josh in particular — and that she has some insecurities herself about being liked.

Insights

One of the best ways to reveal who you are is to show yourself gaining a new insight — a new self-awareness or a new way of seeing the world. While insights can occur for apparently unexplainable reasons, they are most likely to occur when you encounter new ideas or have experiences that change you in some way. Jeff developed a new self-awareness when he participated in Outward Bound, a month-long program that teaches wilderness survival skills.

> Day 13. After three days of not talking to or seeing one single person, I know the three basic necessities of life. Sorry Dad, they are not Stocks, Bonds, and Spreadsheets. And no, Mom, they're not General Hospital, Days of Our Lives, and All My Children. All I have been doing is melting snow for drinking water, rationing my food so it will last, and splitting dead trees in order to get firewood.

In this passage, Jeff reveals not only his sense of humor but also the conflict between his current bleak, snowy circumstances and his comfortable middle-class upbringing — a conflict that leads him to a new way of seeing himself in the world.

Vulnerability

The more honestly you portray your doubts and limitations, the more readers will believe you. Most people can be hurt physically and emotionally by the forces of modern society; few are invulnerable, like comic book super-heroes. In the following example, Rebecca looks at herself in a mirror before going onstage in the *Nutcracker* ballet.

> I glance at one of the mirrors lining the front wall and sigh in relief. Thank God it's a skinny-mirror. Today of all days, I'm not up to a fat-mirror.

Rebecca's admission of anxiety about her looks before a performance rings true to anyone who has been in a similar public situation; readers will feel closer to her because she honestly admits to a touch of vanity.

Change

It is in witnessing change that readers know a character is alive. Readers want to see how a character changes in the course of a narrative. During the several hours of a ballet performance, perhaps the changes would be small and subtle, reflecting the way most change happens in daily life. In newer or more dramatic experiences, where conflict or difficulty is present, more significant changes might be expected. Consider how you can show that the character at the end of your paper differs from the character at the beginning. If the character doesn't change, that too may be an important insight for writer and reader.

WRITING 3

From your list of possible subjects, select three that caused you to change in some significant or inevitable way. Write a paragraph on each one, concentrating on portraying yourself in the act of changing or learning something. Select the one that seems most worthy of further exploration and write a few more paragraphs.

ESTABLISHING PERSPECTIVE (HOW?)

Perspective addresses the question How close in time, distance, or spirit are you to the experience? Do you write as if it happened long ago or yesterday? Do you summarize what happened or put readers at the scene? Do you explain the experience or leave it mysterious? In other words, you can control how readers respond to a story by controlling the perspective, or vantage point, from which you tell it.

Authorial perspective is largely established by point of view, which tells readers how close the narrator is to the events narrated. Using the first person (*I*) puts the narrator right in the story itself, as a participant; this is usually the point of view used in personal experience writing. The third person (*he* or *she*) establishes a distinction between the person narrating the events and the person experiencing them and thus tends to depersonalize the story.

Tense is the other important element of perspective. It establishes the time when the story happened or is happening. Personal experience stories are usually set in either the present or the past.

A good approach may be to write your first draft from whatever perspective seems most natural or easy. As the story becomes clearer, experiment with other possible perspectives and see what you gain and what you lose with each.

Once Upon a Time: Past Tense

The easiest and most natural way to recount a personal experience is to write in the past tense. Lorraine uses this perspective in describing an automobile ride with her Native American grandfather to attend a tribal conference.

> I sat silently across from Grandfather and watched him slowly tear the thin white paper from the tip of the cigarette. He gathered the tobacco in one hand and drove the van with the other. I memorized his every move as he went through the motions of the prayer which ended when he finally blew the tobacco out of the window and into the wind.

Lorraine concludes her five-page narrative with this passage, switching to the present tense in the final sentence. The switch allows Lorraine to evaluate her past experience from her present perspective.

> That day on the mountain was only the beginning of our teachings, but it was the most important because it was shared with our grandfather. Though he has now gone to the spirit world, we continue to give thanks for the lessons he taught us.

Being There: Present Tense

Using the present tense to recount a personal experience provides the illusion that the experience is happening at the moment, with little time for reflection. This strategy invites readers to get more involved with the story, since they have to interpret it for themselves. Two ways of using present tense are the interior monologue, a fictional device that places readers in the writer's mind, and journal or diary entries, a format that allows the writer to pretend to describe the experience only a few hours after it happened. Use the interior monologue to describe a short, intense event; use the journal to provide glimpses of an experience that covers several days or more. (For more information on writing papers in a journal style, see Chapter 24.)

In describing her orchestra rehearsal, Beth writes an interior monologue, pretending that her readers are inside her mind. Writers can know firsthand only their own internal monologues — and even these are hard to capture with any authenticity.

> No you don't really mean that, do you? You do. Rats. Here we go . . .
> Pfff . . . Pfff . . . Why isn't this playing? Maybe if I blow harder . . .
> HONK!! Great, I've just made a total fool of myself in front of everyone.
> Wonderful.

Beth tries to approximate the sounds of attempted oboe playing. She also talks to herself, answers herself, and, all the time, interacts with the rest of the orchestra. She does not describe things with lots of labels, adjectives, and color. The difficulty in writing an interior monologue is one of balance: to sound as if she is authentically talking to herself, Beth cannot fully describe what she sees and hears; at the same time, to help her readers understand, she must provide some clues. Use the interior monologue when you want to put your readers in your shoes at the event but do not want to reflect back on it or its meaning. (See the end of this chapter for a whole essay written in present tense.)

WRITING 4

Write one paragraph of your emerging story using the first person, past tense and a second page using the first person, present tense. From which perspective do you prefer to tell the story? What are the advantages and disadvantages of each?

DESCRIBING THE SETTING (WHERE?)

Experiences happen in some place at some time, and good stories describe these settings. Making your setting vivid and believable contributes to the authenticity of the whole story.

To describe a physical setting, you need to re-create on paper the sights, sounds, smells, and physical sensations that allow readers to experience it for themselves. Try to include evocative, unusual details that will let your readers know you were really there. In the following example, Heather sets the scene on the farm where she spent the summer picking strawberries.

> The sun is just barely rising over the treetops and there is still dew
> covering the ground. In the strawberry patch, the deep green leaves
> are filled with water droplets and many of the strawberries are big and
> red and ready to be picked. The patch is located in a field off the road
> near a small forest of Christmas trees. The white house, the red barn,
> and a checkerboard of fields can be seen in the distance. It is 5:30
> A.M. and the day has begun for the early rising farmers.

Notice the frequency of sight words, some of which convey the time of day (*there is still dew covering the ground*) while others simply paint a vivid picture of the scene (*red strawberries, white house*). In addition, Heather uses a metaphor comparing distant fields to the pattern of a checkerboard.

WRITING 5

Describe in detail one of the settings in which your experience is taking place or took place. Appeal to at least three senses and avoid value judgements as you describe this place.

NARRATING A SEQUENCE OF EVENTS (WHEN?)

In every story, events are ordered one way or another. While you cannot alter the events that happened in your experience, you must always make two choices: which events to portray and the order in which to present the events.

Selecting Events

You have dozens of places to start and end your story, and at each point along the way many possible details and events are worth relating. Your final selection of place should support the theme of your story. In your early drafts, you might want to consider two strategies that writers commonly use to maintain reader interest: showing cause and effect and building suspense.

In cause-and-effect narratives, writers pair one event (having an accident, meeting a person, taking a journey) with another event or events that it caused to happen (undergoing physical therapy, making a friend, learning a new language.)

Writers create suspense when they raise questions or pose problems that they delay answering or solving. If the writer can make the question interesting enough, the problem pressing enough, readers will keep reading to learn the answers — to find out, in other words, what happens. Mary's counseling experience raises the question Will she succeed with this difficult child?

Ordering Events

The most common way to sequence events is to use chronological order, with events presented in the sequence in which they happened. Chronological order can be straightforward, following a day from morning to night as in Heather's narrative about picking strawberries. Jeff's journal account of his Outward Bound experience is also organized chronologically to follow the twenty-two days of his actual experience; however, his paper skips some days on which not very much happened that was relevant to his theme.

Sometimes, the writer deliberately breaks up the order, so that readers are first introduced to an event in the present and then, later in the story, are allowed to see events that happened earlier in time through flashbacks. For example, Jeff's journal could start with the excerpt from day 13, his first day of solo camping, and then flash back to the early days to explain how he got there

Such a sequence has the advantage of stimulating readers' interest by opening with a point of exceptional drama or insight.

WRITING 6

Outline the sequence of events of your story in the order that makes the most sense. Is the arrangement chronological? If not, what is it? How do you decide where to start? Where to end?

DEVELOPING A THEME (WHY?)

Perhaps the most important element in a story is what it means to both writer and reader. Why was this story worth writing in the first place? First drafts of personal experience narratives often do not reveal a clear sense of the story, even to the writers themselves. First drafts are about getting the events down on paper so that writers can see what they look like. In subsequent drafts, the meaning of these events — the theme — becomes clearer. (For more information on how revision helps themes emerge, see Chapters 22–24.)

In personal experience writing, the theme doesn't usually announce it-self in the first paragraph as the thesis statement often does in expository or argumentative writing. Instead, storytellers may create a meaning that is not stated anywhere and that becomes clear only at the end of the narrative. Many themes fall into three categories: slices of life, insights, and turning points.

Slices of Life

Some stories simply let readers see what life is like for someone else. Such stories exist primarily to record the writer's memories and to convey in-formation in an interesting way. Their only theme is "This is what my life is like." When you finish reading Heather's story about strawberry picking, you have learned a little bit about Heather, life on a farm, and strawberries; but you haven't witnessed major changes or dramatic events. After spending five pages relating a day of hard work, she concludes with this paragraph:

> Michelle runs to the car and jumps up and down begging me to let her drive back to the stand. I don't know why, but I let her. As soon as we drive in to the stand, our boss yells, "Girls, go weed the pumpkin patch." Well, it looks like another hard, sweaty, dirty, full day of work-ing on the farm.

Heather is not about to find a moral in her experience — at least not one to tell to her readers. Instead, this bouncy ending shows readers, simply, that life on the farm was hard work and good spirits. When you recount experiences that show everyday life, try to portray the small details that make your experience unique. (See the end of this chapter for a whole slice-of-life paper.)

Insights

In contrast to the paper that shows a slice of life is the paper relating an experience that led to a new insight. The insight itself is the theme of the paper. Such an experience is deeply significant to the writer, and the writer makes sure that readers see the full value of the experience, usually by explicitly commenting on its meaning. Beth does this at the very end of her essay on her music rehearsal. After using interior monologue for nine paragraphs, in the last paragraph she speaks to readers directly and focuses their attention on the significance of her musical education.

> As hard as it is to get up every Saturday morning, and as hard as it is to put up with some people here, I always feel good as I leave rehearsal. A guest conductor once said: "Music sounds how feelings feel." I never really thought about that before, but it's really true. Music evokes emotions that can't be described on paper. Every human feeling and emotion can be expressed through music--pride, sadness, love, hatred. Music is the international language. Once you learn it you can't forget it.

Though Beth has made fun of her music rehearsal throughout her paper, here at the end she gets serious without getting sentimental. In writing narratives that include your explicit insights, use language that is fresh, and avoid putting your message in terms you've heard before.

Turning Points

Many themes fall somewhere in between slices of life and profound insights. In fact, many of the best personal experience stories have change or growth as their themes. Such themes are usually implicit rather than explicit; although they may be implied throughout the story, they usually become clear in a single climactic moment or episode that dramatizes the theme. Mary's camp counselor story shows her progress from insecurity to confidence as she wins the heart of an emotionally disturbed ten-year-old. The following excerpt takes place after she has rescued Josh from ridicule by other campers.

> He ran in and threw himself on my bed, crying. I held him, rubbing his head for over an hour. "I love you, Mary. You're the best big sister in the whole world and you're so pretty! I love you and don't ever want you to leave."

Mary has now learned that she has the skills to help a child in need. Though the narrative continues for another two pages, this event was clearly the turning point in her counseling experience and became the focus of her story.

WRITING 7

Freewrite for ten minutes about the meaning of your story as you have written it so far, addressing some of these questions: What have you discovered about yourself in exploring this topic? Were there any surprises? Does your story remain interesting to you? Why or why not? What do you want readers to feel or know at the end? What word or words best summarize your emerging theme?

SHAPING THE WHOLE PAPER

The finished draft of Rebecca's personal experience paper, "Nutcracker," takes for its subject the day on which Rebecca danced in this famous ballet before a live audience. Rebecca frames the story with her arrival at and departure from the theater, limiting the sequence of events to those that took place in the few hours in between. She relates her story in the present tense to put readers on the scene; the choice of the first person and the backstage setting allows her to give readers an insider's view. Details about the preparations backstage create believability and interest. Through ironic observations and bits of internal monologue she reveals important aspects of her character — her anxiety, sense of humor, and love of music. The event can be seen as one in which Rebecca developed keen insight: by the end of the eighth paragraph, she comes to the realization that she can perform in front of an audience. But she prefers to treat it instead as a single slice of her ballet-dancing life. Rather than ending her paper at the moment of this insight, she continues for four more paragraphs that summarize the rest of the performance and show her unwinding afterward.

Nutcracker

It's eleven o'clock when my parents drop me off at the side door of the Civic Center Theatre. I enter the studio and walk over to an empty place at the barre. Insulation covers the ceiling, and the concrete walls have no windows. The backstage studio is neither airy nor beautiful, yet it's alive with energy. Today, for the first time, we perform the Nutcracker in front of a real audience. I've danced at school in front of our parents, but never on a real stage, under klieg lights, with hundreds of strangers watching my every move.

Dancers are scattered around the room, stretching, chatting, adjusting shoes and tights. Company members, the professionals who are joining us for this performance, wear tattered leg-warmers, sweatpants which have lost their elastic, and old T-shirts over tights and leotards. Their hair is knotted into buns or, in the case of male dancers, held tight with sweatbands. You can tell the students by the runless pink tights, dress-code leotards, and immaculate hair.

I, along with all the 5A students, wear a royal blue leotard and a thick layer of makeup to soften my face under the harsh lights. Our blue and green chiffon costumes look like something Cinderella would wear, the tiaras on top of our lacquered hair oddly resembling blue mountain ranges. The elastic on the plastic wings which complete our costume cuts off the circulation in my arms.

I glance at one of the mirrors lining the front wall and sigh in relief. Thank God it's a skinny-mirror. Today of all days, I'm not up to a fat-mirror.

The room becomes silent as Miss Robbins enters the studio. She wears pink tights, black leotard, and a long black ballet skirt, though no one knows where she finds them small enough for her tiny frame. From pictures we knew that her appearance hasn't changed in over twenty years, since she has been teaching and choreographing, but nobody actually knows how old she is. "OK. Are we ready to start the angels' warmup?" Several company members give us sympathetic looks, remembering the days when they were subjected to Miss Robbins. The music from the theater tells us that the tree is growing, and the Nutcracker is about to turn into a prince, and if we don't get moving soon, we'll be onstage with cold muscles.

We are frozen to the floor. I tightly grasp my lyre, remembering the warnings about dropping props, hair falling out, or pointe shoe ribbons hanging. "When any of these things happens to professionals, they are fined." We assume the same expectations apply to us, so we spray our hair and our shoe ribbons until both look painted on. We stand fast, hold on tight, and wait for the fog.

The fog is our cue. I take one last, long breath of clean air as the toxic cloud rolls closer. I bend toward the floor, placing my head on my outstretched leg. The fog comes closer, the lights dim, and my pointe shoe fades out of sight. Why is this stuff called fog anyway? Smog seems more fitting. There has to be a better way to create the fairyland that opens the second act.

Before we suffocate, the stage lights brighten, and my stomach flutters with excitement. The lines from my false eyelashes make a grid-like pattern in my peripheral vision, but I don't seem to mind. We slowly, and ever so angelically, rise out of the fog and begin to dance. Only an occasional cough tells me people are watching. Miss Leonard was right, under the lights you can't see anything. It's no different from an extra bright rehearsal.

Clara and the Nutcracker Prince come down in a hot-air balloon and are greeted by the Sugarplum Fairy and Cavalier. The professional dancers fill the stage, looking graceful and elegant in stark contrast to their grubby warmup appearance an hour earlier in the studio. I see fifteen other girls gracefully weaving in and out from each other and know that we're halfway through. We continue to dance as if in a trance.

When our part is over we walk upstage to stand on the stairs that form part of the scenery, holding our lyres and looking pleasant. It's funny, but when I hear the <u>Nutcracker</u> in department stores and restaurants, I want to scream and run away, but here, onstage, the music takes over, and I hope it never ends.

After the second curtain call, the applause fades, and we walk down the cold concrete stairs to our dressing room. Miss Robbins is nowhere to be seen. I take off my costume, return it to the closet, and put on my cozy sweatshirt and jeans. I scrub off the thick layer of caked-on makeup from my sore face. I rub the soft cream on my face, then sit in front of my mirror and unpin my lacquered hair. Very slowly I brush it in a vain attempt to soften the hair spray.

It's four o'clock and I'm exhausted. I shove my belongings haphazardly into my ballet bag, toss it over my shoulder, and leave by the side door to find my parents. We do another matinee tomorrow, and maybe then I'll get nervous all over again, but, at least for now, it's over.

Strategies for Writing About Personal Experience

1. Select a subject that interests you but whose meaning still escapes you; the writing will help you capture it.
2. Let your character emerge, not by telling readers what you are like, but by showing yourself in action in difficult or complicated situations.
3. Recount your experience from at least two different perspectives to see which one is most effective.
4. In describing your setting, appeal to as many of the five senses as possible.
5. Explain the sequence of events first in strict chronological order; then write a draft telling it through flashbacks. Use the order that satisfies you the most.
6. Try to focus and select the events of your story so that your theme emerges without your stating exactly what it is.

SUGGESTIONS FOR WRITING AND RESEARCH

Individual

1. Write a personal experience essay based on Writings 2–7 in this chapter. Try to find a topic in which you can show some change or

learning on your part. Plan to write this narrative in several drafts, each one deliberately exploring a different aspect of your experience. Here is a recommended draft sequence:

First draft: Write in your most natural voice and from your most natural point of view, paying attention to the actual sequences of the experience.

Second draft: Write in great detail about the setting and character (you) so that readers can see, hear, touch, and smell this experience. Concentrate on just one or two scenes in your whole story.

Third draft: Limit the focus of this draft to just one small part of the experience — a day, a few hours, a few minutes. Lead off with dialogue, either something overheard or something you participated in. (See Chapter 23.)

Fourth draft: Write this draft from a different point of view or in a different tense from those you have been using so far. Consider, for example, the objective perspective of a journalist reporting the event or the subjective perspective of an interior monologue. (See Chapter 24.)

Fifth draft: Write a final draft of this experience in which you either (1) mix and match elements from your previous drafts, taking parts from different drafts that work successfully together; (2) expand on the previous draft you find most pleasing; or (3) write a fresh draft, using insights you gained in the previous writing. Whichever option you choose, attach to your final draft the previous drafts in the order in which you wrote them.

2. Locate and read a nonfiction narrative in a field of interest to you. Write an essay describing the author's narrative technique and explaining how it works in light of the criteria discussed in this chapter. Good places to find nonfiction narratives are current periodicals such as *The New Yorker, Rolling Stone,* and *Sports Illustrated.*

Collaborative

As a class, write the story of your writing class so far in the semester. Have each class member contribute one short chapter (one page each) to this tale. Each member may choose any moment (funny, momentous, boring, routine) and describe it in such a way that it holds together by itself from beginning to end. Choose two class members to collect all the short narrative chapters and weave them into a larger narrative with a beginning, middle, and end.

Chapter 11

Profiling People

> *When I met Lisa for coffee, it was like the meeting of two total*
> *strangers. But we're both from the south, so when she told me*
> *about growing up in Charleston, we got a lot closer. I still need*
> *to find what makes Lisa uniquely Lisa. We'll meet again.*
>
> — REBECCA

R EADING AND WRITING PROFILES ABOUT PEOPLE teach us not only about others, but also about ourselves. Newspaper and magazine writers commonly profile the rich, famous, and powerful people of the world. Some popular magazines, such as *Vanity Fair* and *Rolling Stone*, feature well-researched profiles in virtually every issue. Weekly newsmagazines, such as *Time, Newsweek,* and *Sports Illustrated*, use short profiles as regular features. And literary magazines, such as *The New Yorker, Atlantic,* and *Esquire*, are well known for their lengthy, in-depth profiles. Profiles are not easy to write, but they are rewarding because the process of writing them inevitably brings the writer and subject closer together.

WRITING A PROFILE

The purpose of a profile is to capture a person's essence on paper. Good profiles generally focus on a single aspect of the subject's life or personality and make some sort of comment on it. In short, a good profile tells a story about its subject.

Profiles are about people other than the writer, but you, the writer, are ultimately in control. You decide what to include, what to omit, how to describe the subject and his or her surroundings, where to begin, and where to end. However, the ultimate purpose of a profile is to convey a sense of who your subject is. You must develop a portrait that is essentially true.

Profiles lie on a spectrum between two related forms, interviews and biographies. Interviews are conversations between a writer and a living person. They are commonly the result of a single visit, though some may be based on multiple visits. Published interviews often transcribe the interviewer's questions followed by the subject's responses.

Biographies are usually book-length studies of people, dead as well as living. A biographer's sources include letters from and to the subject; diaries and notebooks; stories by relatives and acquaintances; newspaper and magazine reports; previously published interviews; legal and medical records; and the subject's published writing or other work — all available resources that shed light on the life and character of the subject.

Like interviews, profiles include direct conversations with living people. Like biographies, they make use of other sources of information about the subject. Profiles are usually longer than interviews, but they are considerably shorter than biographies. Profiles are more tightly focused than both interviews, which may contain questions on a wide variety of subjects, and biographies, which attempt to convey information on all aspects of a subject's life. In contrast, a profile selectively presents information to create a unified portrait.

A common college assignment will ask you to profile a professor or staff member who works at your college or university, people who work in the local community, or other students. Profile writing requires, first, a willing subject; second, time to collect information about the subject; and third, the skill to focus on one aspect of the subject and develop a clear theme.

WRITING 1

Describe any profiles that you recall reading in magazines or newspapers. What details do you remember about the person profiled? Why do you think these details remain in your memory?

FINDING A SUBJECT

Profiles can be written about virtually any person willing to hold still long enough to reveal something about himself or herself. While a list of people whom you might profile is unlimited, some subjects are more accessible than others for students in a college writing class. The profile examples in this chapter are all taken from assignments to profile classmates. But you can select for your own profile subject anyone in whom you are especially interested.

Relatives make good profile subjects because they are usually more than willing to cooperate, and the knowledge resulting from the profile will contribute to your family history. However, sometimes family members are not easily accessible for more than one visit. And family members such as parents, who are emotionally close to you, may be difficult to profile because you may lack the objectivity necessary to portray them realistically.

Members of the campus community are usually willing subjects: professors, librarians, cafeteria workers, resident assistants, alumni staff, and coaches, to name some of the obvious ones. In addition, the local community contains other potential subjects: shopkeepers, street vendors, police officers, city administrators, and various local characters of good and ill repute. The advantage of profiling members of your community is that you can learn about people in various occupations and social circumstances. The disadvantages include the unavailability of busy people for extended interviews and the extra time it takes to conduct off-campus interviews.

Your own classmates can also provide a wealth of characters with varied backgrounds and interests. The advantages of profiling your peers includes their willingness to be profiled, their availability, and the chance to get to know what they are like. The only disadvantage is that writing about a classmate does not expose you to a wider range of people — though this certainly depends on who is in your class. Note, however, that it is very difficult to profile objectively students with whom you're romantically involved.

WRITING 2

Make a list of people in your family, campus community, and local community whom you might be interested in profiling. Make a similar list of classmates who might make good profile subjects. Talk with your instructor about which subjects would be best for a profile assignment.

PROVIDING BACKGROUND INFORMATION

To write an effective profile, you need to learn as much about your subject as possible. You will eventually use some of this background information when you draft the profile itself, to provide a context for the subject's words and actions. Much of it, though, is useful primarily during your planning and invention stages, as you decide on a focus for the profile and a direction for more research.

Finding background information requires good research skills. You must take advantage of all the available sources of information and follow up new leads wherever you find them.

PRELIMINARY INTERVIEWS.   Talking with your subject often is the best place to start. In addition to providing valuable background information, he or she can give you leads to further information. If you are profiling a classmate, interview him or her for ten or fifteen minutes to get started. For other subjects, call ahead and set up a time to meet.

PUBLIC INFORMATION.   If your subject has a résumé, ask to see it. If your subject has published something — whether a letter to the editor or a book — get a copy. If your subject has made a speech or taken a public stand, find a record of it. If the person has been the subject of an interview or biography, read it to see what previous writers have found out.

WRITING PORTFOLIOS. A rich source of recent background information is your subject's writings — especially if your subject is a student. Assigned papers or essay tests will tell you something of the person's intellectual interests, but journals or letters may reveal more personal information.

FRIENDS AND ACQUAINTANCES. An obvious source of background information is the people who know, live, and work with your subject. Each conversation you have with a friend or acquaintance of your subject is itself a small interview. It is a good idea to begin such a conversation with specific questions and to take notes. Good questions include the following: What is this person like? How did you come to know each other? What do you most often do together? Whom does this person admire? What does this person want to do or become next?

WRITING 3

Locate a profile subject and find out as much about his or her background as you can. Take good notes. What further questions are suggested by the subject's responses? Set a time to meet again and probe your subject's history further.

DESCRIBING PHYSICAL APPEARANCE

Often the first thing we notice about people we've just met is their appearance. Profiles, too, commonly introduce the subject through descriptions of how the person looks and acts. In the early stages of your writing process, you may want to take notes on every aspect of your subject's appearance. Later, you should select details that capture your subject's individuality and reveal his or her personality.

When describing your subject, use words that appeal to the senses, that express size, shape, color, texture, and sound. Be as specific as possible. You may want to describe physical appearance, clothing, and habits or gestures.

Pam can capture Mari Anne's appearance by employing all three types of information.

> While sitting at her desk, Mari Anne keeps twirling her hair to help her think and relax. She is dressed in solid colors, black and red, and has a dozen bracelets on her right arm. She smiles as if nervous, but as I got to know her, I found that smile always on her face. She is five feet two inches tall, has naturally curly brown hair, a dark complexion, and dark brown eyes, always smiling. She is a second-generation American since both sets of grandparents came from Greece.

Pam's description tells readers much about Mari Anne's tastes (solid colors, lots of jewelry) and personality (friendly but perhaps a little high-strung). Pam also uses physical description (dark complexion, dark brown eyes) to lead directly to background information (her Greek heritage). It is important to realize how much you, the writer — either consciously or unconsciously — can shape such descriptions. By mentioning Mari Anne's nervous hair twisting at the beginning of the description and her nervous smile a bit later, Pam makes readers see the subject as nervous.

WRITING 4

As an exercise, sit with a classmate and spend ten minutes taking detailed notes on what he or she looks like; pay attention to face, body, height, clothing, gestures, and expressions. Write one to two pages organizing these physical details to convey a dominant impression.

DESCRIBING THE SETTING

Effective description of the setting contributes to realism in a profile and advances readers' understanding of your subject. As in all descriptions, you should note specific details of the physical environment, using sensory words that help readers experience what it was like to be there.

The setting you describe should be the one in which you and your subject met and talked. If this is where your subject lives, you have the opportunity to observe an environment that he or she created and that no doubt reflects much of his or her personality. Do your best to record the details that tell the most about your subject's special interests. If the interview takes place elsewhere, your description may primarily be a way of creating a realistic backdrop, but you may also reveal a great deal about your subject by the way he or she reacts to a less personal environment. Settings can be described on their own — usually near the beginning of the profile — or subtly and indirectly along with the action of the interview.

In the following example, Caleb meets Charles at Charles's favorite off-campus hangout in order to get to know him better; before turning to his subject, Caleb describes the ambiance of their meeting place.

> Charles suggested we meet in the Other Place, a downtown bar commonly referred to as OP. Charles had basketball practice until seven or eight, so he'd meet me there around 9:30. The OP had a dive bar ambiance to it. In the far corner of the bar stood two outdated pinball machines being hugged respectively by a barefoot girl and a portly man wearing jeans and a leather vest. Both were shaking their hips to the noises of their machines. Above the actual bar a mute hockey game was taking place on television.

Caleb describes the "dive" with a good eye for detail, implying in his descriptions of its people that it's not a place he feels comfortable in. But he lets readers know that Charles is comfortable there.

Beth indirectly includes a description of the setting in her profile:

> Becky sits cross-legged at the foot of the bottom bunk on her pink and green homemade quilt. She leans up against the wall and runs her fingers through her brown shoulder-length hair. The sounds of James Taylor's "Carolina on My Mind" softly fills the room. Posters of John Lennon, James Dean, and Cher look down on us from the walls. Becky stares at the floor and scrunches her face as if she is thinking hard.

Beth includes a rich number of sight words about Becky's home away from home — bed, posture, person, posters, and room — letting the detail contribute to the portrait of the person. By including the James Taylor song as well as the three posters, she allows readers to make inferences about what these say about Becky's tastes. Beth slips in the setting details quietly so as not to detract attention from the subject herself.

When including details of setting, think about whether they should strongly reinforce your verbal portrait of the subject, provide a colorful platform for your interaction to take place, or stay quietly in the background.

WRITING 5

If possible, arrange to visit the place where your profile subject lives, and record as much sensory information about that place as you can. Capture what is on the walls and floors, out the windows, on the desk, and on the bed and under it. Also note the brand names of things; their sizes, colors, smells; and the sounds from the CD and from down the hall as well.

LETTING PEOPLE TALK

Interviews allow people to reveal information about themselves that contributes to a portrait. Interviews are the primary source of information about many profile subjects, especially classmates. You can conduct interviews in three ways.

You and your subject can have an informal conversation in which you get to know the subject, usually without notes. In an informal interview, prepared questions may be more intrusive than helpful. If you don't take notes, be sure to capture your recollections of the conversation within twenty-four hours, or you'll forget most of them.

The second method of interviewing is to take notes from the subject's responses to prepared questions. You'll need to write fast in a small notebook, catching the essence of your subject's responses and filling in the details later. Note taking is especially helpful during an interview because it lets you see what information you've got as you go along and sometimes helps you decide where to go next with your questions.

Tape recording captures your subject's language *exactly* as it was spoken. If you plan to bring a tape recorder to the interview, be sure to secure your subject's permission in advance. While reconstructing dialogue from tape may sound easier than reconstructing it from notes, transcribing the conversation accurately and selecting which passages to use in the profile demand a great deal of time and patience. Plan to use especially those ways of speaking that seem most characteristic of your subject.

In all but the most informal interviews, you should come with prepared questions. In your first interview, ask a coherent set of questions to provide you with an overview of your subject. While questions might vary depending on the age, status, and occupation of your subject, the following is a good starting list.

1. Where did you grow up? What was it like?
2. What do your parents do for a living?
3. Do you have any brothers or sisters? What are they like? How are you similar to or different from them?
4. How do you spend your free time?
5. What kinds of jobs have you held?
6. What are your favorite books, movies, or recordings?
7. How did you come to be where you are today?
8. What do you intend to do next?

During subsequent interviews, narrow your questions to a more limited range of interests. For example, if your first interview revealed that photography is your subject's favorite hobby, in your second interview focus several questions on his or her involvement with photography. Your profile will succeed according to the amount of detailed information you get your subject to reveal through interviews.

After Beth interviewed Becky, she wrote the following narrative from her tape transcript.

> Finally, after minutes of silence she says, "I don't ever remember my father ever living in my house, really. He left when I was three and my sister was just a baby, about a year old. My mom took care of us all. Forever, it was just Mom, Kate, and me. I loved it, you know? Just the three of us together."

Beth is aware that if she can capture the small details of Becky's childhood along with her teenage conversational style (*like, you know*), Becky's story will be all the more plausible — which in turn will make Beth's profile more readable. (See Chapter 17 for more on interviews.)

WRITING 6

Interview your profile subject in a place that is convenient and comfortable to you both. If this is a first interview, start with informal, conversational questions like those presented in the text.

SELECTING A POINT OF VIEW

Your profile will be written from either the first-person or the third-person point of view. (See Chapter 6.) The point of view you choose will do much to establish the tone and style of your profile. In the first-person point of view, the narrator (*I*) has a presence in the story. You can use this point of view to let readers know that you are presenting the subject through the filter and perhaps the bias of your own eyes, as Caleb does in the following passage.

> I walked in past the overfilled coatrack and scanned the room for
> Charles. The smell of smoke was overwhelming and it was hard to see.
> It surprised me that Charles would hang out in a joint like this, espe-
> cially since he seemed to be such a disciplined athlete. I spotted him
> with a group of tall guys near the pinball machines. We made eye con-
> tact and he rose to greet me.

In the third-person point of view, *I* is never used, only proper names (*Joan, Sara*), nouns for persons (*athlete, grocer*), and the pronouns *he, she,* and *they*. You can use this point of view to keep yourself out of the narrative, focusing instead on the subject and on the words and actions that any observer might witness. Caleb does this in the following passage as he describes an exchange that takes place where he and Charles are sitting.

> Again the girls came over, accosting Charles. One of them gave him
> a Budweiser, which he gladly accepted.
>
> "You want to play tennis tomorrow?" the shorter girl asked.
>
> "Sure, what time?" Charles asked in a soft voice.
>
> "Whenever you're free."
>
> "How about three? I have a Saturday practice tomorrow morning."

Many profiles are actually written, as Caleb's is, in a combination of first person and third person. Although most of the focus is naturally on the subject, many writers find that, since they select what to report and what to ignore, some acknowledgment of their presence is the most honest approach.

Write your first draft from whatever points of view seem comfortable to you. In the revising stages, you can experiment with increasing or decreasing your presence in the narrative (see Chapter 24), and in editing you will check that the point of view is consistent (see Chapter 25).

WRITING 7

Write one page about your profile subject in the first-person point of view and then one page in the third person, using essentially the same information in each version. Which do you prefer? Why?

DEVELOPING A THEME

Ultimately, profiles tell stories about people. Though you have read only a few examples of student profiles in this chapter, you may already have drawn some conclusions about what these people are like. Profile writers select the details and dialogue and background information that tell the story they want to tell about their subject. Most often, that story builds as the profile progresses so that the last page or paragraph focuses on the most important point the writer wants to make about the subject. This central theme can be revealed *explicitly*, with the writer telling readers what to think, or *implicitly*, with the evolution of the profile making the theme clear.

EXPLICIT THEME. Pam concludes her profile, which focuses on Mari Anne's continued love of gymnastics, with her own summary, a small judgment on what the realities of college life have done to Mari Anne's passion.

> [Mari Anne says,] "I want to be able to judge [gymnastics] here at college, so I will still have to pass part two of the exam. I would especially like to judge creative matches which show each gymnast's unique ability." As of now Mari Anne has not had time to fit gymnastics into her schedule. She is too busy trying to keep up with her studies. But you can bet that next year will find her on the floor or behind the judge's table; Mari Anne has too much passion for the sport to stay out for very long.

IMPLICIT THEME. Beth never suggests what readers should think of Becky. She lets her subject's words end the profile, allowing readers to make their own inferences about who Becky is and what she stands for.

> "I think that because I didn't have my dad, we're closer to my grandparents. Because Mom was so young and they helped us out all the time. They gave us property to build a house and everything. So we're a lot closer because she could always count on them. That's the most important thing, you know, being able to count on people."

WRITING 8

In the profile you are developing, would you like your theme to emerge explicitly or implicitly? If implicitly, how would you conclude the profile so that readers would be most likely to understand the theme you intend?

SHAPING THE WHOLE PAPER

Beth's finished draft of her profile "Becky" is presented here. Notice that Beth chose to shape the profile as if it took place at one sitting in Becky's dormitory room; in fact, she interviewed Becky at several different times and places over several weeks. Beth removes herself almost completely from the profile, letting Becky's own words do most of the characterizing — though at times she also presents information from the dormitory setting and her own summary of background information.

Notice the focus on trust and dependability, which develops early in the profile and carries through to the concluding words that express Becky's attitudes toward men. The final line makes a very strong ending — but be aware that the writer, not her subject, created this ending. Over the course of several interviews, Becky talked about a wide range of subjects, including sports, teacher education, and college life. It was Beth who shaped these many conversations into a coherent essay with a beginning, middle, and end.

Becky

Becky sits cross-legged at the foot of the bottom bunk on her pink and green homemade quilt. She leans up against the wall and runs her fingers through her brown shoulder-length hair. The sound of James Taylor's "Carolina on My Mind" softly fills the room. Posters of John Lennon, James Dean, and Cher look down on us from the walls. Becky stares at the floor and scrunches her face as if she is thinking hard.

Finally, after minutes of silence she says, "I don't ever remember my father ever living in my house, really. He left when I was three and my sister was just a baby, about a year old. My mom took care of us all. Forever, it was just Mom, Kate, and me. I loved it, you know? Just the three of us together."

Becky smiles and continues, "And I remember little things, you know, like we would all sleep together in Mom's bed. We'd all climb in. Little things like, I remember one night there was a bat in the house and Mom is afraid of bats and I was only, like, five, and Mom climbed under the covers with my little sister and I had to go down and call my grandmother to get the bat out of the house.

"But I'm really proud of my mother for bringing up my sister and me on her own. She had to work, sometimes two jobs, and she worked really hard. I don't remember a sad time then, ever. I had the happiest childhood. You know, some of my friends who have whole families complain about fights with their parents, but I have no complaints about anything. I never felt like I needed anything or that I lacked anything."

Becky pauses, hugging her knees close to her chest, rocking slightly. "Hmmm," she mumbles. She traces her lips with the back of her fingernail. "Oh, I always do this when I'm thinking or I'm upset--now I'm just thinking."

Becky Harris grew up in West Granville, a small town where people knew and supported each other. She came to the university to major in elementary education: "I really think those early years are so crucial, when children are first learning how to live in and trust the world."

On campus, she lives in Connors Hall, with Trish, a roommate from Maine who is fast becoming a best friend. Trish agrees, saying, "Outside of classes, we do everything together, share tapes, run on the weekends, borrow clothes, and talk late almost every night. The posters? She put those up. I really like them."

Becky offers me a cup of herbal tea, then makes a cup for herself and resumes her place on the bed. "Anyway, Mom and I have the strangest relationship. It's like we're friends--she's my mom, but we're friends more than she's my mom because, when my dad left, I kinda had to grow up overnight and take care of my sister 'cause my mom was working so much. I mean, she never left us alone or anything, but I had to do things. I had to learn to dress myself and all those little things really fast, earlier than lots of kids because she didn't have time for both of us.

"Oh! I have this watch bear. I put it over my bed, somewhere where it can watch me all the time." She got up from the bed and slid across the linoleum floor to her desk to pick up the little white stuffed animal. "Two years ago, I lost Watch Bear. For almost three whole days, and I didn't have anybody watching over me. But I found him, he was under the bed. I brought him with me to college to sit on my desk to watch over me and to make sure I'm safe like he did when I was little."

Becky carefully places Watch Bear against the wall near her and continues, "Anyway, I hope that if I were ever in the same situation as my mom, I could be as strong as she. 'Cause that would scare me to have a car and this brand new house that they just built and have to take care of everything. 'Cause my dad never paid any money, never a cent of child support, ever in his life to us.

"I've seen him maybe three or four times in ten or twelve years. Once two years ago, at Thanksgiving, I saw him, and that was when he had just gotten remarried, and I met his wife. I really liked her a lot and I really liked their kids. I got along with them, but you know, I don't think of him as part of my family. I don't even really think of him as my father, really. I mean biologically, but that's all. I used to get really sad sometimes that I didn't have a dad. But I don't feel like I've missed anything in my life, ever. I'd rather have my mother happy than to have her live with someone just to make a whole family 'cause I think we had a whole family.

"My mother has never said a bad thing about my father, ever, in her life. And if it was me who got dumped with two children, I would just--I would always be bad-talking, I'm sure. She never wanted us to hate him and wanted us to have the opportunity to get to know him if we wanted to when we could choose to. When he called and asked us to go to Thanksgiving with him a few years ago, I didn't want to, but Mom really encouraged us to 'cause she said maybe he's going to reach out and try to change his ways and be your dad. So we went. Kate, my sister, who was just a year when he left, never knew him at all. She was very uncomfortable there, but I talked to him a little bit."

Becky pauses and traces her lips again. "I used to have really bad feelings towards men in general. Like, I didn't trust them at all 'cause I thought that, you know, they were all sort of like him; you couldn't count on them for anything. I just don't think there's . . . I get so mad that there's people that would just leave someone with children--especially their own, you know? I'm better now. I have a boyfriend and I trust him a lot, but I question everything he does. When he makes commitments I don't really think he's going to come through, you know? I wonder about that a lot because--I don't really have a reason to distrust all men but, you know?

"I think that because I didn't have my dad, we're closer to my grandparents. Because Mom was so young and they helped us out all the time. They gave us property to build a house and everything. So we're a lot closer because she could always count on them. That's the most important thing, you know, being able to count on people."

Strategies for Writing Profiles

1. When interviewing a classmate, agree on guidelines beforehand: whether or not to use tape recorders; where, when, and for how long to exchange visits; where else to meet; what sources of background to share; and so on.
2. Use your own narration to summarize, to provide background and context, and to interpret. Try to strike a balance between writing about your subject and letting him or her speak.
3. Quote interview material directly to reveal your subject's personality and beliefs. Subjects who talk directly to readers characterize themselves and provide living proof to support your inferences about them.
4. Share drafts with your profile subject. When subjects see early drafts, they may tell you important information that will improve your representations of them.
5. You are the author of the profile you write: take your subject's comments into account as much as you can, but maintain ownership of your interpretation and characterization.

SUGGESTIONS FOR WRITING AND RESEARCH

Individual

1. Write a profile of your subject using the information you have collected in Writings 2–7. In doing this assignment, write several drafts and share these with your subject, listen to his or her re-

sponse to your profile, and take those comments into account when writing your final draft. Keep in mind the golden rule of profile writing: Do unto your subject as you would want him or her to do unto you.

2. Write a profile of somebody in the university community who is not a student; a professor, counselor, security officer, cafeteria staff person. Be considerate in arranging interview times; focus on the work this person does; plan to share your resulting profile with the subject.

3. Write a profile of a family member. Interview this person and collect as much information about him or her as you can — letters, yearbooks, photographs. Plan to contribute your final draft to whoever in your family collects such records. (If nobody does, would you want to start collecting yourself?)

Collaborative

1. As a class, select a magazine that interests students or that most students read regularly and that publishes profiles (consider those mentioned at the beginning of this chapter). Send several students to the library and research several years back, making notes about the themes and techniques used in the magazine's profiles. Share information on the qualities that characterize good profile writing, and together develop a set of criteria by which to assess effective profiles.

2. With your classmates, write a profile of your class. First discuss what a class profile might be like: Would it be a collection of individual profiles arranged in some order? Or would it consist of written bits and pieces about people, places, and events, arranged as a verbal collage? Would there be a place for visual components in this class profile? Would you want to challenge other writing classes to develop similar profiles and share them with one another?

Chapter 12

Explaining Things

I hate it when my English teacher is always telling me
to be clear, simple, and direct. And then when I do write this way, she
tells me to add more detail, more description, and to vary my sentences.
What gives?

— BRAD

To EXPLAIN SOMETHING is to make it clear and understandable. Explanation is perhaps the most fundamental act of communication: if we can't make other people understand our ideas, then we're not communicating at all. Explanations are so important that they are part of most other types of writing, such as arguments, interpretations, and reflections (see Chapters 13, 14 and 15). In purely explanatory writing, however, the main purpose is to help readers understand something. Such writing can range from a newspaper feature on baseball card collecting to a magazine article on why dinosaurs are extinct, from a textbook on the French Revolution to a recipe for making chili.

WRITING TO EXPLAIN

The purpose of explanatory writing (also called expository or informational writing) is to help readers understand a subject. Explanations can answer a variety of questions:

- What is it?
- What does it mean?
- How does it work?
- How is it put together?
- How is it related to other things?
- What causes it?
- What will its consequences be?

Explanatory writing is defined not so much by its subject (which can be almost anything) as by the way the subject is treated. First, explanatory writing almost always uses an objective perspective; that is, it emphasizes the thing explained rather than the writer's beliefs and feelings. Second, explanatory writing focuses on the reader's need for information rather than the writer's desire for self-expression. Third, explanatory writing is usually systematic and orderly, having a stated goal, clear explanatory strategies, and a logical organizational structure.

Explanatory writing is objective, reader-focused, and systematic because this writing style simplifies an audience's task of reading to understand. If readers have to stumble through a poorly organized explanation or repeatedly sort fact from opinion, they are likely to give up and look for their information elsewhere.

Taking time to analyze your readers is an important part of writing a successful explanation. You need to find out what they know and don't know, what they care about and don't care about. Only by doing this can you be sure that your explanation is focused on information that readers will find useful and interesting.

In writing classes, explanation usually takes the form of research essays and reports that inform rather than argue, interpret, or reflect. The assignment may ask you to "describe how something works" or to "explain the causes and effects" of a particular phenomenon. To explain anything successfully, you will need to decide on a topic, have a clear sense of who you are writing to, locate information about your topic, develop a working thesis, use clear explanatory strategies, organize predictably, and write with focus on the thing being explained rather than on your feelings and opinions about it.

WRITING 1

How good are you at explaining things to people? What things do you most commonly find yourself explaining? Is it harder to explain things in writing than in speaking? What is the last thing you explained in writing? How did your audience receive it?

FINDING A TOPIC

You can explain only what you understand yourself. It also helps to explain something you're interested in. Even if you are assigned a subject that isn't particularly compelling, try to narrow the subject to one aspect that is more interesting than others. For example, the general subject *stereo systems* is so broad that it's hard to know where to begin or what to say. But a specific aspect of stereo systems, such as compact discs, may interest you; within the subject of CDs, there are probably several topics (their cost, their sound quality, their manufacturing process) that you could write about.

Remember that effective explanations are full of details and carefully developed ideas. This means that even simple explanations may take several pages. For this reason, try to narrow your topic as much as you can. A topic that is too broad will take too many pages to explain or will skip over important points. Even worse, it will probably exhaust both your readers (who are being asked to wade through too much information) and you (who has to find all that information in the first place).

In most instances, an explanatory paper should address one central question, such as Why do CDs cost more than records? Of course, there may be other questions to be answered along the way (How do CDs work? How are CDs made?), but these are secondary.

Once you have a focused topic on a central question, you need to assemble information. If you're not an expert yourself, you'll need to consult an authority on the topic. Even if you are already an expert, finding supportive information from other experts will help make your explanation clear and authoritative. (See Part V for more on researching.) Keep your audience in mind as you begin your research. You don't want to waste time researching and writing about things your audience already knows.

WRITING 2

What would you need to or like to explain? For what purpose? To whom? If you're not sure, do some freewriting or journal writing to help you discover a question.

DEVELOPING A THESIS

A thesis is the writer's declaration of what the paper is about. In explanatory writing, the thesis states the answer to the central question of the paper.

QUESTION   Why do compact discs cost so much?

THESIS   CDs cost more than records because the laser technology required
             to manufacture them is so expensive.

If the question you are answering asks What? or How? rather than Why? When? or Who? then your complete thesis will emerge only after you provide a large amount of varied information. A good thesis for this kind of explanation sums up all the information in a single idea, image, or analogy that gives unity and coherence to your explanation.

QUESTION   How are the various offices of the city government connected?

THESIS   City government offices are like an octopus, with eight fairly inde-
             pendent bureaus as arms and a central brain in the mayor's office.

Because a thesis is important in helping readers understand an explanation, it is usually stated explicitly near the beginning of the paper rather than left implicit or stated only at the end — although for How? or When? questions, you may lead up to it step by step and then state it clearly at the end.

You will probably find yourself revising your thesis as you continue to research, draft, revise, and edit your paper. For example, the more you learn about city government, the less your first analogy may seem to explain: you may discover that city government is more like a centipede than an octopus. Throughout the writing process, keep in mind that your first thesis is a working thesis and should be tentative, flexible, and subject to change; its primary function is to guide further research and help keep your paper focused.

WRITING 3

Write out a working thesis for the topic you are explaining. If you are addressing a When? or How? question, find a controlling image or analogy that will hold together all of the elements of your necessarily longer answer.

USING STRATEGIES TO EXPLAIN

Some methods of explaining are better than others; the key is to select the best method to suit your purpose. The standard explanatory strategies are defining, describing, classifying and dividing, analyzing causes and effects, and comparing and contrasting.

If your paper is on a single, focused topic and answers a narrow, simple question, you may need to use only one strategy. More often, however, you will have one primary strategy that shapes the paper as a whole and several secondary strategies that can vary from paragraph to paragraph or even sentence to sentence. For example, to explain why the government has raised income taxes, your primary strategy would be analyzing cause and effect, but you may also need to *define* terms such as income tax, to *classify* various types of taxes, and to *compare and contrast* them to other options. In fact, almost every explanatory strategy uses other strategies: it's impossible to describe a process without first dividing it into steps, and a comparison-and-contrast explanation is useless if it didn't define the things compared and contrasted.

The primary explanatory strategy you use in a paper will often be determined by the question you are answering.

QUESTION	STRATEGY IN ANSWER
What is it?	Definition
What does it mean?	Definition
What are its important characteristics?	Description
How does it work?	Process description
How is it related to this other thing?	Comparison and contrast
How is it put together?	Classification and division

To what larger group does it belong?	Classification and division
Why did it happen?	Cause-and-effect analysis
What will be the consequences?	Cause-and-effect analysis

The primary explanatory strategy of your paper goes hand in hand with the thesis. It is difficult to develop one without the other. This means that you should expect to reconsider your choice of a primary strategy as you refine your thesis and to reconsider your thesis as you refine your choice of a primary strategy. In your early drafts, focus on using strategies that are appropriate to your purpose and that will be effective with your readers.

Defining

To define something is to identify it, to set it apart so that it can be distinguished from similar things. Writers need to define all terms that might be unclear to readers in order to make points clearly, forcefully, and with authority.

Formal definitions are those found in a dictionary. They usually combine a general term with specific characteristics: "A computer is a *programmable electronic device* [general term] that can *store, retrieve,* and *process data* [specific characteristics]." Another common way to define something is to use a synonym: "Computers, *high-speed electronic calculating machines,* have changed the way people write." You can also define by example: "Small notebook computers, *such as Apple's 8 × 12 inch PowerBook,* can do virtually everything larger desktop computers can."

Usually, defining something is a brief, preliminary step before moving on to another part of the explanation. When you need to define something complex or difficult or when your primary explanatory strategy is definition, you will need an extended definition consisting of a paragraph or more. This was the case with Mark's paper explaining computers, in which he defined each part of a typical computer system. After defining the central processing unit (CPU), he then defined *computer memory.*

> Computer storage space is measured in units called "kilobytes" (Ks). Each K equals 1024 "bytes" or approximately 1000 single typewriter characters. So one K equals about 180 English words, or a little less than half a single-spaced typed page, or maybe three minutes of fast typing.
>
> Personal computers generally have their memories measured in "megabytes" (MBs). One MB equals 1,048,567 bytes (or 1000 Ks), which translates into approximately 400 pages of single-spaced type. A typical personal computer may have one or two or more megabytes of this built-in storage space.

Describing

To describe a person, place, or thing in writing means to create a verbal image so that readers can see what you see; hear what you hear; and taste, smell, and feel what you taste, smell, and feel. In other words, effective descriptions usually appeal to one or more of the five senses. Your goal in describing something is to make it real enough for your readers that they can experience it for themselves.

Good description contains enough to help readers understand your subject, but not so much as to distract or bore them. Above all, descriptive details need to be purposeful. Heed the advice of Russian short-story writer Anton Chekhov: "If a gun is hanging on the wall in the first chapter, it must, without fail, fire in the second or third chapter. If it doesn't fire, it mustn't hang either."

Describing processes — that is, how things work — is slightly more complicated than giving a simple physical description of a person, place, or thing; in addition to showing objects at rest, you need to show them in sequence and motion. In other words, a process description combines the simple description just discussed with some form of orderly action.

To describe a process, you need to divide the process into discrete steps and present the steps in a logical order. For some processes this is easy (making chili, building a garage). For others it is more difficult, either because many steps are all happening at once or because people don't know which steps come before others (manufacturing a car, creating a nation-state, writing a research paper).

In either case, show the steps in a logical sequence that will be easy for readers to understand. Although it is possible to describe a process in reverse chronological order, working from the last event backward to the first, this is far more likely to confuse your readers than chronological order. To orient your readers, you may also want to number the steps, using transition words such as *first, second,* and *third.* (See Chapter 26.)

In the following example, taken from an early draft of his paper, Keith describes the process of manufacturing compact discs.

> CDs start out as a refrigerator-sized box full of little plastic beads that you could sift your hands through. They are fed into a giant tapered corkscrew--a blown-up version of an old-fashioned meat grinder. As the beads pass down the corkscrew, they are slowly melted by the heated walls.
>
> At the bottom of their descent is a "master recording plate" onto which the molten plastic is pressed. The plastic now resembles a vinyl record, except that the disc is transparent. The master now imprints "pits," rather than grooves, around the disc, the surface resembling a ball of Play-Doh after being thrown against a stucco wall--magnified 5000 times.

Comparing and Contrasting

To compare two things is to find similarities between them; to contrast is to find differences. Comparing and contrasting help us understand something better by clarifying how it is related to similar things and how it is distinctive.

College assignments frequently ask you to compare and contrast one thing — an author, a book, a president, a government, a culture, a century, a philosophy, an invention — with another. Comparison-and-contrast analyses can also be used to clarify other explanations.

The two things compared and contrasted should usually be reasonably similar. You *can* compare apples and oranges, but you'll probably learn more if you compare mandarin oranges with navel oranges. You should also compare and contrast the same elements or features of each thing. If you describe the digestive system of one frog species, you should be sure to describe the digestive system of the frog species with which you are comparing it.

There are three common ways to organize a comparison-and-contrast analysis. A point-to-point analysis examines one feature at a time for both similarities and differences. A whole-to-whole analysis first presents one object in its entirety and then presents the other object as a whole; it usually concludes by highlighting important similarities or differences. A similarity-and-difference analysis first presents all the similarities and then all the differences between the two things, or vice versa. Use a point-to-point or similarity-and-difference organization for long comparisons and contrasts of complex things; use a whole-to-whole organization for short subjects that readers can easily comprehend.

In the following whole-to-whole example, Keith compares and contrasts how records and CDs transmit the information that eventually becomes music.

On a record, the stylus (needle) sits in a spiraled groove and reads the depth and width of the groove, from which it receives its audio signal. However, the depth of the groove is constantly changing by fractions of millimeters due to specks of dust and the wear caused by the needle, which reads not only the music but also the dust and wear, passing along all the sound as "music."

On a CD, however, a laser sends out a beam of light, which bounces off an object, like radar, and returns with a message, which becomes the music. The CD player doesn't read an ever-changing and dirty groove. Instead, it reads either a "yes" or a "no"--a pit or no pit--from the disc. On one CD there are hundreds of thousands of tiny pits. . . . The laser in your CD player reads the distance to the disc to determine if there's a pit which will be farther away, or not.

As Keith's example shows, most comparison-and-contrast explanations give equal space to each of the two things examined. This is because both are equally important to the writer's point. If you want to focus on one thing but need to explain it in terms of another, similar thing, then you should use an analogy.

An analogy is an effective way of explaining something new to readers because you can compare something they are unfamiliar with to something they already know about. For example, most of us have never seen a heart beating, but we are used to thinking of it as a pump, a device that we see and use every day. Be sure to use objects and images that will be familiar to your readers in analogies.

Classifying and Dividing

People generally understand short things better than long things, small things better than large things, and simple things better than complex things. To help readers understand a complex or puzzling topic, often it is effective to use classification and division to reduce it to understandable pieces and to put the pieces in context.

To classify something, you put it in a category or class with other things that are like it: *Like whales and dolphins, sea lions are aquatic mammals.* To divide something, you break it into smaller parts or subcategories: *An insect's body is composed of a head, a thorax, and an abdomen.* Many complex systems need both classification and division to be clear. To explain a stereo system, for example, you might divide the whole into headphones, record player, graphic equalizers, tape deck, compact disc player, preamplifiers, amplifiers, radio, and speakers. Then you might classify all these parts into a few categories:

Inputs	FM radio
	Record player
	Tape deck
	Compact disc player
Processors	Preamplifiers
	Amplifiers
	Graphic equalizers
Outputs	Speakers
	Headphones

Combining classification and division is particularly important when your division results in a large number of parts or subcategories. Most readers have a difficult time remembering more than six or seven things, so organize a long list into a few logical groups, as in the preceding list. Also be sure that the categories you use are meaningful to your readers, not simply convenient for you as a writer.

Analyzing Causes and Effects

Nothing happens in isolation. Everything happens because something else happened; then it, in turn, makes something else happen. You sleep because you're tired, and once you've slept, you wake up because you're rested. In other words, you already know about cause and effect because it is a regular part of your daily life. A cause is something that makes something else happen; an effect is the thing that's made to happen.

When you write a cause-and-effect analysis, usually you know what the effect is and you're trying to explain what caused it: Why do CDs cost more than records? Why have the professors formed a union? Why are fish in the lake dying? The thesis for a cause-and-effect analysis should always include the word because: *CDs cost more than records because manufacturing costs are higher.* This sort of analysis often forms part of a larger explanation, but entire papers explaining causes are common, too.

You can also start with the cause and describe possible future effects: *If billboards were banned from state highways, people would be able to enjoy the countryside again.* Unless there is very sound and widely accepted evidence to support the thesis, however, this sort of analysis will almost always result in argumentative or speculative writing. (See Chapter 13.)

In the following example, Tom looks at the shortage of affordable student housing on his campus (the effect) and presents increased enrollment and inadequate planning as the causes.

> The university's policy of "delayed retroactive accommodation" has repeatedly affected housing costs. The last university dormitories were constructed and completed in 1978 when the student population was 7400. By 1985 student enrollment had increased to 8100, which put increased pressure on both existing dorms and city apartments adjacent to the university, causing prices in both to increase substantially. By 1991, the student population had increased to nearly 9000, but since no new dormitories were built during this period, demand and prices for student housing sky-rocketed.

Tom's explanation illustrates the difficulty of analyzing causes and effects. The causes he presents are reasonable, but many other causes — inflation, high taxes, increased cost of construction materials, increased student vandalism — could have contributed to the problem. Most complex situations have multiple causes. If you try to reduce such a situation to just one or two causes, you are making the logical mistake known as oversimplification. (See Chapter 3.) To prove his thesis, Tom would have to present considerably more evidence to demonstrate that the causes he proposes are the most important ones and that any others are merely secondary.

WRITING 4

Decide which of the five strategies described in this section best suits the primary purpose of the explanatory paper you are drafting. Which additional or secondary strategies will you also use?

ORGANIZING WITH LOGIC

Since the information in an explanatory paper will be new and therefore challenging to readers, a strong, easy-to-follow organization is crucial. If you give your readers a good sense of where you're taking them, they will be more willing to follow you at each step. Make sure your method of organization is clear early in the paper; digress as little as possible.

Your method of organization should be as simple, straightforward, and logical as possible, given your subject and audience. For example, if you wanted to explain how a CD stereo system works, you could start your paper with a description of putting a CD on a player and end with the music coming out of the speakers, explaining what happens at each step along the way. You could also describe the system technically, starting with the power source and the amplifier and working outward to the speakers. You could even describe it historically, starting with components that were developed earliest and work toward those that have been invented most recently. For most readers, the first method of organization would be best because it parallels something that they themselves have experienced.

WRITING 5

Outline three possible means of organizing the explanatory paper you are writing. List the advantages and disadvantages of each. Select the one that best suits your purpose and the needs of your audience.

MAINTAINING A NEUTRAL PERSPECTIVE

Your explanatory writing will usually be clearer if you maintain a neutral or objective perspective, one that emphasizes the thing explained (the object) rather than your beliefs and feelings. This perspective allows you to get information to readers as quickly and efficiently as possible without you, the writer, getting in the way.

Of course, a paper written about stereo systems by a stereo enthusiast would be different from one written by someone who thinks only a live performance is worthwhile; it's never possible to be completely objective. The goal is to be as neutral as possible. Write from the third-person point of view, using the pronouns *he, she,* and *it.* Keep yourself (*I*) in the background unless you have a good reason, such as explaining your personal experience with the subject. It is generally a good idea to avoid the second person as well; however, in some instances, speaking directly to the reader (*you*) adds a friendly, familiar tone that keeps readers interested. Present all the relevant information about the topic, both things you like about it and things you dislike. Avoid emotional or biased language. Remember that your goal is not to win an argument but to convey information. (See Chapter 6.)

WRITING 6

Examine the draft you are writing to see if you have maintained as neutral a perspective as possible. Where you find emotional or opinion words, delete them and write from a less biased perspective.

SHAPING THE WHOLE PAPER

Keith's complete essay on the high cost of compact discs is presented here. His topic is narrowly focused on one type of sound medium, CDs, and on one feature of that medium, the high cost. His thesis, that CDs cost more than records because their manufacturing costs are higher, evolves throughout the essay and is revealed only at the end, but it is clearly anticipated by the implicit question: Why do CDs cost so much? His organization is simple and easy to follow. First, the whole essay is framed by a description of a person in a record store wondering why CDs cost more than records. Second, within this framework is a point-by-point comparison of the operational and manufacturing processes of records and CDs. Keith's perspective throughout is that of a knowledgeable tour guide. Although his personality is clear, his biases do not affect the report.

The primary explanatory strategy in Keith's essay is an analysis of causes and effects, but he uses most of the other strategies discussed in this chapter as well: definition, process description, and comparison and contrast. His essay is most remarkable for its effective use of analogy. At various points, he asks his readers to think of radar, the game of telephone, jimmies on an ice cream cone, corkscrews, meat grinders, player pianos, and Play-Doh.

CDs: What's the Big Difference?

The little package in your left hand says $14.95. The larger package in your right hand says $7.95. The question is, do you want to hear James Taylor in true stereo quality or not? Since you don't want to settle for second best, you nestle the larger LP back between some Disney classics and head to the counter with your new JT compact disc. Wandering out of the store you wonder what, besides seven dollars, was the difference between this little CD and that LP record.

Maybe you've heard the term "digital audio," the type of recording used with CDs, as opposed to "analog audio," used with LPs? If you don't know the difference, read on.

The purpose of your stereo system is to interpret recordings and reproduce them faithfully. Of course, nothing's perfect, so your music always has that quaint amount of background fuzz that never goes away. The fuzz is due to your stereo's misinterpretation of the signal it receives from the magnetic tape or vinyl record.

On a record, the stylus (needle) sits in a spiraled groove and reads the depth and width of the groove, from which it receives its audio signal. However, the depth of the groove is constantly changing by fractions of millimeters due to specks of dust and wear caused by the needle, which reads not only the music but also the dust and wear, passing along all the sound as "music."

On a CD, however, a laser sends out a beam of light, which bounces off an object, like radar, and returns with a message, which becomes the music. The CD player doesn't read an ever-changing and dirty groove. Instead, it reads either a "yes" or a "no"--a pit or no pit--from the disc. On one CD there are hundreds of thousands of tiny pits that resemble those of a player piano scroll, telling the piano which keys to hit. The laser in your CD player reads the distance to the disc to determine if there's a pit, which will be farther away, or not.

What's the difference, you ask, in receiving music from grooves versus pits? Do you remember playing the "telephone game" in fifth grade? You know, the one where someone on one side of class whispers something in your ear and it gets passed along until it gets to the last person, who gets to say what he was told? This is much the way in which your stereo works: the LP or CD is like the first person and your speakers are like the last. In the case of the record, I whisper some line in your ear and you pass it on, but by the time it reaches the last person, it's been twisted about and has a few more words attached. In the case of the CD, I whisper either a "yes" or a "no" and by the time it reaches the last person it should be exactly the same--this is where the term "digital" comes from, meaning either there is a signal (yes) or there isn't one (no). After all, how much can you screw up a yes or no?

Even when you understand the difference between a CD and a record, you still feel that seven-dollar difference in your pocket. Why does digital cost so much more?

CDs start out as a refrigerator-sized box full of little plastic beads that you could sift your hands through. They are fed into a giant tapered corkscrew--a blown-up version of an old-fashioned meat grinder. As the beads pass down the corkscrew, they are slowly melted by the heated walls.

At the bottom of their descent is a "master recording plate" onto which the molten plastic is pressed. The plastic now resembles a vinyl record, except that the disc is transparent. The master now imprints "pits," rather than grooves, around the disc, the surface resembling a ball of Play-Doh after being thrown against a stucco wall--magnified 5000 times.

Although a record would be nearly finished at this point, there's still important work to be done on the CD. From here the disc is metallized, a process that deposits a thin film of metal, usually aluminum, on the surface; you see it as a rainbow under a light. Since light won't bounce back from transparent plastic, the coating acts as a mirror to bounce back the laser beam.

The disc is mirrored by a spray-painting process called "sputtering" that must be extremely precise. You couldn't just dip the thing because then the pits would fill in or melt. The clear disc is inserted into a chamber and placed opposite a piece of pure aluminum called a "target," which is bombarded with electricity, causing the aluminum atoms to jump off and embed themselves onto the surface of the disc, like jimmies to an ice cream cone.

To keep fingerprints from this critical surface, it is coated with a polymer resin--sort of like an epoxy glue. The disc is laid flat, while a mask is laid over the center hole and a thin bead of resin is laid down around the center. Then the disc is "spin-coated" with a fine film of resin, which becomes the outer coating on the CD.

Once the resin is cured by a brief exposure to ultraviolet light, your CD is pretty much idiot-proof. As long as you don't interrupt the light path to the film, your CD will perform perfectly, even with small scratches, so long as they don't diffract the laser beam--and even then you may be able to rub them smooth with a finger. In no case does anything ever come in contact with the recorded surface.

The CD is finished when it is either stamped or silk-screened with the appropriate logo and allowed to dry. Though all of these steps take a mere seven seconds to produce one CD, with materials costing no more than a pack of gum, the cost of buying and operating one CD-producing machine is close to that of running a small team of Formula 1 racecars.

So next time you walk into Record Land, you know what you are paying for. A CD may be twice as expensive as a record, but the sound is twice as clear and the disc will last forever.

SUGGESTIONS FOR WRITING AND RESEARCH

Individual

1. Write a paper explaining some thing, process, or concept. As a starting point, use an idea you discovered in Writing 2. When you have finished one draft of this essay, look back and see if there are places where your explanation could be improved by using one of the explanatory strategies explained in this chapter.
2. Select a fiction or nonfiction writer who manages to explain things especially well. Read or reread a sample of his or her work and write an essay in which you analyze and explain the power of the exposition you find there.

Collaborative

Form writing groups based on mutual interests; agree as a group to explain the same thing, process, or concept. Write your explanations separately and then share drafts, comparing and contrasting your different ways of explaining. For a final draft, either (1) rewrite the individual drafts borrowing good ideas from others in the group or (2) compose a collaborative single paper with contributions from each group member.

Chapter 13

Arguing For and Against

When I argued against gun control with my roommates, it was pretty easy to convince them that I was right, but when I wrote out these same arguments, my writing group challenged every one and kept asking me for more evidence and more proof. Do you have to have evidence and proof for everything you write?
– WOODY

ARGUMENT IS DEEPLY ROOTED in the American political and social system, where free and open debate is the essence of the democratic process. Argument is also at the heart of the academic process, where scholars investigate scientific, social, and cultural issues hoping through the give-and-take of debate to find reasonable answers to complex questions. Argument in the academic world, however, is less likely to be about winning or losing — as it is in political and legal systems — than about changing minds or altering perceptions. Through the process of teaching and learning, faculty and students alike spend a great amount of time and energy arguing *for* one interpretation, position, or point of view and *against* another.

Argument as rational disagreement — rather than as quarrels, fights, and contests — most often occurs in areas of genuine uncertainty about what is right, best, or most reasonable. In disciplines such as English, art, history, and philosophy, written argument in scholarly articles and critical reviews commonly takes the form of interpretive arguments, in which the meaning or significance of an idea is disputed. In disciplines such a sociology, political science, engineering, business, and environmental studies, arguments commonly appear as position papers.

WRITING TO CHANGE PEOPLE'S MINDS

Arguments focus on issues about which there is some debate; if there's no debate, there's no argument. College assignments commonly ask that you argue one side of an issue or idea and defend your argument against attacks from skeptical audiences.

A *position paper* sets forth an arguable position on an issue of local or national concern. The position paper is one of the most demanding and, at the same time, most practical forms of argument that you may be assigned in college. A position paper assignment will typically ask you, first, to choose an issue in which you are interested; second, to argue a position on one side or another of the issue; and third, to support your claims with evidence, which you locate through research. (See Chapter 4 for advice about how to approach an assignment.) Position papers and other arguments can be broken down into the following elements.

Purpose

The purpose of argument is to persuade other people to agree with a particular point of view. In the world at large, people argue to get something done: lawyers attempt to win cases; legislators to pass or defeat bills; college committees to ensure a culturally diverse faculty or student body. In your college writing, you attempt to persuade your instructor or classmates to agree that your position is either reasonable or the best one available.

Issue

An issue is something that can be argued about. For instance, *traffic lights* and *cultural diversity* are things or concepts, but not issues. However, they can become issues when questions are raised about them.

ISSUE   Should a traffic light be installed at the corner of Main and 5th streets?

ISSUE   Do American colleges adequately represent the cultural diversity of the United States?

These questions are issues because reasonable people could answer them in different ways; they can be argued about because more than one answer is plausible, possible, or realistic.

Position

Your position is the stand you take on an issue. Virtually all issues can be formulated as yes/no questions; your position, then, will be either *pro* (if the answer is yes) or *con* (if the answer is no).

ISSUE   Should the faculty of Northfield College be more culturally diverse?

PRO   Yes, the faculty should be more culturally diverse.

CON   No, the faculty should not be more culturally diverse.

Claims and Counterclaims

When you argue for or against one side of an issue, you make claims that you want your audience to believe. A *claim* is simply a statement that something is true or should be done. For example, these claims could be made about the issue of cultural diversity at Northfield College:

CLAIM   Northfield College fails to provide good education because the faculty is not culturally diverse.

CLAIM   Northfield College should appoint a committee to recruit faculty to ensure more cultural diversity.

Counterclaims are statements made against your position.

COUNTERCLAIM   The faculty of Northfield College are good scholars and teachers; therefore, their race and gender are irrelevant.

COUNTERCLAIM   A committee on cultural diversity would be a waste of time and money.

The best arguments provide not only good reasons for supporting a given position, but also good reasons for doubting the opposition. Good arguments are made by writers who know the other side as well as their own.

Argumentative Thesis

The primary claim that you make in your argument is called a thesis. In arguing your position you may make other claims, but they all work to support your thesis.

THESIS   Northfield College should enact a policy to make the faculty more culturally diverse by the year 2000.

CLAIM   The faculty at Northfield College is not culturally diverse.

CLAIM   A culturally diverse faculty is necessary to ensure a good education for today's students.

CLAIM   The goal to achieve increased cultural diversity by the year 2000 is achievable and practical.

Evidence

Once you have formulated a thesis, you will need evidence to demonstrate the reasonableness of your claim. For example, to support a claim that Northfield College lacks cultural diversity, you might introduce the following evidence.

EVIDENCE   According to the names listed in the most recent college catalog, sixty-nine of seventy-nine faculty members are male.

EVIDENCE   According to a recent faculty survey, sixty-five of seventy-nine faculty members are white Caucasian.

EVIDENCE   According to Janet Smith, an unsuccessful job candidate for a position in the English Department, one hundred percent of the faculty hired in the last ten years have been white males.

EVIDENCE   Everyone in the 10:00 A.M. section of History 101 is white.

While these pieces of information constitute evidence to support the claimed lack of cultural diversity at Northfield, they could also be called into question. For example, the list of names in a college catalog could be deceptive, since several names — Chris, Pat, Jan — can be either male or female. The faculty survey may be rigorous and impartial, but it was conducted five years ago. And so on. You must strive to assemble evidence that stands up to scrutiny, but you will never be able to supply absolute proofs.

Most arguments become more effective when they include source material gathered through research. However, shorter and more modest argument papers can be written without research and can profitably follow a process similar to that described here.

WRITING 1

An issue debated from time to time by college faculty is whether or not a first-year writing course should be required of all entering college students. Make three claims and three counterclaims about this issue. Write each claim in the most neutral language possible, so it does not suggest a bias on your part. Finally, select the claim you most believe in and write an argumentative thesis that could form the basis for a whole essay.

FINDING AN ISSUE

An issue for a position paper should be phrased as a question with a yes or no answer. In selecting an issue, consider both national and local issues. National issues are those that people in all parts of the United States care about and debate. You are likely to see these issues explained and argued on national television, on the front pages of daily newspapers, and in national newsmagazines; Are SATs a fair measure of academic potential? Should handguns be made illegal? Does acid rain kill forests? The advantage of national issues is their extensive news coverage and the likelihood of wide reader interest. The disadvantage is the difficulty in finding a local expert to interview or a site where the issue can be witnessed.

Local issues have an impact on the community in which you live. You will find these issues argued about in local newspapers and on local news broadcasts: Should a new mall be built on the beltway? Should the school year for the county's elementary school children be extended to 190 days? Should wolves be reintroduced into the nearby national park? The advantage of local issues is that you can often visit a place where the controversy occurs, interview people who are affected by it, and find generous coverage in local news media. The disadvantage is that the subject will not be covered in national news sources.

To write a position paper, select an issue that meets four criteria:

1. It is a real issue, which causes genuine controversy and uncertainty.
2. You can identify at least two distinct positions.
3. You are personally interested in advocating one of these positions.
4. It is narrow enough to be manageable.

Select an issue you care about. If you do a thorough job on this assignment, you will spend quite a bit of time thinking, researching, and writing about it, so select something that matters to you. Frankly, it's best to select an issue you find interesting but about which you have not fully made up your mind: that way, you will conduct your research with more genuine curiosity.

Be sure to focus the issue you select so that it is manageable. The bigger your issue, the more difficulty you will have thinking, researching, and writing about it. It will be easier to sort through and write about information on legalizing marijuana than information on legalizing drugs in general.

Brendan, who is from Wyoming, chose to write about a local issue that also had broader national implications:

ISSUE   Should wolves be reintroduced into Yellowstone National Park?

WRITING 2

Make a list of three national and three local issues about which you are concerned. Next, select the three issues that seem most important to you and write each as a question with a yes or no answer. Finally, write a paragraph on each issue explaining where you stand on it.

ANALYZING AN ISSUE

The most demanding work in writing a position paper takes place after you have selected an issue but before you actually write the paper. To analyze an issue, you need to do the following:

1. Provide a context for the issue.
2. Establish the arguments for your position.
3. Establish the arguments against your position.
4. Compile a list of sources that will support your position.

(For more information on research, see Part V.)

In preparing the material for your argument, you must treat both sides fairly, framing the opposition as positively as you frame your position. Think of it as an honest debate with yourself. Adopting a neutral stance toward your material will help you see clearly all the important claims you must refute to write the most persuasive paper possible. You will also have more empathy for the opposition, therefore qualifying your assertions with terms that suggest some room for honest disagreement. For any reader who sees merit in the opposing side, this strategy will be far more persuasive than absolute assertions.

Establishing Context

Your first search is for the context — social, political, historical, or philosophical — that will allow you, along with your readers, to understand the issue. What is this issue about? Why is it an issue? Where did the controversy begin? How long has it been debated? Who are the people involved?

In the following paragraph, Brendan describes the context for his issue, the reintroduction of wolves to Yellowstone National Park.

> Cattle ranchers killed nearly 81,000 wolves between 1883 and 1918. People believed that if this country was to be domesticated, there was no place for wolves. In 1915 Congress supported the interests of the ranchers and passed legislation for the removal of all wolves from federal lands. Strangely enough, this legislation included national parks, which were originally set aside to conserve wildlife. By 1926 there were no wolves in Yellowstone Park, and within ten years there were no wolves left in the continental United States.

Brendan uses a fairly neutral tone, allowing his statistics to tell a rather grim story about American wildlife management. It's a good idea to use a neutral tone whenever you present the context for an issue in your paper so that your audience witnesses, at the outset, your fairness and reasonableness.

Stating the Claims for (Pro)

List the claims supporting the pro side of the issue. Make each claim a distinctly strong and separate point, and make the best possible case for this position. Here are Brendan's claims supporting the position that *wolves should be reintroduced to Yellowstone National Park.*

1. Wolves would make the park a complete ecosystem; right now these predators are missing.
2. Wolves would help control the current overpopulation of elk, moose, and deer.
3. The Endangered Species Act of 1973 requires wolves to be restored to federal lands.
4. Visitors' experience in visiting Yellowstone would be improved if wolves were present.

Identifying Supporters

After listing the claims, note the authority on which each one rests. You want to identify the most prestigious people or groups who make each one. These are the supporters who will add authority and persuasiveness to your argument (if you decide later to take this position) or whose authority and persuasiveness you will somehow have to counteract (if you decide later not to take this position). Here is Brendan's list of supporters for his pro claims.

1. The National Audubon Society and the Wilderness Society both argue that the purpose of national parks is to preserve the wilderness as it was before civilization moved in.
2. This argument is especially made by biologists and ecologists who believe that the wolf, as the dominant predator of deer, moose, and elk, will once again assume that role in the park.
3. The National Parks and Conservation Association and many environmentalists argue for a strict interpretation of the Endangered Species Act.
4. In a recent survey, the National Park Service found that 74% of Yellowstone Park visitors believed that their park experience would be enhanced by seeing wolves.

Stating the Claims Against (Con)

List the claims supporting the con side of the issue, the counterclaims. It is not important that you have an equal number of reasons for and against, but you do want an approximate balance. Make the best possible case for this position. Here are the counterclaims Brendan identified.

1. Wolves will get out of the park and kill livestock on adjacent ranches.
2. Wolves will reduce the amount of game available to big-game hunters in the Montana-Wyoming-Idaho area.
3. Wolves will be a danger to people, especially park visitors.
4. Introduction of a protected species such as the wolf will limit public and commercial use of adjacent federal land and thus hurt area development.

Identifying Opposition

Now identify the authorities or groups who make the counterclaims. Here is Brendan's list.

1. Sheep and cattle farmers quoted in several articles say they fear for their livelihood, knowing that wolves have been proven livestock killers in the past. They don't want to lose money.

2. Big-game hunters and the Foundation for North American Wild Sheep, which monitors bighorn sheep populations, fear that wolves will not limit their killing to big game within the park itself.

3. Both local citizens and some park visitors believe that wolves harm people, especially children.

4. Loggers, builders, skiers, and campers make the argument that the wolf, as a protected species, would intrude into land near the park and use of that land for humans would cease.

Annotating the References

The next task in preparation for drafting your position paper is to put together, in alphabetical order, the references you consulted during research, briefly identifying each according to the kind of information it contains. The same article may present claims from both sides as well as provide context. Here, for example, is a part of Brendan's reference list.

Bass, R, (1991, October). The wolves' story. Outside, pp. 58–63. [Pro/con/context].

Carey, J. (1987, August–September). Who's Afraid of the big bad wolf? National Wildlife, pp. 4–11. [Pro/context]

Cohn, J. (1990, October). Endangered wolf population increases; planned reintroduction into old territory raises controversy. BioScience, pp. 628–632. [Con/pro]

Edwards, D. (1987, June 13). Recall the wild wolf: recovery plans to reestablish the wolf packs in the wild have diverse groups trapped together in an emotional snare are of politics, economics, and law. Science News, pp.378–379. [Context]

Annotating your list of references before writing the final draft allows you to check, recheck, and rearrange your arguments at any time during the writing process. In addition, if you use the documentation system that you will use in your final paper, your reference list at the end of your paper will be virtually finished. (See Chapter 20 for information about the documentation systems of various disciplines.)

WRITING 3

Select one of the issues you are interested in, establish the necessary context, and make pro and con lists similar to those described in this section, including supporters of each position. Be sure to make the best possible case for each position, pro and con.

TAKING A POSITION

Once you have spread out the two possible positions in the fairest way possible, you need to weigh for yourself which side is stronger. This is a good time to engage in freewriting (see Chapter 7) or journal writing (see Chapter 8), arguing with yourself about which position now makes the most sense to you. Write about each position for a page or so to see how it sounds to you, and determine whether you are more persuaded by one or the other. Select the position that you find most convincing and then state the reasons, most compelling reasons last. This most likely is the position you will defend.

At this point, you need to formulate a thesis, a statement of the position you are going to defend.

THESIS   Wolves should be reintroduced to Yellowstone National Park to
               make the park a complete and balanced ecosystem.

Right now, all you need is a working thesis, something to focus your efforts in one direction and allow you to begin articulating claims and assembling evidence. Writers typically revise their theses as they redirect or narrow their paper and find new evidence.

A good argumentative thesis meets the following criteria:

1. It is interesting to you and your intended audience.
2. It can be managed within the confines of the time and space available.
3. It asserts something specific.
4. It makes a statement about what should be, not what is.
5. It proposes a plan of action.

> **WRITING 4**
>
> Take a position on the issue you have identified. Formulate a working thesis that you would like to support. Test your thesis against the five criteria listed for good theses.

DEVELOPING AN ARGUMENT

Your assignment is the case you will make for your position, the means by which you will try to persuade your readers that your position is correct. Good arguments need two things: good evidence and effective reasoning.

Assembling Evidence

Claims, positions, and theses are meaningless without evidence to support them.

Facts and Examples

Factual knowledge is verifiable and agreed upon by everyone involved regardless of personal beliefs or values. Facts are often statistical. These are facts:

Water boils at 212 degrees Fahrenheit.

Henry David Thoreau is the author of *Walden*, which was published in 1854.

Northfield College employed 79 full-time faculty and enrolled 1143 full-time students in 1992.

Regardless of what you believe about cultural diversity or the quality of education at Northfield College, for instance, all parties to an argument can agree that these faculty and student figures are correct.

Examples can be used to illustrate a claim or clarify an issue. For example, the general claim that "in most situations wolves pose little threat to humans" would gain force by specific examples of peaceful coexistence between wolves and humans.

Facts and examples can, of course, be misleading and even wrong. For hundreds of years malaria was believed to be caused by "bad air" rather than, as we know today, by a parasite transmitted through mosquito bites; however, for the people who believed the bad-air theory, it was *fact*. Be sure that information you present as factual will be accepted as such by your audience.

Inferences

The accumulation of a certain number of facts and examples should lead to an interpretation of what those facts mean — an inference, or generalization. For example, if you attend five different classes at Northfield College and in each class you find no minority students, you may *infer* that there are few or no minority students on campus. If your friends report similar facts about enrollment in specific classes, your inference gets stronger; if after four years you and your friends still encounter no minority students, it gets stronger still. However, while your inference is reasonable, it is not a fact , since the experience of you and your friends does not account for meeting all the possible students at the college.

Neither a fact nor an inference is better or more important than the other; each serves a different purpose. Facts provide information, and inferences give that information meaning. Sometimes inference is all that's available. Statistics describing what "Americans," "college students," or other large groups believe or do are, in fact, inferences about these groups based on information collected from a much smaller number of individuals. To be credible, inferences must be reasonable and based on factual evidence.

Informed Opinion

Informed opinions make good evidence; uninformed ones do not. If you say that Jim Smith is the best teacher at Northfield College, this personal opinion would not count for much in determining whether Smith gets tenure. However, the opinions informed by either research or expertise would be important. For example, if the opinion about Smith were offered by a researcher who had used a reasonable and generally accepted list of criteria for good teaching to evaluate all the faculty at Northfield or by an expert, such as an education professor, it would be taken more seriously than your personal opinion. While informed opinion lends credibility to a claim, it is not generally considered to be as strong as a verifiable fact.

Personal Testimony

An additional kind of evidence that has mixed credibility is testimony based on personal experience. When someone has experienced something firsthand, his or her knowledge cannot easily be discounted — so your opinion that Jim Smith is the best teacher on campus is worth more if you have witnessed his teaching than if you have heard about it. To use personal testimony effectively in supporting a claim, provide details and examples that confirm for readers that you were there and know what you are talking about.

Reasoning Effectively

To build an effective argument out of your evidence, first take a moment to consider your audience again. (See Chapter 5.) To be successful in your argument, you must persuade your audience, and to do this you must know who they are. Of course, your most important audience is your instructor, but consider also all those people who would read your position paper if it had a wider circulation. Ask yourself these questions:

- Who are my potential readers?
- What do they believe?
- Where do they stand on the issue? (All opposed? Some undecided? Some already in favor?)
- How are their interests involved?
- What sort of evidence is likely to be most effective with these people? What will be least effective?

Once you have a sense of who you're trying to persuade, you can begin to build your argument. First, use logic. Make sure each claim and each step in your argument is reasonable and defensible. Make sure you have evidence to support each claim. Present your evidence clearly, make inferences carefully, and avoid errors in logic.

Second, establish your credibility. Your readers will reject even the soundest logic if they don't trust you. Show that you've done your homework and used reliable sources. Establish common ground: begin by identifying elements that both you and the opposition agree on. Be fair. When explaining where you differ with your opponents, state their terms in accurate and neutral language; this way, your arguments cannot be dismissed because you misrepresented theirs. Use an objective and reasonable tone; avoid extremely emotional words or slanted language.

Third, appeal to your audience's emotions. Telling details, vivid and concrete language, compelling examples, persuasive metaphors, and occasionally a more personal or impassioned tone can help your readers' hearts as well as minds. However, do not become sentimental or veer into highly charged language.

WRITING 5

Develop an informal profile of the audience for your position paper by answering the questions posed in this section.

ORGANIZING A POSITION PAPER

After choosing the issue, analyzing it, establishing your position, collecting evidence, and checking your reasoning, you are ready to write your paper. The challenge now is to prepare a strategy for organizing and presenting your position in the best possible way.

Thesis-First Organization

Using this type of organization, writers lead with their thesis and spend the remainder of their essay supporting it, defending their claims against counterclaims.

1. **An issue is introduced as a yes/no question.** This makes clear that there are at least two sides to the issue. (*Should wolves be reintroduced into Yellowstone National Park?*)
2. **A position is asserted as a thesis.** The thesis commonly concludes the paragraph that introduces the issue. (*Wolves should be reintroduced into Yellowstone National Park to restore the natural ecosystem.*)
3. **The counterclaims are summarized.** Squeezing the counterclaim between the thesis and the evidence reserves the strongest places in the essay, the opening and conclusion, for writer's own position. (*If wolves are reintroduced to Yellowstone, they will have damaging effects on both the park and the surrounding region.*)
4. **The counterclaims are refuted.** The writer can actually strengthen his or her position by admitting that in some cases the counterclaims might be true. (*The fear of damage is based on commercial interests and old myths.*)
5. **The writer's claims are supported with evidence.** These claims include *because* statements and constitute the longest and most carefully documented part of the essay. (*Wolves should be reintro-*

duced into Yellowstone because *they will keep the deer population in check, add excitement for visitors, and fulfill the national park mission.*)

6. **The conclusion broadly restates the writer's position.** The conclusion moves beyond the specific claims, synthesizing them into a broad general position. (*Restoring the ecosystem of Yellowstone National Park to its precivilized state is consistent with the mission of the national parks and will be more beneficial than not.*)

There are three distinct advantages to leading with your thesis: (1) Your audience knows where you stand from the first paragraph on; (2) your claim occupies the two strongest places — first and last — in the essay; (3) it is the standard, and the expected, form of academic argument.

Delayed-Thesis Organization

Using this type of organization, the writer introduces the issue, discusses the arguments for and against, but does not obviously take sides until late in the essay. The writer should explain and illustrate his or her position *after* presenting the opposition's position, since the end of the essay provides more emphasis. The delayed-thesis argument follows this pattern:

1. An issue is introduced as a yes/no question.
2. The claims of the opposition are summarized.
3. The claims are refuted.
4. The counterclaims (the writer's position) are summarized.
5. The writer's counterclaims are supported.
6. The conclusion states a thesis based on the counterclaims.

There are three advantages to this indirect form of argument: (1) The audience is drawn into the writer's struggle in arriving at a position by being asked to weigh the evidence and arrive at a claim; (2) the audience is kept in suspense about the writer's position; and (3) the audience understands the difficulty in making a decision.

WRITING 6

Make two outlines for organizing your position paper, one with the thesis first, the other with a delayed thesis. Share your outlines with your classmates and discuss which seems most appropriate for the issue you have chosen.

SHAPING THE WHOLE PAPER

Once you have worked through the pro and con arguments and explored different organizational strategies for presenting your position, you are ready to compose a complete draft. Because you have analyzed the issues extensively prior to composing, you may find that this paper comes together more quickly than some of your other papers. In any case, it's a good idea to test out your position paper on an audience before revising, editing, and turning in the final draft to your instructor.

Following is the finished draft of Brendan's paper, edited in places to shorten it for illustrative purposes. Brendan uses the thesis-first method of organization, as his instructor specified. Because of the complex as well as specialized nature of Brendan's subject, his position paper relies heavily on research. You will notice that he adopts the third-person point of view to present his argument in an objective tone, letting the facts, examples, and informed expert opinion make his case for him. He uses the APA documentation style, which is appropriate to his intended major, political science. (For more information on documentation systems, see Chapter 20.)

The Wolf Should Be Reintroduced into
Yellowstone National Park

Since 1926, there have been no wolves in Yellowstone National Park. The modern wolf inhabited the area of Yellowstone, as well as the greater part of the North American continent, for well over a million years before the Europeans settled the New World. Upon arrival, white settlers began to push the wolf from its natural territory. With the settlers' movement west and with their increased development and agriculture, the wolf's range in the United States rapidly shrunk and eventually disappeared.

In recent years there has been a movement to bring the wolf back to Yellowstone Park. A battle is being waged between environmental conservationists, who support the reintroduction of wolves, and sheep and cattle farmers and western hunters, who oppose it. So far, legislators, representing the farmers and hunters, have been able to block the reintroduction of wolves. The wolf, however, should be reintroduced to Yellowstone National Park.

Wolves need to be in Yellowstone in order to make it a complete ecosystem. Edward Lewis of the Greater Yellowstone Coalition, a regional conservation group, says that wolves are the missing link. They are the only major species that existed in historical times but is missing now. Wolves would help to balance the ecosystem by preying upon deer, elk, and moose. This would reduce the damage that overpopulation of these animals does to the area and limit the numbers of these species that starve during harsh winters.

Many sheep and cattle ranchers, however, feel that if wolves are reintroduced to the park, they will roam outside the park onto the lands where these ranchers keep their animals and will kill the valuable livestock (Bass, 1991). The fact is that wolves in Yellowstone will have relatively little impact on the livestock industry. Steven Fritts, a U.S. Fish and Wildlife Service ecologist, recently compiled a five-year study on the effects wolves have on livestock (Edwards, 1987). In his research he studied wolves in northern Minnesota. There are 12,000 livestock farms, 230,000 cattle, 90,000 sheep, as well as thousands of turkeys and other domesticated animals in the wolves' territory in Minnesota. According to Fritts's study, only about ten animals are killed each year by wolves, which represents only one-fifth of one percent of farm animals. Similar reductions were projected for deer, moose, and bison, and little or no loss was estimated for bighorn and pronghorn. The report also revealed that the grizzly bear (another endangered species) wouldn't be affected at all. Tom France from the National Wildlife Federation says that wolves can be managed and will enhance the hunting experience (Carey, 1987).

Stephen Kellert, a wolf specialist from Yale University, recently conducted surveys of people's attitudes toward wolves. He says that there is a deep-grained bias toward predators among most ranchers and hunters of the West. These attitudes are not necessarily based on facts, but rather superstition and traditional folklore (McNamee, 1986). Nevertheless, many politicians, senators, and representatives from Wyoming, Idaho, and Montana, including Congressman Ron Marlee from Montana, have an obligation to side with the farmers and hunters whom they represent. Many of these politicians are hunters or were farmers themselves and, therefore, share the same negative feelings about wolves returning. They feel that they must please the people they represent in order to get reelected and keep their jobs, so they are reluctant to side with anyone besides those who are most likely to vote them back into office (Joyce, 1990).

Yellowstone Park alone consists of 2.2 million acres of wilderness; the greater Yellowstone ecosystem consisting of Grand Tetons National Park, seven national forests, and other federal and state land totals about 14 million acres. David Mech, America's leading wolf expert from the U.S. Fish and Wildlife Service, says that Yellowstone "literally begs to have wolves. It's teeming with prey. Wolves would add an element to the ecosystem that would help restore it to a more natural state, and that would allow the public to better enjoy the park" (Cohn, 1990, p. 630). In a recent poll, 74% of Yellowstone visitors felt wolves would improve the experience of visiting the park (Cohn, 1990). Reasons for this include the fact that wolves are presently not found in the wild anywhere in the United States, with a few exceptions in Canada-bordering states. Many people feel wolves are exciting animals because they have seen the results of studies that have shown how wolves possess many of the family-oriented characteristics that humans value.

The National Park Service is the leading preservation agency in the United States; part of the purpose of the National Park Service is to preserve the natural wilderness as it was before the white settlers disturbed it. Yellowstone is somewhat of a role model for public land management in our times, a symbol of "whole ecosystem management," says William Turnage, the executive director of the Wilderness Society. "Of course the wolf belongs here" (O'Gara, 1986, p. 20).

The Endangered Species Act of 1973 states that federal agencies are to use "all methods and procedures necessary" to restore endangered species that have been driven out, and not just "methods and procedures [that are] convenient, economically painless, and politically expedient" (Williams, 1990, p. 33). The three subspecies of the gray wolf that once occupied the continental United States are listed as endangered. The Endangered Species Act then not only gives the National Park Service the power to work toward the reintroduction of the wolf into areas such as Yellowstone, but also requires it to do so. Today, however, there are no wolves in the park. Conservation organizations, such as the Wilderness Society and the National Parks and Conservation Association as well as the National Park Service, feel that if this issue was worth the time, effort, and money for Congress to pass this act, then it should be enforced. Our leading conservation agency should not be prevented from enforcing this act of Congress.

The reintroduction of wolves to Yellowstone National Park is both an important and a reasonable proposal. In this age of environmental abuse and excessive development by human beings, it seems only appropriate to set aside areas for the complete preservation of nature. Our National Parks are the ideal place for this. The wolf was once an integral part of the Yellowstone environment. Its reintroduction would complete the ecosystem and improve the natural situation. The arguments posed by farmers and hunters are insubstantial. An act of Congress requires government agencies to return the wolf to its original habitat. Why, then, are there still no wolves in Yellowstone?

References

Bass, R. (1991, October). The wolves' story. Outside, pp. 58–63.
Carey, J. (1987, August–September). Who's afraid of the big bad wolf? National Wildlife, pp. 4–11.
Cohn, J. (1990, October). Endangered wolf population increases; planned reintroduction into old territory raises controversy. Bioscience, pp. 628–632.
Edwards, D. (1987, June 13). Recall the wild wolf: recovery plans to reestablish the wolf packs in the wild have diverse groups trapped together in an emotional snare of politics, economics, and law. Science News, pp. 378–379.
Joyce, C. (1990, June 2). Yellowstone lets the wolf through the door. New Scientist, p. 21.
McNamee, T. (1986, January). Yellowstone's missing element. Audubon, pp. 12–19.
O'Gara, G. (1986, November–December). Filling in a missing link. Sierra, pp. 20–21.
Williams, T. (1990, November). Waiting for wolves to howl in Yellowstone. Audubon, pp. 32–34.

SUGGESTIONS FOR WRITING AND RESEARCH

Individual

1. Write a position paper on the issue you have been working with in Writings 2–6. Follow the guidelines suggested in this chapter to write the paper, using as much research information as you deem appropriate.
2. Write a position paper on an issue related to your writing class. Consider topics such as (a) student voice in writing topics, (b) the seating plan, (c) the value of writing groups versus instructor conferences, or (d) the number of writing assignments. For supporting or opposing views, interview classmates and your instructor.

Collaborative

1. In teams of two or three, select an issue; divide up the work so that each group member contributes some work to (1) the context, (2) the pro argument, and (3) the con argument (to guarantee that you do not take sides prematurely). Share your issue analysis with another group and receive feedback. Finally, write position papers individually, using the best evidence available.
2. Follow the procedure for the first collaborative assignment, sharing the research and receiving feedback, but write your final position paper collaboratively, either blending, weaving, or sequencing the voices of group members.

Chapter 14

Interpreting Texts

When I read, I've learned to ask a lot of questions, such as Who's telling the story? What's the character like? Why does a certain action happen? What do symbols mean? Things like that. But I never find as much meaning in the stories as my teachers do.

— DIANE

WHEN YOU INTERPRET SOMETHING, you address the question What does it mean? When most of us encounter something new and interesting, we try to make sense of it by figuring out how it works, by comparing it to similar things, by analyzing our reactions to it, and by trying to determine why it affects us the way it does. Interpreting things is how we learn to understand and value them.

We usually think of texts as the written material found in books and periodicals. However, virtually all symbolic works can be considered texts open to interpretation — video and audio recordings, films, music and dance performances, exhibits, paintings, photographs, sculptures, advertisements, artifacts, and even whole cultures.

You are probably familiar with the reviews that are commonly written about these texts, such as a review in a newspaper or magazine telling you whether a film is worth seeing. A review is a form of interpretation that not only answers the interpretive question What does it mean? but also asks the evaluative question Is it good? Most interpretive essays in writing classes focus on written texts and are more interpretive than evaluative.

WRITING TO INTERPRET

Our initial reactions to a new text of any kind are often a jumble of impressionistic thoughts, feelings, and memories — seldom fully realized interpretations. To write an interpretive essay, you must take the time to analyze this jumble and develop a reasonable, systematic understanding of what the text means and why. Since all texts have more than one possible meaning and are open to more than one interpretation, in an interpretive essay you also try to make the best possible case that your reading is a good one and deserves attention.

A fully developed interpretation *explains* what the text says, in and of itself. It also *argues* for a particular interpretation of the text's meaning — what the text implies or suggests in a larger sense. Like any argument, an interpretive essay should be as persuasive as possible, but it can never be an absolute proof.

Interpretive essays, which are also called critical, analytical, or review essays, are among the most frequent college writing assignments. A typical assignment may ask you to interpret a poem, a story, an essay, a newspaper or magazine article, or even a historical document. Writing a good textual interpretation will require various writing strategies. To explain a text, you will usually have to describe its people and situations, summarize its events, and define important concepts or terms. You may also need to analyze the various parts of the text and explain how they work together as a whole, perhaps by comparing the text to others. To argue for your interpretation, you will have to develop a strong thesis and defend it with sound reasoning and effective evidence. In many cases, you will also be expected to evaluate the text's worth and reflect on its significance to you.

The following essay and the two responses to it, demonstrate the art of interpretive writing. It was written by Angel Fuster, a senior majoring in English and enrolled in an advanced writing class. After you have read his essay, study the various strategies for writing about it, as well as two essays — one objective and one subjective — written by first-year students who read and interpreted Angel's story.

While Fuster's essay is autobiographical and therefore nonfiction, many of the texts you will be asked to analyze in college will be fiction or poetry. But the techniques for interpreting works of fiction and nonfiction are the same.

Angelique's Letter

Angel Fuster

– 1 –

The letter is written on standard grade-school paper, the blue lines far enough apart for any kid to learn on. Her name, "Angelique," at the top of the page, is done in her fanciest style. But the characters are boxy and it looks as though they were done especially slow.

– 2 –

"Just like a nice restaurant's name," my nine-year-old sister said.

I wanted to say how proud I was that she was learning script, but instead replied, "Yeah, like those restaurants only rich white people go to."

She gazed at her name and smiled wishfully. "Yeah, if I was white, I'd make a restaurant with those letters."

"Don't worry, Mamma, if you go to college like me, you could get whatever you want."

I felt guilty for using her artistically written "Angelique" to teach her about racism, especially since I knew what I had said was a bit oversimplified and inaccurate. But what could I do? How could I ensure that she grows up questioning things? I had to keep her from getting pregnant and dropping out of school as many of her classmates will, as my older sister did, and as my mother before her. And she was already talking about boys.

– 3 –

The boys loved to talk about Sorada Rodriguez, but none loved her like I did. One day I walked up to her on the playground and, without thinking, took out my pencil and poked her in the thigh.

She was sent to the nurse. I waited after school and told her I was sorry, and she just gave me the worst stare and screamed at me.

I walked her the two blocks to her side of the projects without saying a word. When we got to the empty apartment, I kissed her on the mouth. Then, still without saying a word, she took off her clothes, like in the movies, and I took off mine. I was embarrassed because I had no hair and she had a lot.

– 4 –

I would have to get Angelique interested in important issues, things that would excite her, make her want to develop her mind so she would grow into a thinking person. My strategy was twofold: I would give her enormous pride in her people, then I would teach her to act on that pride to improve herself. But in order to keep her interested in these issues, I would have to show that they directly affect her, using every opportunity I could to bring up the subject.

– 5 –

"Chino, play Barbie with me. You could be her," Angelique said, holding up a blond doll dressed in a bikini bathing suit.

"No, I don't want her. I want the one with the black hair. It isn't fair that all the Barbies are blond. Black hair is beautiful too. They don't even make Puerto Rican Barbies."

She studied the long wiry blondness. "I wish they make Puerto Rican Barbies."

I felt like telling her I was only kidding.

– 6 –

Under "Angelique," her words are written in large print that allows only four or five words to fit between the pink margins.

Dear Chino,
  How are you doing?
  remember you said to write
  you a song or a story? Well, I
  am goging to write bouth of them.
  Are you happy?

Indeed, I was very happy. My plan to educate Angelique was working. Getting her to write was one step in encouraging her to be a thinking person. I knew that in her grade school, the same one I went to, little encouragement is given to write. I regretted my educational background from the moment I was assigned my first college paper.

– 7 –

Why did these white people know how to write so much better than I? Why did they go to the best schools while I went to run-down schools like Seward Park? Why didn't someone encourage me to write?

I would push Angelique as hard as I could. I would get her angry at the injustice around her, make her want to prove herself. If she learned to enjoy writing, I would be that much closer to making her a thinking person.

– 8 –

She wrote me like I asked her to, at first mostly drawing pictures and writing the standard "How are you doing" and "I miss you." Soon, however, her letters became more substantial. She wrote about the games she played in school, her new shoes, and why she still likes to watch *Ducktails*, even though her classmates say it's a baby cartoon.

– 9 –

do you love scary stoys? Well
you are going to loike this one
get wety here it is "HA" "HA" "HA" "HA"

FRITE NIGHT FOR ANGELIQUE
It all started on Friday morning
It was 6 am I saw red drops from
my seling! Somehing is happing in
the adek I seid. I ran up the stars.
I herd a scem. I opened the door slowly
it was my mom. She was merded she was
stab. She is laing on the floor.
I scemed like I was going to die myself.
I called Chino. He came in a ower.
Every one we knew was dead. Some one was
kning on the door. It was the mertira.
I kict him in the nust. He drope the
gun and I pict up and seid if you toch
that rabbit your dead. He kick the rabbit.
I shot him in the hart thak his mask off
and it was Chino alalong.

– 10 –

I was proud of her.	She is learning to be a good writer.
I liked her surprise	Is the ending a subconscious
ending — an	slip?
unexpected twist.	

did I push her too hard?   No. After all, is it not I who plays
                            Barbie with her, who encourages
                            her and who thinks about what is
                            best for her? How could I be chok-
                            ing her?
I am sorry.   But I have to push hard.

                            – 11 –

That's What Siste'rs are for
And I neve thought I
felt this way
and I'm glad I got a chanse to say

that I do beleve I love you
and if I should ever go away
Well then close your eye
and trie
the thing we do today
and that if you can remmber
keep smiling, keep shing
Thrus me doling — thats
what sisters for.

                            – 12 –

                            Guilt

WRITING 1

Can you recall interpretive essays you have written in the past?
Describe your experience in writing one of these assignments,
successful or not.

WRITING 2

After reading "Angelique's Letter," freewrite for ten minutes about
your initial reaction to the text. You may want to consider how your
experience is similar to or different from Angel's and why.

EXPLORING A TOPIC

To develop an interpretation, you need to read a text carefully — and
more than once. The first time (or first few times) you read a text, you will be
reading to understand, sorting out what the text says on the literal level: who

is involved, where they are, what happens, how it all concludes. You need to move beyond this, however, to critical reading, in which you develop an understanding of the author's larger theme or purpose.

To do this, you will want to pay close attention to the text — every word the author chose, every thing he or she described (or left undescribed) is significant. It is important, though, to let your own ideas roam freely at this point. Don't try to force every last detail in the text into a tidy pattern; focus on questions, not answers. Freewriting, journal writing, clustering, outlining and annotating are helpful invention and discovery techniques at this stage.

Like a good issue for a position paper, a good topic for an interpretive essay must involve an interesting question that has more than one possible answer. Without the possibility of more than one answer, there is no debate, no argument, and no real interpretation. If the topic is not interesting, you will bore not only your readers but also yourself. Here are some suggestions for finding and exploring topics for interpretive essays.

Identify Questions, Problems, or Puzzles

Annotate the text with questions in the margins as you read the text or discuss it in class. Later you can explore each question to see if a suitable topic emerges. Good topics arise from material that is difficult to understand. Here, for example, are some of the questions that could be raised during a reading of "Angelique's Letter":

- Why does Angel Fuster focus so much on Angelique's writing?
- Why does he include the story about his own early sexual encounter in stanza 3?
- Why does Angelique identify Chino as the murderer in stanza 9?

Find Patterns of Repeated Words, Ideas, and Images

By repeating words, ideas, and images, writers call extra attention to them, often indicating that they are important to the meaning of the text. Often these patterns are strong enough to be called a theme — a major idea with which the work is concerned. For example, in "Angelique's Letter," the concepts of writing, race, sex, and guilt arise more than once.

Consider the Style, Organization, or Form

Careful writers try to make these elements contribute to the meaning of a text. As a critical reader you should try to decide why the writer made the choices he or she did. For example :

- Why does Fuster number his prose paragraphs as if they were poetic stanzas?

- Why does he arrange stanza 9 in opposite parallel columns?
- What is the effect of including Angelique's letters exactly as she wrote them?

Consider the Larger Context

You can often find an interesting topic by comparing the text with another, either one by the same author or a similar work by a different author. Carefully examine similarities and differences, looking for clues to why the author made the choices he or she did. For example, you could compare Fuster's essay with chapters in Mike Rose's *Lives on the Boundary* (1989) or with Julia Alvarez's *How the Garcia Girls Lost Their Accents* (1991), which also deal with growing up Hispanic in America. If the work you are interpreting has been published, consider reading what other reviewers or critics have said about it.

WRITING 3

Use at least three of the methods described in this section to find and explore potential topics for a text you are currently reading. Write journal entries, outlines, or rough notes about the possibilities, but do not, at this time, worry about developing your ideas thoroughly.

EXPLAINING A TEXT

Once you have explored several topics and settled on one, you will need to begin the task of explaining the text. You need to give your readers a grasp of the text as a whole, so that they can follow your interpretation as well as join in the act of interpreting themselves. This process is also valuable because it forces you to reexamine the details of the text.

Explanatory information in your essay should usually be written from an objective stance because you are focusing on the text, not yourself. Try to provide readers with all the information they will need to understand and evaluate your interpretation.

Identify and Summarize the Text

Your first job in writing about any text is to identify it thoroughly, yet briefly, so that readers know from the start what you are talking about. Identify its author, title, subject, and genre (what type of text it is — essay, poem, novel, and so on).

If the text tells a story, summarize the plot, character, and setting. If the text provides another kind of information (if it is, say, a poem or an argument), summarize the main ideas. In the following opening paragraph, Bob summarizes, "Angelique's Letter."

> "Angelique's Letter," an essay by Angel Fuster, explores one of the many struggles that minority families face in deteriorating inner cities throughout the country. Chino, the author and older brother, would like to see his nine-year-old sister, Angelique, rise above the lackluster education of her ghetto school. He does not want her to get pregnant and cut her education short as his mother and older sister did. Nor, however, does he want to stifle her with too much big brother advice.

Explain the Form and Organization

No matter what the text, some principle or plan holds it together and gives it structure. Texts that tell stories are often organized as a sequence or events in chronological order. Other texts may alternate between explanations and examples or between first-person and third-person narrative. You will have to decide which aspects of the text's form and organization are most important for your interpretation. Rebecca explains the unusual stanza organization of "Angelique's Letter":

> After Angelique's scary story, we see both sides of Angel's conscience in an argument made visible by writing it in two columns. On the left is the soft side of him who would like to praise her. On the right is the voice that wants to control and educate her. He concludes this section with "I don't know."

Describe the Author's Perspective

Describing the author's perspective provides your readers with clues about the author's theme and purpose, which will probably be important elements in your interpretation. In some cases, you will need to differentiate the author's perspective from those of the characters. In *The Color Purple*, for instance, novelist Alice Walker uses the voice of fourteen-year-old Celie as her narrator. "Angelique's Letter," however, is nonfiction, so Angel the author is the same person as the character his sister calls Chino. John attempts to describe Fuster's perspective:

> Angel writes as an angry but goal-driven older brother intent on protecting his sister from the destructive forces of the urban ghetto. At the same time, he views his attempt to save her as itself destructive. The resulting essay is more ironic and self-deprecating than angry and revolutionary.

Explain the Thesis or Theme

Tell your readers what the main point of the text is. In fiction, poetry, and reflective essays, the main point usually takes the form of an implicit theme, while in most nonfiction it appears as a thesis, either stated or un-stated. Remember that the theme or thesis of a text is different from your inter-pretation as a reader. A theme or thesis is what the text says it is about: *"Angelique's Letter" is about the difficulties of growing up Hispanic and the obstacles encountered by Hispanic youth in their attempts to make a better life for themselves and their families.* An interpretation is the larger or deeper meaning that you, as a critical reader, find in the story: *"Angelique's Letter" is about the author's uneasi-ness with his well-educated self, which he fears has killed his neighborhood self.*

Place the Work in a Historical, Cultural, or Biographical Context

No text exists in isolation; it was created by a particular author in a par-ticular place at a particular time. Describing this context provides readers with important background information and indicates which conditions you think were most influential. After learning more about the author through a personal interview, Rebecca describes the circumstances that provide the background to Fuster's essay:

> I particularly liked "Angelique's Letter" because it shows some of
> the experiences, anger, and frustration that nonwhite children, includ-
> ing Angel, faced growing up in the city. Angel drew on his own experi-
> ence of living in the Seward Park housing project on the Lower East
> Side of New York City.

WRITING 4

Look at the text you are now interpreting, and make brief notes addressing each of the five elements described in this section.

TAKING A STAND

When you write an interpretation, you explain how a text works and take a stand on what the text means, arguing from the most persuasive point of view possible.

Understanding Interpretive Communities

The communities to which you belong shape who you are, how you see, what you hear, and how you respond to the world. All of us belong to many communities: families (parents and siblings, entire ethnic cultures), social and economic groups (students or teachers, rich or poor), organizations (Brownies, Boy Scouts, Democrats, Masons), neighborhoods (rural or urban, North or South), and institutions (school, church, fraternity).

Those communities that influence you most strongly are your interpretive communities — they determine how you interpret the world. People who belong to the same community as you are likely to have similar assumptions and are therefore likely to interpret things as you would. People who belong to different communities are likely to have perspectives different from yours.

College is, of course, a large interpretive community. It is made up in turn of many smaller communities called disciplines — English, history, chemistry, business, and so on. To study a discipline for several semesters is to consciously adopt that community's way of looking at the world. Within any discipline are several established ways of interpreting texts. Within the field of English literature, for example, there are feminist critics and Marxist critics, scholars who rely heavily on biographical information about authors and those who look at only the words on the page.

When you take a stand in an interpretive essay, you will often do so from the perspective of a traditional academic interpretive community. Take care to follow the conventions and strategies of that community. Remember, though, that your view of the world is influenced by many other communities. Acknowledging these other communities — such as class, gender, race, family — and examining how they affect your reading can often lead to interesting insights and interpretations.

Choosing a Perspective

Many college assignments will ask that you interpret a text fairly, neutrally, and objectively — that you focus on the *object* (text) under study instead of the *subject* doing the study (yourself). This would seem to ask you to avoid showing any of those biases that inevitably come with your membership in various interpretive communities. Realistically, however, you can be objective only to a certain degree.

What such assignments really ask is that you adopt an objective stance, interpreting the text *as objectively as possible*, trying to see things as they exist apart from your preconceived way of viewing them. An objective stance is fair to the text, because you focus on the text itself without letting your feelings get in the way. Treating texts fairly and objectively — even those with which you strongly disagree — lays the foundation for strong and believable criticism: readers will be more willing to listen to your interpretations and evaluations if you have first demonstrated that you are unbiased.

When using an objective stance, write from the third-person point of view. Keep yourself and references to yourself out of your writing, and use language that is emotionally neutral and unbiased.

A few college assignments that call for interpretation will ask — or allow— you to take an admittedly subjective stance. Such assignments encourage you to acknowledge frankly the interpretive communities to which you belong. Instead of keeping your opinions or emotions out of the assignment, you incorporate them as it suits your purpose.

A subjective stance can be honest in admitting that complete objectivity is impossible. However, subjective writing sometimes becomes self-centered, with the writer digressing from the text into personal experience and opinion. The subjective stance is often distrusted in academic writing because it can divert attention from the object under study and misdirect it toward the writer.

When you write interpretive papers from a subjective stance, do so carefully. Use the first-person point of view, but not excessively or in every sentence. Refer to personal experience only when it supports your purpose. Make value judgments, but with care, caution, and respect for opposing opinions.

Some of the most accessible, readable, and honest interpretative writing is a mix of objective and subjective points of view: the writer focuses on the text and supports all assertions with evidence from the text, yet admits his or her own opinions and values at carefully selected points. Frequently, interpretive essays use an objective stance for explaining the text and a more subjective stance for interpreting it.

Developing and Supporting a Thesis

The thesis of your interpretive essay gives a clear, concise statement of your interpretation. It should answer the question that you identified as the topic of the paper.

QUESTION	Why does Angel Fuster focus so much on Angelique's writing?
THESIS	In "Angelique's Letter," Angel Fuster focuses on education and on writing in particular because he believes they will lead to a better life for Angelique and others like her.

Like an argumentative thesis, an interpretive thesis should answer an interesting question and should be focused enough that you can support it within the confines of your paper. Unlike an argumentative thesis, it does not propose a plan of action; rather, it proposes a way of seeing. A clear thesis not only helps readers understand what you are saying but also helps persuade them that your interpretation is careful and reasonable.

Stating your interpretation is one thing, persuading readers to believe it is another. You need to support your interpretation with examples from the text itself. To explore your topic and develop your thesis, you probably marked, collected, and copied passages from your reading. These passages will form the basis for your evidence. In addition, you may want to bring in other expert sources, such as those found through library research or interviews, to support your ideas.

When you draw on other sources to support your view, be careful how you bring that information into your text. You will need to decide when to summarize, when to paraphrase, and when to quote directly. Regardless of how you bring the outside information into your paper, remember that you must document each idea; to fail to do so is plagiarism. (For a complete explanation of using and documenting source material, see Chapter 19.)

WRITING 5

Write three possible statements about a text you are studying. Identify two quotations in the text that would support each statement. Conclude by freewriting about which thesis you would prefer to develop into a full-fledged interpretive essay.

SHAPING THE WHOLE PAPER

Angel Fuster's essay "Angelique's Letter" was read and interpreted by a class of first-year students. The assignment was in three parts. The first draft was to be an objective interpretation. The second draft was to be subjective, in the form of a personal letter to the author. And the third and final draft was to be a revision of whichever interpretation the student preferred. Two final drafts are reproduced here. The first is objective, the more common form of interpretive writing you will be asked to do in college. The second is subjective, a less common form of interpretive writing that is nonetheless powerful and important.

Objective Stance

Heather's essay "Slowing Down" is written from an objective stance. The writer is not present until the last paragraph, where Heather felt it necessary to step in personally and affirm her own feelings about Fuster's essay. Heather's organization follows Fuster's essay from beginning to end. Because she believes that Fuster's own words convey a great deal of power, she quotes him directly rather than paraphrasing or summarizing his text; notice that she integrates her quotes smoothly and grammatically with her own sentences.

Slowing Down

"Angelique's Letter" tells a story about how a Puerto Rican college student named Angel decides to see his nine-year-old sister Angelique grow up having pride in herself and her culture, despite the disadvantages she will have to face throughout her life because of her race and economic background. Understanding the importance of education and achievement, Angel sets out to instill in his sister a sense of value toward these things, hoping that will help her become all that she is capable of being.

The story begins with young Angelique displaying her excitement about learning. Using her newly acquired ability to write in script, she has written "Angelique" in her "fanciest style" on a sheet of blue-lined notebook paper. Looking for praise from her older brother, whom she calls by the family name Chino, she proudly displays her letter to him.

Rather than with praise and encouragement, however, Chino replies sarcastically, "like those restaurants only rich white people go to."

Chino's response is harsh, but he intends it to provoke thought and encourage his sister to become as angry as he is at the system that makes Puerto Ricans second-class citizens. However, Chino appears to worry about his own reaction, as he confesses to feeling "guilty for using her artistically written 'Angelique' to teach her about racism."

These first two passages are important in several ways. First, they show Chino's influence on his younger sister. Second, they introduce Chino's drive to make sure Angelique does not become pregnant and drop out of school "as many of her classmates will." Third, they show Chino's dedication to act on his resolve by turning innocent situations into lessons about inner-city life. Finally, the second passage ends with a clear warning that time is short, "and she was already talking about boys." If Chino wants to have an impact on his sister's life, he has to start now.

Chino's flashback about Sorada Rodriguez illustrates how little time he has to lose if he is going to make a difference in Angelique's life. Girls in this environment are forced to grow up very quickly. Chino has to prevent her from becoming too sexually active, like Sorada, at such a young age if she is to stay in school and do well.

Chino continues with his strategy to ensure that Angelique "grow into a thinking person." He shows how hard he will have to push, "using every opportunity . . . to bring up the subject." When Angelique offers him a blond Barbie, he replies, "No, I don't want her. I want the one with the black hair." So again he uses her simple game as a lesson in racial discrimination, and again he feels guilty, ending the episode with "I felt like telling her I was only kidding."

When Chino returns to school, Angelique writes to him as he has requested. He knows what it is like to grow up in a poor educational environment, since that is where he grew up too. Chino is still "bitter" because the other kids at college know how to write better, went to the best schools, and had the best teachers. But his bitterness leads him to push her too hard, too fast, as her scary story "Frite Night" makes clear to him; she has cast Chino in the role of the murderer. On the one hand, Chino is proud of the long imaginative story she has written, but on the other hand he wonders if he is "choking her." He ends his essay with the single word "Guilt"--his clear admission that, despite his good intentions, he is doing his sister wrong.

I do not pretend to understand the situation Chino and his sister are facing, so I really cannot judge whether Chino is right or wrong. His intentions are the best; however, I question whether instilling anger in a young child is a good thing to do. Anger is a powerful emotion, but it is also dangerous. There are other emotions, such as love, that encourage learning and self-improvement. Children need to be children, and childhood is the only time they can be that. There is nothing wrong with educating his sister, but, as Chino realizes himself by the end of his essay, he has to learn where and when to stop. If he does not stop, at least he knows he must slow down.

Subjective Stance

Pat takes a personal approach to finding meaning in Fuster's text, yet he supports his assertions in two important ways: first, by sharing relevant elements of his own experiences and, second, by quoting specific passages from Fuster's text that are important to him. While Pat's essay/letter is not analytic in a strict academic sense, it does analyze the text in light of his own experience.

Dear Angel,

I grew up in rural Vermont, a long way from places like Seward Park. My little town is surrounded by high mountains, not tall skyscrapers. But your paper made me think about Bethlehem, Pennsylvania, where I lived before my family moved to Vermont, nine years ago. We lived close to the projects, where both black and Hispanic families lived, and which my parents warned us to stay away from. I wonder what it is like now in my old neighborhood and what the future is of the people who live there. How many children have older brothers looking out for them, wanting them to grow up "questioning things"?

I learned a lot from "Angelique's Letter," not only about your life, but about mine as well. Though Angelique has formidable obstacles to overcome--especially since she is female--I learned that she has a powerful advocate in you, her older brother. You are a role model for her as well as for all of her friends who are trapped in that system. Your plan to make her a "thinking person" by writing letters is working, even though you worry about pushing her too hard. Remember that in addition to writing "Frite Night" she copied out the song "That's What Sisters Are For" and sent it to tell you she loved you. You have no choice; she does need to read, write, and become better educated to escape her life in the projects.

I also learned that I take my own educated life for granted. You "regretted [your] educational background from the moment [you were] assigned [your] first college paper." Well, compared to you, I have been handed everything on a silver platter, including a safe, comfortable, middle-class home, college prep classes, parents who nourished me, teachers who encouraged me. Reading and writing must have come easy to me since I seem to have been doing them all of my life.

What touches me most is your great concern for Angelique's future. Most people in your situation would be out for themselves and not thinking about what's best for the family they left behind. Instead you are trying to share your success with them, worrying, pushing, and keeping track of enough emotions for two people. Thank you for sharing your story with me.

Sincerely,

Pat

Strategies for Writing Interpretive Essays

1. Identify the text, your subject, and yourself fully and correctly.
2. State the thesis of your essay up front or lead up to it and state it at the end — but be sure to state it.
3. Use the third person (objective voice) in most interpretive writing. Use first person when you want to add relevant personal information or are writing deliberately from the subjective stance.
4. Write interpretive essays in a comfortable, semiformal style. Avoid both contractions and pretentiousness. Write in neutral, unemotional language that shows your interpretation to be careful and rational.
5. Provide a brief summary of what happens in the text, first to last, but keep your focus on *interpretation*, or what the text means.
6. When providing evidence for your assertions, quote directly to capture the special flavor of an author. Use summaries and paragraphs for other evidence.
7. Document any assertions not your own or any passages of text that you quote or paraphrase.

SUGGESTIONS FOR WRITING AND RESEARCH

Individual

1. Write the interpretive essay that you have been exploring in Writings 3–5. Write the first draft from an objective stance, withholding all personal judgments. Write the second draft from a subjective stance, including all relevant personal judgments. Write your final draft by carefully blending elements of your first and second drafts.
2. Locate at least two reviews of a current text (book, recording, exhibit) with which you are familiar, and analyze each to determine the author's critical perspective. Write your own review of the text, and agree or disagree with the approach of the reviewers you analyzed. If you have a campus newspaper, consider offering your review to the editor for publication.

Collaborative

As a class or small group, attend a local concert, play, or exhibition. Take good notes and, when you return home, write a review of thisevent that includes both an interpretation and a recommendation that readers attend it (or not).

Share these variations on the same theme with others in your class or group and explore the different judgments that arise as a result of different perspectives.

Chapter 15

Reflecting On the World

*Imagine and create. Never be content with just retelling
something. And never be content with your first telling. Dive deeply
into your mind and give the reader something to dream about.*

— CHRISSIE

REFLECTIVE WRITING RAISES QUESTIONS about any and all subjects, reflecting
these subjects back to readers, allowing a clearer view and exposing new dimensions, as if a mirror had been held up before them. Reflective writing allows both writer and reader to consider things thoughtfully and seriously, but
it demands neither resolution nor definitive answers.

Reflective essays are the closest modern form to the kind of writing that
began the essay tradition some four hundred years ago when French author
Michel de Montaigne first published his *Essais* in 1580. An *essai* (from the
French, meaning "to try") was a short piece of writing meant to be read at a
single sitting on a subject of general interest to a broad spectrum of citizens.
Montaigne's essays explored education, truth, friendship, cruelty, conversation,
coaches, cannibals, and many other subjects. Essays were never intended to be
the last word on a subject, but rather, perhaps, the first thoughtful and speculative word. E. B. White, Virginia Woolf, and George Orwell are among the
best-known essayists in the twentieth century; among the best-known living
essayists are Joan Didion, Russell Baker, and Ellen Goodman.

WRITING TO REFLECT

When you write to reflect, part of your motivation is to figure out something for yourself in addition to sharing your reflections with somebody else.
A piece of reflective writing is both *the result of* and *an account of* the act of
speculation, and it invites readers into the game of reflection, speculation, and
wonder as well. Such writing is commonly characterized by a slight sense of

indirection — as if the writer were in the actual process of examining a subject closely for the first time. This appearance of spontaneity is, of course, an illusion, as most good reflective writing — unlike journal writing — has been thoroughly rewritten, revised, and edited to achieve just the right tentative and spontaneous tone. (See Chapter 6.)

It is tone along with purpose that distinguishes reflective writing from other types of writing. In reflective essays, writers ask Why?: Why do people live and behave the way they do? Why does society develop this way rather than that? Why does one thing happen rather than another? In asking such questions — and offering possible answers — writers try to make sense of the world.

Reflective writing can be on any subject under the sun (or moon, for that matter). However, unlike in explanatory or argumentative writing, the subject that causes the reflection in the first place is seldom the actual focus or topic of the essay. The topic of reflective writing is the meaning the writer finds in the subject. In other words, in reflective essays the subject is often treated as a metaphor: the writer observes or experiences something concrete, thinks about it, and then extends that thinking into a more abstract speculation. For example, visiting the library (subject) could stimulate a reflection on knowledge and creativity (topic). The everyday experience comes to stand for larger issues and ideas.

Unlike many college writing assignments, reflective essay assignments ask for your opinion. Assignments that contain a direction word such as *imagine, speculate,* or *reflect* invite a kind of writing that features your ability to see a given subject from several sides and to offer tentative answers to profound questions. (See Chapter 4.) For these assignments, it may be important to include factual information; however, such information is background, not foreground, material. While reflecting, writers may narrate a story, explain, interpret, or argue while reflecting on something; however, neither the story, explanation, interpretation, nor argument is foremost on their minds.

Reflective essays are as varied as the thought processes of the people who write them, but a typical pattern does exist. Many reflective essays describe a concrete subject or actual situation, pause for a moment and focus on the true topic, make a point, and then conclude by coming back to the subject that prompted the reflection.

Reflective essays are about something that's on your mind, perhaps something bothersome, distracting, or intriguing to you — but you may not always be conscious of what that is. No matter where or with what you start, try to bring that concern into focus — mirror it — and allow both yourself and your reader to look at it in a steady light.

WRITING 1

Describe your past experiences writing reflective essays. Did you enjoy writing them? How did readers respond to them?

FINDING AND DESCRIBING A SUBJECT

The subject of a reflective essay is the concrete, observable, actual thing or occurrence that prompts you to make more abstract reflections. It can be any *person,* any *place,* any *thing* — in other words, everything imaginable is a possibility. To find a subject, you may want to start by remembering something that has always interested or puzzled you, even if you don't know why — finding out is part of the process. You may want to review old journal entries, do some freewriting, or use other discovery techniques to find a possible subject; looping and clustering may help you decide whether a subject is a fertile one for reflection. (See Chapter 7.)

No matter what your subject, begin with concrete description and actual circumstances — a particular concert, a specific case of plagiarism. Record as much detail as you can, appealing to all five senses. Try to make your subject visible and tangible before considering its more abstract dimensions and associations.

Through accurate observation and description, you ground your reflection in the everyday world. If you faithfully record things that readers themselves have seen or can easily imagine, they will be more willing to trust and follow you on your reflective journey. By providing a concrete description before you let readers know what your point of view will be, you allow them to do some reflection themselves. This in turn makes them more curious to read your reflections later.

In your final draft, you will want details that subtly suggest your ultimate point without giving it away: a child's weary expression for a reflection on domestic violence, the spring fashions in a department store window for a reflection on annual rebirth. You will continue the careful layering of details throughout the revising and editing stages. For now, concentrate on collecting impressions that seem particularly interesting or meaningful, even if you don't know exactly what they mean.

People

Chapter 11 discusses writing profiles of people, which requires getting to know subjects well by interviewing, doing background research, visiting their homes, and so on. However, for subjects of reflective essays, brief and casual encounters with strangers may work as well as more developed relationships. In fact, reflecting on chance encounters almost guarantees speculative and inconclusive thoughts: Why is she doing that? Where does he live? How is their life like mine? Unlike profile writing, where the writer seeks real answers to such questions from the subject, the reflective author turns the encounter into a prompt to ponder other subjects. Reflective writing about people often leads to comparisons with the writer's own circumstances, character, or behavior. What makes such writing especially interesting, of course, is that no two writers who encountered or witnessed the same person would speculate, muse, or wonder in the same way.

In the following passage, Mari writes about a chance encounter one Saturday morning.

> The sign on the front door says the store opens at eight o'clock. It's 7:56, so I put the bag of bottles on the ground.
>
> An old woman with a shopping cart full of bottles stands in front of Pearl Street Beverage Mart. Most of her long gray hair is tucked into a Red Sox baseball cap, but some of it hangs in twisted strands about her face. She wears an oversized yellow slicker, a striking contrast against the crystal blue morning sky. She looks at the bottles and her lips are moving as if she's telling them a story.
>
> Then the bottle lady turns and speaks to me: "These bottles in my cart here, you see which I mean? Well, I'm gonna get five hundred dollars for them and get me a fine stylin' dinner tonight. It's a good thing there's bottles, yes?"

In this early part of her essay, Mari first focuses on locating the circumstance in a particular time and place and on describing the appearance of the woman. She provides enough detail so that the readers can see the woman and, perhaps, join the writer in asking questions: Why is she wearing a raincoat when the sky is blue? Why is she speaking to the bottles?

WRITING 2

Make a list of people whom you have encountered or observed within the past few weeks and who have, for one reason or another, made a sharp impression on you. Did any of them trigger reflective thoughts? Do they now? What are those thoughts?

Places

Places make good reflective subjects; writers can generally return to a place again and again for further information and ideas. You can, of course, reflect on just about any place under the sun, including those in your memories to which you cannot return. But you can also turn to places right under your nose and make something interesting and reflective from those too. Reflective essays that begin by describing a physical place often end up focusing on places of the heart, mind, and spirit.

In the following passage, Judith turned the university library into an object for reflective thought. The first part of the essay is narrative. We follow Judith as she locks her apartment door and hurriedly walks to the library. This description locates her place in a particular time and circumstance. Once at the library, she slows her self and her essay down.

Inside the smoke-colored doors, the loud and busy atmosphere vanishes, replaced by the soft soothing hum of air conditioning and the
hushed sound of whispering voices. The repetitive sound of the copy
machine has a calming effect as I look for a comfortable place in which
to begin my work.

I want just the right chair, with a soft cushion and a low sturdy
table for a leg rest. The chairs are strategically positioned with comfortable personal space around each one, so you can stretch your arms
fully without touching a neighbor. . . . People seem to respect each
other's need for personal space.

Like her search for the right chair, Judith's description is detailed and
concrete. At the same time, she introduces the importance of quiet space to
her peace of mind. She concludes with a generalization triggered by the space
she describes, hinting at but not stating the topic of her reflection.

WRITING 3

Make a list of places that would provide you with material for writing
a reflective essay. Think about places you've visited in the recent past
and those you still have access to. What associations do these places
conjure up? What questions do they raise? Write a paragraph about
each of three places on your list and see which offers the best
prospect for further writing.

Things

Any thing can be a subject for reflection, so long as you treat it accordingly. Perhaps the first things that come to mind are physical objects. But a
very different kind of a thing is an event, whether public (a political rally, a
basketball game) or private (drinking a cup of coffee, fishing for trout). And a
still more abstract kind of thing is a concept (plagiarism, campus parking). In
other words, to reflect on a thing allows you to reflect on virtually anything!

Scott opens his essay with a generalized statement about water fountains:

There is something serene about the sound of a water fountain. The
constant patter of water splashing into water. The sound of endless
repetition, the feeling of endless cycle. . . .

Two paragraphs later, he moves to the campus water fountain.

The fountain pipe has eighty-two nozzles. Two weeks ago, only
fifty-five of them were spraying water vigorously, eleven sprayed
weakly, and sixteen didn't spray at all. This week eighty-one are spraying; someone has fixed the fountain.

Even though Scott starts with a preliminary generalization, he quickly gives the reader a careful, even technical description. The implication that Scott is writing from direct observation at a particular time (this week) and place roots the description in a specific circumstance. Readers are likely to believe Scott's reflection because he has taken pains — or at least appears to have done so — to be accurate in his observation, and so they are likely to believe the rest of his account as well. While Scott has made it clear that listening to fountains is peaceful for him, in the early paragraphs of his essay readers still do not know why he chooses to write about them.

WRITING 4

Make a list of things that interest you, cause you to pause, or raise questions. Do so either from memory or by walking around your room, house, neighborhood, or campus. Write a paragraph or so on three of the things you encounter and see which offers the best prospect for further writing.

Strategies and Describing Subjects for Reflection

Select any or all of the following strategies for starting a reflection paper.

1. Remember a person, place, or thing that has always interested you. Close your eyes, ransack your memory, freewrite to bring it closer for more speculative examination.
2. Go someplace and notice someone or something. Examine this person, place, or thing carefully, look at it from many sides, take good notes so that you can reproduce it accurately in your essay.
3. Recapture a prior reflection about anything — even something you have written about before. Then attach to it recent or local examples to bring it back to life.
4. Read examples of good reflective writing, such as Montaigne's early essays or Joan Didion's contemporary ones. Read newspaper columnists such as Ellen Goodman and Russell Baker. Browse among the *New York Times* best-selling nonfiction in a bookstore and look for titles that sound reflective or works called *essays*.

Pausing

The three reflective examples we have seen so far have taken everyday people, places, and things — a bottle woman, a library, a water fountain — as the subjects on which to reflect. The advantage of common over spectacular subjects is that everyone has some experience with them and is automatically curious to see what you make of them. At the same time, you need to make sure your reflection itself goes beyond the commonplace and introduces readers to new dimensions or perspectives. Your subject alone will carry interest just so far: the rest is up to your originality, creativity, and skill as you present the topic of your essay, the deeper and more speculative meaning you have found.

After introducing your subject through careful description, you need to execute a pause, saying to the reader, in effect, "Wait a minute, there's something else going on here — stop and consider." The pause is a key moment in both the writing and the reading of reflective essays. It signals to the writer that it's time for maximum creativity, time to generate connections between the present and the past, the concrete and the abstract, the literal and the symbolic. It signals to the reader that the essay is about to move in a new and less predictable direction.

Often the pause is accompanied by a slight shift in voice or tone. Suddenly the writer is either a little more personal or a little more formal, slightly more biased or slightly more objective. the exact nature of the shift will, of course, be determined by the point the writer wants to make.

After describing the bottle woman in some detail, but without judgment, Mari steps back and shifts from the woman to the common objective that has brought them both to the store, returning bottles for a refund.

> I guess I had never thought about it before, but the world is full of
> bottles. They're everywhere, on shelves, in trash cans, on park
> benches, behind bushes, in street gutters. In the modern city, bottles
> are more common than grass.

By calling attention to her own new thoughts about bottles, Mari causes her readers, too, to think about a world full of bottles and about what, if anything, that may mean.

In the following passage, Scott stops observing the campus water fountain and begins wondering and remembering.

> I'm not sure where my love of fountains comes from. Perhaps it's
> from my father. When I was very young he bought a small cement
> fountain for our backyard. Its basin was an upturned shell and there
> was a little cherubic boy who peed into it.

This pause signals that it is not, in fact, water fountains that are on Scott's mind, but memories of his father. He now moves away from observing the campus fountain in the present toward memories of fountains in the past.

WRITING 5

Select one of the topics you have explored in Writings 2–4. Once you have firmly and concretely described or defined it, create a reflective pause by writing one or two pages about what, besides itself, this person, place, or thing makes you think about.

MAKING THE POINT

In explanatory, argumentative, or interpretive writing, the point of the paper is commonly stated as an explicit thesis, often in the first paragraph. In a successful narrative or profile, however, the point may be conveyed only indirectly and nearly always emerges at the end rather than the beginning of the essay. That way, readers are drawn into the act of reflecting themselves and become more and more curious to find out what the writer thinks. In other words, reflective writers are musing rather than arguing. In fact, reflective essays are most persuasive when least obviously instructive or assertive.

Mari includes her observation of the bottle woman first by re-creating the shopkeeper's sarcastic response to the woman after he totals the deposit her bottles have earned her.

> "Eight dollars and thirty-five cents, Alice. You must have new competition or else bottles are getting scarce. You haven't broken ten dollars in days."

As readers perhaps suspect, Alice has grossly overestimated the value of the bottles in her cart. However, this transaction has a transforming effect on the observer/writer, who now adds her own bottles to the old woman's pile.

> . . . I realized then that my bottles were more nuisance than necessity. They were cluttering up our back hall--the landlord had already complained once--and tonight my roommates and I were making chicken curry for our boyfriends. That wasn't the case with Alice, who seemed to have neither roommate, dinner, nor boyfriend.
>
> "Here you go, Alice. Maybe you can break ten bucks with these." I gave them to her freely, at the same time realizing their true value for the first time.

Though the essay begins with a narrative about a trip to the bottle store and an encounter with an old woman, it ends somewhere else. At the end, Mari is still ignorant of any real details about the woman's life, history, or prospects — though she, like us, has made educated guesses. Alice remains frozen in the essay for all time as the "bottle woman." It is what Mari makes of her — or what we make of her — that is the real topic of this essay. The trip to the bottle store, her encounter with Alice, and her thoughts about bottles have caused Mari to reassess, if ever so briefly, on her own relatively comfortable and privileged life as a college student with her whole future ahead of her.

Mari's essay is strong precisely because it doesn't hit readers over the head with a message or champion a particular cause. Instead of writing an editorial about poverty or the homeless, Mari has raised a question about the relative value of bottles for different people in a throwaway society.

Scott's essay about water fountains has progressed from fountains in general to the campus fountain in particular, then to the memory of fountains, which remind him of his father. Only in the last paragraph does he reveal more:

> My father died just after my twentieth birthday. It was very sud-
> den and very surprising and everything felt very unfinished. They say
> I am a lot like him in many other ways, but I'm not sure. What I do
> know is that like him, I love the sound of water.

Even at the end, Scott's point emerges by implication rather than explication — he never states outright why he began this reflection or what he hopes readers will take from it. Some readers will infer that Scott's reflection is on the nature of reflection itself, how observation stimulates memory and how memory itself becomes part of people's everyday reality. In other words, even very personal reflective writing can open new insights for readers.

This proved to be an especially difficult topic for Scott to write about; in fact, he may not have chosen "water fountains" had he known in advance exactly where they were to lead him. Scott's early drafts focused on water and fountains and people sitting around them — but did not mention his father. The deliberate attention to mental processes that writing demands actually caused this particular reflection to emerge. A writer may select to write about an object with only a vague idea of why it's attractive, interesting, or compelling. Commonly it's only through the act of reflective writing that the writer finds out the nature of the attraction, interest, or compulsion.

Remember that reflective essays raise issues but do not need to resolve them. The tradition of essay writing is the tradition of *trying* and *attempting* rather than *resolving* or *concluding*. Ending by acknowledging that you see still other questions invites your readers to join in the search for answers.

At the very end of your essay, it is a good idea to return to the specific person, place, or thing that prompted the reflection. This brings about a sense of closure — if not for the topic itself, at least for this particular essay.

WRITING 6

Write two conclusions to the reflective essay you have been working on. In one, state your point openly near the end of your paper; in the other, let it emerge gradually without spelling it out.

SHAPING THE WHOLE PAPER

The finished draft of Judith's short reflective essay "Writing in Safety" follows the structure described in this chapter. It has a loosely narrative pattern and is written in the present tense to convey a sense of the event unfolding as it is read. It is structured from start to finish by her walk to and from the library. Her essay does not, however, actually tell a story since nothing happens in a physical sense — unless you count walking and sitting down. The journey emerges as a mental, almost spiritual, quest for safety — safety in which to think and create without fear. At the same time, the physical dimensions of her journey and the attention to descriptive detail contribute to make her journey believable and to ground readers in a reality they too have most likely experienced.

The point of Judith's reflection is articulated in the paragraph before the concluding paragraph: "I am beginning to understand the importance of felling safe in order to be creative and productive." The final paragraph, retracing her path home, returns us to the place where the essay began, suggesting that this reflection is over, at least for the time being.

Writing in Safety

It is already afternoon. I fiddle with the key to lock the apartment door after me. I am not accustomed to locking doors. Except for the six months I spent in Boston, I have never lived in a place where I did not trust my neighbors. When I was little, we couldn't lock our farmhouse door; the wood had swollen and the bolt no longer lined up properly with the hole, and nobody ever bothered to fix it. I still remember the time our babysitter, Rosie, hammered the bolt closed and we had to take the door off the hinges to get it open.

I heft the book bag on my shoulder and walk up College Street toward the library. The morning is clear and cold and the colorful leaves look like confetti on the sidewalk. As I pass and am passed by other students, I scrutinize everything around me, hoping to be struck with a creative idea for a topic for my English paper. Instead, my mind fills with a jumble of disconnected images, like a bowl of alphabet soup: the letters are there, but they don't form any words. Campus sidewalks are not the best places for creativity to strike.

Approaching the library, I see skateboarders and bikers weaving through students who talk in clusters on the library steps. A friendly dog is tied to a bench watching for its owner to return. Subjects to write about? Nothing strikes me as especially interesting, and besides, my heart is still pounding from the walk up the hill. I wipe my damp forehead and go inside.

Inside the smoke-colored doors, the loud and busy atmosphere vanishes, replaced by the soft soothing hum of air conditioning and the hushed sound of whispering voices. The repetitive sound of the copy machine has a calming effect as I look for a comfortable place in which to begin my work.

I want just the right chair, with a soft cushion and a low sturdy table for a leg rest. The chairs are strategically positioned with comfortable personal space around each one, so you can stretch your arms fully without touching a neighbor. I notice that if there are three chairs in a row, the middle one is always empty. If people are seated at a table, they sit staggered so they are not directly across from one another. People seem to respect each other's need for personal space.

Like a dog who circles her bed three times before lying down, I circle the reading room looking for the right place to sit. I need to feel safe and comfortable so I can concentrate on mental activity. Some students, however, are too comfortable. One boy has moved two chairs together, covered himself with his coat, and is asleep in a fetal position. A girl sits at a table, head down, dozing like we used to do in first grade.

I find my place, an empty chair near a window, and slouch down into it, propping my legs on the low table in front. If my mother could see me, she'd reprimand me for not sitting up straight. I breathe deeply, close my eyes for a moment, and let myself become centered, forgetting both last night's pizza and tomorrow's philosophy exam. I need a few minutes to acclimate to this space, relax, and feel safe before starting my work.

Two weeks ago, a female student was assaulted not far from where I live--that's why I've taken to locking my door so carefully. I am beginning to understand the importance of feeling safe in order to be creative and productive. Here, in the library, I feel secure, protected from real violence and isolated from everyday distractions. There are just enough people for security's sake but not so many that I feel crowded. And besides, I'm surrounded by all these books, all these great minds who dwell in the hallowed space! I am comfortable, safe, and beginning to get an idea.

Hours later--my paper started, my exam studied for, my eyes tired--I retrace the path to my apartment. It is dark now, and I listen closely when I hear footsteps behind, stepping to the sidewalk's edge to let a man walk briskly past. At my door, I again fumble for the now familiar key, insert it in the lock, open the door, turn on the hall light, and step inside. Here, too, I am safe, ready to eat, read a bit, and finish my reflective essay.

Strategies for Writing Reflective Essays

1. Begin your reflection with something concrete (a person, place, or thing) that interests you.
2. Describe your subject carefully and locate it in a specific circumstance, using sensory details where appropriate.
3. Pause and move deliberately away from the actuality of your subject to the larger or different issue it brings to mind — the topic of your reflection.
4. Organize your essay to move from the concrete and specific toward the abstract and general.
5. Use a reflective voice — tentative, questioning, gentle — to advance your reflective point.
6. Let your point emerge, explicitly or implicitly, near the end of your essay.
7. Conclude by reminding your readers where your reflective journey began.

SUGGESTIONS FOR WRITING AND RESEARCH

Individual

1. Review your responses to Writings 2–6. Select the reflective possibility that interests you most; then compose a whole essay on the subject. When you have finished a draft, follow the suggestions at the end of the chapter to help you write your second draft.
2. Find an object in your room, dormitory, house, or neighborhood that seems especially commonplace or routine or that you otherwise take for granted (a chair, rug, window, comb, glass, plant, newspaper, fire hydrant). Describe it carefully and fully and draft an essay in which you reflect on its possible meaning or value.
3. Look up one of the authors mentioned in the chapter — Michel de Montaigne, Joan Didion, Russell Baker, Ellen Goodman — or a similar writer of your choice. Read several of his or her essays; analyze the work in terms of the characteristics of reflective essays described in this chapter. Write a review of this author as an essayist.

Collaborative

1. As a class, select a place or event that has reflective possibilities. Write your own reflection on the subject, limiting each reflection to two single-spaced pages. Elect two class members to edit the collection of essays and publish them in bound volumes for the whole class, complete with table of contents, and editor's introduction, and an afterward by the course instructor.
2. Break into small groups and each group select an essayist, living or dead, and research his or her writing (you can use writers mentioned in this chapter or a local newspaper columnist). Group members share findings with others in the group and together prepare a report to teach the class about the writer. Select and hand out readings in advance of your presentation.

CONDUCTING RESEARCH

Chapter 16

How Writers Research

You know, this isn't my best writing. We had to have fifteen references from at least ten different sources and I was really struggling to find that many and in the end I just sort of stuck them in to get it done with. You shouldn't really read this one.

— MEGAN

BEFORE AGONIZING TOO LONG OVER YOUR NEXT RESEARCH PROJECT, stop to consider what, exactly, research entails. Keep in mind that in your nonacademic life you conduct practical research of one kind or another every time you search the want ads for a used car, browse through a library or video store in search of a book or movie, or read a book, movie, or music review. You may not make note cards or report the results in writing, but whenever you ask questions and then look systematically for answers, you are doing research.

In college, the research you conduct is academic rather than practical. In other words, it's designed to result in a convincing paper rather than a purchase or action. Academic research is part of the writing process for most of your papers. You rarely begin writing an explanation, argument, or interpretation already knowing all the facts and information you'll need: to fill in the gaps in your knowledge, you conduct research. However, one particular assignment, the *research essay*, is specially designed to introduce you to the process of conducting research and writing a paper based on research findings. Research essays are generally longer, require more extensive research, use a more formal style and format, and take more time than other types of papers.

The most meaningful research grows out of your own curiosity and interest: you've thought hard about the questions and you care about the answers. Real research is exciting work. It is when you are assigned research questions you don't care about that research seems dull and mechanical. Yet even then, thoughtful digging into a new subject may turn out to be more interesting than you first imagined. This chapter focuses on research as a challenging, engaging, and exciting process and offers suggestions for stimulating interest in research topics even where none existed before.

UNDERSTANDING RESEARCH

Practical Research

In preparing to write this chapter, I reconstructed the process I went through the last time I did research of a substantial nature, when I recently bought a motorcycle. My current motorcycle was a 750cc black BMW that I used for riding to school and taking short trips but that proved underpowered for riding double and not very comfortable for longer trips. It was time, I thought, to buy my first new motorcycle, one big enough for comfortable long-range touring with an additional rider as a regular passenger. To find the right machine meant shopping carefully, which meant asking good questions: What kinds of motorcycles were best for touring? How large should it be, and how much should it weigh? What brand was most reliable? How much would it cost? When was the best time to purchase one? What accessories were available? Who were the best dealers, and how trustworthy were they? And where, besides dealers, could I find motorcycle information?

Here's how I researched my questions about buying a new motorcycle:

- First, over a period of several weeks I talked to people who knew a lot about motorcycles — some old friends, the mechanic at the shop where my old bike was serviced, a neighbor who owned two different touring machines.
- Second, I subscribed to *Motorcyclist* and *Rider* magazines; I found the latter more interesting since it focuses primarily on touring motorcycles. The more I read, the more familiar I became with current terminology (*ABS, fairings*), brands (BMW, Harley-Davidson), models (sport tourers, roadsters), and performance data (roll-on speed, braking distance). On a corner of my desk, I piled the most useful magazines with many dog-eared pages.
- Third, I looked up back issues of *Rider* magazine in the local library to gain a historical perspective. I made photocopies in the library of the most relevant articles, underlined key findings, and made notes in the margins of photocopies.
- Fourth, I visited the local chapter of the BMW Motorcycle Club. Here I met more people who seemed to be expert motorcyclists (all, of course, recommending BMWs) and bought a copy of *BMW Motorcycle Owners News.*
- Fifth, I ordered ten recent back issues of *BMW News* for $1 each to learn more about BMW motorcycle touring. I liked the tone of the writing and was struck by the loyalty of this brand's owners.
- Sixth, I rented the video *On Any Sunday* (1971), considered by many to be the best film ever made about motorcycles, and watched it three times.
- Seventh, I approached Lester, the owner of Frank's Motorcycle Shop, and asked about the virtues of certain BMW models on dis-

play. I was most impressed by two models, the K75RT and the K100RS, both of which I sat on but did not ride. I left with literature and, at home, reread this along with other published articles about BMWs — and even wrote in my journal about the dreams motorcycles inspired and the difficult choices they required.

- Eighth, I visited local dealers who sold Honda, Kawasaki, Yamaha, and Suzuki motorcycles and listened to sales pitches explaining the features of their best touring machines. I found some too racy and others too large, but still took notes about each to facilitate my comparison. I also wrote in my journal to keep track of differences.
- Ninth, I returned to Frank's and test-drove the two BMW models, finding the K75RT smoother and cheaper, the K100RS more powerful and expensive. Still I was undecided. I asked about deals and discounts and the trade-in value of my old motorcycle. (Not much.)
- Tenth, after weighing the relative merits of smoothness versus power versus money, and taking into account my intentions of touring two-up, I returned to Frank's Motorcycle Shop and bought the more powerful K100RS, receiving an end-of-season discount — after which I retreated into a long Vermont winter and waited for motorcycle season to resume in the spring.

As my personal example illustrates, the business of research can be a serious part of our everyday lives. Think about the research you may have done to find the right college, vacation spot, automobile, or stereo system. Of course, there are important differences between the research we conduct for personal and practical reasons and that required for academic assignments, but let's look first at the basic similarities.

WRITING 1

What research outside of school settings have you conducted recently? Think about major changes, moves, or purchases that required you to ask real questions and then find a plan for answering them. Make a list of these questions, and then list the steps you took to answer them. Finally, what was the result of this research?

Academic Research

While the search for motorcycle knowledge is practical rather than academic, it serves nevertheless to introduce most of the elements common to all research projects, argumentative or informational, in school or out.

1. **The researcher has a genuine interest and curiosity in the topic.** It's difficult to fake curiosity, but it is possible to develop it. My interest in motorcycles was long-standing, but the decision to

purchase a new one caused a resurgence of interest; the more I investigated and learned, the more I wanted to know. Some academic assignments will allow you to pursue personally important issues; others will require that you dive into the research itself and generate interest as you go. In either case, the more you investigate, the more you learn; and the more you learn, the more you want to know.

2. **The researcher asks questions.** The first questions were more general than specific, as I explored the broad scope of the subject. However, as I gained more knowledge, the questions became more sharply focused and specific. No matter what your research assignment, you need to begin by articulating questions, finding out where the answers lead, and then asking more questions.

3. **The researcher seeks answers from people.** I talked to both friends and strangers who had more knowledge than I about my subject. The people to whom I listened most closely were specialists with expert knowledge. All research projects profit when you ask knowledgeable people to help you answer questions or point you in directions where answers may be found.

4. **The researcher visits places where information can be found.** I went not only to ask questions of experts, but to observe and examine and experience firsthand. No matter how much other people told me, my knowledge increased when I was able to visit places, make my own observations, and take notes about what I found there. In many forms of academic research, especially in the sciences and social sciences, research in the field is as important as research in the library.

5. **The researcher examines texts.** I read motorcycle magazines and brochures and watched videotapes to become more informed. I consulted texts available at home and in my local community; I also ordered texts I did not own; I visited the library to find out more historical and expert opinion. I did not limit my examination to verbal texts, but sought information from visual ones (*On Any Sunday*) as well. While texts are helpful in consumer research, they are crucial in academic research.

6. **The researcher evaluates sources.** As the research progressed, I double-checked information to see if it could be confirmed by more than one source. I asked experts about the reliability of other sources and checked these opinions against published sources as well. In consumer research, your ability to distinguish between one source and another, between fact and opinion, plays an important role in your satisfaction with the product you purchase. In academic research, your ability to evaluate your sources plays a major part in the credibility of your research paper.

7. **The researcher writes.** I made field notes (in the cycle shops) to help remember what I learned, to facilitate comparison, and to aid

my decision making in general. I made notes about my library sources. And at home I also wrote in my journal, exploring the pros and cons of the different bikes I saw, rode, and read about. Even in practical research, writing helps find, remember, and explore important information. In academic research, writing is even more important, since the results must be reported in writing that is clear, logical, correct, and interesting.

8. **The researcher tests and experiments.** In my practical research, testing was simple and fairly subjective — riding different motorcycles to compare the qualities of each. In this case, I needed to please only myself. But testing was, perhaps, the turning point in the decision-making process. In the sciences and social sciences, testing and experimentation are regular parts of many research projects. However, since the goal of academic research is establishing knowledge that is true for a community much larger than the researcher's self, the testing must be systematic and rigorous if the conclusions are to be credible.

9. **The researcher synthesizes information to arrive at a conclusion.** The information led to a conclusion — my decision to purchase one motorcycle rather than another. In academic research, the synthesis of diverse sources of information leads not to a consumer purchase, but to a well-supported thesis that will convince a skeptical audience the research findings are correct and believable.

These, then, are the elements that are part of any research project: (1) an interesting subject to explore, (2) focused questions to answer, (3) people to provide answers, (4) sites to visit, (5) texts to read, (6) sources to evaluate, (7) notes to write, (8) tests to make, and (9) a conclusion to be reached. Despite the practical nature of my motorcycle research, the elements involved are more similar than different from those in academic research. What I did not do, of course, in buying the motorcycle is the step most directly concerned with the subject matter of this handbook — publish the results of my investigation. So for academic research, there is one more activity to consider — writing.

WRITING 2

Explain how the research activities described in this section were part of an investigation you once conducted, in school or out. Did you at one time or another, go through the same steps? What other activities did you engage in that are not listed here?

PREPARING FOR RESEARCH

Research papers are usually major products meant to occupy a span of weeks or months; they usually make a strong contribution to your course grade. Consequently, it pays to study the assignment carefully, begin working on it immediately, and allow sufficient time for the many different activities involved.

Understanding the Assignment

First, reflect on the course for which the research paper is assigned. What is the aim of this field of study? What themes has the instructor emphasized? How would a research assignment contribute to the goals of this course? In other words, before even considering a topic, assess the instructor's probable reasons for making the assignment and try to predict what he or she expects from your finished project.

Next, study the assignment directions carefully. Identify both the subject words and the direction words. *Subject words* specify the precise area of the investigation — the novels of Toni Morrison, weather patterns in the northeast. *Direction words* specify your purpose for writing — whether you should explain or report or argue.

Finally, examine the assignment requirements: the perspective to be taken, the most appropriate style, the preferred format, the sources expected, the documentation system required, the due dates, and the paper length. Thinking about these issues early rather than late in the research process may save time and help avoid false steps.

Developing a Research Question

Since research papers are among the most lengthy and involved of all college assignments, make the project as interesting and purposeful as you can by developing a research question that will be exciting for you to answer. Your instructor may assign a specific topic or only a general subject, or the choice of a subject and topic may be left completely up to you. If you need to find a topic, think hard about how your interests dovetail with the content of the course. What subjects or issues in the course do you enjoy most? What discussions, lectures, or labs have you found most engaging? What has happened recently in the news that both interests you and relates to the course material? Take the answers to these questions and do some freewriting or clustering to find the topic that seems most promising to you. (See Chapter 7.) Be sure to narrow your topic to one that will be interesting to you and your readers and manageable given the time, space, and resources available.

TOO BROAD	Ben and Jerry's ice cream franchise
TOPIC	The effect of Ben and Jerry's franchise on the Vermont economy
TOPIC	The reasons for the rapid success of Ben and Jerry's ice cream franchise.

Research projects are designed to answer questions, so you need to develop a research question about your topic. What makes a good research question? First, it's a question that you really want to know the answer to. Second, it requires more than a yes or no answer. The question "Does my state have a bottle law?" can be answered with one phone call. A better question would be "What are the benefits and liabilities of bottle laws?" Third, it's a question to which you do not already know the answer. If you are knowledgeable about the new state law governing solid waste disposal, you might pursue aspects of the law with which you are not familiar — or a different law altogether. And fourth, it's a question that you have a reasonable chance of answering. If you ask "What effect will a new condominium development have on the environment?", make sure you have access to the people or documents that can provide you with that information.

RESEARCH *QUESTION*	Why has Ben and Jerry's ice cream franchise become such a success?

Whether or not you already have a tentative answer to your research question will determine what type of research you undertake. Informational research is conducted when you don't know the answer to the question or have a firm opinion about the topic. You enter this kind of investigation with an open mind, focusing on the question, not on a predetermined answer. In some cases, this kind of research will lead you to an argumentative position; in others, you may report the results of your research in an explanatory essay. In either case, you will need eventually to develop an answer to your question — a thesis — and the purpose of informational research is to help you find it. Such research might be characterized as thesis-finding.

Argumentative research is conducted to prove a point. You enter the project already knowing your thesis — the answer to your question, the side of the debate you want to support. "Should handguns be abolished? Yes, handguns should be abolished." You conduct research to further buttress your position. The research question helps focus your investigation, but this kind of research is really thesis-driven. To be sure, the process of researching may lead to a revised or entirely different thesis; in fact, you should consider any thesis you have in mind at this point a working thesis, subject to extensive revision, redirection, and clarification. Nonetheless, your working thesis colors your investigation from the start.

Before you commit yourself to pursuing a question or developing a specific thesis, visit your library and make a quick survey of relevant information. Locate some of the periodicals in your field and see what kinds of information they contain. Check the book titles in your subject area — are the books plentiful and current? You can save yourself a lot of frustration by knowing that periodicals, books, and special collections that you will need are available. If you find you will need to special order most of your resources, consider revising your topic or thesis to one for which resources are available in your college library.

Finally, ask your instructor to respond to your intended topic before you invest too much time in it. Your instructor will help direct you to topics that are consistent with the goals of the assignment or course and steer you away from questions that are too large, too common, or too offbeat.

WRITING 3

Select a subject area that interests you and that is compatible with the research assignment. List ten questions that you have about this subject. Freewrite for ten more minutes about the question that most interests you. Why does it interest you? Where would you start looking for answers?

Starting a Research Log

A research log can help you keep track of the scope, purpose, and possibilities of any research project. Such a log is essentially a journal in which you write to yourself about the process of doing your research, asking questions and monitoring the results. Questions you might ask include the following:

- What are my questions today?
- Have my questions changed since I last wrote? How so?
- What have I found so far?
- What do I still need to find?
- Where am I most likely to find it?
- Can I articulate my thesis succinctly?
- What evidence best supports my thesis?
- What evidence challenges my thesis?
- If there are contradictions, how should I handle them?

Answering such questions as you visit the library, look for and read sources, review note cards, and write various drafts helps all your research and writing stay on course.

Research logs can make research more efficient. Novice researchers often waste time tracking down sources that are not really useful. Because writing in a research log forces you to continually articulate the research project, it can help you better understand for yourself what your quest is really about.

Here, for example, are some entries from a first-year student's research log for an investigation of ozone holes in the atmosphere.

> November 12 Checked the subject headings and found no books on
> ozone depletion. Ref. librarian suggested magazines because it takes so
> long for books to come out on new subjects. In the General Science
> Index I found about twenty articles to check out--I've got them all on a
> printout. Need to come back tomorrow afternoon to actually start read-
> ing them.

November 17 Conference today with Lawrence about the ozone hole thesis--said I don't really have much of a thesis, rather a lot of information aiming in the same direction. Suggested I look at what I've found already and then back up to see what question it answers--that will probably point to my thesis. I didn't really understand before that a thesis is just an answer to a question!

When a project requires you to investigate only a few sources of information to support a short essay or report, you may choose to keep all your bibliographic and research information in your research log — or in a separate part of your class notebook. Record what you find as if you were keeping separate note cards. And write to yourself as you would in any research log, monitoring your research as you go along.

Some students keep their logs on computers, treating their entries as if they were in a notebook. The computer has the advantage that information from log entries can be transferred directly into actual drafts of the paper without recopying.

WRITING 4

Keep a research log for the duration of your research assignment. Write in it daily and record everything you think of or find in relation to the project.When your project is finished, write an account of the role the log played in completing the project.

Making a Research Plan

After you have developed some sense of the range and amount of information available, write out a plan scheduling when you will do what on your project. For example, plan a certain amount of time for trips to the library. Find out if any of the books you need are checked out by somebody else and allow time for the library to call those in. Arrange needed interviews well in advance, with time to reschedule in case an interview has to be canceled. And allow enough time not only for writing, but also for revising and editing. As you accomplish each task or complete each stage of the research project, you may want to check off that item in your plan or note the date. If you find yourself falling behind schedule or if you discover additional tasks to be accomplished, revise your plan.

WRITING 5

On one page of your research log, design a research plan to include both library and field investigations. In this plan, list sources you have already found as well as those you hope to find.

Consulting a Range of Sources

To conduct any kind of research, you need to identify appropriate sources of information, consult and evaluate those sources and take good notes recording the information you collect. You also need to understand how each source works as evidence.

Primary sources contain original material and raw information. Secondary sources report on, describe, interpret, or analyze someone else's work. For example, if you were exploring the development of a novelist's style, the novels themselves would be primary sources, and reviews and critical interpretations of the novels would be secondary sources. What constitutes a primary source will differ depending on the field and your research question. The novel *Moby Dick* is a primary source if you are studying it as literature and making claims about what it means. It is a secondary source if you are investigating nineteenth-century whaling and referring to Melville's descriptions of harpooning for information about what that activity was like. An actual whaling log kept by a captain of a ship would be a primary source for that paper.

Most research essays use both primary and secondary sources. Primary sources ground the essay in firsthand knowledge and verifiable facts; secondary sources supply the context for your discussion and provide support for your interpretation or argument.

Many college research papers are based on library research, since libraries contain so much of the collective knowledge of the academic community. However, some of the most interesting research papers are based on field research. Field research involves firsthand interviews with people who have expert knowledge of your subject. Field research is also what you find simply by being in the field: for example, touring the local sewage treatment plant to see how the treatment actually happens.

Owning the Topic

Whenever you undertake research, you join an ongoing conversation among a select community of people who are particularly knowledgeable about the subject. As you collect information, you too become something of an expert, an *author*-ity, gaining an authoritative voice, becoming a stronger, more powerful writer. Plan to become enough of an expert on your topic that you can teach your readers — your classmates and instructor — something they didn't know before. The best way to exercise your newfound authority is to write in your own words all the important information and major ideas connected with your research project, either periodically in log entries or when you draft. Finding your own language to express an idea makes that idea yours and increases your understanding of and commitment to the topic; this is especially important if you are only lukewarm about your topic when you begin. Writing about the topic will actually make you more interested in it.

Keeping an Open Mind

Don't be surprised if, once you begin doing research, your questions and answers multiply and change. Keep in mind that the process of research often circles back on itself. You ask one question, find the answer to another, pursue that, and then stumble onto the answer to your first question. Be prepared, at times, to ramble, wander, travel in circles, find dead ends where you expected thoroughfares — but also thoroughfares where you expected dead ends. Good research will, at some point, become focused research.

For example, say you start out researching local recycling efforts, but you stumble upon the problem of finding buyers for recycled material. One source raises the question of manufacturing with recycled materials, while another source turns the whole question back to consumer education. All of these concerns are related, but if you attempt to study them all with equal intensity, your paper will be either very long or very superficial. It is wiser to use some information for context, some for the main focus of your research, and some not at all. Follow your strongest interests, and try to answer the question you most care about.

Similarly, what began as informational research may become argumentative, as the process of research turns up information to tip your original neutrality one way or another. Or a research investigation that starts out to prove a thesis may result in a mere neutral, informative paper if you uncover multiple causes or complications in what had seemed a straightforward case.

Research must remain flexible if it is to be vital and exciting; but you also need to conclude your research and write a focused paper. Keep an open mind, but also keep focusing your topic.

Developing an Outline

Making an early outline of your research project — what you intend to do, where you think it will go — and updating it as you go along are crucial research activities. Research usually takes place over a period of weeks or months. If you don't organize your information as you go along, you risk losing track of it as well as losing sight of your objective. When you locate and collect research information, make notes in your outline about where the information might go and what kind of evidence it provides. Revise your outline as necessary to accommodate new information and any new focus your research might take.

Stating a Thesis

Whether your research essay makes an argument or reports information, it needs a thesis. An argumentative thesis states a position on an issue. An informational thesis makes a statement about the information presented in the paper but does not advance one position over another.

ARGUMENTA-	To reduce the annual number of violent deaths in the United
TIVE THESIS	States, Congress should pass a law to mandate a waiting period of
	ten days before any handgun can be purchased in this country.
INFORMA-	Compact discs cost more than records because the laser tech-
TIONAL THESIS	nology required to manufacture them is so expensive.

If your research is argumentative, you will probably begin with a working thesis. If your research is informational, you will probably begin with a research question, and a thesis will evolve as you find answers. In most cases, your final thesis will be based on this working thesis but will be revised according to the information and insights you found through research.

Writing out a focused thesis statement is an important step in the process of completing a first draft. A good thesis not only helps readers understand your paper, it also helps you organize your thoughts and energies when writing. Look over your research log, notes, journal entries, and any preliminary drafts to remind you of the questions you've asked and the answers you've found. Then try drafting a thesis statement that's as complete, focused, and accurate as possible. Ask yourself the following questions, and revise the thesis as you think necessary:

1. Is the thesis interesting? An informational thesis should answer a question that is worth asking. An argumentative thesis should take a position on a debatable issue and should probably include a proposal for change.
2. Is the thesis as precise and specific as possible? Try to sharpen both your understanding of the thesis and the language you use to express it. Don't say *a waiting period* if you mean *a waiting period of ten days.* This will help you define the exact nature of your paper and will result in a final thesis that is more interesting to readers.
3. Is the thesis manageable? You may have collected more information than you actually write about, given the time available and the number of pages required. If necessary, take this opportunity to narrow both the thesis and the paper.
4. Does the thesis adequately reflect your research and the expected shape of your paper? Try to state explicitly all the major points you want to make in your paper. Consider also whether you have evidence or information to support each point.

Most research essays are long and complex enough that the thesis should be stated explicitly rather than left implicit. However, the thesis you include in your paper may be different from the one you developed to help you write the paper. For example, after asking the four questions given here, Zoe developed this detailed statement of her thesis.

To get an internship with a professional photographer in today's competitive and heavily commercialized market, you need to sell yourself effectively to busy people by developing a small and varied portfolio, making contact with potential employers early and often, and demonstrating that you understand the difficult and unglamorous work involved.

In her paper, however, her explicit thesis focused on only part of this statement.

> I've learned the steps to setting up an internship: First, establish contact through writing a letter and sending a résumé, then push your portfolio.

She developed her other points — about the competitive marketplace and the unglamorous work involved in being an assistant — elsewhere in her paper.

Many research essays give the thesis at the beginning, somewhere in the first or second paragraph, where it acts as a promise to the reader of what will follow. Some research papers present the thesis at the end, where it acts as a conclusion or a summary. If you take this approach, be sure that the topic and scope of your paper are clear to readers from the very beginning.

Drafting, Revising, and Editing

Research writing, like all important writing, benefits from the multistage process of drafting, revising, and editing — processes explained in detail in other parts of this book. In research writing, however, managing information and incorporating sources present special problems. Be sure that when you write your first draft, you allow room and time for further research if it is needed. In addition, be aware that incorporating sources smoothly into your prose may take more time and require special attention to the conventions of documentation; you will also need to spend more time editing and proofreading than for papers not based on research.

Keep in mind that since you are on your way to becoming an expert on your research topic, you will need to explain, define, and clarify many terms and concepts to your readers, including your instructor, who will know less than you do. You'll also want to make sure that you have remained focused on a topic that appeals to your potential readers. For both these reasons, you may want to ask your classmates and instructor to read and respond to your paper at several points along the way — for example, when you have a detailed outline or thesis, when you have completed your first draft, and when you are ready to edit.

COLLABORATIVE RESEARCH PROJECTS

Of all writing assignments, those involving extensive research profit most from collaboration. If your assignment lends itself to collaboration, and if your instructor approves of joint ventures, find out with which classmates you could work. The following suggestions will aid collaboration.

Topics. Either form a group you want to work with and then choose a topic you all want to research, or choose a topic that interests you and see if you can interest others to join you.

Size. Prefer small groups (two to three people) to large groups because it will be much easier to find time to meet outside of class and to synthesize the information you have found.

Organization. Divide tasks early in your project, specifying who will do what when. Divide the tasks equitably so that everyone contributes an equal amount. Divide the tasks so that members make maximum use of their different skills, abilities, and interests.

Research. Two or three people gathering information will result in a lot of information. Agree to take careful notes on texts or interview subjects and to duplicate the notes so that each group member has full source information. Shared research can result in separate papers written individually by the members or in one paper written collaboratively by all members.

Composing. A whole group writing a single paper can result in a paper that is longer and more detailed than individual papers on the same subject. The group can write together by (1) blending voices, passing the drafts back and forth, each writer overwriting the others each time; (2) sequencing voices,with each writer writing a different section; (3) weaving voices, so that the final product has different writers' voices emerging at different times throughout the paper. It is a good idea for all members to participate in drafting the paper.

Thesis. In the early stages of collaborative writing, it is a good idea for each group member to write his or her own version of what the research suggests. These early drafts should be shared, with each writer reconsidering the thesis and direction in light of points made by the other writers.

Revision and Editing. At the end, responsibilities can be divided equitably according to abilities, with different members volunteering to type, prepare references, edit, proofread, and reproduce the final paper. This is also a good time to even out the workload; if, for example, one member has done substantially more research, the others should do more with to produce the final text.

Responsibility and Evaluation. If all group members adhere to the agreed-upon responsibilities and deadlines, all should receive the same assessment for the work.

SUGGESTIONS FOR WRITING AND RESEARCH

Individual

1. Select a research topic that interests you and write an explanatory draft about it. First, write out everything you already know about the topic. Second, write out everything you want to know about the topic. Third, look for experts to talk to, and go to the library.

Finally, make a list of questions you need answered in order to write a more complete essay. Plan to put this paper through a process that includes not only planning, drafting, revising, and editing but also locating, evaluating, and using sources.

2. With the research question you developed in individual assignment 1 in mind, visit the library and conduct a search of available resources. What do you find? Where do you find it? Show your question or questions to a reference librarian and ask what additional sources he or she would suggest.

3. After completing individual assignments 1 and 2, find a person you have reason to believe knows something about your topic, and ask him or her for leads about doing further research on the topic. Whom else would he recommend you speak with? What books or articles would she recommend? What's the first thing this expert would do to find information?

Collaborative

1. Join with a classmate or classmates to write a collaborative research essay. Go through the suggestions for conducting an individual research project presented in this chapter, and develop plans for dividing tasks among members of the group.

2. After completing collaborative assignment 1, conducting you research, and writing your essay, write a short report in which you explain the collaborative strategies your group used and evaluate their usefulness.

3. Create a team of two to four classmates who would like to join you in researching a project you planned in individual assignment 1. Plan the necessary activities to make the collaboration work. Divide the labor so that each of you brings back some information to the group by next week's class meeting. Make a copy of your research information for each group member, including typed transcripts of interviews and photocopies of visual information. You may each write an individual paper based on your collective research, or you may team up and write a longer paper.

Chapter 17
===

Conducting Field Research

Talking to the author was a lot different from reading her book. She was actually there, friendly, smiling sometimes, thinking out loud, telling me inside stories and trade secrets, and when she didn't know an answer, she didn't pretend that she did. Her stories really make my paper come alive.

— MARY

RESEARCH IS AN ACTIVE AND UNPREDICTABLE PROCESS requiring serious investigators to find answers wherever they happen to be. Academic research is not confined to libraries. Depending on your research question, you may need to seek answers by visiting museums, attending concerts, interviewing politicians, observing classrooms, or following leads down some other trail. Investigations that take place outside the library are commonly called *field research*.

Field researchers collect information that is not yet written down, that cannot be read and examined in books. Because the information they collect has not been previously recorded or assessed, field researchers have the chance to uncover new facts and develop original interpretations. To conduct such research, you need to identify the people, places, things, or events that can give you information you need. Then you must go out in the field and either *observe* by watching carefully or *interview* by asking questions of one particular person. You should also take careful notes to record your observations or interviews and critically evaluate the information you've collected.

PLANNING FIELD RESEARCH

Unlike a library, which bundles millions of bits of every kind of information in a single location, "fields" are everywhere — your room, a dormitory, cafeteria, neighborhood, theater, mall, park, playground, and so on. Field information is not bundled, cataloged, organized, indexed, or shelved for your convenience. Nor is there a person like a reference librarian to point you to the best resources. In other words, when you think about making field research a part of your research project, you start out on your own. Successful field research requires diligence, energy, and careful planning.

First, you need to find the person, place, thing, or event most helpful to you and decide whether you want to collect observations, conduct interviews, or do both. Consider your research question as you've developed it thus far and the sources most likely to give you the answers you need. Also consider what sort of information will be most effective in your final paper.

Second, you need to schedule field research in advance and allow enough time for it. People, things, and events will not always hold still or be exactly where you want them to be when it's most convenient for you. Allow time for rescheduling a visit or interview or returning for more information.

Third, you need to visit the library before conducting extensive field research. No matter who, where, or what you intend to collect information from, there's background information at the library that can help you make more insightful observations or formulate better interview questions.

Finally, you need to keep a *research log* so you can keep track of all the visits, questions, phone calls, and conversations that relate to your research project. Write in your log as soon as you receive your assignment and at each step along the way about topics, questions, methods, and answers. Even record dead-end searches to remind you not to repeat them.

WRITING 1

In your research log, write about the feasibility of using field research information to help answer your research question. What kind of field research would strengthen your paper? Where would you go to collect it?

INTERVIEWING

A good interview provides the researcher with timely, original, and useful information that often cannot be obtained by other means. Getting such information is part instinct, part skill, and part luck. If you find talking to strangers easy, then you have a head start on being a good interviewer. In many respects, a good interview is simply a good conversation. If you're not naturally comfortable talking to strangers, you can still learn how to ask good interview questions that will elicit the answers you need. Of course, no matter how skillful or prepared you are, whether your interview results in good answers also depends on your interview subject — his or her mood, knowledge and information, and willingness to spend time talking with you.

Your chances of obtaining good interview material increase when you've given some thought to the interview ahead of time. The following guidelines should help you conduct good interviews.

Select the right person. People differ in both the amount and kind of knowledge they have on a subject. Not everyone who knows something about your research topic will be able to give you the specific information you need. In other words, before you make an appointment with a local expert because he or she is accessible, consider whether that expert is the best person to talk to. Ask yourself (1) exactly what information you need, (2) why you need it, (3) who is likely to have it, and (4) how you might approach them to gain it. Most research projects benefit from various perspectives, so you may want to interview several people. For example, to research Lake Erie pollution, you could interview someone who lives on the lake shore, a chemist who knows about the pesticide decomposition, and the president of a paper company dumping waste into the lake. Just be sure the people you select are likely to provide the information you really need.

Do your homework. Before you talk to an expert about your topic, make sure you know something about it yourself. Be able to define or describe your interest in it, know what the general issues are, and learn what your interview subject has already said or written about it. Having become familiar with your topic, you will ask sharper questions, get to the point faster, and be more interesting for your subject to talk with.

Plan appropriate questions. A good interview doesn't follow a script, but it usually starts with one. Before you begin an interview, write the questions you plan to ask and arrange them so that they build on each other — general questions first, specific ones later. If you or your subject digresses too much, your questions can serve as reminders about the information you need.

Ask both open and closed questions. Different kinds of questions elicit different kinds of information. Open questions place few limits on the kinds of answers given: Why did you decide to major in business? What are your plans for the future? Closed questions specify the kind of information you want and usually elicit brief responses: When did you receive your degree? From what college? Open questions usually provide general information, while closed questions allow you to zero in on specific details.

Ask follow-up questions. Listen closely to the answers you receive, and when the information is incomplete or confusing, ask follow-up questions requesting more detail or clarification. Such questions can't be scripted; you've just got to use your wits to direct your interview subject toward the information you consider most important.

Use silence. If you don't get an immediate response to a question, wait a bit before rephrasing it or asking another one. In some cases, your question may not have been clear, and you will need to rephrase it. But in many cases your subject is simply collecting his or her thoughts, not ignoring you. After a slight pause, you may hear thoughtful answers that are worth waiting for.

Read body language. Be aware of what your subject is doing when he or she answers questions. Does he look you in the eye? Does she fidget and squirm? Does he look distracted or bored? Does she smile or frown? From these visual cues you may be able to infer when your subject is speaking most frankly, when he or she doesn't want to give more information, or when he or she is tired of answering questions.

Take good notes. Most interviewers take notes, using a pad that is spiral-bound on top, which allows for quick page flipping. Don't try to write down everything, just major ideas and important statements in the subject's own language that you might want to use as quotations in your paper. Omitting small words, focusing on the language that is most distinctive and precise, and using common abbreviations (like *b/c* for *because*, *w/* for *with*, and & for *and*) can make note taking more efficient.

Also take notes about your subject's physical appearance, facial expressions, and clothing and about the interview setting itself. These details will be useful later to help you reconstruct the interview and represent it more vividly in your paper.

If you plan to use a tape recorder, ask your subject's permission in advance. The advantage of tape recording is that you have a complete record of the conversation. Sometimes on hearing the person a second time you notice important things that you missed the first time. The disadvantages are that sometimes tape recorders make subjects nervous and that transcribing a tape is time-consuming work. If you use a tape recorder, it's still a good idea to have a pen in your hand to catch points of emphasis or jot down questions that occur as the conversation continues.

Confirm important assertions. When your subject says something you judge to be especially important or controversial, read your notes back to your subject to check for accuracy and allow your subject to elaborate on the topic. Some interviewers do this as the interview progresses, others at the end of the interview.

Review your notes as soon as possible. Notes taken during an interview are brief reminders of what your subject said, not complete quotations. You need to write out the complete information as soon after the interview as you can, certainly within twenty-four hours. Supplement the notes with other remembered details while they are still fresh, by recording the information on note cards or directly into a computer file that you can refer to as you write your paper.

WRITING 2

Describe any experience you have had as either interviewer or interviewee. Drawing on your own experience — or on watching TV interviews — what additional advice would you give to researchers setting out to interview a subject?

WRITING 3

If you are planning a research project, whom could you interview to find out useful and relevant information? Make a list of such people. Write out first drafts of possible questions to ask them.

OBSERVING

Another kind of field research calls for closely observing people, places, things, and events and then describing them accurately to show readers what you saw and experienced. While the term *observation* strictly speaking denotes visual perception, it also applies to information collected on site through other senses. The following suggestions may help you conduct field observations more effectively.

Select a good site to visit. As with interviewing, observing requires that you know where to go and what to look for. You need to have your research question in mind and then to identify those places where observation will yield useful information. For example, a research project on pollution in Lake Erie would be enhanced by on-the-scene observation of what the water smells, feels, and looks like. Sometimes the site you visit is the primary object of your research, as when the purpose of your paper is to profile people and activities you find there. At other times the on-site observation provides supplemental evidence but is not the focus of the paper itself.

Do your homework. To observe well, you need to know what you are looking for and what you are looking at. If you are observing a political speech, know the issues and the players; if you visit an industrial complex, know what products are manufactured there. Researching background information at the library or through other means will allow you to use your time on site more efficiently.

Plan your visit. Learn not only where the place is located on a map but also how to gain access; call ahead to ask directions. Find out where you should go when you first arrive. If relevant, ask which places are open to you, which are off limits, and which you could visit with permission. Find out about visiting hours; if you want to visit at odd hours, you may need special permission. Depending on the place, after-hours visits can provide detailed information not available to the general public.

Take good notes. At any site there's a lot going on that casual observers take for granted. As a researcher you should take nothing for granted. Keep in mind that without notes, as soon as you leave a site you forget more than half of what was there. As with interview notes, be sure to review your observation notes as soon after your site visit as possible.

You can't write everything down, though, so be selective. Keep your research question in mind and try to focus on the impressions that are most important in answering it. Some of your observations and notes will provide the background information needed to represent the scene vividly in your paper. Some will provide the specific, concrete details needed to make your paper's assertions believable. Make your notes as precise as possible, indicating the exact color, shape, size, texture, and arrangement of everything you can.

Use a notebook that has a stiff cover so you can write standing, sitting, or squatting, as a table may not be available. Double-entry notebooks are useful for site visits, because they allow you to record facts observed in one column and interpretations of those facts in the other. If visual images would be useful, you can also sketch, photograph, or videotape. You can use a tape recorder and speak your notes into it; this way, you will also pick up the characteristic sounds of the site.

WRITING 4

Describe a time when you used close observation in a piece of writing. When and where was it? Was it deliberate or by accident? What was your readers' response?

WRITING 5

If you are currently conducting research, list at least three sites you could visit that would add relevant information to your study. Then follow the suggestions in this chapter and visit at least one of them.

THINKING CRITICALLY ABOUT FIELD SOURCES

When you've found a potentially useful field source, you need to examine it and assess its value just as carefully as you would a source found in a library. To do this requires critical thinking, a process much like critical reading. You need to analyze the assumptions and reasoning of the source, determine whether it is reliable and credible, and develop an interpretation of what it means to you and your research question. Ask yourself the following questions when you are thinking critically about field sources.

1. **What is the most important point this source makes?** How does it address my research question? How would I articulate this point in writing?
2. **What evidence did the source provide that supports this point?** Is it strong or weak? Can I use it? Build on it? Should I question it? Refute it?
3. **Does the information collected from this source support my working thesis?** If so, how? Can I express in writing the precise nature of the support?
4. **Does the information challenge my working thesis?** If so, how? Can I refute the information or contradiction? Or should I revise my thesis to take the new information into account?
5. **Does the information support or contradict information collected from other sources?** How so? How can I resolve any contradictions? Do I need to seek other sources for confirmation?
6. **Is the source reliable?** Is any of the information from this source illogical or incredible? Has any of the information been conclusively contradicted by a more authoritative source? If so, is this enough to cast all of the information from this source in doubt?

7. **Is the source biased?** Does the interview subject have a reason to
    be biased in any way? Does he or she have a reputation to protect
    or a vested interest in the thing I'm researching? Would the selec-
    tion of a different site have resulted in different information?

WRITING 6

If you are conducting a research project using field sources, explain
how you have evaluated your field sources to test their accuracy and
reliability.

SUGGESTIONS FOR FIELD RESEARCH PROJECTS

Individual

Plan a research project that focuses on a local place (park, playground, street, building, business, or institution) and make a research
plan that includes going there, describing what you find, and interviewing somebody.

Individual

Plan a research project that begins with an issue of some concern to
you. Identify a local manifestation of this issue that would profit from
some field research. Conduct the research, using field techniques appropriate to your topic.

Chapter 18

Conducting Library Research

I am beginning to understand the importance of feeling safe in order to be
creative and productive. Here, in the library, I feel secure, protected from
real violence and isolated from everyday distractions. There are just enough
people for security's sake, but not so many that I feel crowded. And besides,
I'm surrounded by all these books, all these great minds who dwell in this
hallowed space! I am comfortable, safe, and beginning to get an idea.

— JUDY

LIBRARIES ARE THE HEART — or perhaps the head — of the academic community. Libraries provide the primary knowledge base that allows professors to teach and conduct research in their fields. And libraries provide students with many sources of information that allow them to investigate more deeply and more broadly any area of study.

The modern library is a complex and multifaceted place. You should visit your own college library early and get to know it well. At first, a college library may appear intimidating, but the more you use it, the more friendly it will become.

PLANNING LIBRARY RESEARCH

To learn about the library, you need to go there, stroll through it, read the informational signs that identify special desks, rooms, and departments; poke your nose into nooks and crannies that look interesting; and open a few books or magazines to get the feel of the place. If there's an introductory video explaining the library, pause to see it. If there's a self-paced or guided tour, take it. Read informational handouts or pamphlets. Be sure to locate the following:

The book catalog, computerized or on cards, that tells you which books your library owns and where they are located.

The book stacks, where books, periodicals, pamphlets, and other materials are stored.

The circulation desk, usually on the first floor, where you check out and reserve books and get information on the library's procedures and resources.

The reference desk, also on the main floor, which is the best place to find help locating the library's resources.

The periodical room, which houses recent issues of magazines, journals, and newspapers. Older issues are either shelved in the book stacks or stored on microfilm or microfiche.

The reference room, which contains general reference works such as dictionaries and encyclopedias along with guides and indexes that point you to more specific sources of information.

To take full advantage of library resources, keep the following suggestions in mind.

Visit the library early and often. As soon as you receive a research assignment, visit the library to find out what resources are available for your project, and plan to return often. Even if your initial research indicates a wealth of material on your topic, you may not be able to find everything the first time you look. A book you need may be checked out, and the process of having it called in may take several days. Your library may not own a particular book or subscribe to a particular periodical containing important information, and you may need to order it on interlibrary loan, a process that takes some time.

Prepare to take notes. If you take careful notes from the sources you find, you will save yourself time and write a better paper. Bring index cards to the library — 3″ × 5″ cards for bibliographical information and 4″ × 6″ cards for notes — from your first visit on.

In addition, writing in a research log, perhaps daily as you work on your research project, will help you find ideas to research, plan your course of action, change directions if necessary, pose and solve problems related to your topic, and keep track of where you have been so far and what you have tried.

Check general sources before specific ones. During your first or second visit to the library, check general sources — dictionaries, encyclopedias, atlases, and yearbooks — for information about your topic. An hour or two spent with these general sources will give you a quick overview of the scope and range of your topic, which will help you focus the topic and will lead you to more specific information.

Ask for help. Talk to librarians whenever you need their help. At first you might show them your assignment and describe your topic and your research plans; later you might ask them for help in finding a particular source; finally, when you are nearly finished, you might ask if they know of any sources that you have not checked yet. Keep in mind, however, that reference librarians are busy people — don't ask questions to which you know the answers or ones that you haven't tried to answer for yourself.

Strategies for Talking with Librarians

1. Before you ask for help, try to answer your questions yourself.
2. Bring with you a copy of the research assignment, preferably the instructor's original handout.
3. Be ready to explain your understanding of the assignment in your own words: purpose, expected format, length, number of required or expected sources, and due date.
4. Identify any special requirements about sources: Should information come from government documents? Special or rare book collections? Films?
5. Describe the particular topic you are researching and the tentative question you have framed to address the topic.
6. Describe any work you have done so far: books read, periodicals looked at, log entries written, people interviewed, and so on.

WRITING 1

Visit your college library and locate the areas and materials discussed in this section. Then look for a place that's comfortable, sit down, and write about which of these might be of most use to you as you begin a research project.

WRITING 2

Write an entry in your research log in which you outline a tentative plan for using the library in your current project. Include (1) the subject and the topic of your research, (2) a time line for how long you expect the project to take, (3) specific dates that you reserve to visit the library, (4) the sources you plan to consult first, and (5) a question about the library (plan to ask the reference librarian about this).

FINDING SOURCES OF INFORMATION

Most of the information you need to find at the library will be contained in reference books, in other books, or in periodicals — journals, magazines, and newspapers. Reference books are fairly easy to locate: there are relatively few of them and they are usually placed in one room or section of the library. However, even a moderately sized college library owns hundreds of thousands of books and periodicals. To simplify the researcher's task of finding the relevant ones, bibliographies and indexes have been developed. These resources either indicate which books or periodical articles have been published on a given topic or attempt to present comprehensive lists of sources in an easy-to-use format. Once you know which book or periodical might be useful, you still need to find it. The library's catalogs tell you whether the library owns the source. To use catalogs efficiently, look for sources of information by using this four-step process:

1. Consult general reference works to gain background information and basic facts.
2. Consult bibliographies and indexes to learn which books, periodicals, and articles are relevant.
3. Consult your library's catalogs to see if it owns the books and periodicals you want.
4. Consult other sources as needed.

In most cases, the research source you eventually find and use will be printed on paper. However, many of the bibliographies and indexes that lead you to these sources will be available in electronic form, either through an on-line service (which your library's computers access through a telephone line and a modem) or on a CD-ROM disc (a compact disc containing data that can be read by a computer with a CD drive). One research tool that is available only in electronic form is the database. Databases are large electronic indexes. Often they provide summaries or outlines in addition to bibliographic information on the sources they list; occasionally they contain copies of the sources themselves. Databases can be either on-line or on CD-ROM. Many library catalogs today are computerized as well; they are essentially on-line databases.

Searching through electronic indexes, databases, and catalogs is much easier if you have identified the key words for your research topic. A key word is an important word describing your topic, either a word for the topic itself, a word for the general subject, or a word describing parts of the topic. Sometimes titles and author names can also be used as key words. For example, key words for a research paper investigating the pottery of Native Americans in the western United States would include *Indian, art,* and *California.* Because a computer can search only for the words you give it and because building an electronic database is a new process with noticeable oversights, the key words you select can mean the difference between success and failure. For example, in most databases, a search including the word *Sioux* would turn up nothing, but a search including the word *Dakota* (the preferred term for this group) would result in a number of sources. To find good key words for your topic, consult the *Library of Congress Subject Headings*, a bound guide — actually a thesaurus — that cross-lists related terms and identifies the term under which a subject is classified. This bound volume is usually located at the reference desk.

Reference Works

General reference works provide background information and basic facts about a topic. The summaries, overviews, and definitions you find in these sources can help you decide whether to pursue a topic further and, if you do, where to turn next for information. The information in these sources is necessarily general and will not be sufficient by itself as the basis for most research projects; you will also need to consult specialized sources and full-length works about your topic.

Specialized reference works contain detailed and technical information in a particular field or discipline. They often include articles by well-known authorities and sometimes contain bibliographies and cross-references that can lead you to other sources. Two useful guides to finding specialized reference books are *Guide to Reference Books*, edited by Eugene P. Sheehy (10th edition, 1986) and *Walford's Guide to Reference Material* (4th edition, 1980–86). Although specialized reference works provide more detailed and technical information than that found in general reference works, you should still use them primarily for exploratory research and background.

While many reference works are published as books, increasingly they are available on CD-ROM. The following lists contain the most common and most useful references, although there are many more in each category.

ALMANACS AND YEARBOOKS. Almanacs and yearbooks provide up-to-date information on politics, agriculture, economics, and population along with statistical facts of all kinds.

Facts on File: News Digest (1941–present). A summary and index to current events reported in newspapers worldwide. (Also, CD-ROM, 1980–present.)

Statesman's Year-Book (1863–present). Contains annual statistics about government, agriculture, population, religion, and so on for countries throughout the world.

World Almanac and Book of Facts (1868–present). Reviews important events of the past year and provides data on a wide variety of topics, including sports, government, science, business, and education.

ATLASES. Atlases such as the *Hammond Atlas,* the *National Geographic Atlas of the World,* and the *New York Times Atlas of the World* can help you identify places anywhere in the world and provide basic information on population, climate, crops, industry, and so on.

BIOGRAPHICAL DICTIONARIES. Biographical dictionaries contain information on people who have made some mark on history in many different fields; biographical indexes tell you how to locate additional sources.

Contemporary Authors (1967–present). Includes short biographies of authors who have published books during the year.

Current Biography (1940–present). Contains articles and photographs of people in the news.

Who's Who in America (1899–present). The standard biographical reference for living Americans.

DICTIONARIES.   Dictionaries contain definitions, derivations, and histories of words and information on their correct usage.

ENCYCLOPEDIAS.   Encyclopedias are excellent places to start any research investigation. They provide elementary and superficial information, explanations, and definitions of virtually every topic, concept, country, institution, historical person or movement, or cultural artifact imaginable. One-volume works such as the *Random House Encyclopedia* and *The New Columbia Encyclopedia* give brief overviews. Larger works such as *Collier's Encyclopedia* (24 volumes) and the *New Encyclopaedia Britannica* (32 volumes) contain more detailed information.

SPECIALIZED REFERENCE WORKS.   Each discipline has many reference works; here is a small sampling.

LANGUAGES AND LITERATURE

Cassell's Encyclopedia of World Literature
Handbook to Literature
McGraw-Hill Encyclopedia of World Drama
Oxford Companion to American Literature

HUMANITIES

Cambridge Ancient History
Dictionary of the Bible
Encyclopedia of Philosophy
Encyclopedia of Religion
Encyclopedia of World History
New Grove Dictionary of Music and Musicians
Oxford Companion to Art

SOCIAL SCIENCES

Dictionary of Education
Encyclopedia of Anthropology
Encyclopedia of Crime and Justice
Encyclopedia of Psychology
Encyclopedia of Social Work
Political Handbook and Atlas of the World

SCIENCES

Encyclopedia of Biological Sciences
Encyclopedia of Chemistry

Encyclopedia of Computer Science and Technology
Encyclopedia of Physics
McGraw-Hill Dictionary of Science and Technology

BUSINESS

Encyclopedia of Banking and Finance
Encyclopedia of Economics
McGraw-Hill Dictionary of Modern Economics

WRITING 3

Look up information on your potential research topic, using at least three of the reference sources described in this section.

BIBLIOGRAPHIES, INDEXES, AND DATABASES

Bibliographies, indexes, and databases are tools — they help you locate books and periodicals that contain the information you need. Periodicals are magazines, journals, and newspapers, works that are published at set periods throughout the year. Periodicals focus on particular areas of interest, and their information is usually more current than that found in books. Because so many periodical issues are published each year and because every issue can contain dozens of articles on different topics, using a periodical index or database is essential to finding the periodical and article you need.

Bibliographies

Bibliographies are lists of books, given alphabetically by title, by author, or by subject. Many books include a bibliography of the works consulted by the author in researching the book; always consult the bibliography of a book you have found helpful. Other bibliographies are published separately as reference tools. Some of the most useful are listed here.

Bibliographic Index: A Cumulative Bibliography of Bibliographies. New York: Wilson, 1938–present. This index lists the page numbers of bibliographies in books over a wide variety of subjects. Such bibliographies provide lists of related sources already compiled by another author on a subject similar to your own. Some may be out of date, but they can still be useful.

Books in Print. New York: Bowker, 1948–present. The latest edition of this yearly index lists by author, subject, and title all books currently in print. It is also available on-line and on CD-ROM.

Paperbound Books in Print. The latest edition of this semiannual index lists paperback books currently in print by author, subject, and title. It is also available on-line and on CD-ROM.

MLA Bibliography of Books and Articles in the Modern Languages and Literature (1921–present). It is also available on-line and on CD-ROM.

Indexes

Indexes are guides to the material published within works, sometimes within books but more often within periodicals. Each index covers a particular group of periodicals. Make sure that the index you select contains the journals, magazines, and newspapers that will be useful to you as sources.

Indexes list works alphabetically by author or by subject. To conduct an effective subject search, you'll need to make use of the key words you've identified for your topic. Check under every subject heading that you think might be relevant. Many periodicals use the subject headings in the *Library of Congress Subject Headings,* but others use their own lists.

Most indexes are available both in printed form and in computerized form (either on-line or on CD-ROM). Many are also available on microfiche or microfilm — media that provide copies of the printed page that must be read on special machines. Indexes in book form are usually the most comprehensive; those presented on microfilm, on microfiche, or electronically usually cover only the past ten or twenty years.

Using computerized indexes provides a distinct advantage because it allows you to focus your search strategy more effectively. By combining your key words in certain ways, you can have the computer generate a list of works that closely match your topic. For example, if your research topic is the art of Dakota Indians, you might try searching for all works with the key word *Dakota* in their subject descriptions. This would result in hundreds of works, a few on art but many others on other topics, such as politics, economics, history, and so on. Something similar would happen if you searched for *art.* But if you search for *Dakota and art* the computer will list only those works with both words in their subject descriptions, a much more useful list, given the research topic. You can also combine key words using *or:* Searching for *Dakota and art or fiction* would result in a list of works that all have the word *Dakota* in their subject descriptions, some of which also have *art* and some of which also have *fiction.*

Some of the more helpful periodical indexes are listed here.

GENERAL PERIODICAL INDEXES.   These indexes list articles published in a wide variety of periodicals, most of interest to the general public.

InfoTrac. This monthly index is available only on CD-ROM. It contains three separate indexes. The *Academic Index* covers nearly 1000 commonly used scholarly publications. The *General Periodical Index* covers over 1000 general-interest publications. The *Newspaper Index* covers large-circulation newspapers. Many entries include summaries.

New York Times Index (1851–present). This bimonthly index lists every article that appears in the *New York Times.* Short summaries are provided for many articles. It is also available on-line.

Readers' Guide to Periodical Literature (1900–present). This semimonthly index lists articles in over 200 magazines of general interest, such as *Time, Newsweek, Popular Science, The New Yorker,* and *Rolling Stone.* On-line and CD-ROM versions are also available (1983–present).

SPECIALIZED PERIODICAL INDEXES. These indexes list articles in periodicals that focus on specific disciplines or fields of interest. They are usually much more helpful than general periodical indexes for college-level research. Here are some of the most common.

America: History and Life
Applied Science and Technology Index
Art Index
Biological and Agricultural Index
Business Periodicals Index
Dissertation Abstracts International
Education Index
Essay and General Literature Index
General Science Index
Humanities Index
Index to Legal Periodicals
Music Index
Psychological Index
Social Science Index

Databases

Databases are large collections of electronically stored information that function like indexes. Often they provide summaries or outlines in addition to bibliographic information on the sources they list; occasionally they contain copies of the sources themselves.

The database most commonly found in college libraries is DIALOG, which keeps track of more than a million sources of information. DIALOG is divided into many smaller, more specialized databases, some 987 of which are listed in the current manual, *DIALOG Blue Sheets.* Some of the most commonly used databases within DIALOG include Arts and Humanities Search (1980–present), ERIC (Educational Resources Information Center, 1965–present), PsychINFO (1967–present), Scisearch (1974–present), and Social Scisearch (1972–present). You must decide which specialized database you need to use before you begin your search.

DIALOG and similar databases are available on-line. To use an on-line database, you will usually need the assistance of a reference librarian, who will ask you to fill out a form listing the key words you have identified for your project. The library is charged a fee for each search, calculated according to the time spent and the number of entries retrieved. Some libraries have the person requesting the search pay the fee; others limit the time allotted for each search. Be sure to ask what your library's policy is.

Some databases, including some of the specialized databases within DIALOG, are also available on CD-ROM. You can usually search through these databases without the aid of a reference librarian.

```
SilverPlatter 3.11   Journal Articles (1/74 - 12/86)   F10=Commands
                                                        F1=Help
```
....
```
TI: Teacher expressiveness: More important for male teachers than
female teachers?
AU: Basow.-Susan-A.; Distenfeld, -M. -Suzan
IN: Lafayette Coll
JN: Journal-of-Educational-Psychology; 1985 Feb Vol 77(1) 45-52
```
AB: 55 male and 62 female undergraduates viewed a videotape of a
male or female actor giving a short lecture using expressive or
nonexpressive communication and rated each teacher on a 22-item
questionnaire that yielded 5 factors (Rapport, Student Orientation,
Stimulates Interest, Organization, and Knowledge of Material).
Findings show that the expressive teacher received the highest
student evaluations on the basis of a global evaluation score and
on the 5 factor scores. The nonexpressive male teacher received low
ratings on Organization and Stimulating Interest. Ss who viewed
this tape also had the poorest performance on a subsequent content
test. Ss who viewed a nonexpressive female teacher had the
highest performance on the content test. It is hypothesized that
differential attention as a function of sex-role-appropriate
characteristics is a mediating variable. It is suggested that in
studies of teaching performance and
....
```
MENU: Mark Record Select Search Term Options  Find  Print  Download

Press ENTER to Mark records for PRINT or DOWNLOAD.
Use PgDn and PgUp to scroll.
```

Partial Entry in a CD-ROM Database

WRITING 4

For your current research project, use one of the bibliographies, indexes, or databases described in this section to find information on a relevant book or periodical. Locate the work and record the results of your search in your research log.

The Library Catalog

The library catalog lists every book a library owns; many libraries also catalog their periodicals. At one time all catalogs were card catalogs, with the information printed on small cards and stored in drawers. Several decades ago, many libraries began transferring their catalogs to more convenient formats: microfiche and microfilm. These are copies of the printed cards that are read in a special machine. More recently, libraries began computerizing their catalogs, which are now known as on-line catalogs (or circulation computers). Often on-line catalogs can be accessed through telephone lines and modems from locations outside the library.

Regardless of the format, all catalogs provide the same basic information. They list each book by author, title, and subject; provide basic information about its physical format and content; and tell you where in the library to find it.

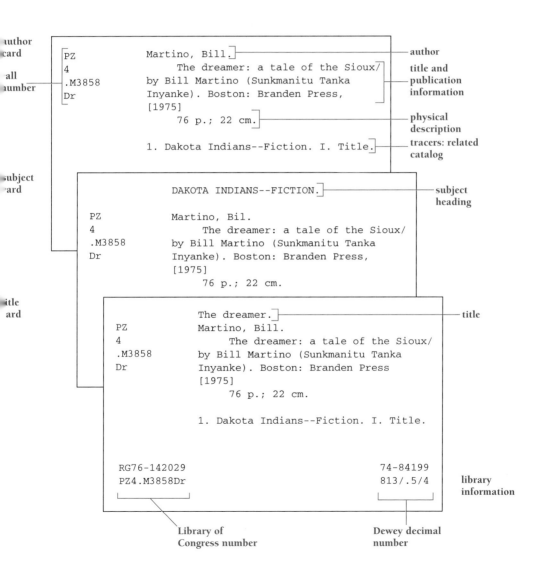

Cards from a Traditional Card Catalog

During the course of your research project, you will probably use the library catalog in two different ways. Sometimes you will already know — through research conducted in reference works or in bibliographies, indexes, or databases — the title of a work you want to find. The catalog can confirm that your library owns the work and can tell you where to find it. At other times, you will use the catalog as you would an index or a database, searching for works that are relevant to your topic. This sort of search is called *browsing*. On-line catalogs are particularly good for browsing and usually have several special features designed to facilitate it.

Even if you discover through the catalog that your library doesn't own the source you want, don't despair. Many libraries can obtain a work owned by another library through an interlibrary loan, although this usually takes a few days. Ask your librarian.

Consulting On-Line Catalogs

Computerized catalog systems vary slightly from library to library, though all systems follow the same general principles. Specific instructions for conducting a search in your own library will be posted next to the terminals. The following sections briefly describe four search procedures to locate the book *Love Medicine*, Louise Erdrich's novel about Native American life on a North Dakota reservation.

AUTHOR SEARCH.   If you know the name of the author of the book you are looking for, follow the on-screen directions for searching by author; in some systems, you would type

a=Erdrich, Louise

and the following would appear on the monitor:

```
Search Request:  A=ERDRICH, LOUISE                            LUIS
Search Results:  5 Entries Found                      Author Index
----------------------------------------------------------------- T259
   ERDRICH LOUISE
      1     BEET QUEEN A NOVEL <1986> (BH)
      2     CROWN OF COLUMBUS <1991> (BH)
      3     JACKLIGHT <1984> (BH)
      4     LOVE MEDICINE A NOVEL <1984> (BH)
      5     TRACKS A NOVEL <1988> (BH)
-----------------------------------------------------------------
```

This is an alphabetical listing of all of the books in the library's collection by Louise Erdrich, each followed by the date of publication and the initials identifying the library in which the book is found, in this case BH for Bailey Howe. Since many campuses house more than one library — art and medical, for instance — it is important to note in which campus library your book is located. In addition, the list indicates that the full title includes the word *A Novel*.

Typing the number 4 brings up more information on *Love Medicine* and the following screen appears:

```
Search Request: T=LOVE MEDICINE                              LUIS
BOOK - Record 1 of 5 Entries Found                      Brief View
----------------------------- Screen 1 of 1 ----------------------- T259
Author:      Erdrich, Louise.


Title:       Love Medicine : a novel
Edition:     1st ed.


Published:      New York : Holt, Rinehart, and Winston, c 1984.
-------------------------------------------------------------------
       LOCATION:              CALL NUMBER          STATUS:
  1.  Bailey/Howe Stacks     PS3555.R42 L6 1984   Not checked out
  2.  Bailey/Howe Stacks     PS3555.R42 L6 1984   Not checked out
-------------------------------------------------------------------
```

This screen provides a brief view of basic information about the book, identifying the edition, place of publication, name of publisher, and date of publication. Below the dotted line is the information needed to find the book: *Love Medicine* is located in the book *stacks* under the Library of Congress *call number* PS3555.R42 L6 1984. In addition, the screen indicates that the book is not checked out, so it should be on the shelf as indicated.

TITLE SEARCH.   If you did not know the author's name, you could also locate the book by its title, *Love Medicine*, by typing

    t=Love Medicine

and the following would appear on the monitor:

```
 Search Request:  T=LOVE MEDICINE                            LUIS
 Search Results:  5 Entries Found                     Title Index
----------------------------------------------------------------- T259
   1  LOVE MEDICINE A NOVEL. ERDRICH LOUISE <1984> (BH)

      LOVE MEDICINE AND MIRACLES
   2     SIEGEL BERNIE S <1986> (BH)
   3     SIEGEL BERNIE S <1988> (DA)

      LOVE MEDICINE MIRACLES LESSONS LEARNED ABOUT SELF HEALING FROM A
         SURGEONS EXPERIENCE WITH EXCEPTIONAL PATIENTS
   4     SIEGEL BERNIE S <1986> (BH)
   5     SIEGEL BERNIE S <1988> (DA)
-----------------------------------------------------------------
```

The computer located five separate entries with the words *Love Medicine* in the title. There are, however, only three individual books here — two by Siegel, each listed twice, indicating that they can be found in two different libraries on campus. The first listing is the book by Erdrich.

SUBJECT SEARCH.   A subject search will tell you how much material your library has on any given subject. For example, you might do a subject search at the beginning of a research assignment to find out if the library holds enough material to proceed. It also describes the subtopics into which the information in a particular area is divided. You can use subject search to locate a specific book if you can't remember who wrote it or what it is called, but if you know either author or title, one of these search procedures is more direct and faster.

To find out how many items the library has on the general subject of Indians, for example, you could type

s=Indians

and the following information might appear on the monitor:

```
Search Request:  S=INDIANS                                    LUIS
Search Results:  5000 Entries Found                  Subject Guide
-----------------------------------------------------------------T256
LINE    BEGINNING ENTRY:                             INDEX RANGE:
  1     INDIANS                                        1 - 358
  2     INDIANS--ORIGIN                              359 - 716
  3     INDIANS OF CENTRAL AMERICA--COSTA RICA--ART  717 - 1074
  4     INDIANS OF MEXICO--ANTIQUITIES              1075 - 1432
  5     INDIANS OF MEXICO--OAXACA                   1433 - 1790
  6     INDIANS OF NORTH AMERICA                    1791 - 2148
  7     INDIANS OF NORTH AMERICA--AGED--MENTAL HEALTH  2149 - 2506
  8     INDIANS OF NORTH AMERICA--ANTIQUITIES       2507 - 2864
  9     INDIANS OF NORTH AMERICA--ART               2865 - 3222
 10     INDIANS OF NORTH AMERICA--CALIFORNIA        3223 - 3580
 11     INDIANS OF NORTH AMERICA--CANADA
           --ECONOMIC CONDITIONS                    3581 - 3938
 12     INDIANS OF NORTH AMERICA--CANADA EASTERN    3939 - 4296
 13     INDIANS OF NORTH AMERICA--CONNECTICUT
           --LEDYARD--CLAIMS                        4297 - 4654
 14     INDIANS OF NORTH AMERICA--EDUCATION         4655 - 5000
-----------------------------------------------------------------
```

This screen indicates under the heading "Search Results" that that library has 5000 entries on Indians. In other words, you could do any number of substantial research projects on Indians. This large number of items also shows that subject searches are more useful if your topic is narrow; even the more limited entry *Indians of North America* contain over 300 items, many more than you would have time to look through.

To limit the subject search still further, you could add additional qualifying words. Adding the word *Sioux* to *Indians* to identify a specific tribe, the following appears on the screen:

```
Search Request:   S=SIOUX INDIANS                           LUIS
Search Results:   1 Entry Found                      Subject Index
------------------------------------------------------------------- T256
          SIOUX INDIANS
   1      *Search Under: DAKOTA INDIANS
```

This entry says that the preferred name for this Native American tribe is Dakota Indians, and that entries are cataloged under that name.

If the computer does not provide the cross-reference, you can look it up in the *Library of Congress Subject Headings*.

When you type:

s=dakota indians

results in the following list on the monitor:

```
Search Request:   S=DAKOTA INDIANS                          LUIS
Search Results:   155 Entries Found                  Subject Guide
------------------------------------------------------------------- T256
LINE:    BEGINNING ENTRY:                         INDEX RANGE:
  1      DAKOTA INDIANS                               1 -  12
  2      DAKOTA INDIANS                              13 -  24
  3      DAKOTA INDIANS                              25 -  36
  4      DAKOTA INDIANS--ART                         37 -  48
  5      DAKOTA INDIANS--CLAIMS                      49 -  60
  6      DAKOTA INDIANS--GOVERNMENT RELATIONS        61 -  72
  7      DAKOTA INDIANS--INDUSTRIES                  73 -  84
  8      DAKOTA INDIANS--LAND TRANSFERS              85 -  96
  9      DAKOTA INDIANS--LEGAL STATUS LAWS ETC--SOURCES  97 - 108
 10      DAKOTA INDIANS--RELIGION AND MYTHOLOGY     109 - 120
 11      DAKOTA INDIANS--TREATIES                   121 - 132
 12      DAKOTA INDIANS--WARS 1862 1865             133 - 144
 13      DAKOTA INDIANS--WARS 1876                  145 - 156
------------------------------------------------------------------------
```

In searching through these thirteen headings, you would find many interesting books on the Dakotas; however, until you limit your topic, this quantity of information would serve no purpose. If you are still searching for a topic, browsing through the lists and noticing how the information is organized may suggest topic possibilities.

You need to ask, "What about the Dakotas interests me most?" If you decided to look for novels depicting Dakota life, none of the headings so far would be helpful because the subject is not classified that way. So rather than further subject searching, you could turn to a key word search.

KEY WORD SEARCH.   The advantage of a key word search is that the computer simultaneously searches all three catalogs (author, title, and subject) to locate books on the key word or words you specify.

To search by key word you identify key descriptive words about the subject and join them with either *and* or *or* to locate sources. If you join the key words with *and*, you narrow your search to only those sources that include *both* terms — for example, *Dakota Indians and fiction*. If you join your key words with *or*, you will get all library entries that have *either* term included — for example, all entries with *Dakota Indians or* all with *fiction*, resulting in many more entries. To further limit the search, you would type

> k=Dakota Indians and fiction

and the following would appear on the screen:

```
Search Request:  K=DAKOTA INDIANS AND FICTION                       LUIS
Search Results:  7 Entries Found                          Keyword Index
----------------------------------------------------------------T256
     DATE  TITLE:                                  AUTHOR
  1  1988  A circle unbroken                       Hotze, Sollace
  2  1988  Waterlily                               Deloria, Ella Cara
  3  1984  Love medicine : a novel                 Erdrich, Louise
  4  1983  Good Thunder : a novel                  Solensten, John
  5  1979  Hanta yo                                Hill, Ruth Beebe
  6  1973  When the tree flowered;an authentic tale Neihardt, John Gnei
  7  1968  Dahcotah : or, Life and legend <microfilm> Eastman, Mary Hende
----------------------------------------------------------------------
```

The library has seven novels about the Dakotas, including *Love Medicine*. By typing the number 3, you would locate the same identifying information located through the author and title searches. However, the key word search has also identified six other books on the same topic, all written within twenty years, making it possible for you to compare other authors to Erdrich, if you choose. A key word search can thus help find and limit a research topic.

Using Call Numbers

Once you have determined through the catalog that your library owns a book you want to consult, you will use that book's call number to locate it in the stacks. Most academic libraries use the *Library of Congress system*, whose call numbers begin with letters. Some libraries still use the *Dewey decimal system*, whose call numbers consist entirely of numbers. In either case, the first letters or numbers in a call number indicate the general subject area. Because libraries shelve all books for a general subject area together, this tells you where in the library to find the book you want.

Be sure to copy down a book's call number exactly as it appears in the catalog. Most college libraries have *open stacks*, in which you can retrieve the book yourself. One wrong number or letter could lead you to a completely incorrect part of the library. If your library has *closed stacks*, you will need to give the call number to a librarian, who will go into the stacks and retrieve the book for you. If you have given the librarian the wrong call number, you won't get the book you want.

WRITING 5

Use the library's catalog to see what holdings it contains on your topic. Retrieve one of these books from the stacks, and check to see if it contains a bibliography that could lead you to other books. Record these findings in your research log.

Other Sources of Information

Many libraries own materials other than books and periodicals. Often these do not circulate. If you think one of the sources listed here might contain information relevant to your research, ask a librarian about your library's holdings.

GOVERNMENT DOCUMENTS.   The U.S. government publishes numerous reports, pamphlets, catalogs, and newsletters on virtually every issue of national concern. Reference books that can lead you to these sources include the *Monthly Catalogue of United States Government Publications* (monthly) and the *United States Government Publications Index,* both available on CD-ROM and on-line.

NONPRINT MEDIA.   Records, audiocassettes, videotapes, slides, photographs and other media are generally cataloged separately from book and periodical collections.

PAMPHLETS.   Pamphlets and brochures published by government agencies and private organizations are generally stored in a library's vertical file. The *Vertical File Index: A Subject and Title Index to Selected Pamphlet Material* (1932/35–present) lists many of the available titles.

SPECIAL COLLECTIONS.   Rare books, manuscripts, and items of local interest are commonly found in a special room or section of the library.

WRITING 6

For your current research project, identify one relevant source of information in your library's holdings other than a book or a periodical. Locate it and take notes in your research log on the usefulness of the source and the process you used to obtain it.

EVALUATING LIBRARY SOURCES

You will uncover many sources through your library research, but not all of them will be equally useful. So that you don't waste time and energy taking careful notes on sources that are only loosely related to your topic or that contain unreliable information, make sure to read each source critically by previewing, responding, and reviewing.

To preview a text, either read it through once quickly or read selected parts of it such as the chapter titles of a book or the abstract of a journal article. Your purpose in previewing is to determine whether the source is related closely enough to your topic to be useful and to decide whether you should read it further.

If you decide that the source will probably be useful, you need to read it more carefully and take notes on it. Critical reading at this stage consists of *responding* — entering into a conversation with a text while you read — and *reviewing* — coming to a critical understanding of the text as a whole. See Chapter 2 for more information on these activities.

One critical reading activity, *reviewing to evaluate,* is particularly important when writing a research essay. Whenever you review to evaluate, you are trying to determine the worth or validity of a source and the information it contains. This is crucial in library research because your final research essay will probably require several sources of sound information. If you determine that a source is irrelevant, unreliable, or out of date, you'll need to find a new one. Because you obviously want to know this as soon as possible, make the effort to evaluate each source continually — when reading, when taking notes, and when considering how to incorporate the source into your final research paper.

Evaluating Sources Yourself

The more you research a topic, the more of an expert you become at determining if a source is reliable and useful. When in doubt, confer with your instructor or a librarian. Here are some questions you can ask yourself.

SUBJECT.   Is the subject of the source directly related to my research question? Does it provide information that supports my view? Does it provide helpful context or background information? Does it contain quotations or facts that I will want to quote in my paper?

AUTHOR.   What do I already know about the author's reputation? Does the book or periodical provide any biographical information? Has my search uncovered any other works by this author? (They may be a clue to his or her expertise.) Is this author cited by other sources? Am I aware of any biases that might limit the author's credibility?

DATE.   When was this source published? Do my field and topic require current, up-to-date sources? Or would classic, well-established sources be more credible?

PUBLISHER. Who published this source? Is it a major publisher, a university press, or a scholarly organization that would subject material to a rigorous review procedure? Is it a special-interest publisher that produces works intended for particular audiences? What does this tell me about the nature of the source?

Using Professional Reviews

You can get expert help in evaluating books by consulting book reviews. To avoid a tedious hit-and-miss search, consult one of the several indexes that identify where and when a book was reviewed.

Book Review Index. This bimonthly index lists reviews of major books published in several hundred periodicals.

Current Book Review Citations. This annual index lists reviews published in more than 1000 periodicals.

WRITING 7

For at least one source you are considering for your research paper, consult three of the book review indexes listed in this section. Make a list of the references identified in each and notice the different information provided by each. Look up some of these reviews and take careful notes.

TAKING NOTES

Taking good notes will make the whole research process easier — from locating and remembering sources to using them effectively in your writing. For short research projects requiring only a few sources, it is easy to take careful notes in a research log or class notebook and refer to them as needed when writing your paper. Or you can *photocopy* whole articles or chapters and take them home for further study. However, for any research project requiring more than a few sources, you should develop a card-based system for recording the sources you consult and the information you find in them.

Bibliographic Cards

When you locate a useful source, write all the information necessary to find that source again on a 3″ × 5″ index card, using a separate card for each work consulted. You will need to provide complete bibliographic information for all the sources you use in your paper, so preparing the cards as you go along will make it easy, at the end, to arrange them in alphabetical order and prepare your reference list. (See Chapter 20.) The information to be included on the bibliographic cards includes:

FOR BOOKS

1. Call number or other location information
2. Full name(s) of author(s)
3. Full title and subtitle
4. Edition or volume number
5. Editor or translator
6. Place of publication
7. Publisher and date of publication
8. Inclusive page numbers for relevant sections in longer works

FOR PERIODICALS

1. Full name(s) of author(s)
2. Full title and subtitle of article
3. Periodical title
4. Periodical volume and number
5. Periodical date
6. Inclusive page numbers of articles
7. Library call number or other location information

PE
1405
.U6
M55
1991

Miller, Susan. Textual Carnivals.
    Carbondale: Southern Illinois UP,
    1991.

Bibliographic card using MLA documentation style

Note Cards

Note cards are used to record the relevant information you find in the research sources you consult. When you write your research essay, you will be working from these note cards, so be sure they contain all the information you need from every source you intend to use. Also try to make them *focused* on your particular research question, so that their relevance to your topic is immediately clear when you read through them later.

To fit as much information as possible on each note card, use 4″ × 6″ index cards. Using different sizes for bibliography cards (3″ × 5″) and note cards will also help you keep the two sets separate. Each note card should contain only one piece of information or one idea. This will allow you to arrange and rearrange the cards and thus the information in different ways as you think and write. At the top of each note card, identify the source by author and title, and note the page numbers on which the information appears. Many writers also include the category of information or a particular theme, subject, or argument for which the note provides support. Personal notes, including ideas for possible use of the information or cross-references to other information, should be clearly distinguished from the notes from the source — perhaps by putting the personal notes at the bottom in parentheses.

Lewis, Green Delusions, p. 230

Reasons for overpopulation in poor countries

Some experts believe that birth rates are linked to the "economic value" of children to their parents. Poor countries have higher birth rates because parents there rely on children to work for the family and to take care of them in old age. The more children, particularly sons, the better off the family is financially. In wealthier countries, parents have fewer children because they cost more in terms of education and they contribute less.

(Based on Caldwell and Cain——check these further?)

Note card containing a paraphrase

When recording information on your card, you must avoid *plagiarism*. You can do this by making distinctions between quoting directly, paraphrasing, and summarizing. A *direct quotation* is an exact duplication of the author's words in the original source. Put quotation marks around direct quotations on your note cards so that you will know later that these words are the author's, not yours. A *paraphrase* is a restatement of the author's words in your own words. Paraphrase to simplify or clarify the original author's point. A paraphrase is not necessarily shorter than the original source, but it must restate the original facts or ideas fully and correctly. A *summary* is a condensation or distillation of the main point of the original source. Like a paraphrase, a summary should be in your own words and all facts and ideas should be accurately represented.

Deciding when to quote, when to paraphrase, and when to summarize will require judgment on your part. The major advantage of quoting is that it allows you to decide later, in the course of writing the paper, whether to include a quotation or to paraphrase or summarize. However, copying down many long quotations can be time-consuming. Also, simply copying down a quotation may prevent you from thinking about the ideas expressed and from making them your own in a way that will benefit your understanding of the topic. In general, copy direct quotations only when the author's words are particularly lively or persuasive. Photocopying machines make it easy to collect direct quotations, but be sure to highlight the pertinent material or make notes to yourself on the copy so you can remember later what you wanted to quote and why. For ease of organizing notes, many researchers cut out the pertinent quotation and paste it to a note card.

A good paraphrase can help you better understand a difficult passage by simplifying complex sentence structure and vocabulary into language you are more comfortable with. Keep in mind, though, that in paraphrasing you have a responsibility to the source: be careful not to distort the author's ideas. Use paraphrases when you need to record details, but not exact words.

Because a summary boils a source down to its essentials, it is particularly useful when specific details in the source are not important or are irrelevant to your research question. You may often find that you can summarize several paragraphs or even an entire article or chapter in just a few sentences without losing any useful information. It is a good idea to note when a particular card contains a summary so you'll remember later that it leaves out detailed supporting information.

WRITING 8

Reread this chapter as though you were researching the question "What are the most important things students need to learn about a library?" First, create a bibliographic card for *The Working Writer*. Then write the following note cards: (1) a direct quotation; (2) a paraphrase of a passage (two to three paragraphs); (3) a summary of a longer section in one to three sentences. On the back of each note card, explain why you handled the material in the manner you chose.

WRITING 9

Describe the most important, useful, or surprising thing you have learned about the library since exploring it as part of your research project. Share your discovery with classmates, and listen to theirs. Are you comfortable in the library? Why or why not?

Chapter 19

Writing with Sources

*I really don't mind doing the research. The library, once you get to
know it, is a very friendly place. But when I go to write the paper I keep
forgetting all the rules about what to quote, and what not to
quote, and how to introduce quotations and not make them too long
or too short. It seems like that part could be less confusing.*

— JASON

LOCATING POTENTIAL SOURCES FOR A RESEARCH PROJECT IS ONE THING; deciding
which ones to include, where to use them, and how to incorporate them is
something else. Some writers begin making use of their sources in their very
earliest explanatory drafts, perhaps by trying out a pithy quotation to see how
it brings a paragraph into focus. Others prefer to wait until they have all or
most of their note cards in neat stacks in front of them before making any decisions about what to include. No matter how you begin writing with sources,
there comes a time when you need to incorporate them finally, smoothly, effectively, and correctly into your paper.

CONTROLLING YOUR RESOURCES

Once you've conducted some research and are ready to begin drafting,
you need to decide which sources to use and how to use them. You can't make
this decision based on how much work you spent finding and analyzing each
source; you have to decide based on how useful the source is in answering
your research question. In other words, you need to control your sources
rather than letting them control you.

Papers written in an effort "to get everything in" are source-driven and
all too often read like patch jobs of quotations loosely strung together. Your
goal should be to remain the director of the research production, your ideas
on center stage and your sources the supporting cast.

You may find that a potential source you decided not to take notes on
has become crucial, while notes that initially seemed central are now irrele-

vant. Don't be discouraged. Real research about real questions is vital and dynamic, which means it's always changing. Just as you can't expect your first working thesis to be your final thesis, you can't expect to know in advance which sources are going to prove most fruitful. And, of course, you can collect more information once you've begun drafting. At each step in the process you see your research question and answer more clearly, so the research you conduct as you draft may be the most useful of all.

The best way to ensure that you and your thesis remain in control is to make an outline first and then organize your notes according to it. (If you compose your outline on a word processor, it will be easier to make changes later.) If you do it the other way around — organizing your notes in a logical sequence and then writing an outline based on the sequence — you'll be tempted to find a place for every note and to gloss over areas where you haven't done enough research. By outlining first, you let the logical flow of your ideas create a blueprint for your paper. (Of course, your outline may change as your ideas continue to develop.) If you can't outline before you write, then be sure to begin writing before you arrange your note cards.

Once you've outlined or begun drafting and have a good sense of the shape of your paper, take time to organize your notes. Set aside bibliographic and note cards for sources that you don't think you're going to use. Put the rest of the bibliographic cards in alphabetical order by the authors' last names and arrange your note cards so that they correspond to your outline. Integrate field research notes as best you can. Finally, you may want to go back to your outline and annotate it to indicate which source goes where. This will also show you if there are any ideas that need more research.

Keep in mind that referring more than two or three times to a single source — unless it is itself the focus of your paper — undercuts your credibility and suggests overreliance on a single point of view. If you find you need to refer often to one source, make sure that you have sufficient references to other sources as well.

WRITING 1

Describe your experiences writing research papers. Were there requirements for using a certain number or kind of sources? Did you or your sources control the paper?

WRITING 2

If you haven't already done so, use your research log to draft a tentative thesis and working outline for your research paper. Then arrange your note cards according to that working outline.

QUOTING, PARAPHRASING, AND SUMMARIZING

Once you know which sources you want to use in your paper, you still have to decide how to use them. The notes you made during your research are in many forms. For some sources, you will have copied down direct quotations; for others you will have paraphrased or summarized important information. For some field sources you may have made extensive notes on background information, such as your interview subject's appearance. For some library sources you may have photocopied whole pages, highlighting useful passages. Simply because you've quoted or paraphrased a particular source in your notes, however, doesn't mean you have to use a quotation or paraphrase from this source in your paper. Once again, you must remain in control. Make decisions about how to use sources based on your goals, not on the format of your research notes.

Whenever you quote, paraphrase, or summarize, you must acknowledge your source through documentation. Different disciplines have different conventions for documentation. The examples in this chapter use the documentation style of the Modern Language Association (MLA), the style preferred in the languages and literature. (See Chapter 20 for details about the MLA system as well as the American Psychological Association [APA] style used in the social sciences.)

Quoting

To quote a source, you use the writer's or speaker's own words, reproducing them exactly as they were in the original source.

Direct quotation provides strong evidence and can add both life and authenticity to your paper. However, too much quotation can make it seem as though you have little to say for yourself. Long quotations also slow readers down and often have the unintended effect of inviting them to skip over the quoted material. Unless the source quoted is itself the topic of the paper (as in a literary interpretation), limit brief quotations to no more than two per page and long quotations to no more than one every three or four pages.

Deciding When to Quote

Direct quotations should be reserved for cases in which you cannot express the ideas better yourself. Using only strong, memorable quotations will make your writing stronger and more memorable as well. Use them when the original words are especially precise, clear, powerful, or vivid.

> **Precise.** Use direct quotations when the words are important in themselves or when they've been used to make fine but important distinctions.

> **Clear.** Use quotations when they are the clearest statement available.

Powerful. Let people speak for themselves when their words are especially strong. Powerful words are memorable; they stay in the reader's mind long after the page is turned.

Vivid. Use direct quotation when the language is lively and color-ful, when it reveals something of the author's or speaker's character and individuality.

Quoting Accurately and Effectively

To quote, you must use an author's or speaker's exact words. Slight changes in wording are permitted in certain cases but these must be clearly marked as your changes.

Although you can't change what a source says, you do have control over how much of it to use. Use only as long a quotation as you need to make your point. Remember that quotations should be used to support your points, not to introduce or make them. Be sure that when you shorten a quotation, you have not changed its meaning.

If you omit words within quotations for the sake of brevity, you must in-dicate that you have done so by using ellipsis points. Any changes or additions must be indicated with brackets.

ORIGINAL

The human communication environment has acquired biological complex-ity and planetary scale, but there are no scientists or activists monitoring it, theorizing about its health, or mounting campaigns to protect its resilience. Perhaps it's too new, too large to view as a whole, or too containing — we swim in a sea of information, in poet Gary Snyder's phrase. All the more rea-son to worry. New things have nastier surprises, big things are hard to change, and containing things are inescapable.

— STEWART BRAND, *The Media Lab*

INACCURATE QUOTATION

In The Media Lab, Steward Brand describes the control that is exerted by watchdog agencies over modern telecommunications: "The human communication environment . . ." (258).

By omitting certain words, the writer has changed the meaning of the original source.

INEFFECTIVE QUOTATION

In The Media Lab, Steward Brand notes that we have done little to mon-itor the growth of telecommunications. "Perhaps it's too new, too large to view as a whole, or too containing . . . All the more reason to worry. New things have nastier surprises, big things are hard to change, and containing things are inescapable" (258).

By quoting too much, the writer has allowed the quotation to introduce an important point rather than support it.

ACCURATE AND EFFECTIVE QUOTATION

In The Media Lab, Steward Brand notes that we have done little to monitor the growth of telecommunications. Modern communication technology may seem overwhelmingly new, big, and encompassing, but these are reasons for more vigilance, not less: "New things have nastier surprises, big things are hard to change, and containing things are inescapable" (258).

Integrating Quotations into Your Paper

Direct quotations are most effective when you integrate them smoothly into the flow of your paper. Readers should be able to follow your meaning easily and to see the relevance of the quotation immediately.

USING EMBEDDED OR BLOCK FORMAT. Brief quotations should be embedded in the main body of your text and enclosed in quotation marks. A brief quotation consists of four or fewer typed lines according to MLA style guidelines.

> Photo editor Tom Brennan took ten minutes to sort through my images and then told me, "Most photography editors wouldn't take more than two minutes to look at a portfolio."

Longer quotations should be set off in block format. Begin a new line, indent ten spaces (for MLA), and do not use quotation marks.

> Katie Kelly also focuses on Americans' peculiarly negative chauvinism, in this case the chauvinism of New York residents:
>> New Yorkers are a provincial lot. They wear their big city's accomplishments like blue ribbons. To anyone who will listen they boast of leading the world in everything from Mafia murders to porno moviehouses. They can also boast that their city produces more garbage than any other city in the world. (89)

INTRODUCING QUOTATIONS. Introduce all quoted material so that readers know who is speaking, what the quotation refers to, and where it is from. If the author or speaker is well known, it is especially useful to mention his or her name in an introductory signal phrase.

> Henry David Thoreau asserts in Walden, "The mass of men lead lives of quiet desperation" (5).

If your paper focuses on written works, you can introduce a quotation with the title rather than the author's name, as long as the reference is clear.

> Walden sets forth one individual's antidote against the "lives of quiet des-
> peration" led by the working class in mid-nineteenth-century America
> (Thoreau 5).

If neither the author nor the title of a written source is well known (or the
speaker in a field source), introduce the quotation with a brief explanation to
give your readers some context.

> Mary Catherine Bateson, daughter of anthropologist Margaret Mead, has
> become, in her own right, a student of modern civilization. In Composing
> a Life she writes, "The twentieth century has been called the century of
> the refugee because of the vast numbers of people uprooted by war and
> politics from their homes" (8).

EXPLAINING AND CLARIFYING QUOTATIONS.   Sometimes you will need to
explain a quotation in order to clarify why it is relevant and what it means in
the context of your discussion.

> In A Sand County Almanac, Aldo Leopold invites modern urban readers to
> confront what they lose by living in the city: "There are two spiritual dan-
> gers in not owning a farm. One is the danger of supposing that breakfast
> comes from the grocery, and the other that heat comes from the furnace"
> (6). Leopold sees city dwellers as self-centered children, blissfully but
> dangerously unaware of how their basic needs are met.

You may also need to clarify what a word or reference within the quotation
means. Do this by using square brackets.

> *UNCLEAR*
>
> Observing the remains of earwigs, sow bugs, moths, and spiders, Dillard
> reminds us that everything is changing, even in death: "Next week, if
> the other bodies are any indication, he will be shrunken and gray,
> webbed to the floor with dust."

> *CLEAR*
>
> Observing the remains of earwigs, sow bugs, moths, and spiders, Dillard
> reminds us that everything is changing, even in death: "Next week, if
> the other bodies are any indication, [the earwig] will be shrunken and
> gray, webbed to the floor with dust."

INTEGRATING QUOTATIONS GRAMMATICALLY.   A passage containing a quotation must follow all the rules of grammatical sentence structure — tenses
should be consistent, verbs and subjects should agree, and so on. If the form
of the quotation doesn't quite fit the grammar of your own sentences, you can
either quote less of the original source, change your sentences, or make a
slight alterations in the quotation. Use this last option sparingly, and always
indicate any change with brackets.

GRAMMATICALLY INCOMPATIBLE

If Thoreau thought that in his day, "The mass of men lead lives of quiet desperation" (Walden 5), what would he say of the masses today?

GRAMMATICALLY COMPATIBLE

If Thoreau thought that in his day, the "mass of men [led] lives of quiet desperation" (Walden 5), what would he say of the masses today?

GRAMMATICALLY COMPATIBLE

If Thoreau thought that in his day, the masses led "lives of quiet desperation" (Walden 5), what would he say of the masses today?

GRAMMATICALLY COMPATIBLE

In the nineteenth century, Thoreau stated, "The mass of men lead lives of quiet desperation" (Walden 5). What would he say of the masses today?

WRITING 3

Read through your research materials, highlighting any quotations you might want to incorporate directly into your paper. Use your research log to explore why you think these words should be quoted directly.

Paraphrasing

To paraphrase, you restate a source's ideas in your own words. The point of paraphrasing is to make the ideas clearer (both to your readers and to yourself) and to express the ideas in the way that best suits your purpose.

Deciding When to Paraphrase

In taking notes you may have written down or photocopied many quotations instead of taking the time to put an author's or speaker's ideas into your own words. As you draft, however, you should paraphrase or summarize most such information so that your paper doesn't turn into a string of undigested quotations.

Paraphrasing should generally re-create the original source's order, structure, and emphasis, and they should include most of its details. This means that a paraphrase is not usually much briefer than the original. Use paraphrases only when the original is already quite brief or when you need to present an author's or speaker's ideas in detail; otherwise, use a summary.

Paraphrasing Accurately and Effectively

Restate the source's ideas, but do so in your own words. You may need to rewrite a paraphrase several times in order to get it fully into your own voice. A paraphrase should say neither more nor less than the original source, and it should never distort the meaning of the source. The best way to make an accurate paraphrase is to stay close to the order and structure of the original passage and to reproduce its emphasis and details. However, don't use the same sentence patterns or vocabulary or you will risk inadvertently plagiarizing the source.

If the original source has used a well-established or technical term for a concept, you do not need to find a synonym for it. If you believe that the original source's exact words are the best possible expressions of some points, you may use brief direct quotations within your paraphrase, as long as you indicate these with quotation marks.

Keeping in mind the reason that you are including the source will help you decide how to paraphrase the ideas. Be careful, though, not to introduce your own comments or reflections in the middle of a paraphrase, unless you make it clear these are your thoughts, not the original author's or speaker's.

ORIGINAL

The human communication environment has acquired biological complexity and planetary scale, but there are no scientists or activists monitoring it, theorizing about its health, or mounting campaigns to protect its resilience. Perhaps it's too new, too large to view as a whole, or too containing — we swim in a sea of information, in poet Gary Snyder's phrase. All the more reason to worry. New things have nastier surprises, big things are hard to change, and containing things are inescapable.

— STEWART BRAND, *The Media Lab*

INACCURATE PARAPHRASE

In The Media Lab, Brand points out that the "communication environment" we live within is as complex and vast as any ecosystem on the planet. Yet no one monitors this environment, keeping track of its growth and warning us if something is about to go wrong. This is because the communication environment has become so large and all-encompassing in such a short time that we don't worry about it (258).

This paraphrase distorts the original passage by changing speculation ("perhaps") to assertion ("This is because").

ACCURATE PARAPHRASE

In The Media Lab, Brand points out that the "communication environment" we live within is as complex and vast as any ecosystem on the planet. Yet no one monitors this environment, keeping track of its growth and warning us if something is about to go wrong. This may be understandable, since the communication environment has become so large and all-encompassing in such a short time that we often overlook it. But this is exactly why we should worry: it's the very qualities of being recent, large, and all-encompassing that makes this environment potentially so dangerous (258).

WRITING 4

Read through your note cards for any passages you quoted directly from an original source. Find notes that now seem wordy, unclear, or longer than necessary for your purposes. Paraphrase any of these notes that you expect to use in your paper. Exchange your paraphrases and the originals with a classmate. Assess each other's work: Have you paraphrased the original source accurately? Have you used your own words and sentence structure to express the original idea?

Summarizing

To summarize, distill a source's words down to the main ideas and state these in your own words. A summary includes only the essentials of the original source, not the supporting details, and is consequently shorter than the original.

Deciding When to Summarize

Use summaries whenever your readers need to know only the main point that the original source makes, not the details of how the original makes this point.

You may have taken extensive notes on a particular article or observation only to discover in the course of drafting that all the detail you included is not necessary, given the correct focus of your paper. In such a case, you may be able to summarize your notes in a few sentences that effectively support your discussion.

Keep in mind that summaries are generalizations and that too many generalizations can make your writing vague and tedious. You should occasionally supplement your summaries with brief direct quotations or evocative details collected through observation in order to keep readers in touch with the original source.

Summarizing Accurately and Effectively

Summaries vary in length, and the length of the original source has no necessary relationship to the length of the summary you write. Depending on the focus of your paper, you may need to summarize an entire novel in a sentence or two, or you may need to summarize a brief journal article in two or three paragraphs. Remember that the more material you attempt to summarize in a short space, the more you will necessarily generalize and abstract it. Reduce a text as far as you can while still providing all the information your readers need to know. Be careful though, not to distort the original's meaning.

ORIGINAL

The human communication environment has acquired biological complexity and planetary scale, but there are no scientists or activists monitoring it, theorizing about its health, or mounting campaigns to protect its resilience. Perhaps it's too new, too large to view as a whole, or too containing — we swim in a sea of information, in poet Gary Snyder's phrase. All the more reason to worry. New things have nastier surprises, big things are hard to change, and containing things are inescapable.

— STEWART BRAND, *The Media Lab*

INACCURATE SUMMARY

The current telecommunications networks comprise a nasty, unchangeable, and inescapable environment (Brand 258).

ACCURATE SUMMARY

Steward Brand warns that we may soon regret not keeping a closer watch on the burgeoning telecommunications networks (258).

Guidelines for Using Quotation, Paraphrase, and Summary

Below are some rules of thumb to help you decide how to use sources in your paper.

QUOTATION

- To quote, use the author's or speaker's exact words.
- A quotation is the same length as in the source, although words may be omitted for brevity if the omission is indicated with ellipsis points.
- Use a quotation when the language of the original is particularly precise, clear, powerful, or vivid.

PARAPHRASE

- To paraphrase, put the author's or speaker's ideas in your own words.
- A paraphrase is about the same length as the passage in the source.
- Use a paraphrase when you need to include all or most of the details in the source.

SUMMARY

- To summarize, reduce the author's or speaker's ideas to the main points, and express these in your own words.
- A summary is shorter than the passage in the source.
- Use a summary when you need to include only the essential points in the source.

WRITING 5

Review your notes to find any sources on which you have taken particularly extensive notes. Would it be possible to condense these notes into a briefer summary of the entire work? Would it serve the purpose of your paper to do so? Why or why not?

USING DOCUMENTATION AND AVOIDING PLAGIARISM

Documentation is a systematic method for acknowledging sources. Documentation is important not only as an acknowledgment of indebtedness but also as a service to your readers and to later scholars. Knowledge in the academic community is cumulative, with one writer's work building on another's. After reading your paper, your readers may want to know more about a source you cited, perhaps in order to use it in papers of their own. Correct documentation helps these readers find the source quickly and easily. (See Chapter 20 for details of the MLA and APA styles.)

You do not need to document *common knowledge,* even if it is mentioned in or by your sources. Common knowledge is information that an educated person can be expected to know or any factual information that can be found in multiple sources. Examples include the dates of historical events, the names and locations of states and cities, the workings of political and economic systems, the general laws of science, and so on. However, when you read the work of authors who have specific opinions and interpretations of a piece of common knowledge and you use their opinions or interpretations in your paper, you need to give them credit through proper documentation.

Plagiarism is stealing ideas or information from somebody else and passing them off as your own. Whenever you introduce ideas or information from a source into your text, you need to cite the source for those ideas. Failing to cite a source is an unethical practice and at most colleges is grounds for discipline or even dismissal.

Not all plagiarism is intentional. Many writers are unaware of the guidelines for correctly indicating that they have borrowed words or ideas from someone else. Nevertheless, it is the writer's responsibility to learn these guidelines and follow them.

Keep in mind that when you paraphrase or summarize a source, you need to identify the author of those ideas just as surely as if you had quoted directly. The most common kind of inadvertent plagiarism is a paraphrase or summary of a source that stays too close to the writing or sentence structure of the original, sometimes including whole phrases from the original without quotation marks. To avoid plagiarism, use your own words to replace unimportant language in the original, place any particularly effective language within quotation marks, and be sure to cite the author and page number where you found the ideas in the source.

ORIGINAL

Notwithstanding the widely different opinions about Machiavelli's work and his personality there is at least one point in which we find a complete unanimity. All authors emphasize that Machiavelli is a "child of his age," that he is a typical witness to the Renaissance.

— ERNST CASSIER, *The Myth of the State*

PLAGIARIZED PARAPHRASE

Despite the widely different opinions about Machiavelli's work and personality, everyone agrees that he was a representative witness to the Renaissance (Cassier 43).

ACCEPTABLE PARAPHRASE

Although views on the work and personality of Machiavelli vary, everyone agrees that he was "a typical witness to the Renaissance" (Cassier 43).

Guidelines for Avoiding Plagiarism

1. When taking notes, include complete bibliographic or other source information for each note.
2. Enclose even short phrases borrowed from other sources within quotation marks.
3. Credit any paraphrased and summarized material as well as direct quotations.
4. Do not document common knowledge. Learn what is considered common knowledge within your community or the discipline within which you are writing your paper; if in doubt, ask your instructor.

WRITING 6

Read the following quotation from Mike Rose's *Lives on the Boundary*; then examine the three sentences that follow and explain why each is an example of plagiarism.

"The discourse of academics is marked by terms and expressions that represent an elaborate set of shared concepts and orientations; alienation, authoritarian personality, the social construction of self, determinism, hegemony, equilibrium, intentionality, recursion, reinforcement, and so on. This language weaves through so many lectures and textbooks, it is integral to so many learned discussions, that it is easy to forget what a forgein language it can be." (192)

1. The discourse of academics is marked by expressions that represent shared concepts.
2. Academic discourse is characterized by a particular set of coded words and ideas that are found throughout the college community.
3. Sometimes the talk of professors is as difficult for outsiders to understand as a forgein language is to a native speaker.

Chapter 20

Documenting Sources: MLA

E<small>ACH DISCIPLINE HAS DEVELOPED</small> its own conventions for documentation. The languages and literature use the style recommended by the Modern Language Association (MLA). Other fields in the humanities use a system of endnotes or footnotes. Social sciences use the style recommended by the American Psychological Association (APA). Natural sciences use the style recommended by the Council of Biology Editors (CBE) or a related style. You should use the documentation of the discipline for which you are writing; if you are in doubt, ask your instructor.

This chapter presents the most commonly used documentation system, the MLA.

MLA GUIDELINES

The Modern Language Association (MLA) system is the preferred form for documenting research sources in the languages and literature. The MLA system requires that all sources be briefly documented in text by an identifying name and page number (generally in parentheses) and that there be a Works Cited section at the end of the paper listing full publication information for each source cited. The MLA system is explained in detail in the *MLA Handbook for Writers of Research Papers*, 3rd ed. (New York: MLA, 1988), the book on which the information in this section is based.

Conventions for In-Text Citations

In-text citations identify ideas and information borrowed from other writers. They also refer readers to the end of the paper for complete publication information about each original source. The fields of languages and literature are not primarily concerned with when something was written but focus instead on writers and the internal qualities of texts. In-text citations of the MLA system therefore feature authors' names, book and article titles, and page numbers. The places and dates of publication are found only at the end in the Works Cited list. Following are some examples of how MLA in-text citation works. (See Chapter 21 for sample papers using this style of documentation.)

Single Work by One or More Authors

When you quote, paraphrase, or summarize the work of an author, you must include in the text of the paper the author's last name and the page or pages on which the original information appeared. Page numbers are inserted parenthetically, without the word *page* or abbreviation *p.* or *pp.*; authors' names may be mentioned in the text sentence or included parenthetically preceding the page number(s).

> Lewis Thomas notes that "some bacteria are only harmful to us if they make exotoxins" (76).

> In his 1974 book Lives of a Cell, Lewis Thomas explains simply and elegantly why bacteria endanger the human organism (74-79).

> We need only fear some bacteria "if they make exotoxins" (Thomas 76).

> Exotoxins make bacteria dangerous to humans (Thomas 76).

Note that a parenthetical reference at the end of a sentence comes before the period. There is no punctuation between the author's name and the page number(s).

If a work cited is by two or three authors, the text sentence or the parenthetical reference must include all the names: (Rombauer and Becker 715), (Child, Bertholle, and Beck 215). For works by more than three authors, you may list all the authors or, to avoid awkwardness, use the first author's name and add "et al." (Latin for "and others") without a comma: (Britton et al. 395).

Two or More Works by the Same Author

If your paper includes references to two or more works by the same author, your citation needs to distinguish the work to which you are referring. Either mention the title in your sentence or include a brief title in your parenthetical citation.

According to Lewis Thomas, "many bacteria only become dangerous if they manufacture exotoxins" (Lives 76).

"Many bacteria only become dangerous if they manufacture exotoxins" (Thomas, Lives 76).

Note that if a *parenthetical* citation includes both the author's name and a title, the two are separated by a comma; there is no comma between the title and the page number.

Unknown Author

When an author is unknown, as in some pamphlets, documents, and periodicals, identify the complete title in your sentence or include an abbreviated title in the parenthetical citation along with the page number.

According to Statistical Abstracts, the literary rate for Mexico stood at 75% for 1990, up 4% from census figures ten years earlier (374).

The government's ban on ivory even extends to piano keys, which now can be only plastic-coated ("Key Largo" 42).

Corporate or Organizational Author

When no author is listed for a work published by a corporation, organization, or association, indicate the entity's full title in the parenthetical reference: (Florida League of Women Voters 3).When such names are long, cite the organization in your sentence and put only the page number in parenthesis.

Authors with the Same Last Name

When you cite works by two or more authors with the same last name, include each author's first name either in your sentence or in the parenthetical citation: (Janice Clark 51).

Works in More than One Volume

When your sources include more than one volume of a multivolume work, indicate the pertinent volume number for each citation by placing it before the page number, followed by a colon and one space: (Hill 2: 70). If your sources include only one volume of a multivolume work, you need not specify the volume number in your in-text citation (you will specify it in your Works Cited list).

One-Page Works

When you cite a work that is only one page long (such as a newspaper or magazine article), it is not necessary to include the page number parenthetically. The author (or title if the author is unknown) is sufficient for readers to find the exact page number in your Works Cited list.

Quote from an Indirect Source

When a quotation or any information in your source is originally from another source, use the abbreviation "qtd. in."

> Lester Brown of Worldwatch feels that international agricultural pro-
> duction has reached its limit and that "we're going to be in trouble on
> the food front before this decade is out" (qt. in Mann 51).

Literary Works

In citing classic prose works that are available in various editions, provide additional information (such as chapter number or scene number) for readers who may be consulting a different edition. Use a semicolon to separate the page number of your source from this additional information: (331; bk. 10, ch. 5). In citing poems, use only line numbers, indicating that you are doing so by including the word *line* or *lines* in the first reference.

> In "The Mother," Gwendolyn Brooks remembers " . . . the children you
> got that you did not get, / The damp small pulps with a little or with no
> hair . . ." (lines 1-2). Later she recalls children that "never giggled or
> planned or cried" (30).

Cite verse plays using arabic numberals for act, scene, and line numbers, separated by periods: (*Hamlet* 4.4.31–39.)

More than One Work in a Citation

To cite more than one work in a single parenthetical reference, separate the references with semicolons: (Aronson, *Golden Shore* 177; Didion 49–50).

Long Quotation Set Off from Text

For quotations of four or more lines, which are set off from the text by indenting ten spaces, the parenthetical citation follows any end punctuation and is not followed by a period.

Conventions for Endnotes and Footnotes

MLA style allows notes only for comments, explanations, or information that cannot be accommodated in the text of the paper, for citation of several different sources, or for comments on sources. In general, omit such additional information unless it is necessary for clarification or justification of the text.

If notes are necessary, insert a raised (superscript) numeral at the reference point in the text; the note itself should be introduced by a corresponding raised numeral and indented.

TEXT WITH SUPERSCRIPT

The standard ingredients for guacamole include avocadoes, lemon juice, onion, tomatoes, coriander, salt, and pepper.[1] Hurtado's poem, however, gives this traditional dish a whole new twist (lines 10-17).

NOTE

[1]For variations see Beard 314, Egerton 197, Eckhardt 92, and Kafka 26. Beard's version, which includes olives and green peppers, is the most unusual.

Complete publication information for the references listed in the note would appear in the Works Cited list. Footnotes are placed, single-spaced, at the bottom of the page on which their text references appear. Endnotes are placed, double-spaced, on a separate page at the end of the paper (before the Works Cited), with the title *Note* or *Notes*. (For examples of format and use of endnotes, see Chapter 21.)

Conventions for Works Cited

All sources mentioned in a paper should be identified in a list of Works Cited at the end of the paper. The Works Cited list should follow specific rules for formatting and punctuation so that the reader can readily find information.

FORMAT.   After the final page of the paper, title a separate page "Works Cited," an inch from the top of the page, centered, but not underlined and not in quotation marks. (If you are required to list all the works you have read in researching the topic, title the list "Works Consulted.") Number the page, following in sequence from the last page of your paper.

Double-space between the title and first entry. Begin each entry at the left margin and indent the second and subsequent lines of the entry five spaces. Double-space both between and within entries. If the list runs to more than a page, continue the page numbering in sequence but do not repeat the Works Cited title.

ORDER OF ENTRIES.   Alphabetize your list of entries according to authors' last names. For entries by an unknown author, alphabetize according to the first word of the title (excluding an initial *A*, *An*, or *The*).

FORMAT FOR ENTRIES.   There are many variations on the following general formats to accommodate various kinds of sources. The following formats are the three most common.

GENERAL FORMAT FOR BOOKS

two spaces   two spaces

Author(s). |Book Title. |City of publication, with country or state postal
Indent 5
spaces| abbreviation if needed: ¦Publisher, ¦year of publication.

one space   one space

GENERAL FORMAT FOR JOURNAL ARTICLES

two spaces   two spaces   one space   one space

Author(s). | "Article Title." ⌐Journal Title ↓volume number (year):
Indent 5
spaces| inclusive page numbers.   one space

GENERAL FORMAT FOR MAGAZINE AND NEWSPAPER ARTICLES

two spaces   two spaces   one space

Author(s). | "Article Title." ¦Publication Title date: inclusive page
Indent 5
spaces| numbers.   one space

PUNCTUATION.   In general, each major item of information (author, article or book title, edition, publication information) is followed by a period; such periods are followed by two spaces. For books, a colon separates the city from the publisher; for periodicals, a colon separates the date of publication from the page number(s). Commas separate multiple authors' names; commas also separate a book's publisher from the year of publication. The publication year of a journal is enclosed in parentheses.

AUTHORS.   The first author in an entry is listed last name first, followed by a comma and the first name or initial(s). For a work with more than one author, subsequent names are listed first name first. When more than one work is included by the same author, three hyphens are used for the name in entries after the first.

TITLES.   Titles and subtitles are listed in full. Capitalize the first, last, and all principal words. Underline the titles of books and periodicals; put quotation marks around the titles of essays, poems, articles, short stories, and so forth, that are part of a larger work.

PUBLISHERS.   Abbreviate publishers' names as discussed under "Abbreviations." If the title page indicates that a book is published under an imprint (for example, Arbor House is an imprint of William Morrow), list both imprint and publisher, separated by a hyphen (Arbor-Morrow).

DATES AND PAGE NUMBERS.   For books and journals, give only the year of publication. The year for books is followed by a period; the year for periodicals is within parentheses and is followed by a colon. For dates of weekly magazines and newspapers, use no commas to separate elements, and put the day before the month (25 Sept. 1954). For monthly magazines, give the month and the year, not separated by a comma. In the latter three cases, the date is followed by a colon.

Inclusive page numbers are separated by a hyphen with no space before or after (36-45); use all digits for second page numbers up to 99 and the last two digits only for numbers above 99 (130-38) unless the full sequence is needed for clarity (198-210). If subsequent pages do not follow consecutively (as is the case in a newspaper story), use a plus sign after the final consecutive page (39+, 52-55+).

ABBREVIATIONS.   In general, do not use state and country names with the city of publication. But when the state or country is necessary for clarity (to distinguish between Newark, NJ, and Newark, DE, for instance), use the post office abbreviations. Publishers' names are abbreviated by dropping the words *Press, Company,* and so forth ("Blair" for "Blair Press"); by using only the first in a series of names ("Farrar" for "Farrar, Straus & Giroux"); and by using only the last name of a person ("Abrams" for "Harry N. Abrams"). *University* and *Press* are abbreviated "U" and "P," with no periods (Columbia UP; U of Chicago P). All months except May, June, and July are abbreviated. For a book, if no publisher or date of publication is given, use the abbreviations "n.p." or "n.d."

Following are some examples of the Works Cited format for a variety of different sources. For sample Works Cited lists, see the first three papers in Chapter 21.

Documenting Books

Book by One Author

Thomas, Lewis. Lives of a Cell: Notes of a Biology Watcher. New York:
    Viking, 1974.

Book by Two or Three Authors

Fulwiler, Toby, and Alan Hayakawa. The Blair Handbook. Boston:
    Blair-Prentice, 1994.

Book by More than Three Authors

Britton, James, et al. The Development of Writing Abilities (11-18).
    London: Macmillan Education, 1975.

If there are more than three authors, you have the option of using the Latin abbreviation "et al." ("and others") or listing all authors' names in full as they appear on the title page.

Book by a Corporation, Association, or Organization

U.S. Coast Guard Auxiliary. Boating Skills and Seamanship.
    Washington: Coast Guard Auxiliary National Board, 1988.

Alphabetize by the name of the organization.

Revised Edition of a Book

Hayakawa, S. I. Language in Thought and Action. 4th ed. New York:
    Harcourt, 1978.

Edited Book

Hoy, Pat C., II, Esther H. Shor, and Robert DiYanni, eds. Women's
    Voices: Visions and Perspectives. New York: McGraw, 1990.

Book with an Editor and Author

Britton, James. Prospect and Retrospect. Ed. Gordon Pradl. Upper
    Montclair, NJ: Boynton, 1982.

Book in More than One Volume

Waldrep, Tom, ed. Writers on Writing. 2 vols. New York: Random,
    1985-88.

When separate volumes were published in different years, include inclusive dates.

One Volume of a Multivolume Book

Waldrep, Tom, ed. Writers on Writing. Vol. 2. New York: Random,
    1988.

When each volume has an individual title, list the volume's full publication information first, followed by series information (number of volumes, dates).

Churchill, Winston S. Triumph and Tragedy. Boston: Houghton, 1953.
    Vol 6. of The Second World War. 6 vols. 1948-53.

Translated Book

Camus, Albert. The Stranger. Trans. Stuart Gilbert. New York:
    Random, 1946.

Book in a Series

Magistrale, Anthony. Stephen King, The Second Decade: Danse
    Macabre to The Dark Half. Twayne English Authors Ser. 599. New
    York: Twayne-Macmillan, 1992.

Add series information after the title. Book titles within another title are not
underlined.

Reprinted Book

Hurston, Zora Neal. Their Eyes Were Watching God. 1937. New York:
    Perennial-Harper, 1990.

Add the original publication date after the title; then cite the current edition
information.

Introduction, Preface, Foreword, or Afterword in a Book

Holroyd, Michael. Preface. The Naked Civil Servant. By Quentin
    Crisp. New York: Plume-NAL, 1983.

Odell, Lee. Foreword. Writing across the Disciplines: Research into
    Practice. Ed. Art Young and Toby Fulwiler. Upper Montclair, NJ:
    Boynton, 1986.

Work in an Anthology or Chapter in an Edited Collection

Donne, John. "The Good-Morrow." The Metaphysical Poets. Ed. Helen
    Gardner. Balitmore: Penguin, 1957. 58.
Gay, John. The Beggar's Opera. British Dramatists from Dryden to
    Sheridan. Ed. George H. Nettleton and Arthur E. Case. Carbondale:
    Southern Illinois UP, 1975. 530-65.
Lispector, Clarice. "The Departure of the Train." Trans. Alexis
    Levitin. Latin American Writers: Thirty Stories. Ed. Gabriella
    Ibieta. New York: St. Martin's, 1993. 245-58.

Enclose the title of the work in quotation marks unless the work was originally
published as a book, in which case underline it. At the end of the entry, add
inclusive page numbers for the selection. When citing two or more selections
from one anthology, list the anthology separately under the editor's name.

Selection entries will then need to include only a cross-reference to the anthology entry.

> Donne, John. "The Good-Morrow." Gardner 58.

Periodical Article Reprinted in a Collection

> Emig, Janet. "Writing as a Mode of Learning." College Composition
> and Communication 28 (1977): 122-28. Rpt. in The Web of
> Meaning. Ed. Janet Emig. Upper Montclair, NJ: Boynton, 1983.
> 123-31.

Include the full citation for the original periodical publication, followed by "Rpt. in" ("Reprinted in") and the book publication information. Give inclusive page numbers for both sources.

Article in a Reference Book

> "Behn, Aphra." The Concise Columbia Encyclopedia. 1983 ed.
> Miller, Peter L. "The Power of Flight." The Encyclopedia of Insects.
> Ed. Christopher O'Toole. New York: Facts on File, 1986. 18-19.

If the article is signed, begin with the author's name. For commonly known reference works, full publication information and editor's names are unnecessary. Page and volume numbers are unnecessary when entries are arranged alphabetically.

Anonymous Book

> The World Almanac and Book of Facts. New York: World Almanac-
> Pharos, 1993.

Alphabetize by title, excluding an initial *A*, *An*, or *The*.

Government Document

> United States. Central Intelligence Agency. National Basic Intelligence
> Fact Book. Washington: GPO, 1980.

If the author is identified, begin with that name. If not, begin with the government (country or state), followed by the agency or organization. The Government Printing Office is abbreviated GPO.

Dissertation

> Kitzhaber, Albert R. "Rhetoric in American Colleges." Diss. U of
> Washington, 1953.

Put the title in quotation marks. Include the university name and the year. For a published dissertation, underline the title and add publication information as for a book, including the order number if the publisher is University Microfilms International UMI.

Documenting Periodicals

Article, Story, or Poem in a Monthly or Bimonthly Magazine

Linn, Robert L., and Stephen B. Dunbar. "The Nation's Report Card
    Goes Home." Phi Delta Kappan Oct. 1990: 127-43.

Abbreviate all months except May, June, and July. Hyphenate months for bimonthlies (July-Aug. 1993). Do not list volume or issue numbers.

Article, Story, or Poem in a Weekly Magazine

Updike, John. "His Mother inside Him." New Yorker 20 Apr. 1992:
    34-36.

The publication date is inverted.

Article in a Daily Newspaper

Brody, Jane E. "Doctors Get Poor Marks for Nutrition Knowledge."
    New York Times 10 Feb. 1992, natl. ed.: B7.
"Redistricting Reconsidered." Washington Post 12 May 1992: B2.

If the article is unsigned, begin with its title. Give the name of the newspaper as it appears on the masthead, but drop any introductory *A, An,* or *The.* If the city is not in the name, it should follow the name in brackets: El Diario [Los Angeles]. Include with the page number the letter that designates a separately numbered section; if sections are numbered consecutively, list the section number (sec. 2) before the colon, preceded by a comma.

Article in a Journal Paginated by Volume

Harris, Joseph. "The Other Reader." Journal of Advanced Composition
    12 (1992): 34-36.

If page numbers are continuous from one issue to the next throughout the year, include only the volume number and year, not the issue number or month.

Article in a Journal Paginated by Issue

Tiffin, Helen. "Post-Colonialism, Post-Modernism, and the
    Rehabilitation of Post Colonial History." Journal of Commonwealth
    Literature 23.1 (1988): 169-81.

If each issue begins with page 1, include the volume number followed by a period and the issue number. Do not include the month of publication.

Editorial

> "Price Support Goes South." Editorial. Burlington Free Press 5 June
> 1990: A10.

If signed, list the author's name first.

Letter to the Editor and Reply

> Kempthorne, Charles. Letter. Kansas City Star 26 July 1992: A16.
> Massing, Michael. Reply to letter of Peter Dale Scott. New York
> Review of Books 4 Mar. 1993: 57.

Review

> Rev. of Bone, by Faye Myenne Ng. New Yorker 8 Feb. 1992: 113.
> Kramer, Mimi. "Victims." Rev. of 'Tis Pity She's a Whore. New York
> Shakespeare Festival. New Yorker 20 Apr. 1992: 78-79.

If a review is unsigned and untitled, begin the entry "Rev. of"; alphabetize by the name of the work reviewed. If the review is unsigned but titled, begin with the title. If the review is of a performance, add pertinent descriptive information such as director, composer, or major performers.

Documenting Other Sources

Pamphlet

Cite as you would a book.

Cartoon

> Roberts, Victoria. Cartoon. New Yorker 13 July 1992: 34.
> MacNelly, Jeff. "Shoe." Cartoon. Florida Today [Melbourne] 13 June
> 1993: 8D.

Computer Software

> Fastfile. Computer software. Computerworks, 1992. MS-DOS, disk.

List title first if the author is unknown. Name the distributor and the year published. List other specifications (such as the operating system, the units of memory, and the computer on which the program can be used) as helpful.

Film or Videocassette

Casablanca. Dir. Michael Curtiz. With Humphrey Bogart and Ingrid
  Bergman. Warner Bros., 1942.

Begin with the title followed by the director, the studio, and the year released.
Including the names of lead actors and other personnel following the director's
name is optional. If your essay is concerned with a particular person's work on
a film, lead with that person's name.

Lewis, Joseph H., dir. Gun Crazy. Screenplay by Dalton Trumbo. King
  Bros., 1950.

Personal Interview

Holden, James. Personal interview. 12 Jan. 1993.
Morser, John. Professor of Political Science, U of Wisconsin.
  Telephone interview. 15 Dec. 1993.

Begin with the interviewee's name, and specify the kind of interview and the
date. Identify the individual's position if it is important to the purpose of the
interview.

Published or Broadcast Interview

Steinglass, David. Interview. Counterpoint. 7 May 1970: 3-4.
Lee, Spike. Interview. Tony Brown's Journal. PBS. WPBT, Miami.
  20 Feb. 1993.

Begin with the interviewee's name. Include appropriate publication information for a periodical or book, and appropriate broadcast information for a radio or television program.

Unpublished Lecture, Public Address, or Speech

Graves, Donald. "When Bad Things Happen to Good Ideas." NCTE
  Convention. St. Louis, 21 Nov. 1989.

Begin with the speaker, followed by the title of the address (if any), the meeting (and sponsoring organization if needed), the location, and date. If untitled,
use a descriptive label (such as *Speech*) with no quotation marks.

Personal or Unpublished Letter

Friedman, Paul. Letter to the author. 18 Mar. 1992.

Begin with the name of the letter writer, and specify the letter's audience.
Include the date written if known, the date received if not. To cite an unpub-

lished letter from an archive or private collection, include information that locates the holding (for example, "Quinn-Adams Papers. Lexington Historical Society. Lexington, KY").

Published Letter

> Smith, Malcolm. "Letter to Susan." 15 Apr. 1974. The Collected Letters of Malcolm Smith. Ed. Sarah Smith. Los Angeles: Motorcycle, 1989. 23.

Cite a published letter like a selection from an anthology. Specify the audience in the letter title. Include the date of the letter immediately following its title. Also include the page number(s) following the publishing information. In citing more than one letter from a collection, cite only the entire work and list dates and individual page numbers in the text.

Map

> Northwest United States. Map. Seattle: Maps Unlimited, 1978.

Cite as you would a book by an unknown author. Underline the title and identify it as a map or chart.

Performance

> Rumors. By Neil Simon. Dir. Gene Saks. Broadhurst Theater, New York. 17 Nov. 1988.
> Bissex, Rachel. Folk Songs. Flynn Theater, Burlington, VT. 14 May 1990.

Identify the pertinent details such as title, place, and date of performance. If you focus on a particular person (such as the director or conductor), lead with that person's name. For a recital or individual concert, lead with the performer's name.

Recording

> Marley, Bob, and the Wailers. "Buffalo Soldier." Legend. Island Records, 422 846 210-4, 1984.
> Mahler, Gustav. Symphony no. 5. Compact disc. Cond. Seiji Ozawa. Boston Symphony Orch. Philips, 432 141-2, 1991.

Depending on the focus of your essay, begin with the artist, composer, or conductor. Enclose song titles in quotation marks, followed by the recording title underlined. (Do not underline musical compositions identified only by form, number, and key.) Specify the recording format for a tape or compact disc. End with the company label, the catalog number, and the date of issue.

Television or Radio Program

"Emissary." Star Trek: Deep Space Nine. Teleplay by Michael Pillar.
    Story by Rick Berman and Michael Pillar. Dir. David Carson. Fox.
    WFLX, West Palm Beach. 9 Jan. 1993.

If the program is not an episode of a series or the episode is untitled, begin
with the program title. Include the network, the station and city, and the date
of broadcast. Including other information (such as narrator, writer, director,
performers) depends on the purpose of your citation.

Work of Art

McIntyre, Linda. Colors. Art Inst. of Chicago.
Holbein, Hans. Portrait of Erasmus. The Louvre, Paris. P. 148 in The
    Louvre Museum. By Germain Bazin. New York: Abrams, n.d.

Begin with the artist's name. Follow with the title, and conclude with the location. If your source is a book, give pertinent publication information.

Documenting More than One Source by the Same Author

Subsequent Source by the Same Author

Thomas, Lewis. Lives of a Cell: Notes of a Biology Watcher. New York:
    Viking, 1974.
---. The Medusa and the Snail: More Notes of a Biology Watcher. New
    York: Viking, 1979.

The three hyphens stand for the same name (or names) in the previous publication.

Handout: Photocopy, Mimeograph, or Unpublished Paper

Clarke, John. "Issue Tree." Handout, History of Education, U of
    Vermont, 1983.

Illustration: Drawing, Photograph, or Transparency

"Vital Statistics." Chart. Car and Driver Aug. 1992: 74.

If your essay deals, for example, with the work of a particular photographer,
you should lead with the creator's name. Otherwise, lead with the title, or, if
untitled, lead with the identifying label without quotation marks.

Chapter 21

Research Essays: A Sampler

T HIS CHAPTER PROVIDES SAMPLES OF FOUR RESEARCH PAPERS, three following Modern Language Association (MLA) format and documentation conventions and one following American Psychological Association (APA) conventions. Each of the student papers has been edited slightly for publication but remains largely as originally written. Each paper contains annotations explaining the format and documentation conventions. (For a full discussion of these conventions, see Chapter 20.)

PERSONAL RESEARCH ESSAY: MLA STYLE

The following research essay, "How to Become a Photographer's Assistant," resulted from an assignment asking students to investigate a career interest and report on it in an informal paper. Zoe Reynders writes in her own casual, personal voice yet uses careful library research (and some field research), which she documents according to the conventions of the Modern Language Association (MLA).

Reynders' paper illustrates the simple MLA style of identifying the writer of the paper and other pertinent academic information in the upper left-hand corner of the first page, followed by the title, centered. Page numbers are in the top right corner, without further punctuation or identification. Some instructors want students to put their last names at the top of each page, just before the page number, and others consider this unnecessary, although it is specified as MLA style.

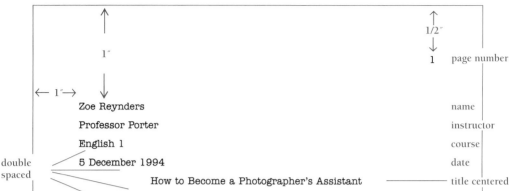

1/2″

1   page number

Zoe Reynders   name

Professor Porter   instructor

English 1   course

5 December 1994   date

How to Become a Photographer's Assistant   ——— title centered

double spaced

Writer opens with question to raise interest.

What makes a good advertising photograph? For Clint Clemens, a commercial photographer out of Boston, the answer is simplicity, and he thinks that many photographers lose sight of that. "They complicate it too much," he said in a recent interview. "Too often there isn't a simple statement or any purity of thought or elegance"

Clemens is quoted in source written by Redmond.

(qtd. in Redmond 35). He practices what he preaches; in many a magazine you will see examples of his work: sleek, black cars or a shiny, silver pen on a dark background.

Writer introduces two different answers to her question.

Annie Leibovitz, the portrait photographer of the nineties, head photographer for Vanity Fair magazine, and onetime Rolling Stone magazine staff photographer, has a different approach. Her photos range from Bette Midler lounging naked in a bed of roses to Dolly Parton standing juxtaposed against Arnold Schwarzenegger's biceps. "My pictures are really based on the encounter I have with the person,"

Author is introduced in paragraph; only page reference is necessary.

Liebovitz says. "I'm sure what I do know about them before I meet them is thrown in, but it's really based on the timing and the moment" (23). This type of vague guidance makes it hard for confused and inexperienced students like me to grasp any clue as to what is really wanted, what is necessary to succeed in the ever more competitive market of photography.

Writer introduces herself and her problem.

Here I am then, a lowly college student without access to a good darkroom, having no portfolio to show, attempting to get a commercial photography internship in New York City for the summer as a first step toward becoming a professional photographer. With a little research, however, I've learned the steps to setting up an internship: First, establish contact through writing a letter and sending a résumé, then push your portfolio--mail it, drop it, call, recall, pester. In the

2

process I've also learned that in commercial photography the emphasis is on commercial. Talent alone really isn't enough. If you don't represent yourself correctly, you may never get the chance to show off your photography talents.

First person and contractions establish informal tone.

This is understandable. An average photo shoot that will cover one full page in a relatively popular magazine can be worth anywhere from $2,000 to $200,000 and can take anywhere from one hour to three weeks to shoot. And the better known you are, the more you can charge, and the more you are used. According to Catherine Calhoun, "The current depressed market . . . is characterized by tried-and-true imagery, slick professionalism, and intense competition." But all this seemed, at first, irrelevant to me. I thought, I'm just in it for the experience, not the money, not the glamour nor the fame. Photography is fun, it is something I enjoy. Wrong.

Author is introduced in signal phrase.

No page number is needed for one page source.

Writer structures paper according to her quest for information.

I've already learned that not every aspect of taking photographs is that much fun. "Practically every photographer has a preconceived notion of what he will shoot and what he won't shoot," writes Richard Sharabura in his lively book Shoot Your Way to a $-Million. He continues, "This is probably one of the most common stumbling blocks to financial success" (56). Commercial photographers cannot pick and choose to do only the assignments they want or they would lose clients.

Fragment is acceptable in informal paper.

Writer continues informal approach by directly addressing the reader.

What? You're not interested in shooting a cat food ad? This can deter creative photographers because it seems more obvious today that companies approach advertising conservatively. Special-effects photography and the unconventional photo don't sell products. John Jay, creative director of Bloomingdale's, reiterates this: "There's a lot more money on the line than there used to be. . . . There's not a lot of encouragement for experimentation" (qtd. in Redmond 35).

Book title introduced because it is popular and catchy.

Position of author mentioned to lend authority.

I've also learned that becoming a photographer's assistant is a creative void and does not entail ever taking any actual pictures. Committing myself to interning this summer won't mean blissful photo shoots with famous people. It will mean ten hours a day of getting up

3

before the sun, packing photography equipment, carrying supplies, load-
ing cameras, setting up lights, answering phones, and walking someone's dog. Nevertheless, you have to prove that you are also competent. A highly paid photographer is not going to risk having an idiot
load preexposed film into a camera. This is where the importance of
the portfolio comes in. You are not showing your portfolio to get a commercial photography job for yourself; you have to demonstrate that you
understand and respect the art of a finely produced photo.

Structure based on quest for information continues.

So, after writing my polite letters to incredibly famous New York
photographers, I next took about 50 of what I consider my best images
to the leading photographer at the University of Vermont, in hopes of
identifying 10 or 15 of my pictures that may be portfolio quality. Photo
editor Tom Brennan took ten minutes to sort through my images and
then told me, "Most photography editors wouldn't take more than two
minutes to look at a portfolio."

Date of personal interview can be found on Works Cited page.

Again, I became nervous, not because I don't think I could handle
the job, but because of the strict professionalism of these people. I
question if my photos are strong enough to make an impact, if I have
what it takes to stand apart from the crowd of would-be photographers.
Brennan chose 12 images he thought would be good. They do not have
a consistent theme or subject; some are in black and white, others are
slides or color negatives. "What I am looking for are your photos that
show some kind of feeling or atmosphere," he said. Some of the photos
he chose, I would have too. Others, I wouldn't have looked twice at. It's
clear that I will include everything from a landscape to a portrait
of my father to pictures of kids, and even an egg. The more variety,
the better to demonstrate a wide range of skills.

Further citation of Brennan is unnecessary because source is clear.

Henrietta Brackman, author of The Perfect Portfolio, carefully outlines how to edit photos for a portfolio: First the work has to be good.
(Who could have guessed?) But it is also important to examine every
detail, to make sure that the photo is printed and developed at its best
and that the picture is intelligible to the eventual viewer. I've done lots

Paraphrased information is documented.

4

Partial quotation is worked into the sentence in a grammatically correct way.

of trick photography, but I am going to stick to my traditional photographs. Bob Lynn, the graphics director of The Ledger-Star, says he "hopes to find surprises, not clichés" (qtd. in Upton 23). I know my photos don't belong in the family album; they are not clichés.

Lost in the technicalities of this whole process, I almost forgot why I really want this internship in the first place--for the practice and hands-on experience. But I hope to learn a more important lesson--to understand how and when to take career chances. An internship, I remind myself, will also make the outside world seem a little less frightening.

Writer concludes with her own ideas rather than borrowed ones.

So, I'll keep sitting around hoping for a break. I can't guarantee that this research method for landing an internship will work; it still remains to be tried and tested. To my knowledge there is no foolproof formula for a successful start. Like everybody else before me, I'm creating my own method as I go along.

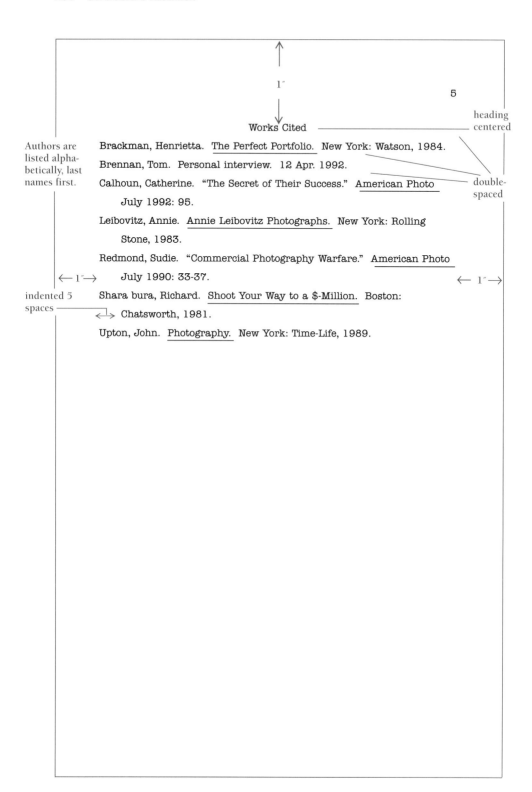

1″

5

Works Cited

heading
centered

Authors are
listed alpha-
betically, last
names first.

Brackman, Henrietta. The Perfect Portfolio. New York: Watson, 1984.

Brennan, Tom. Personal interview. 12 Apr. 1992.

Calhoun, Catherine. "The Secret of Their Success." American Photo

July 1992: 95.

double-
spaced

Leibovitz, Annie. Annie Leibovitz Photographs. New York: Rolling

Stone, 1983.

Redmond, Sudie. "Commercial Photography Warfare." American Photo

← 1″ →   July 1990: 33-37.

← 1″ →

indented 5
spaces

Shara bura, Richard. Shoot Your Way to a $-Million. Boston:

Chatsworth, 1981.

Upton, John. Photography. New York: Time-Life, 1989.

LITERARY RESEARCH ESSAY: MLA STYLE

In literary research essays, students are expected to read a work of literature, interpret it, and support their interpretation through research. The research in such papers commonly uses two kinds of sources: primary (the literary works themselves, from which students cite passages) and secondary (the opinions of literary experts found in books or periodicals).

The following paper was written by Andrew Turner in a first-year English class. Students were asked to focus on a topic of personal interest about the author Henry David Thoreau and to support their own reading of Thoreau's work with outside sources.

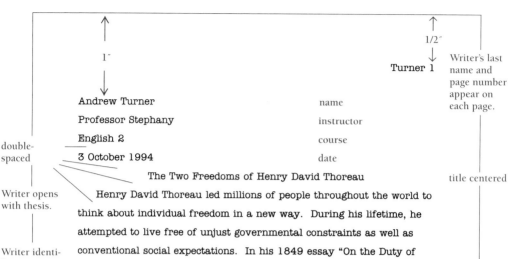

1″

1/2″

Turner 1

Andrew Turner — name

Professor Stephany — instructor

English 2 — course

double-spaced

3 October 1994 — date

The Two Freedoms of Henry David Thoreau — title centered

Writer opens with thesis.

Henry David Thoreau led millions of people throughout the world to think about individual freedom in a new way. During his lifetime, he attempted to live free of unjust governmental constraints as well as

Writer identifies two works to be examined.

conventional social expectations. In his 1849 essay "On the Duty of Civil Disobedience," he makes his strongest case against governmental interface in the lives of citizens. In his 1854 book Walden, or, Life in the Woods, he makes the case for living free from social conventions and expectations.

Only the page number is needed when source is introduced in the sentence.

Thoreau opens "Civil Disobedience" with his statement that "that government is best which governs not at all" (222). He argues that a

Abbreviated title is used after work has been identified by full title.

government should allow its people to be as free as possible, providing for the needs of the people without infringing on their daily lives. Thoreau explains, "The government does not concern me much, and I shall bestow the fewest possible thoughts on it. It is not for many moments that I live under a government" ("Civil" 238). In other words, in his daily life he attends to his business of eating, sleeping, and earning a living and not dealing in any noticeable way with an entity called "a government."

Short title is added to page number because two works by the author appear on Works Cited page.

Because Thoreau did not want his freedom overshadowed by governmental regulations, he tried to ignore them. However, the American government of 1845 would not let him. He was arrested and put in the Concord jail for failing to pay his poll tax--a tax he believed unjust because it supported the government's war with Mexico as well as the immoral institution of slavery. Instead of protesting his arrest, he celebrated it and explained its meaning by writing "Civil Disobedience," one of the most famous English-language essays ever written. In it, he ar-

Turner 2

gued persuasively that: "Under a government which imprisons any un-
justly, the true place for a just man is also in prison" (230). Thus the
doctrine of passive resistance was formed, a doctrine that advocated
protest against the government by nonviolent means:

> How does it become a man to behave toward this American
> government today? I answer that he cannot without disgrace
> be associated with it. I cannot for an instant recognize that
> political organization as my government which is the slave's
> government also. (224)

According to Charles R. Anderson, Thoreau's other writings, such as
"Slavery in Massachusetts" and "A Plea for Captain John Brown," show
his disdain of the "northerners for their cowardice on conniving with
such an institution" (28). He wanted all free American citizens, north
and south, to revolt and liberate the slaves.

In addition to inspiring his countrymen, Thoreau's view of the sanc-
tity of individual freedom affected the lives of later generations who
shared his beliefs. "Civil Disobedience" has the greatest impact because
of its "worldwide influence on Mahatma Gandhi, the British Labour
Party in its early years, the underground in Nazi-occupied Europe, and
Negro leaders in the modern south" (Anderson 30). For nearly one
hundred and fifty years, Thoreau's formulation of passive resistance
has been a part of the human struggle for freedom.

Thoreau also wanted to be free from the everyday pressure to conform to society's expectations. He believed in doing and possessing
only the essential things in life. To demonstrate his case, in 1845 he
moved to the outskirts of Concord, Massachusetts, and lived by himself
for two years on the shore of Walden Pond (Spiller et al. 396-97).
Thoreau wrote Walden to explain the value of living simply, apart
from the unnecessary complexity of society: "Simplicity, simplicity, simplicity! I say, let your affairs be as two or three, not a hundred or a
thousand" (66). At Walden, he lived as much as possible by this

---

Margin annotations:

indented 10 spaces

Quotation of more than 4 lines presented in block format.

Partial quotation is worked into sentence in a grammatically correct way.

Writer switches to discussion of a work after discussion of first work is completed.

Identification for work with more than three authors.

Page number only is used because the context identifies the work.

Signal phrase introduces the name of the secondary source author.

Abbreviated popular title is listed after work's first reference.

Short title is added to page number because two works by the author appear on Works Cited page.

Turner 3

statement, building his own house and furniture, growing his own food, bartering for simple necessities, attending to his own business rather than seeking employment from others (Walden 16-17).

Page numbers for paraphrase are included.

Living at Walden Pond gave Thoreau the chance to formulate many of his ideas about living the simple, economical life. At Walden, he lived simply in order to "front only the essential facts of life" (66) and to center his thoughts on living instead of on unnecessary details of mere livelihood. He developed survival skills that freed him from the constraints of city dwellers whose lives depended upon a web of material things and services provided by others. He preferred to "take rank hold on life and spend [his] day more as animals do" (117).

Page numbers alone are sufficient when context makes the source clear.

While living at Walden Pond, Thoreau was free to occupy his time in any way that pleased him, which for him meant writing, tending his bean patch, and chasing loons. He wasn't troubled by a boss hounding him with deadlines nor a wife and children who needed support. In other words, he wasn't expected to be anywhere at any time for anybody except himself. His neighbors accused him of being selfish and did not understand that he sought most of all "to live deliberately" (Walden 66), as he felt all people should learn to do.

Then as now, most people had more responsibilities than Thoreau had, and could not just pack up their belongings and go live in the woods--if they could find free woods to live in. Today, people are intrigued to read about Thoreau's experiences and inspired by his thoughts, but few people can actually live or do as he suggests in Walden. In fact, most people, if faced with the prospect of spending two years removed from society would probably think of it as a punishment or banishment, rather than as Thoreau thought of it, as the good life.

Turner 4

Writer's conclusion repeats thesis assertion.

Practical or not, Thoreau's writings about freedom from government and society have inspired countless people to reassess how they live their lives. Though unable to live as he advocated, readers everywhere remain inspired by his ideal, that one must live as freely as possible.

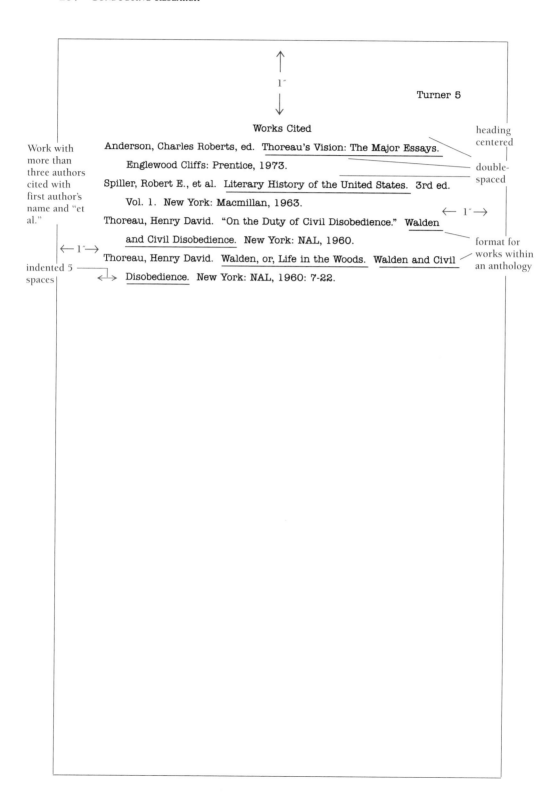

Turner 5

Works Cited

Anderson, Charles Roberts, ed. Thoreau's Vision: The Major Essays.
  Englewood Cliffs: Prentice, 1973.

Spiller, Robert E., et al. Literary History of the United States. 3rd ed.
  Vol. 1. New York: Macmillan, 1963.

Thoreau, Henry David. "On the Duty of Civil Disobedience." Walden
  and Civil Disobedience. New York: NAL, 1960.

Thoreau, Henry David. Walden, or, Life in the Woods. Walden and Civil
  Disobedience. New York: NAL, 1960: 7-22.

Work with more than three authors cited with first author's name and "et al."

heading centered

double-spaced

← 1″ →

format for works within an anthology

indented 5 spaces

← 1″ →

← 1″ →

COLLABORATIVE FIELD RESEARCH ESSAY: MLA STYLE

"Ben and Jerry's: Caring Capitalism" is the result of assigning students in a first-year composition class to collaboratively investigate local institutions or issues with local impact. The research-writing teams ranged in size from three to five. The topics investigated included pollution in Lake Champlain; the homeless in downtown Burlington, Vermont; underage drinking; the Ronald McDonald House; the Ben and Jerry's ice cream franchise; and the Vermont beer industry.

The team that investigated the Ben and Jerry's ice cream franchise was the largest in the class and wrote the longest paper — twenty-one pages in final form. The version appearing here has been edited slightly for publication.

The title page, optional under the MLA system, is centered top to bottom, right to left, and double-spaced. Each subsequent page is numbered with the first author's name followed by the page number in the upper right-hand corner, according to MLA style. Such running heads provide a safeguard in case pages are mislaid or mixed up. The outline is optional, but some instructors require one.

no page
number

centered on
page top to
bottom, right
to left

Ben and Jerry's: Caring Capitalism

Michelle Anderson, Pamela Jurentkuff, Sandi Martin,

Heather Mulcahy, and Jennifer Stanislaw

Professor Fulwiler

English 1

30 October 1994

title

writers

instructor

course

date

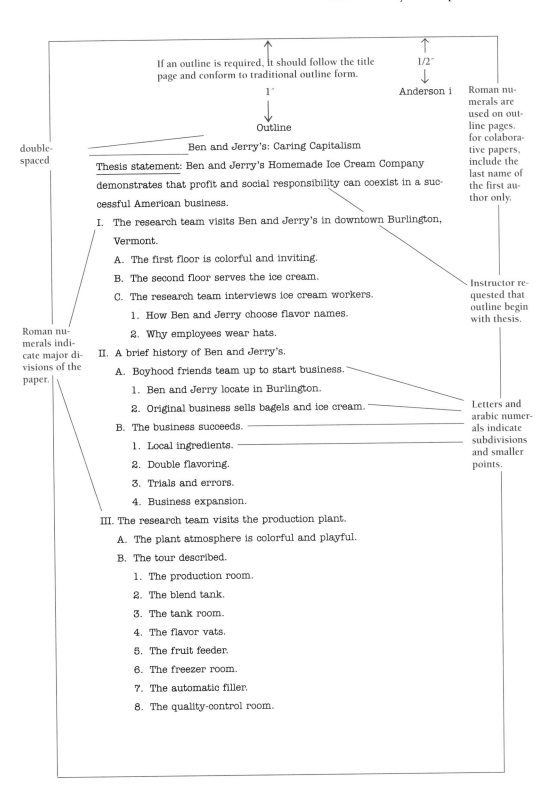

If an outline is required, it should follow the title page and conform to traditional outline form.

1/2″

1″

Anderson i

Roman numerals are used on outline pages. for colaborative papers, include the last name of the first author only.

Outline

double-spaced

Ben and Jerry's: Caring Capitalism

Thesis statement: Ben and Jerry's Homemade Ice Cream Company demonstrates that profit and social responsibility can coexist in a successful American business.

I. The research team visits Ben and Jerry's in downtown Burlington, Vermont.

   A. The first floor is colorful and inviting.

   B. The second floor serves the ice cream.

   C. The research team interviews ice cream workers.

      1. How Ben and Jerry choose flavor names.

      2. Why employees wear hats.

Roman numerals indicate major divisions of the paper.

II. A brief history of Ben and Jerry's.

   A. Boyhood friends team up to start business.

      1. Ben and Jerry locate in Burlington.

      2. Original business sells bagels and ice cream.

   B. The business succeeds.

      1. Local ingredients.

      2. Double flavoring.

      3. Trials and errors.

      4. Business expansion.

III. The research team visits the production plant.

   A. The plant atmosphere is colorful and playful.

   B. The tour described.

      1. The production room.

      2. The blend tank.

      3. The tank room.

      4. The flavor vats.

      5. The fruit feeder.

      6. The freezer room.

      7. The automatic filler.

      8. The quality-control room.

Instructor requested that outline begin with thesis.

Letters and arabic numerals indicate subdivisions and smaller points.

     9. The hardening tunnel.

  C. The employees enjoy their work.

IV. The company's concept of "caring capitalism and social activism."

  A. High profits lead to hippy guilt.

  B. The company contributes to the world community.

     1. Seven and one half percent of profits is donated to the community.

     2. One percent for peace.

     3. Rainforest Crunch helps Brazil.

  C. The company's environmental guidelines.

     1. Recycling successes.

     2. Recycling problems.

Title is repeated on first page of a paper with a title page.

1/2˝

Anderson 1

1˝

double-spaced

Anonymous source identified by shortened title. No page number is needed for a one-page source.

In long papers informative subheadings help explain the paper's organization.

arabic numerals used on text pages.

Thesis is implicit in first paragraph.

Purpose for research is stated.

Raised number refers to explanatory note on Notes page.

information from field research.

Dialogue is added to create sense of authenticity. Identification of source not necessary.

Ben and Jerry's: Caring Capitalism

Ben and Jerry's Homemade Ice Cream Company has developed an international reputation for making "the best ice cream in the world" while, at the same time, setting a new standard for social responsibility ("They All Scream"). Numerous trips to the local scoop shop had already convinced our research team--Pam, Sandi, Heather, Michelle, and Jennifer--that Ben and Jerry's ice cream was good; now we wanted to find out the rest of the scoop.[1]

The Scoop (Shop)

When you enter the front door of Ben and Jerry's Homemade Ice Cream shop in downtown Burlington, Vermont, you find yourself standing on a clean, tiled, black-and-white checkered floor. To the left are three dark red booths with white tables. Painted on the opposite wall are eight black and white spotted cows standing in a lush, green field probably somewhere in Vermont. The sky above them is a bright blue with several white, puffy clouds.

Upstairs, the first thing you see is a blue plastic bin with a sign that says, "We are now recycling spoons!" To the right is the ice cream counter. Behind it a colorful wooden sign reads "Today's Euphoric Flavors" and lists 29 flavors, including Cherry Garcia, Chocolate Chip Cookie Dough, Chunky Monkey, Heathbar Crunch, Coffee Heathbar Crunch, New York Super Fudge Chunk, and Rainforest Crunch. To the left of the flavors is a white sign with black writing that tells the prices--$1.44 for a small, $1.84 for a medium, $2,60 for a large.

We asked the person behind the counter, "How do you get the names of the flavors for the ice cream?"

"Most of them are pretty basic. Well, like Cherry Garcia was thought up by a Grateful Dead fan in Maine. Some lady in New Hampshire wrote in with the idea for Chunky Monkey. They gave her a lifetime supply of the ice cream and it turns out she doesn't even like it."

The three workers behind the counter all seemed to be having fun while scooping ice cream and joking with the steady line of customers.

Anderson 2

They were all wearing Ben and Jerry's t-shirts, but different hats--a blue beret, a baseball cap, a beanie. "Why do you all wear hats?" we asked.

"Actually, it's a health regulation. We have to keep our hair back. In the factory they have to wear an elastic cap and all-white sanitary outfits. Here we're encouraged to have fun with it. We wear all different types. I'm known for my Viking hat that I often wear." *(margin note: Dialogue contributes to the thesis that the company is a caring organization.)*

Another scooper adds: "There are some limitations. Like they wouldn't let me wear a hat made out of a pair of jeans or one out of a paper bag. But I have a great hat planned for Christmas. It's a secret though."

It was clear from our visit to Ben and Jerry's main scoop shop in downtown Burlington that both eating and serving ice cream could be fun. How, we wondered, did such a funky business get started?

In the Beginning

Ben and Jerry's Homemade Ice Cream Company began when two old friends from Long Island, Ben Cohen and Jerry Greenfield, decided to honor a childhood pact that one day they would go into business together and "do something more fun" (Hubbard 73). At the time, Ben was working with emotionally unstable children in New York, and Jerry was a lab technician in North Carolina. They selected Burlington, Vermont, as just the right sized rural college town for a small food business--a food and ice cream emporium, as they first envisioned it. An old run-down gas station on the corner of St. Paul and College streets proved the ideal location for their first shop, which opened a week earlier than planned on May 5, 1978.

At first they tried to sell both bagels and ice cream. As Jerry tells it, "At first it was almost like a race to see who would sell the most. Would it be Ben with his bagels covered with marinated artichoke hearts, mushroom, and sliced cucumber? Or Jerry with his Sweet Cream Oreo ice cream?" (Greenfield).[2] But everybody bought the ice cream and nobody bought the bagels, so at the end of 1979, Ben joined Jerry in the ice cream business. *(margin note: The note explains the source of the interview.)*

Anderson 3

The ice cream succeeded because it was handmade in an old-fashioned rock salt ice cream maker, the flavors were original and fun, and it claimed to be made from strictly natural Vermont dairy products. Ben and Jerry also double flavored their ice cream, making it with twice as much flavor as a recipe normally called for. How did they know how much flavoring was enough? "Well, when we first started, I made the ice cream and Ben tasted it. If Ben couldn't tell what flavor the ice cream was with his eyes closed, he would tell me it needed more flavoring" (Greenfield).

It took time and practice to perfect their recipes. Jerry remembers, "I once made a batch of Rum Raisin that stretched and bounced" (Hubbard 73). By 1981, however, through the process of trial and error, they were noted in <u>Time</u> magazine for making "the best ice cream in the world" ("They All Scream").

By 1983, the small shop in downtown Burlington could not generate enough ice cream to keep up with the streams of customers who poured in each day, so they relocated their main store to Cherry Street and their production facilities to the outskirts of town. In time they needed an even larger plant, so they reestablished their headquarters in Waterbury, Vermont, some 40 miles east of Burlington, where they continue to produce most of their ice cream (Smith).

The end of the historical discussion includes a transition to the next section.

Making the "World's Best Ice Cream"

On November 7, 1990, our research team toured the Ben and Jerry's Ice Cream plant in Waterbury. On entering the plant, we noticed the smell of peppermint and a lobby packed with people, strolling from one wall to the next, looking at newspaper and magazine articles and pictures of Ben and Jerry. Almost everyone was holding a dish or a cone filled with their favorite euphoric flavor of Ben and Jerry's ice cream in one hand and a t-shirt, sweatshirt, bumper sticker, or pair of boxer shorts in the other. We were surprised to find so many people in the middle of the week, especially since it was only 35 degrees outside.

Details provide color and add liveliness to the research report.

Entire section is based on field research; no further references are needed after this first one.

Anderson 4

The writers
include refer-
ences to
themselves in
this section
to lend au-
thenticity to
information
collected
through field
research.

We got there just in time to take the tour. About 15 of us slowly followed our guide, Rick, into a long corridor with light green trees, pale yellow flowers, and bright pink birds painted on the walls. A tape recording of toucans and other tropical birds played in the background-- "Vermont's only tropical rainforest," Rick explained.

Next we visited the production room where the ice cream is made. The number 44,560 was painted in big, black, bold numbers on the wall--the plant's record pint production for a 17-hour period, enough ice cream for an individual to eat a pint a day for 196 years. You might think that this is a lot of ice cream, but every employee takes home three pints a day. "It's a wonderful benefit," Rick explained, "but not too good for the waistline, which is why Ben and Jerry's also offers a free health club membership to everyone who works there."

Dialogue is
added for
reader inter-
est and also
to advance
the theme of
"caring capi-
talism."

This section
is organized
chronologi-
cally accord-
ing to the se-
quence of the
field re-
search.

Ben and Jerry's ice cream begins in the blend tank, a 240-pound stainless steel tank that combines Vermont milk, cream, egg yolks, un- refined sugar, and the flavor of the day. From there, the mix is sent to the 36-degree tank room, where it sits for 4 to 8 hours before it re- ceives further flavoring, which on this day was Coffee Heathbar Crunch.

The source of
the informa-
tion is the
field re-
search; no
other citation
is necessary.

From the tank room, the mix moves into four 300-gallon flavor vats, so the coffee extract can be added. From the flavor vat, the mix goes to the fruit feeder, where big chunks of Heath Bar are mixed in. The ingredients are next sent through a freezer that holds 750 gallons, which is turned by a crank to add air to the ice cream. Ice cream man- ufacturers are allowed up to a 100% overrun, which would mean that for every 1 gallon of mix, 2 gallons of ice cream would come out. However, Rick told us that "Ben and Jerry's has a 20% overrun, mak- ing it much thicker than standard commercial ice cream found in su- permarkets."

The automatic filler fills the pints, and the packaged ice cream is then sent to the spiral hardening tunnel to be frozen solid at 35 de- grees below zero, where a life-size doll, called "Freezer Fred," watches the ice cream as it passes through the tunnel on its way to be stored prior to shipping.

We were impressed by the cleanliness and efficiency of the whole operation and also by the fact that all the workers we met seemed to enjoy their jobs. The benefits to the workers seemed clear, but we still wondered where Ben and Jerry's reputation as a "socially responsible company" came from, so we continued our investigation.

"Caring Capitalism and Social Activism"

In 1984 Ben realized, "We're no longer ice cream men, but businessmen" ("Ben and Jerry's"). Since their opening in 1978, their annual profits increased every year. Their most recent net sales for the quarter ending September 29, 1990, were $21,705,512, a 24% increase from $17,525,279 for the same time the previous year (Severance 6). Being businessmen instead of ice cream men, however, made the two old friends nervous. As Ben said in a Washington Post interview, "We were sitting at desks, and we were people's bosses and giving orders. Growing up in the '60s, being a businessman wasn't a cool thing to do. I started feeling we were a cog in the economic machine" (qtd. in Kurtz).

However, Ben and Jerry also realized that just because they were successful businessmen who made money, they didn't have to change what they believed in. In fact, their substantial annual income allows them to make a profit and give to their community at the same time. Jerry explained, "Early on, we knew that if we stayed in business, it was because of the support of a lot of people, so it seemed natural to want to return that support" (Hubbard 74).

Ben and Jerry believe in a concept called "Caring Capitalism and Social Activism," which means giving a percent of the profits back to the community (About Ben and Jerry 5). Every day 7.5% of the company's profits go to a worthy social, nonprofit organization and to preserving the environment. According to the company's promotional material, "Underlying the mission of Ben and Jerry's is the determination

---

The subheading is a phrase from a pamphlet, which is explained within the discussion.

Transition to the next section is made by raising a question.

Shortened title is provided for anonymous source. No page number is needed for one-page source.

No page number is needed for one-page source.

Source is identified as company produced and not objective.

Anderson 6

to seek new and creative ways of addressing both social and economic missions, while holding a deep respect for the individuals, inside and outside the company, and for the communities of which they are a part" (About Ben and Jerry 5).

Part of Ben and Jerry's social mission is evident in the program called "One Percent for Peace," a campaign that advocates redirecting 1% of the United States defense budget to a global effort "to solve world problems of hunger, disease, the environment, poverty, and human rights" (Kurtz). Whenever you buy a Peace Pop, chocolate-covered ice cream on a stick, you help promote this campaign.

Ben and Jerry's also promotes environmental issues, such as saving the rain forests in Brazil. They send a percentage of all profits from the ice cream Rainforest Crunch, made with Brazilian cashew nuts, to Cultural Survival, a nonprofit human rights organization promoting nut processing plants owned and operated by natives of Brazil.

Closer to home, Ben and Jerry's promotes the safety of the environment. At every Ben and Jerry's scoop shop there are big buckets to put used spoons in, for recycling purposes. On every table are napkin dispensers with a sign saying, "Save a tree, please take only one napkin." Presently the company recycles approximately 60% of its paper products and is now experimenting with an alternative for their plastic-coated pint containers. "As a result of [our] recycling efforts, we have reduced our solid waste volume by about 30% this year" (Severance 6).

Ben and Jerry's is a growing enterprise which shows promising signs of worldwide expansion, not only for its excellent ice cream, but for responsibility as well. Through caring capitalism Ben and Jerry have gained the support of both environmentalists and the business community. We believe Ben and Jerry's provides a good model of corporate responsibility as America enters the twenty-first century.

Transition is made from global to local concerns.

Conclusion returns to main theme of essay.

Change in quotation for grammatical consistency is indicated by brackets.

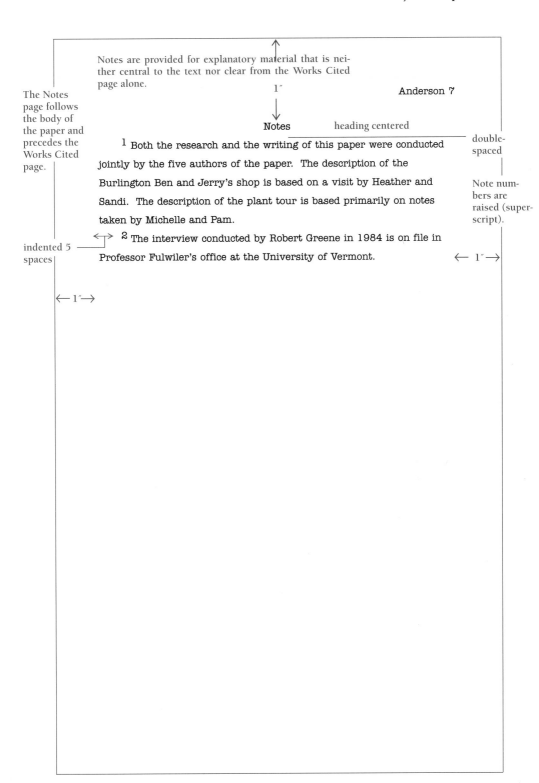

Notes are provided for explanatory material that is neither central to the text nor clear from the Works Cited
page alone.

1″

Anderson 7

The Notes
page follows
the body of
the paper and
precedes the
Works Cited
page.

Notes   heading centered

double-
spaced

¹ Both the research and the writing of this paper were conducted
jointly by the five authors of the paper. The description of the
Burlington Ben and Jerry's shop is based on a visit by Heather and
Sandi. The description of the plant tour is based primarily on notes
taken by Michelle and Pam.

Note num-
bers are
raised (super-
script).

indented 5
spaces

² The interview conducted by Robert Greene in 1984 is on file in
Professor Fulwiler's office at the University of Vermont.

← 1″ →

← 1″ →

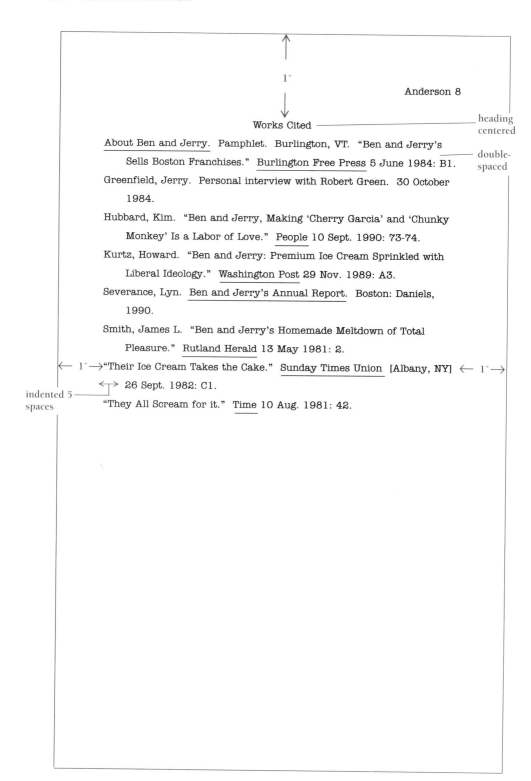

1″

Anderson 8

Works Cited ——————————————— heading
centered

About Ben and Jerry. Pamphlet. Burlington, VT. "Ben and Jerry's ——— double-
spaced

    Sells Boston Franchises." Burlington Free Press 5 June 1984: B1.

Greenfield, Jerry. Personal interview with Robert Green. 30 October

    1984.

Hubbard, Kim. "Ben and Jerry, Making 'Cherry Garcia' and 'Chunky

    Monkey' Is a Labor of Love." People 10 Sept. 1990: 73-74.

Kurtz, Howard. "Ben and Jerry: Premium Ice Cream Sprinkled with

    Liberal Ideology." Washington Post 29 Nov. 1989: A3.

Severance, Lyn. Ben and Jerry's Annual Report. Boston: Daniels,

    1990.

Smith, James L. "Ben and Jerry's Homemade Meltdown of Total

    Pleasure." Rutland Herald 13 May 1981: 2.

← 1″ →"Their Ice Cream Takes the Cake." Sunday Times Union [Albany, NY] ← 1″ →

indented 5 ————→ 26 Sept. 1982: C1.
spaces

    "They All Scream for it." Time 10 Aug. 1981: 42.

COLLABORATIVE LIBRARY RESEARCH ESSAY:
APA STYLE

The following research essay, "New Brew: Vermont's Diverse Beer Culture," is the result of shared library research and shared writing by Pat Quimby and Stephen Reville in a first-year writing class. "New Brew" is documented according to American Psychological Association (APA) conventions and includes a title page, an abstract, and an outline.

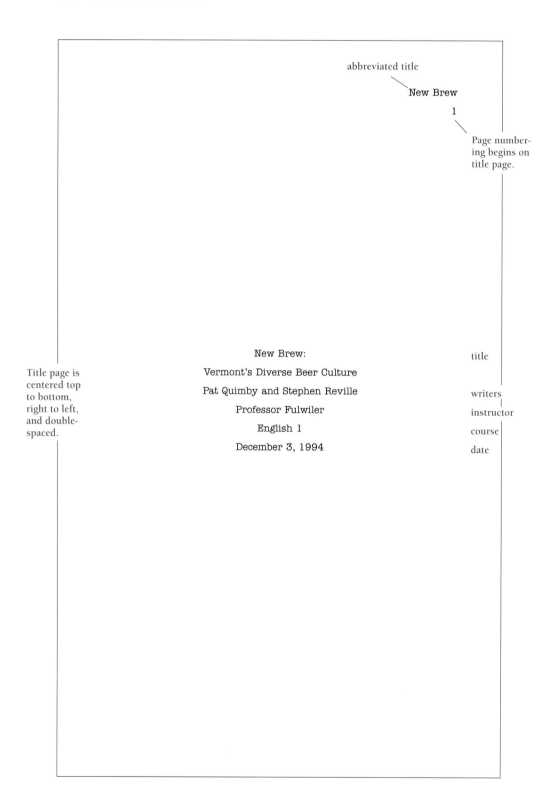

abbreviated title

New Brew

1

Page numbering begins on title page.

Title page is centered top to bottom, right to left, and double-spaced.

New Brew:

Vermont's Diverse Beer Culture

Pat Quimby and Stephen Reville

Professor Fulwiler

English 1

December 3, 1994

title

writers

instructor

course

date

If an abstract is required, it should be printed on a separate page following the title page and preceding the paper.

New Brew

2

heading centered

no paragraph indent

Abstract

double-spaced

Beer has a long and diverse history which has been severely threatened as a result of the monopolization of the American beer industry by huge corporate breweries. Recently, however, microbreweries have begun to challenge the monopoly of national breweries. These small local brewers who make alternative beer have found a successful market niche and begun to turn a profit. This paper describes how this national trend has affected beer drinking in the state of Vermont.

The abstract summarizes both the theme and the findings of the entire paper.

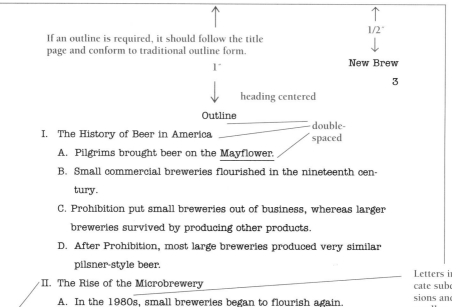

If an outline is required, it should follow the title
page and conform to traditional outline form.

1″

1/2″

New Brew

3

heading centered

Outline

I. The History of Beer in America
    — double-spaced

    A. Pilgrims brought beer on the Mayflower.

    B. Small commercial breweries flourished in the nineteenth cen-
        tury.

    C. Prohibition put small breweries out of business, whereas larger
        breweries survived by producing other products.

    D. After Prohibition, most large breweries produced very similar
        pilsner-style beer.

II. The Rise of the Microbrewery

    A. In the 1980s, small breweries began to flourish again.

    B. Microbreweries offer diverse kinds of beer.

    C. In 1987, the Catamount Brewery opened in Vermont and the
        industry began to expand in that state.

    D. Other small producers include brew pubs, bars or restaurants
        that produce and sell their own beers.

    E. One such brew pub, the Vermont Pub and Brewery in Burlington,
        Vermont, is typical in its distinctive beer and diverse clientele.

III. Conclusion

Roman nu-
merals indi-
cate major di-
visions of the
paper.

Letters indi-
cate subdivi-
sions and
smaller
points.

New Brew:

Vermont's Diverse Beer Culture

The beer industry in the United States grosses 40 billion dollars a year. Ninety-nine percent of those profits are made by giant corporations such as Anheuser-Busch, Miller, and Coors. But today, even though dollars are tight and industries are struggling to hold their ground, several microbreweries have gained a foothold in Vermont and they are fighting for their share of the profits (Shaw, 1990). This paper examines the options available to the Vermont beer drinker and explains what distinguishes locally produced beers from their national competitors.

The History of Beer in America

Understanding the recent interest in locally produced, alternative beers requires first an understanding of some beer history. The earliest proven evidence of the existence of beer dates back over 5000 years to Mesopotamian and Egyptian times where residues have been found in casks and jugs. The Pilgrims brought beer with them on the Mayflower, although apparently not enough of it. According to the captain, they were forced to land at Plymouth, rather than their original destination farther south, because they "could not take time for further search, our victuals being much spent, especially our beer" (Baron, 1972, p. 15).

The earliest immigrants to the New World were forced to brew their own beer. George Washington, Thomas Jefferson, William Penn, and Samuel Adams were all home brewers. But eventually commercial breweries sprang up. At the beginning of this century there were thousands of breweries spread all across the country, each brewing unique styles of beer (Mares, 1984, p. 34). This practice can still be seen in many European countries where beer is very much part of the regional history.

However, the broad and diverse beer culture here in America was almost completely destroyed in 1920 by laws prohibiting the sale or consumption of alcoholic beverages. Prohibition forced all of the small

---

Title is repeated from the title page.

titles are double-spaced

The informative subheadings help explain the paper's organization.

Partial quotation is worked into the text in a grammatically correct way.

Transition words signal a change in direction.

Most citations give author's name and date in parentheses.

The informational thesis is stated at the end of the first paragraph.

Author's name, year of publication, and page numbers are included in parentheses for a direct quotation or a specific part of the source.

New Brew

5

local breweries and taverns to close, so for the next fourteen years the only beer in the United States was illegally smuggled across the border or secretly and illegally brewed in private homes. In Vermont, for example, home brewing during Prohibition was as common as baking bread. Vermonters made beverages from anything available: maple sap, spruce needles, herbs, spices, fruits, and berries (Morris, 1984, p. 25).

The only breweries still in business in December of 1933, when Prohibition was repealed, were the largest of the commercial breweries, such as Anheuser-Busch and Miller, who had been able to convert their operations over to other products for the food industry (Papazian, 1991). According to Baron (1972), "The kitchen kettle of yesteryear has given way to the tremendous factory covering several city blocks" (p. 32). These large breweries became the giants of today's American beer industry without the competition of their small-scale rivals.

> The publication date of a source immediately follows the author's name, and the page number follows the direct quotation.

And they all brewed essentially the same beer. The warm climate over most of the United States, at least for part of the year, combined with the availability of rice and corn as cheap grains and the economic value of using fewer grains in the brew, suggested a very light-bodied and mild-flavored beer (Roberts & Russett, 1981). The result is what is known as the American light lager or pilsner beer, stemming from a traditional style from the town of Plzen, Czechoslovakia. This style was adopted by all of the major national brands in the United States, leaving only expensive imported or homemade beers for an alternative (Papazian, 1991).

> Both authors' last names are listed, joined with an ampersand.

The Rise of the Microbrewery

In the early 1980s, the movement to bring back the small breweries of the early part of the century began (Morris, 1984). Microbreweries, breweries which produce fewer than 30,000 barrels of beer each year, started cropping up across the United States, especially in California and the western states. Jack McAuliffe, one of the pio-

neers of the microbrewery industry, gave this impression of the

changes that were coming in the industry back in 1982:

double-
spaced

> As the industry continues to shrink, the products you make
>
> have to become more and more alike in taste. You want to of-
>
> fend as few people as possible. When you own a large brewery,
>
> you can't afford to make specialty beer. In that sense, there is
>
> more and more opportunity for the specialty brewer. In this
>
> country there is a choice of brands, but no choice of style.
>
> People are becoming more interested in food that tastes different
>
> and a broadened taste will support more specialty beers.
>
> (Mares, 1984, p. 119).

indented 5
spaces

Colon is used
to introduce a
long quota-
tion.

Quotations
over 40
words are
presented in
block format.

No paragraph
is needed
when the text
following the
indented pas-
sage refers
back to it.

Unfortunately McAuliffe's company, the New Albion Brewing Company,

in California, was unable to make a profit competing against the na-

tional giants, and New Albion closed within three years. But many oth-

ers did survive, companies such as Anchor Brewing Co. in San

Francisco and the Boston Beer Co., brewers of Samuel Adams. In fact,

according to Chris Fisher, a local home brewer and authority on the in-

dustry, "In the past year the national breweries are down twelve per-

cent in profits while the microbreweries as a whole are up about three

hundred percent" (personal communication, October 29, 1992).

However, Budweiser alone still produces more beer in a single day than

all the microbreweries produce in a year (Mares, 1984, p. 121).

Field source
is identified
completely
here, so not
included on
reference
page.

Authors'
names should
be worked
into the text
whenever
possible to
clarify source
information.

According to Shaw (1990), the home brewing revolution did not be-

gin in Vermont until February 1987 when Stephen Mason and Alan

Davis opened Catamount Brewery, which offered golden lager, an am-

ber ale, and a dark porter as well as several seasonal brews. This was

only the beginning. In September 1992, the first Vermont Brewers

Festival was held at Sugarbush Resort. Sixteen breweries participated

and the forty-plus beers present ranged from American light lagers to

German-style bock and everything in between. The beers included such colorful names as Tall Tale Pale Ale, Black Fly Stout, Slopbucket Brown Ale, Summer Wheat Ale, Avid Barley Wee Heavy, and Hickory Switch Smoked Amber Ale.

In addition to new breweries are brew pubs such as McNeill's Brewery in Brattleboro and the Vermont Pub and Brewery in Burlington. These are bars or restaurants that feature their own selection of beers brewed and served in-house only. Greg and Nancy Noonan, the owners of the Vermont Pub and Brewery, will be celebrating the fifth anniversary of their successful venture in December.

According to Greg, their business has been better than they had predicted. He said, "Our first expectations were based on worst-case scenarios" (personal communication, November 17, 1992). In fact, for the Vermont Pub and Brewery there has not been any recession. Greg attributes this success to the consistency of the Burlington economic base and the increase of Canadian tourism: "Our Canadian business doubled or tripled since we opened on November 11, 1988."

The Vermont Pub and Brewery beer selection changes with the seasons, with a core of regular favorites including Burly Irish Ale, Dogbite Bitter, and Smoked Porter. The seasonal specialties range from Oktoberfest in the fall to Maple Ale in the spring. Even the casual observer can see that the patrons at the Vermont Pub and Brewery do not fit into any neat categories. Greg described his intentions this way: "We're not appealing to primarily blue collar or white collar people, not any specific age bracket. We're definitely not a shot and a beer bar. We always knew that we didn't want to be a college bar."

Conclusion

Microbreweries have gone to great lengths to provide a rich alternative diversity to the normal pilsner American-style beer offered by the national breweries. The interest in locally made beer has found a niche in Vermont. The search for quality and variety has led the beer drinker away from the industry giants to the newly established local alternatives.

Field research is smoothly integrated.

The thesis is repeated in the conclusion.

New Brew

8

heading centered

double-spaced

Authors are listed alphabetically.

References

Baker, P. M. (1979). New brewers handbook. Westpoint, MA: Crosby and Baker.

Baron, S. (1972). Brewed in America: A history of beer and ale in the U.S. New York: Arno.

Mares, W. K. (1984). Making beer. New York: Alfred A. Knopf.

indented 3 spaces

Morris, S. (1984). The great beer trek. Brattleboro, VT: Stephen Greene.

Article titles are not underlined and not enclosed in quotation marks.

Papazian, C. D. (1991). The new complete joy of home brewing. New York: Avon.

Roberts, A. K., & Russett, G. H. (1981). The new brewers. National Brewing Digest, 3 (4), 129-138.

Shaw, K. (1990, April 12). Micro breweries are hopping in Vermont. The Burlington Free Press, p. 2.

In book and article titles, only first words and proper names are capitalized. Book titles are underlined.

Periodical titles are capitalized normally. Volume number is underlined, and issue number is placed in parentheses.

REVISING

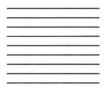

Chapter 22

How Writers Revise

Writing. I'm more involved in it. But not as attached. I used to really cling to my writing, and didn't want it to change. Now I can see the usefulness of change. I just really like my third draft, but I have to let it go. But that's not what it's all about. I can still really enjoy my third draft and still create another exciting paper.

— KAREN

A FIRST DRAFT IS A WRITER'S FIRST ATTEMPT TO GIVE SHAPE TO AN IDEA, argument, or experience. Occasionally, this initial draft is just right and the writing is done. More often, however, the first draft shows a broad outline or general direction that needs further thinking, further revision. An unfocused first draft, in other words, is not a mistake, but a start toward a next, more focused draft.

No matter how much prior thought writers give to complex composing tasks, once they begin writing, the draft begins to shift, change, and develop in unexpected ways. In other words, the act of writing itself produces new questions and insights that must be dealt with and incorporated into the emerging piece of writing. That's where active and aggressive revision strategies can help.

For many novice writers, revising is an alien activity that neither makes sense nor comes easy. Experienced writers, though, know that revising is the very essence of writing, the primary way of developing thoughts and preparing them to be shared with others. The rest of this chapter introduces strategies and procedures for effective revision.

UNDERSTANDING REVISION

Revising, editing, and *proofreading* are sometimes used to mean the same thing, but there is a good reason to understand each as a separate process, each in its own way contributing to the production of good writing. When you *revise,* you reread, rethink, and reconstruct your thoughts on paper until they match those in your mind. Revising is, literally, reseeing your focus, thesis, argument, evidence, arrangement, and conclusion and making major changes that affect the content, direction, and meaning of your paper. Revising generally takes place at the paragraph level.

When you *edit*, you change your language more than your ideas. After you know what you want to say and have written it, you edit by testing each word or phrase to see if it is necessary, accurate, and correct and if it conveys your intended tone and style. Editing takes place at the level of the sentence or word. The many dimensions of editing, including proofreading, are treated in Part VII.

When you *proofread*, you check very specific sentence elements for correctness: mainly spelling, punctuation, and capitalization. Proofreading is the final stage of the editing process, so it makes most sense to do it at the very end, when you have addressed style and grammar and simply want to make sure your paper contains no errors to distract or confuse readers.

There are two good reasons to revise before you edit. First, when you revise you may cut out whole sections of a draft because they no longer suit your final purpose. If you have already edited those sections, all your careful sentence-level work goes for naught. Second, if you've invested time in carefully editing sentences, you may be reluctant to cut them — even though cutting may make your paper better. Of course, writers are always circling back through the stages, mixing them up, editing after drafting, revising as they invent, drafting new paragraphs when they intend only to edit. Nonetheless, your work will probably be more productive (and you will probably be happier) if you resist as much as possible the urge to edit before you revise.

Revision is a complex and dynamic process. Exactly how to approach it is up to you, of course, but you may want to take advantage of some of the tried-and-true revision strategies described here. These will guide you in thinking profitably about revising and will ensure that your revising is thorough and appropriate.

WRITING 1

Describe one paper that you spent a long time revising. What was the assignment? How did you approach it? Did you plan to revise or did you just fall into the process? How many drafts did you write? Can you single out when you "drafted," when you "revised," and when you "edited"? What was the result of your revision work? Were you pleased? Was your audience?

ASKING REVISION QUESTIONS

Learning to revise means learning to ask careful questions about the purpose of your text, the audience for whom it's intended, and yourself as its author. The answers to these questions will help you decide what aspect of your paper to change when revising.

Ask Questions About Your Purpose

Revising is your last opportunity to modify your paper's purpose. While it's important to think about purpose when planning and drafting a paper, it's crucial to get the purpose straight when you revise. In fact, it's often easier to see your purpose — or lack thereof — most clearly after you have written a draft or two. Expect to return to the basic questions about purpose that you asked during planning (see Chapter 4):

1. Why am I writing this paper?
2. Do all elements and parts of the paper advance this purpose? If not, why not?
3. What was the assignment? Does my paper fulfill the assignment's requirements?
4. What is the aim of the paper? To narrate, explain, interpret, argue, reflect, or something else? Will my readers be able to tell that this is what I'm doing?
5. What is my theme or thesis? Have I expressed it clearly?

Ask Questions About Your Audience

You also need to make sure your paper is aimed accurately at your audience. If in planning and drafting you have been most concerned with gathering information and putting your ideas together in a coherent manner, at some point you need to switch your attention to your audience, asking questions like these:

1. Who is my audience for this paper?
2. What do my readers know about this subject? Have I told them too much that they already know?
3. What do my readers not know about this subject? Have I given them the context they need?
4. What questions or objections do I anticipate my audience raising? Can I answer any of them before they are asked?
5. Are my tone and style appropriate to this audience?

For more information on writing to specific audiences, see Chapter 5.

Ask Questions About Yourself

Perhaps the best reason for revising is to know for yourself that you have written the best paper possible. Revise so that when you read the paper you enjoy both its ideas and its language. If you are writing from personal experience, make that experience ring true; if you are writing an argument, develop one you believe in. When you please and convince yourself, you improve your chances of pleasing and convincing others as well. Ask questions like these:

1. Do I believe everything I've written in this paper? If not, why not?

2. What doubts do I have about my paper? Can I still address these?
3. Which passages do I most enjoy reading? How can I make the rest of the paper more like them?
4. Which passages do I find difficult to read? What can I do to change them?

USING REVISION STRATEGIES

This section lists more than a dozen time-tested revision strategies that may be useful to you. While they won't all work for you all the time, some will be useful at one time or another. Notice that these suggestions start with larger concerns and progress toward smaller ones.

Plan for Revising

You cannot revise if your haven't first written. If you are used to writing papers the day or night before they are due, you will not leave yourself time for revising. Plan from the outset to write early and to make time for all subsequent stages of the writing process, including revising.

Keep a Revision Notebook

If you regularly keep a journal, you can use it to write about revision plans. If you don't already keep one, you might consider using a portion of your class notebook for revision ideas. Be sure to record notes about books or articles related to your project as well as ideas about theme, direction, and purpose. Making time to write about your writing may contribute in surprising ways to the writing itself. (See Chapter 8 for further suggestions about keeping a journal.)

Impose Due Dates

After you write the due date for the final draft in your calendar or appointment book, add self-imposed due dates for revising and editing. Leave yourself time to return to your draft before your instructor's due date.

Establish Distance

The most important condition for revising well is to gain some distance from your first-draft thoughts. Even letting a draft sit overnight and then returning to it the next day allows you to see it differently — more objectively, more clearly. When you reread the whole piece, you'll almost always see places that satisfied you yesterday, but now, by the light of a new day, don't. Allow time to expect this possibility rather than dread it.

You can also achieve distance by typing rather than handwriting drafts and by asking others to read your paper with fresh eyes and without your preconceptions.

Type All Drafts

Handwriting can be too friendly, too familiar to allow you to see your thoughts clearly. As soon as you can, type your thoughts so you can look at them on a computer screen or piece of paper. Seeing your thoughts may make it easier to change, expand, or delete them. Typing drafts on a computer will also encourage revising and editing, since you can change your words, phrases, and sentences without retyping every one.

Request Response

It always helps to share a draft of your paper with readers you trust. No matter how good a writer you are or how good you feel about a particular paper, getting another opinion will give you new ideas. When you ask for a response, be sure to specify what kind of response you want. In an early draft, for instance, you might request a response to your larger ideas; in a later draft, you might request more attention to matters of tone, style, or detail; in a final draft you may simply want help with proofreading.

Reconsider Everything

When you return to your draft for revision, reread and reconsider the whole text. First, reconsider it in light of the assignment: Does the paper address the question it was supposed to address? Next, reread the whole paper from the start; every time you change something of substance, reread the whole thing again. Remember that revision is conceptual work in which you try to get your thoughts just right and in the right order. If you change the information on one page, you may need to change ideas, questions, or conclusions on another page. Finally, if a classmate or instructor has made comments on some parts of the paper and not on others, do not assume that those are the only places where revision is needed.

Believe and Doubt

Reread your draft as a believer (imagine a supportive friend), putting checks in the margins next to passages that are most convincing — the assertions, the dialogue, the details, the evidence. Then reread the draft as a skeptic (imagine your most critical teacher), putting question marks next to all passages that seem questionable. Finally, review the paper, being satisfied at the check marks that assure you the paper is on the right track and answering the doubts raised by the question marks.

Test Your Theme or Thesis

Sometimes while revising, you generate new ideas, raise new questions, add and subtract information, and end up with a theme or thesis quite different from the one you set out to demonstrate. Consequently, it's a good idea whenever you revise to return periodically to your thesis to make sure it still corresponds to what you've actually written. If not, you can either realign your paper, making it conform to the theme or thesis you originally envisioned, or change the theme or thesis to reflect the content of your paper.

Evaluate Your Evidence

To make any theme or thesis convincing, you need to support it with evidence. Check to see if your evidence, examples, and illustrations provide that support. Ask the following questions:

- Do the evidence and examples support my thesis or advance my theme?
- What objections can be raised about my evidence?
- What additional evidence will answer these objections?

Make a Paragraph Outline

Each paragraph in your paper should be a group of sentences focused on the same main idea. The whole paper is a series of such paragraphs. A paragraph outline at the revision stage creates a map of your whole paper and lets you see where organization is effective and changes need to be made. To make a paragraph outline, number each paragraph and write a phrase describing its main idea. When you are finished you can see whether adjacent paragraphs develop your overall topic or theme in a logical manner. If not, you can reorganize them first in the outline and then in the paper itself. A word processor makes it especially easy to make an outline and then move items around until they fit most logically. (For more information on paragraphs, see Chapter 26.)

Limit and Cut

Professional writers often use revision to cut out, delete, and simplify their writing; in writing as in living, less is often more. When you revise, eliminate all passages that do not contribute necessary information to the point you want your paper to make. This is especially important when you have collected a lot of research information and try to make it all fit into your paper; information that doesn't fit confuses readers more than it impresses them. (For more information on limiting and cutting, see Chapter 23.)

Add and Amplify

Sometimes even as you limit and cut your text, you may also need to expand on some ideas. When you revise, keep asking yourself whether you have explained every concept clearly and added the information, illustrations, and examples to make your paper convincing. (For more information on adding and amplifying, see Chapter 23.)

Switch and Transform

Reconsider your existing draft in light of new possibilities: What would happen if you switched the tense in which it is written or the point of view from which it is told? What would happen if you recast it into a different form? Look at your current draft and ask whether it could communicate even better if you switched or transformed the material. (For more information on switching and transforming, see Chapter 24.)

Listen for Your Voice

When your paper is nearly finished, read it out loud and see if it sounds like you talking. In many informal and semiformal papers, your language should sound like you, a real human being, speaking. If it doesn't, you should attempt to revise it so that it does. In more formal papers, such as science and research reports, the language should not sound like you talking; if it does, revise to make it less personal and more objective. And in some papers, you may want different sections to sound like different voices speaking. Keep in mind that while the complex concept of voice includes tone and style, it includes the writer's values and choices, and what he or she stands for. Ask these questions about your voice:

- Where do I hear or see evidence of my voice: in which words, phrases, sentences, or paragraphs?
- What does my voice sound like: confident, questioning, diplomatic, uncertain, arrogant, friendly, or humorous?
- What do I want to sound like?

Let Go

The spirit of revision is the welcome acceptance of change, the belief that no matter how good something is, it can always be made better. But many writers become attached to their words, proud to have generated so many of them in the first place, reluctant to abandon them once generated. When writers learn to let go, they have learned to trust that their power, creativity, and authority can generate exciting writing again and again, on demand. Letting go can imply dropping whole sections or even whole drafts.

Consider revising by starting a completely new second draft. After you have written and reread your first draft, start a new one as if you no longer have a written draft to tinker with. Sometimes your best writing will result from a new start on old material as you automatically delete and edit out dead-end ideas and are not constrained from finding better ones. This approach is especially easy if you are writing on a computer. You can make a new file for the new draft and keep the old one in a backup file just in case you change your mind.

WRITING 2

Return to an early draft of a paper you are writing and examine it in light of the strategies suggested in this section. Which suggestions proved most useful? Do you know why?

REVISING WITH A COMPUTER

A computer can make every stage in your writing process easier and can help you improve many aspects of your writing. In addition, it can make writing more fun. Word processing programs have virtually revolutionized how writers work, allowing them to draft, revise, experiment, reshape, and edit any number of times before committing to a final draft. And they can catch and correct spelling mistakes in the final draft.

It really doesn't matter what brand of computer you use, whether you own it or not, which word processing program you have, or what kind of disk your computer is equipped with. A computer aids revision in numerous ways.

A computer makes it easier to move back and forth in your text as you revise. It facilitates the typical nonlinear writing process in which you may jump around from planning to drafting to researching to revising, keeping everything fluid until you call it finished.

A computer offers distinct advantages at each stage in your writing: when looking for ideas, the computer makes everything — from freewriting to list-making and outlining — fluid, flexible, and instantly changeable — as early draft plans need to be. When you're drafting and revising, the computer stores text and so makes it, at the same time, changeable, moveable, and re-coverable. When you're editing, it allows you to easily rearrange words. A computer also makes it easy to add new research; some software programs provide on-line help and automatic formatting with documentation conventions.

A computer can help create the distance you need for effective revising. As they appear on a computer screen or as printed in good-looking type on fresh sheets of paper, your ideas may be easier to reread with detachment. Be careful, though: a good-looking typeface may make your thoughts look more professional and profound than they may really be; don't be lulled into complacency just because the type looks good.

If you need to add details or supporting evidence, a computer can help you find new information easily and quickly. When equipped with a *modem*, your computer can gain access to library information from your home or dorm. Instead of traveling physically to locate books, periodicals, and special collections, you can search for and often even print out some information from sources within the library. In addition, you can share your drafts with other writers via electronic mail, sending text and comments back and forth.

Sophisticated and powerful software can help you improve your final draft by checking your spelling, grammar, and style.

And of course, when you're finished revising and editing, you can produce a professional-looking, visually exciting paper using the computer's fonts and graphics capabilities. Keep in mind, however, that fancy fonts and graphics are no substitute for clear language, logic, and organization.

WRITING 3

If you currently write on a computer, explain the major advantage of this writing tool. If you do not write with a computer yet, make a resolution to get thee to a computer lab on campus and learn.

Review to Revise

1. Reread the *assignment* and state it in your own words. Does your first draft adequately address the assignment?
2. Advance your *purpose*. Draw a vertical line in the margin next to passages that most clearly advance your purpose; plan to return to these and make them even stronger.
3. Question your *purpose*. Place a question mark in the margin next to passages that do not clearly advance your purpose and consider eliminating or rewriting them.
4. Describe your *audience*. What do they already know or assume? What context or background do they need? On what points do they already agree with you? On what points will you need to persuade them?
5. Underline the sharpest statement of *thesis* or *theme* in your paper. Do you have such a statement? Should you? Where is it located? Can it be made stronger?
6. Put a check mark next to each specific paragraph that contains *evidence* to support your thesis or theme. Do you introduce your strongest evidence first or last? Can you think of other examples, illustrations, or quotations that would provide more or stronger evidence?
7. *Outline* the paper, paragraph by paragraph. Is it clear which paragraphs contain *coordinate* ideas? Are these supported by paragraphs that contain *subordinate* ideas?
8. Read your paper *out loud* and see if you believe it and like it.

SUGGESTIONS FOR WRITING AND RESEARCH

1. Select any paper that you wrote and considered finished in one draft but that you believe would profit from revision. Revise the paper by using some of the revision strategies suggested in this chapter.

2. Go to the library and research the revision habits of a favorite or famous writer. If you cannot find such information, interview a professor, teacher, or other person on your campus or in your community who writes and publishes frequently. Find out about the revision process he or she most often uses. Write a report explaining the concept of revision as understood and used by a professional writer.

Chapter 23

Limiting and Adding

I want my audience to feel like they're actually attending the game, that they're sitting just behind the bench, overhearing coach telling us how to defend against the inbounds pass, and I can do this if I just close my eyes while I write and remember being there — I can put you at the game.

— KAREN

IN THEIR FIRST DRAFTS, writers often try to cover too much territory in too little detail. Not surprisingly, they end up with drafts that are overgeneralized and not very interesting. Overgeneralization can take many forms, but it usually results from the same cause: writers doing their best to get information down on paper and make some sense of it. In first drafts of personal experience papers, for example, writers may try to summarize the whole story and its meaning. In first drafts of argumentative and informational papers, writers may offer capsule summaries of their opinions. These approaches are expected — even necessary — in an exploratory first draft but would seriously damage the effectiveness of the final paper.

The problem of overgeneralization can be combatted with two apparently contradictory revision strategies. *Limiting* involves focusing on a narrow portion of a topic and eliminating extraneous material. *Adding* involves incorporating new details to make writing more vivid and powerful. Used together, the strategies of limiting and adding can help turn a bland, overgeneralized first draft into an energetic, focused paper.

RECOGNIZING OVERGENERALIZATION

The first step in fighting overgeneralization is learning to see it in your own writing. Here, for example, are several overgeneralized openings, some of which come from the early drafts of finished essays found elsewhere in this book.

Life is so full of ups and downs that it sometimes drives me crazy. Last summer was like that, up one week, down the next. Picking eggs every day nearly drove me crazy, but it was better than picking potatoes, which I did at the end of the summer.

Last winter I spent nearly a month with the Outward Bound program. This action-packed winter camping trip proved to be almost more than I could handle. From the tragedy of a close friend nearly drowning to my own experience nearly freezing to death, I discovered a new side of myself and became a new person.

The American timber wolf, the most noble of all North American predators, has been methodically and tragically exterminated from every state in the country due to greed, misunderstanding, and fear.

Anybody who has ever tasted a Ben and Jerry's ice cream cone knows that they make the best ice cream in the world. Since Ben and Jerry make their ice cream right here in Burlington, Vermont, we wanted to find out the secret of their success.

These openings provide several clues to the problems typical of first-draft writing: they contain summaries, platitudes, prejudgments, overstatements, misstatements, and misdirection.

SUMMARY.   Some of the preceding examples offer a summary rather than particulars about the essay to follow: the ups and downs of potato picking, the action-packed trip. While summaries are useful at many points in writing, the particulars and details are more likely to attract and hold attention. Starting an essay with a summary asks readers to take on trust rather than by example that what follows will be interesting and true.

PLATITUDE.   When readers are told that life has its "ups and downs" or that an experience made the writer "a new person," they are hearing a platitude, a cliché about life. Platitudes decrease readers' expectations for fresh, original insights.

PREJUDGMENT.   Some of these passages tell readers how they should react to the information about to be related. The story is either action-packed, a rebirth, or tragic — judgments made for readers by the writer. When writers prejudge an experience or idea, they take the act of interpretation away from readers, unwittingly decreasing readers' involvement in the paper.

OVERSTATEMENT.   Some of the preceding passages make very large claims that will be difficult to substantiate: that the wolf is the "most noble of all North American predators," for example. Since critical readers distrust exaggeration, these passages are warnings that the writers' assertions are not to be trusted.

MISSTATEMENT.   In an effort to make their writing powerful and emphatic, some of these writers have misstated the facts. It is not true, for example, that Ben and Jerry's ice cream is still made in Burlington, since the plant has moved to Waterbury. A reader who finds such a misstatement, small though it may be, will read cautiously and skeptically thereafter.

MISDIRECTION.   In addition, though you cannot tell it from reading only the opening lines of the four examples, some of these writers don't know yet what their theme, thesis, or story really is.

Writers who do not yet know the full extent of their subject see it as if from a distance — and from a distance even cities and mountains look small, well defined, and manageable. Writers have the choice of staying far away, letting the first-draft generalizations stand, or moving in close, narrowing and sharpening the focus, adding details. Doing real writer's work means exploring the geography up close, finding out which path to follow home.

The best way to handle overgeneralizations is to get them down on paper where you can examine them. Let the first-draft writing take you where it will. Let it get you started — but don't settle for it. Plan in the second draft to limit your focus and in the third draft to begin building it back up, making it clearer, sharper, more believable each time.

LIMITING SCOPE

Writers often overgeneralize in first drafts because their topics are too broad. To write about them fully would require a book rather than an essay. One way to fight overgeneralization is therefore to limit the scope of your paper, the conceptual ground you are trying to cover. You can do this by focusing on a narrower topic or by focusing on a topic that's closer to home; often writers do both at once.

To limit the scope by narrowing your topic, try to identify the many subtopics *within* your topic and to find one that especially interests you. Instead of trying to cover endangered wildlife in general, for example, could you limit it to a particular issue, species, or habitat? Or, better still, to a particular species in a particular habitat?

In Brendan's first draft of his argumentative paper about American timber wolves, he had already limited the topic to one species of wildlife in one country. However, even that topic proved too broad. As he read and researched, he limited his topic still further, to the reintroduction of wolves into Yellowstone National Park. The final draft of Brendan's paper (see Chapter 13 for the complete draft) now begins this way:

> Since 1926, there have been no wolves in Yellowstone National Park. The modern wolf inhabited the area of Yellowstone, as well as the greater part of the North American continent, for well over a million years before the Europeans settled the New World. Upon arrival, white settlers began to push the wolf from its natural territory. With the settlers' movement west and with their increased development and agriculture, the wolf's range in the United States rapidly shrunk and eventually disappeared.

Another way to limit your scope is to restrict your investigation to a local issue or to a local manifestation of a national issue. This not only will help narrow your topic but also will allow you to do field research and experience some dimension of your topic firsthand.

For example, the collaborative research and writing group that set out to investigate Ben and Jerry's, the Vermont ice cream company, began by asking broad questions about "the secret of the company's success." However, they quickly decided to limit their investigation to what they could observe through field research at local ice cream shops and production facilities. This in turn resulted in a more focused topic, the company's surprising combination of business success and social responsibility. (See Chapter 21 for a complete draft of this paper.)

WRITING 1

Block out a portion of your journal or class notebook exclusively for notes on the revision of one paper. In this section, try to limit the scope of your paper first by narrowing the topic and second by focusing on a local aspect of the topic.

LIMITING TIME AND PLACE

Another way to fight overgeneralization is to limit time and place. Rather than limiting your paper's topic as an idea or concept, you limit its chronological and physical boundaries: focusing on days rather than years, neighborhoods rather than cities. Of course, limiting time and place often results in a more limited scope as well.

Consider, for example, this paragraph from a first draft by Amanda, a first-year student from Scotland, writing a paper entitled "Waitressing":

> For most of this summer I again worked on the farm, where I removed rotten, diseased potato shaws from a field all day. But I was in the sun all the time with a good bunch of people so it was quite good fun. . . . My waitressing job was nothing to get excited about either. I signed up with an employment agency and got a waitressing job in Aberdeen, a city thirty miles north of our farm. It was only for one week, but I didn't mind--it was the first job that I had got myself and I felt totally independent.

Amanda has squeezed into one paragraph two jobs (waitressing and farming), two locations (Aberdeen and the farm thirty miles away), and a whole summer. To cover all of this, she has room only for broad generalizations — both in this paragraph and in the rest of her draft.

To limit her paper, Amanda chose one time and place (October and on the farm) and focused on those in the next draft.

> [Digging potatoes] was always in October, so the weather was never very good. It either rained or was windy, often both. Some days it would be so cold that we would lie in between the drills of undug potatoes to protect ourselves from the wind.

As you can see, once Amanda began to *limit*, she intuitively began to *add* interesting specifics and details that make writing informative and enjoyable.

After witnessing the life and energy in her second draft, Amanda revised again, not about what *usually* occurred in October, but about what occurred on one particular day in October.

> Potatoes, mud, potatoes, mud, potatoes, that was all I saw in front of me. They moved from my right side to my left, at hip level. A conveyor belt never stopping. On and on and on.
>
> I bounced and stumbled around as the potato harvester moved over the rough earth, digging the newly grown potatoes out of the ground, transporting them up a conveyor belt and pushing them out in front of me and three other ladies, two on either side of the belt.
>
> The potatoes passed fast, a constant stream. My hands worked deftly, pulling out clods of dirt, rotten potatoes, old shaws, and anything else I found that wasn't a potato. They were sore, rubbed raw with the constant pressure of holding dirt. They were numb, partly from the work and partly from the cold. It was October, the ground was nearly frozen, the mud was hard and solid. Cold. Dirt had gotten into my yellow and yet brown rubber gloves, had wedged under my nails increasing my discomfort.

In this draft, Amanda found her story. The specific idea to limit the time frame had made all the difference, and had Amanda not gone back and revised her paper, she wouldn't have found the story that most interested her.

Strategies for Limiting

The following ideas will tighten the focus of your paper.

1. Ask yourself what your paper is about; don't settle for first hunches. Try writing in your journal about what your paper means to you personally.
2. When you are investigating an issue, consider a local topic that allows you to observe a place and interview the people involved.
3. When you are writing about something you have experienced personally, consider limiting your attention to one time or one place.

WRITING 2

Read again the last version of Amanda's potato paper. Which lines or words stand out as especially strong writing? Explain what makes them strong.

ADDING DETAILS

Generalization is death to good writing. The problem with most generalizations, including this one, is that everyone has heard them and no one fully believes them. We all hear that smoking is hazardous to our health, that the ozone layer is in trouble, and so on. But hearing these generalizations over and over again numbs us rather than makes us more attentive.

What makes people pay attention to these and other issues are the details that bring them to life. One of the key qualities of interesting writing is that it teaches readers something they did not already know — something beyond the generalizations they've already heard. When a subject is explored through careful research and exposed through thoughtful writing, readers find themselves learning something new and wanting to learn more.

Once you have limited your paper's scope, time, or place, two important things will happen: first, you will find more to say of a specific nature, and second, your paper will have more room to include these specifics.

The research team investigating the success of Ben and Jerry's wrote a generalized first draft full of familiar phrases about a good product and happy employees. But after limiting their investigation to local ice cream stores and production facilities, the writers found that they could incorporate the telling details they gathered by firsthand observation.

> Around the corner are five black steps that lead to the upstairs where the ice cream is sold. At the top of the stairs, next to a white metal wastebasket, is a blue bucket that says "We are now recycling spoons." On every table in the room are napkin dispensers saying "Save a tree, please take only one napkin."

On the one hand, this is an example of detailed descriptive writing meant to give readers the feel of the ice cream store. On the other hand, the recycling signs provide readers with concrete evidence that supports the claim that Ben and Jerry's cares about the environment, an important theme in the research report. Details not only add life, they add power and authority by lending credibility to your assertions.

WRITING 3

Identify a place that contains information relevant to a paper you are writing. If possible, visit this place and describe any concrete details that you find there, especially any that may relate to a theme you are developing. If you are writing from memory, close your eyes and visit this place in your imagination and describe the details you find there.

ADDING QUOTATIONS

When you add quotations to your writing, you let other people speak in their own words. This is a natural complement to limiting time and place, like putting living characters on sets you have created. Unlike summaries and paraphrases of past action, quotations re-create action as if it were happening at the moment, so that readers become witnesses and interpreters instead of passive recipients of already-digested information. (For more on quotations, paraphrases, and summaries, see Chapter 19.)

In many cases, the most powerful quotations are not from written sources but from living people, those who were actually on the scene at the moment you're writing about. If your subject is a personal experience, you will probably add quotations in the form of re-created dialogue and interior monologue; if you are writing an argumentative or informational paper, you will probably add quotations collected in interviews. When you integrate quotations, the voices of other people will enhance and complement your own voice, making your paper both more lively and more authoritative.

Adding dialogue requires remembering what was said sometime in the past or, more likely, re-creating or inventing what was probably said. Of course, nonfiction writers are not allowed to create fiction, that is, to invent something that never happened. But they are allowed some license in bringing back the past since nobody remembers *exactly* every word, sentence, or paragraph of conversation. Adding interior monologue requires capturing yourself in the act of talking silently to yourself. You won't remember *exactly* what you thought, but your re-creation should be plausible and should sound like you.

In response to an assignment to write a paper based on a significant personal experience, Karen used her first draft to describe her whole basketball season in fewer than three pages, concluding with the team playing in the Massachusetts semifinals.

> We lost badly to Walpole in what turned out to be our final game. I sat on the bench most of the time. The coach refused to put me in until the fourth quarter when there were five minutes left and we were already twenty points behind.

As you can see, Karen's first draft included much summary ("We lost badly") and paraphrase ("The coach refused"), storytelling techniques that allow writers to cover ground rapidly but do little to involve readers or create excitement.

In her second draft, Karen limited her paper to the last eight minutes of the final game. She re-created the same scene described in her first-draft paragraph, this time using dialogue and interior monologue.

> "Girls, you have got to keep your heads in the game. Don't let them get you down," Coach Gleason shouted. "You've worked so hard all season. You are just as good as them, just look at our record, 18–2–0."
>
> "Coach, they're killing us," Allison said. "They're making us look like fools, running right by us. We're down by twenty with eight minutes to go. It's hopeless."
>
> "I don't want to hear anyone talk like that. You girls have worked too hard to get to this point and give up. You can't quit now."

> Yeah, think of every sweat-dripping, physically grueling, suicide-sprinting, drill-conditioning Saturday morning practice this year. ("OK girls, for every missed foul shot it's one full suicide!") Oh, yes, I remember those practice sessions just fine.

This draft puts readers on the bench with Karen, hearing what she heard, experiencing her frustration as she did at the time.

If you are writing an explanatory or argumentative paper, you will probably add quotations from interviews, perhaps the most powerful kind of field research. In an interview, you ask someone for his or her observations, interpretations, and opinions — expert and otherwise — on the issue you are investigating.

A group of first-year writing students collaboratively investigated the role of the Ronald McDonald House in providing housing for out-of-town parents while their children stayed in local hospitals. In their first draft the writers reported the following information from newspaper sources:

> The McDonald's corporation actually provided less than 5% of the total cost of starting the Ronald McDonald House. The other 95% came from local businesses and special-interest groups.

By the time they wrote their second draft, however, the group had visited the house and interviewed the director, whose words now add both life and authenticity to the report.

> "Our biggest problem is that people think we're supported by the McDonald corporation. We have to get people to understand that anything we get from McDonald's is just from the particular franchise's generosity--and may be no more than is donated by other local merchants. Martins, Hood, and Ben and Jerry's provide much of the food. McDonald's is not obligated to give us anything. The only reason we use their name is because of its child appeal."

In the final draft the writers included both pieces of information, one written with the authority of statistics, the other spoken with personal authority.

Whether you are re-creating dialogue or adding interview material, make sure the quotations serve your purpose and advance the paper. Because the sound of people talking adds life to writing, it is sometimes tempting to keep adding and inventing human voices, making the paper lively but sometimes losing the point in the process. Use careful judgment and strive for balance.

Strategies for Adding

The following ideas will add life to your papers.

1.   When you visit places, take careful notes including details that appeal to the senses of sight, sound, touch, smell, and taste. These specific words will help you add convincing details when you write your paper.

2. When you include interview material, be faithful to the spirit of the occasion and the character of the person talking.
3. When you re-create dialogue or interior monologue from memory, close your eyes, visualize the experience, and make your re-created words faithful to the spirit of the occasion.
4. When you include quotations, write with respect for the speaker and represent him or her as you would like to be represented yourself.
5. Be judicious in your use of quotations: summary and paraphrase work well to cover ground or time rapidly or to set up a context for more detailed discussion.

WRITING 4

Interview a classmate about anything (favorite food, worst class, last night) for a few minutes and take notes to capture the essence of what he or she says. Now reconstruct a paragraph from theses notes. What do you choose to summarize? What do you carefully leave in the person's own language? Why?

SUGGESTIONS FOR WRITING AND RESEARCH

Individual

1. Write the first draft of a personal experience paper as an overview of the whole experience. Write the second draft by limiting the story to one day or less of this experience. Write the third draft by limiting it to one hour. For your final draft(s), revise the version that most pleases you.
2. Write the first draft of an argumentative or interpretive paper as an overview of the whole issue you intend to deal with. In the second draft write three pages about something you cover in one page in the first draft. In the third draft write three more pages about something covered in one page in the second draft. For your final draft, revise the version that most pleases you.
3. In revising a personal experience paper, locate a place where you paraphrase yourself or somebody else speaking, and replace the paraphrase with reconstructed dialogue or interior monologue.

Collaborative

In revising a collaborative paper based on research, locate a place in the paper where interview information would add life or credibility; find several appropriate people to interview, divide responsibilities, and add that information to your paper.

Chapter 24

Switching and Transforming

I never realized before that in revising you can do drafts from totally different perspectives and keep experimenting with your ideas. When you write the final draft, it could be totally different from how you expected it to come out in the beginning.

— GARY

THE LAST CHAPTER DESCRIBED TWO OF THE MOST COMMON REVISING STRATEGIES: limiting a paper's focus and adding new information. The strategies described in this chapter — switching and transforming — are less common but equally capable of advancing a draft. Writers revise by *switching* when they change their paper's tense or point of view. Writers revise by *transforming* when they change the paper's genre from one kind (a report or essay) to another (a letter or a play).

Both of these revising strategies work according to the same principle. Every type of paper has certain conventions that the writer is expected to follow: personal experiences are related in the first person and the past tense, research essays are objective and formal, and so on. These conventions establish a certain way of seeing; they predispose the reader — and the writer — to interpret and experience the information in the paper in a certain way. By changing a mechanical element such as tense or form, writers hope to provoke a conceptual reassessment both in themselves and in their readers.

These strategies are useful revising tools because they create distance by forcing writers to resee the events in their papers from a different perspective. Finally, they are fun and exciting — which is often exactly what writers need after working long and hard to put together a first draft.

When and under what circumstances should you try switching and transforming? There are no rules, but you might try them when your language seems stuffy or boring. Or you might plan to write one draft using a switching or transforming strategy, just to find out what you learn by doing so. Most writers try switching or transforming entire papers, but you can also use these strategies on just a limited part of the paper, to see where it leads you.

It's important to weigh gains and losses whenever you use a radical revision technique such as switching or transforming. Conventions have been developed because they aid readers' understanding, and if you disregard the conventions you risk confusing your readers. Always consider whether you have gained more than you have lost.

Like anything else, switching and transforming are not irreversible. You can experiment with them to refresh and challenge yourself and then use a more conventional approach in your next draft. Or, if your instructor is receptive to such approaches, you can hand in a switched or transformed version of your assignment. If your instructor would prefer papers written according to traditional conventions, reserve the strategies of switching and transforming for intermediate drafts only.

The following pages focus on personal experience papers and research essays in particular, but remember that these switching and transforming strategies can be used with any piece of writing.

SWITCHING TENSE

An interesting technique for switching the way you see an experience, story, issue, or idea is to write a draft in a verb tense different from the tense you've used in previous drafts. The most common way to recount personal experiences that have taken place in the past is to use the past tense: *Once upon a time* or *Last night* or *When I visited England.* The past tense is also conventionally used in research essays, both because the events reported have already occurred and because the past tense establishes scholarly distance and detachment. But both personal experience papers and research essays can benefit from being put into the present tense.

Switching in Experience Papers

Dawn used the past tense in a first draft about her summer experience as a nurse's aide in a hospital.

> Well, I walked into the first room, expecting to see women, but no, there were men lying in their beds. My face turned red with embarrassment. I didn't expect that I would have to take care of men. So Charlene gave me a washcloth and a towel and told me to wash and dress them. As I washed them, I thought to myself, I can deal with this.

Dawn's past-tense draft recounts a past summer's experience in convincing, graphic detail. However, she decided to try another draft in present tense.

> Up the steps through the big white door again. The full odor of urine strikes my nose. Sounds quiet . . . of course it is, it's 6:30 in the morning. Time to punch in already! Seems like I just got here.

Another eight hours for a small paycheck. I hope my feet stay under me.

   "Dawn, you have assignment five!" yells Terri.

   "Gee, thanks. Why do I get stuck with the men's section? Just because I'm younger?"

Dawn uses some of the same material here (being assigned the men's ward) but presents it as if it were just happening, putting readers with her on the ward. Notice that she uses dialogue and internal monologue as an easy and natural part of the present-tense experience, which, in turn, adds detail and authenticity to her account. For her final draft Dawn switched her entire paper to the present tense and limited her story to the experiences that happened on one eight-hour shift.

Switching in Research Papers

   The following example is taken from a collaborative research essay investigating the effect of lake pollution on city beaches. The paper was based on substantial library and field research, and the early drafts were written in a conventionally formal and objective voice, using the past tense. For a later draft, the team decided to switch to the present tense.

   How do you close down a public beach? You can't barricade the water, can you? But people know the sewage system is dumping raw sewage into the lake, and they won't swim there. The newspaper always calls the contamination "fecal coliform," which according to the dictionary is "bacteria that indicate human waste." But you know what they're talking about.

Switching to the present tense resulted in a number of other changes in perspective and tone, which combined to create a direct, honest, informal student voice. The writers decided to preserve this voice for the introductory part of their paper, since their readers included other students in the class. Most of the twenty pages that follow, however, are written in a conventionally objective manner, usually in the past tense.

Weighing Gains and Losses

   The advantage of switching to the present tense is that it lets you resee the experience or information as unfinished and still open to interpretation, which in turn allows you to reexamine, reconsider, and reinterpret it as well — all essential activities for successful revision. The advantage for readers is that the present tense puts them closer to the story, side by side with the writer, causing them to wonder what will happen next and to read with a sense of mystery and suspense.

The disadvantage is that the present tense makes it difficult for you to reflect on, process, or summarize the experience or information. So long as writers maintain the present tense, they must pretend — in their language — to have no more distance from, perspective on, or understanding of their experience than their readers have. Essays written in the present tense may also seem more like fiction and thus less believable since readers know that the experience cannot really be happening at the same time it is being written about. Consequently, though it is a good idea to try at least one draft in the present tense, it may not work in the final draft unless it especially suits your purpose.

WRITING 1

Write several pages in your journal about a past experience, using the present tense as if you were reliving what you are writing about. Then reread the passage and describe its effect on you as both writer and reader.

SWITCHING POINT OF VIEW

Switching the point of view means switching the perspective from which a story, essay, or report is related by the writer. For example, in recounting a personal experience, the most natural point of view is the first person (*I, we*), with the writer relating each event as it happened to him or her: *On Friday I went to a concert.* In recounting the results of research, the most conventional point of view is third person (*he, she, it*), with the writer keeping to the background or disappearing completely: *The prison is surrounded by high brick walls.* Sometimes it is useful to switch from the conventional point of view, if only for just a draft: describing a personal experience in the third person or the results of research in the first person.

Switching in Experience Papers

Sometimes it is useful for writers to attempt to see themselves and their experience from the outside, as others do. You can do this by simply changing all first-person pronouns to third-person pronouns, so that *I* becomes *he* or *she*. Or you can adopt the role or persona of another person looking at the events and refer to yourself as *he* or *she*.

In the following passage from an intermediate draft, Karen recounts the last five minutes of a basketball game in which her team was competing for the Massachusetts state championship. In previous drafts she told the story from the first-person point of view. For this draft, she adopts the perspective of the play-by-play announcer calling the game and describes her own entry into the game in the announcer's voice.

Well, folks, it looks as if Belmont has given up. Coach Gleason is preparing to send in his subs. It has been a rough game for Belmont.

> They stayed in it during the first quarter, but Walpole has run away
> with it since then. Down by twenty with only six minutes left,
> Belmont's first sub is now approaching the bench.
>
> Megan Sullivan goes coast to coast and lays it in for two. She has
> sparked Walpole from the start.
>
> The fans have livened up a bit, but oddly they aren't Walpole's fans,
> they're Belmont's. Cheers for someone named Karen are coming from
> the balcony. . . . Number eleven, Karen Kelly, replaces Michelle
> Hayes.

In this example, Karen actually becomes another person, not only referring to herself in the third person, as *Karen*, but also adopting the role of a play-by-play announcer. By adding this voice, Karen was able to resee and retell her own story with added drama and suspense. Karen decided to open her final draft from the announcer's point of view, switching after the first page back to the first-person perspective.

Switching in Research Papers

Switching point of view can also enhance research writing. The following example is taken from the paper investigating the effect of lake pollution on city beaches. After several early drafts written from the third-person point of view, the research team rewrote the paper as a story told by a first-person fictional narrator. The research essay begins with a fictional dialogue between two bicyclists riding next to the lake.

> We both started to cycle and I followed her down a path near the lake.
> "I'm just amazed by the beauty of the water. It is great to see the islands out
> there in front of us. This is paradise," I said.
>
> "Well, there are some problems with the lake. The sewage treatment
> plant." She paused and continued, "It's taken a lot of the beauty away."
>
> "What do you mean?" I asked, and she proceeded to tell me this story. . . .

The fictional opening uses a framing device often used by both short story writers and television documentary writers to raise audience curiosity and provide an excuse for telling a story. Here it serves the same initial purpose. The remainder of the paper recounts the bike riders' attempt to find out what is wrong with the lake, using a more conventional third-person point of view.

Weighing Gains and Losses

When you switch to unorthodox points of view, you gain distance from your experience or ideas, seeing details and implications perhaps invisible before. Your readers gain, too, from the additional details and insights, from the stylistic and tonal variety that makes technical information accessible to them as lay readers, and from the realism of the mixed perspective — which is, perhaps, the fairest representation of reality as most individuals experience it.

If you switch points of view without good reason, however, your writing may appear gimmicky rather than interesting. For example, to narrate life on the urban streets from the perspective of a homeless person may help your readers see the story in a new and useful light; choosing to narrate the same story from the perspective of a fire hydrant or a toy poodle may seem silly.

Strategies for Switching

These suggestions will help you see your paper from a new perspective.

1. Switch tense and point of view when revising intermediate drafts to create distance and stimulate new insights.
2. Signal changes in tense or point of view within the same piece of writing by giving clear typographical signals (subheads, indentations, type changes, or white space) or by carefully using transitional phrases.
3. Switch from past to present tense to create a sense of immediacy, suspense, and surprise. Switch back to past tense to synthesize, summarize, and reflect.
4. Switch your point of view by changing pronouns from third person (*he, she, it*) to first person (*I*). Or switch by referring to yourself in the third person when the assignment allows you to create a fictional voice.
5. Keep tense and point-of-view changes in the final draft only when they suit your purpose and are acceptable to your audience. Be careful not to switch back and forth so often within the paper that the effect is confusing rather than clarifying and interesting.

WRITING 2

Write several pages in your journal about yourself, using the third-person point of view. Reread what you have written and then describe the effect this perspective creates and whether or not such writing causes you to see your experience differently.

TRANSFORMING EXPERIENCE PAPERS

To transform a text is to change its form by casting it into a new genre. In early drafts, writers often attend closely to the content of their stories, arguments, or reports but pay little attention to the form in which these are presented, accepting the genre as a given. However, recasting initial ideas and information into a different genre presents them in a different light.

The possibilities for presenting information in different genres are endless, limited only by the writer's imagination. Consequently, keep in mind that some transformations are useful primarily to help you achieve a fresh perspective during revision while other transformations can be carried into the final draft when you find that they are the best way for you to present information to readers.

Personal experience assignments often benefit from transformation. Suppose, for example, that you are writing a paper about a week-long trip you took last year to someplace new and exciting. In your first draft or two you try to recapture the events, scenes, details, and dialogue of this experience, but you pay little attention to the form in which you tell your story, since you expect it to be an essay. This may be exactly what you want. However, before calling your final paper finished, suppose you imagine other genres in which you can tell the same story. What would happen to your account, for instance, if you recast it as a series of excerpts from an imaginary travel journal kept on the trip, a set of letters back home, or a column for a travel magazine or local newspaper? Each of these transformations can open up new possibilities.

Writing Journals

In the following example, Mary transformed a first-draft personal essay into a set of journal entries to capture the immediacy of her experience at a camp for emotionally disturbed children. She took advantage of the informal, conversational language characteristic of journal writing and of the fact that at the end of each entry the writer does not know what will happen the next day. In other words, using the journal genre helped Mary tell her story in a suspenseful manner.

> August 14. Tomorrow I leave for Camp Daybreak. I thought it was a good idea in May, when I applied for the job, but tonight I'm having second thoughts. I don't know anything at all about emotional disturbances--What will the kids be like? What will the camp be like? How will we be paired with the campers?

Note that in this single entry Mary uses past, present, and future tenses to capture her ambivalent feelings the night before setting off for camp. In other entries, Mary is able to work in the details of people, settings, and events by presenting them as memories of something that happened in the recent past. In the end, Mary re-created one entry per day over a six-day period for a twelve-page paper.

The journal form encourages informal, conversational language, creates a sense of chronological suspense, is an ideal form for personal reflection, substitutes dates for more complex transitions, and proves especially useful for conveying immediate experience over a long period of time.

Experimenting with Other Genres

In addition to journal writing, you might experiment with these other forms associated with personal experience.

LETTERS.   An experience might be rendered in a lively and interesting way by casting it as an exchange of letters between the writer and a trusted audience. The advantages of this genre are that all readers are familiar with letters and that, as in journals, the writer can adopt a friendly, informal voice, use dates for transitions, and maintain immediacy over a long period of time. The key advantage of a letter exchange over journals is the ease with which other voices (people writing letters in response) can be included.

POEMS.   Poetry can offer writers a powerful medium for conveying emotional experiences. The language can be condensed and transitions handled by the stanza form. While some types of poetry (the sonnet, for instance) must conform to certain structures, in modern poetry there are virtually no rules of form, style, reason, or rhyme. For novice writers, poems may be especially effective in conveying short, intense experience; it is more difficult to write long poems (more than a page or so) that will sustain readers' interest.

DRAMA.   A personal story can also be told by re-creating the setting where something happened and placing characters, including yourself, in that setting. In the dramatic genre, writers must convey their meaning through what the characters say out loud since the writer cannot relate what transpires inside the characters' minds. It is an excellent genre with which to create suspense, describe settings in vivid detail, and use the lively language of informal talk to advance your point.

WRITING 3

Describe the genre with which you are most familiar and comfortable: journals, letters, drama, or poetry. With which genre are you most comfortable as a reader? As a writer? Why do you think this is so?

TRANSFORMING RESEARCH PAPERS

In the world outside of college it is common for research information to be imported in different genres to different audiences: a report to a manager, a letter to the president, a pamphlet for the stockholders, and a news release for public media might all contain the same information. Similarly, information collected for a research paper can be presented in a variety of ways. An argumentative research paper can be transformed into a College Bowl debate or a series of letters to the editor of a local paper. An informational research paper can be transformed into an investigative report for *Newsweek* magazine or a "Reporter at Large" piece for *The New Yorker*. In other words, if you have initially drafted a research report as an academic paper, it might take on new life if you revised it into an alternative genre.

Writing Scripts

Chapter 23 contains samples of a research report on the Ronald McDonald House. The writers struggled through several rather vague and undefined drafts until, in their final draft, they turned their report into an imaginary script for the CBS news show *60 Minutes*. Since these first-year writers are not reporters for the television show, the form they chose is, of course, fictional. But the content remains real, consisting of the factual information and statistical data uncovered by both library and field research.

The transformed paper uses a combination of monologue, dialogue, and description. The script opens with a monologue by a fictional "John Smith," who is meant to be a television reporter like Chris Wallace or Diane Sawyer, standing before a camera.

> SMITH: Hello, this is John Smith reporting for *60 Minutes*. Our topic this week is the Ronald McDonald House. Here I am, in front of the house, but before I go inside, let me fill you in on the history of this and many other houses like it.
>
> In 1974, Fred Hill, a Philadelphia Eagles football player, opened the first Ronald McDonald house in downtown Philadelphia. Hill's daughter was suffering from leukemia, so he knew what families with hospitalized children were going through. . . .

When writing a script for the fictional Smith, the researchers sought to adopt the clear, simple language of TV reporters, which helped them focus their information. The script also includes dialogue, as Smith learns about the house by going on a walking tour with a volunteer hostess named Robin (a real person) and interviewing her.

Within the script are descriptive scenes called "Camera Eye" that portray the house from the objective view of the TV camera. They are set in italic type to distinguish them from the rest of the script.

> *Toward the back of the house, three cars and one camper are parked in an oval-shaped gravel driveway. Up three steps onto a small porch are four black plastic chairs and a small coffee table. On top of the table is a black ashtray filled with crumpled cigarette butts.*

This procedure both mimics the conventions of *60 Minutes* and allows the writers to accomplish one of their central goals — showing readers what the Ronald McDonald House looks like.

When these writers decided to use the TV documentary genre, they were looking for an interesting way to tell a story based on field research. But the new genre raised new questions: How could they make Smith sound like a real reporter? How should they indicate the difference between what a TV audience would hear and what it would see? How should they keep the whole thing moving along? Finding the answers to these questions proved interesting and fun, and the team learned a great deal about presenting information in a powerful, engaging fashion.

Experimenting with Other Genres

Research writing may take innumerable forms. Here are some of the possibilities.

STORIES.   One way to present research information is to adopt an obviously fictional form, such as a story, and embed the factual information in a made-up setting. For example, the beach pollution research paper discussed earlier includes fictional narrators but employs authentic tours of the treatment plant, some interviews with merchants and shoppers, and statistical results from a survey.

BOOKS WITH CHAPTERS.   Several authors can collaborate on writing a short book with several chapters. Such a form could include a table of contents, preface, foreword, afterword, introduction, and so on. One such example was written by four students about the plight of the homeless in a small city. This paper was written as a short book with four five-page chapters, one by each of the four writers, and a collaborative introduction.

ARTICLES FOR MAGAZINES.   If you are investigating consumer products, such as VCRs, computers, stereo equipment, motorcycles, automobiles and the like, you can write the results of your investigation as if it were a report for *Consumer Reports*. If you are investigating an issue, write about it as if for *Time* or *Newsweek*.

Strategies for Transforming

The following ideas will present your paper in a new light.

1. Try a new form only when you have time. If it doesn't work, you can still write a final draft in conventional form.
2. You will not know the effect of a new form until you actually write in it for awhile. Don't try to just *imagine* what the form will do to your ideas.
3. Use a form that complements and enhances the content of the paper. Don't use a new form just for the sake of doing so.
4. Be consistent within the form you choose. For example, if you write an article for *Consumer Reports*, follow that publication's style and conventions all the way through.
5. First check with your instructor before writing a final draft as a transformation.

SUGGESTIONS FOR WRITING AND RESEARCH

Individual

1. To gain a perspective in writing a personal experience paper, write the next draft from the third-person point of view, as if somebody else were observing you from the outside or as if you were watching yourself from a distance.
2. Write a draft of a paper based on either memory or research in which you deliberately weave multiple points of view and tenses. Consider the advantages and disadvantages of this draft before deciding how to proceed in the next one.
3. Select any paper you are writing and rewrite it in a different genre. Before you start writing, make a list of the genres that have the greatest possibilities for your paper so you see the range you have to choose from.

Collaborative

1. For a class research project, interview college instructors in different departments concerning their thoughts about transforming academic papers into other genres. Are they agreeable or reluctant to encourage such writing? Write up the results in any form that seems useful.
2. As a class, compile a catalog in which you list and describe as many alternative forms for college papers as you can.

EDITING

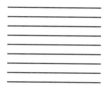

Chapter **25**

Working Paragraphs

Paragraphs tell readers how writers want to be read.
— WILLIAM BLAKE

WHILE THERE ARE NO HARD AND FAST RULES FOR EDITING, there are important points to keep in mind as your essay nears completion. Once you are satisfied with the general shape, scope, and content of your paper, it's time to stop making larger conceptual changes — to stop revising — and start attending to smaller changes in paragraphs, sentences and words — to begin editing. When you edit, you shape these three elements (paragraphs, sentences, and words) so that they fulfill the purpose of the paper, address the audience, and speak in the voice you have determined is appropriate for the paper.

This chapter describes the way in which you design and shape effective paragraphs. Chapter 26 examines the specialized paragraphs that open and close your paper. And Chapter 27 shows you how to put together sentences and choose words for maximum effect.

THE WORK OF PARAGRAPHS

Most texts of a page or more in length are subdivided by indentations or breaks — paragraphs — that serve as guideposts, or as Blake puts it, "that tell readers how writers want to be read." Readers expect paragraph breaks to signal new ideas or directions; they expect each paragraph to have a single focus as well and to be organized in a sensible way; and they expect clear transition markers to link one paragraph to the next.

In truth, however, there are no hard and fast rules for what makes a paragraph, how it needs to be organized, what it should contain, or how long it should be.

I could, for instance, start a new paragraph here (as I have just done), leaving the previous sentence to stand as a single-sentence paragraph and so call a little extra attention to it. Or I could connect both that sentence and these to the previous paragraph and have a single five-sentence paragraph to open this section.

Most experienced writers paragraph intuitively rather than analytically; that is, they indent almost unconsciously, without thinking deliberately about it, as they develop or emphasize ideas. Sometimes their paragraphs fulfill conventional expectations, presenting a single well-organized and -developed idea, and sometimes they serve other purposes — for example, creating pauses or breathing spaces or points of emphasis.

The example paragraphs that follow are excerpts from student papers that have already appeared in this textbook. The paragraphs do different kinds of work, and although each is a good example, none is perfect. As you study them, bear in mind that each is illustrative of various purposes and organization, not definitive.

WRITING WELL-ORGANIZED PARAGRAPHS

Unity: Stick to a Single Idea

Paragraphs are easiest to write and easiest to read when each one presents a single idea, as most of the paragraphs in this textbook do. The following paragraph, from Brendan's essay on reintroducing wolves to Yellowstone National Park, focuses strictly on the role of wolves in the park.

> In recent years there has been a movement to bring the wolf back to Yellowstone Park. A battle is being waged between environmental conservationists, who support the reintroduction of wolves, and sheep and cattle farmers and western hunters, who oppose it. So far, legislators, representing the farmers and hunters, have been able to block the reintroduction of wolves. The wolf, however, should be reintroduced to Yellowstone National Park.

Focus: Write a Topic Sentence

One of the easiest ways to keep each paragraph focused on a single idea is to include a *topic sentence* in it, announcing or summarizing the topic of the paragraph, with the rest of the sentences supporting that main idea. Sometimes topic sentences conclude a paragraph, as in the previous example, where the topic sentence is also the thesis statement for the whole essay. More commonly, however, the topic sentence introduces the paragraph, as in the next example, also from Brendan's essay.

> Wolves need to be in Yellowstone in order to make it a complete ecosystem. Edward Lewis of the Greater Yellowstone Coalition, a regional conservation group, says that wolves are the missing link. They are the only major species which existed in historical times but is missing now. Wolves would help to balance the ecosystem by preying upon deer, elk, and moose. This would reduce the damage that overpopulation of these animals does to the area and limit the number of these species that starve during harsh winters.

The sentences after the first one support and amplify the topic sentence, explaining how wolves would make the park "a complete ecosystem."

Most of the following examples have topic sentences, and all focus on single subjects. Note, however, that not all paragraphs need topic sentences. For example, if a complicated idea is being explained, a new paragraph in the middle of the explanation will create a pause point. Sometimes paragraph breaks are inserted to emphasize an idea, like my own one-sentence paragraph, earlier, which is a topic and a support sentence all in one. Additionally, paragraphs in a personal experience essay seldom have a deliberate topic sentence since these sorts of essays are seldom broken into neat topics (see, for example, Judith's paragraph below). Nevertheless, in academic writing, there is great reverence for topic sentences because they point to clear organization and your ability to perform as an organized and logical thinker within the discipline. Thus, when you write academic papers, attend to topic sentences.

WRITING 1

Examine the paragraphs in a recent draft, and pencil in brackets around those that stick well to a single idea. Put an X next to any sentences that deviate from the main idea in a paragraph, and note whether you want to delete that sentence or use it to start a new paragraph. Finally, underline each topic sentence. If a paragraph does not have one, should it? If so, write it.

Order: Follow a Recognizable Logic

On first drafts, most of us write sentences rapidly and paragraph intuitively. However, when we revise and edit, it pays to make certain that paragraphs work according to a recognizable logic. There are dozens of organizational patterns that make sense; here we look at five of them: free association, rank order, spatial, chronological, and general to specific.

When ideas are organized according to *free association*, one idea triggers the next because it is a related one. Free association is especially common in advancing a narrative, as in a personal experience essay. It is quite fluid and suggestive and seldom includes topic sentences. In the following paragraph, Judith allows the first act of locking a door to trigger memories related to other locked doors.

> It is already afternoon. I fiddle with the key to lock the apartment door after me. I am not accustomed to locking doors. Except for the six months I spent in Boston, I have never lived in a place where I did not trust my neighbors. When I was little, we couldn't lock our farmhouse door; the wood had swollen, and the bolt no longer lined up properly with the hole, and nobody ever bothered to fix it. I still remember the time our babysitter, Rosie, hammered the bolt closed and we had to take the door off the hinges to get it open.

Notice that Judith uses a reverse chronological arrangement to order her associations, that is, she moves backward from the present — first to Boston, then to childhood — thereby using one pattern to strengthen another, helping us still further to follow her.

When ideas are arranged by *rank order*, that is, order of importance, the most significant idea is reserved for the end of the paragraph. The writer leads with the idea to be emphasized least, then the next most important, and so on. This paragraph is commonly introduced by a topic sentence alerting readers that an orderly list is to follow. Heather edited the following paragraph to summarize the importance of four ideas in her interpretive essay.

> These first two passages [in "Angelique's Letter"] are important in several ways. First, they show Angel's influence on his younger sister. Second, they introduce Angel's drive to make sure Angelique does not become pregnant and drop out of school "like the other girls in the neighborhood." Third, they show Angel's dedication to act on his resolve by turning innocent situations into lessons about inner-city life. Finally, the second passage ends with a clear warning that time is short, "And she was already talking about boys." If Angel wants to have an impact on his sister's life, he has to start now.

Notice that enumerating the ideas (first, second, etc.) helps readers keep track of each one. Heather could have edited her first sentence more sharply to set up the rest of the paragraph by replacing the vague phrase *in several ways* with the more precise *in four ways*, to reinforce the distinctiveness of each point. The result of paying attention to detail is improved readability.

When ideas are arranged *spatially*, each is linked to the next. Thus, the reader's eye is drawn through the paragraph as if through physical space. For example, a writer might describe a landscape by looking first at the field, then the forest, then the mountain, then the sky. In the following paragraph, Beth begins by showing Becky in the spatial context of her dormitory room; her description moves from bed to walls to floor.

> Becky sits cross-legged at the foot of the bottom bunk on her pink and green homemade quilt. She leans up against the wall and runs her fingers through her brown shoulder-length hair. The sound of James Taylor's "Carolina on my Mind" softly fills the room. Posters of John Lennon, James Dean, and Cher look down on us from her walls. Becky stares at the floor and scrunches her face as if she were thinking hard.

Becky's subtle, silent actions carry readers through the paragraph as Beth describes her sitting, leaning, listening, and staring — actions that set up the next paragraph in her paper in which Becky speaks.

When ideas or facts are arranged *chronologically*, they are presented in the order in which they happened, with the earliest first. Sometimes it makes sense to use *reverse chronology*, listing the most recent first and working backward in time. The following paragraph from a research paper illustrates normal chronology; it begins with the first microbrewery and then moves to a full-fledged brewers' festival five years later.

> According to Shaw (1990) the home brewing revolution did not begin in Vermont until February 1987 when Stephan Mason and Alan Davis opened Catamount Brewery, which offered golden lager, an amber ale, and a dark porter as well as several seasonal brews. This was only the beginning. In September 1992, the first Vermont Brewers Festival was held at Sugarbush Resort. Sixteen breweries participated and the forty-plus beers present ranged from American light lagers to German-style bock and everything in between. The beers included such colorful names as Tall Tale Pale Ale, Black Fly Stout, Slopbucket Brown Ale, Summer Wheat Ale, Avid Barley Wee Heavy, and Hickory Switch Smoked Amber Ale.

Notice that starting in the middle of the paragraph, another supportive pattern is at work here: the pattern of general to specific. It is unlikely that the first draft of this paragraph contained these mutually supportive organizational patterns; careful editing made sure the final draft did.

A *general to specific pattern* begins with an overall description or general statement and moves toward a description of smaller, more specific details. In the preceding paragraph, the general idea is "all breweries"; the specific idea is "Catamount beer."

The following two paragraphs in the same research essay are also organized general to specific, the first starting with the general category of brew pubs and moving to the specific Vermont Pub and Brewery, the next beginning with business in general and moving to Canadian business in particular.

> In addition to new breweries are brew pubs such as McNeill's Brewery in Brattleboro and the Vermont Pub and Brewery in Burlington. These are bars or restaurants which feature their own selection of beers brewed and served in-house only. Greg and Nancy Noonan, the owners of the Vermont Pub and Brewery, will be celebrating the fifth anniversary of their successful venture in December.

> According to Greg their business has been better than any of their predictions. He said, "Our first expectations were based on worst-case scenarios" (personal communication, November 17, 1992). In fact, for the Vermont Pub and Brewery there has not been any recession. Greg attributes this success to the consistency of the Burlington economic base and the increase of Canadian tourism: "Our Canadian business doubled or tripled since we opened on November 11, 1988."

Notice that the second paragraph does not start in a different direction or with a different topic from those in the first paragraph, though it is unified and has its own topic sentence. Instead it provides specific support for paragraph 1; its unifying subject is the speaker, Greg Noonan. In a previous draft, this paragraph was connected to the previous one; a new paragraph was created to hold the focus on the brewery. When we consider both paragraphs together, however, the principal organization of general to specific continues — from brew pubs in general to a specific brew pub to a specific brew pub owner talking.

Note, too, that *specific to general*, the reverse of the previous pattern, is also common and has a recognizable logic. For example, the brewery paper could have begun with two people sharing a specific beer in a specific pub; the writer then could have moved on to a description of the industry as a whole. The point here, as it is in all writing, is to edit carefully for pattern so that you lead your reader through the paper.

HELPING THE READER

Most of this discussion has focused so far on structures within paragraphs. When editing, it's important to know how to rewrite paragraphs to improve essay readability. However, you can improve readability in other ways as well. One of them is to break up lengthy paragraphs.

Paragraph breaks help readers pause and take a break while reading, allowing them, for example, to imagine or remember something sparked by the text and yet find their place again with ease. Breaking into a new paragraph can also recapture flagging attention, especially important in long essays, reports, or articles where detail sometimes overwhelms readers. And you can emphasize points with paragraph breaks, calling a little extra attention to what follows.

WRITING 2

Review a near-final draft of a paper you are working on, and identify the organizational pattern in each paragraph. Do you find a pattern to your paragraphing? Identify paragraphs that contain a single idea carefully developed and paragraphs that need to be broken into smaller paragraphs. What editing changes would you now make in the light of this review?

TRANSITIONS BETWEEN PARAGRAPHS

Your editing is not finished until you have linked the paragraphs, so that readers know where they have been and where they are going. In early drafts, you undoubtedly focused on getting your ideas down and paid less attention to clarifying relationships between ideas. Now, as you edit your final draft, consider the elements that herald transitions: words and phrases, subheads, and white spaces.

WORDS AND PHRASES.   Writers often use transitional expressions without consciously thinking about them. For example, in writing a narrative, you may naturally use sequential transition words to indicate a chronology: *first, second, third*; *this happened, next this happened, finally this happened*; or *last week, this week, yesterday, today*. Here are some other transitional words and phrases and their functions in paragraphs:

Contrast or change in direction: *but, yet, however, nevertheless, still, at the same time, on the other hand*

Comparison or similarity: *likewise, similarly*

Addition: *and, also, then, next, in addition, furthermore, finally*

Summary: *finally, in conclusion, in short, in other words, thus*

Example: *for example, for instance, to illustrate, specifically, thus*

Concession or agreement: *of course, certainly, to be sure, granted*

Time sequence: *first, second, third; (1), (2), (3); next, then, finally, soon, meanwhile, later, currently, eventually, at last*

Spatial relation: *here, there, in the background, in the foreground, to the left, to the right, nearby, in the distance, above, below*

There is no need to memorize these functions or words; you already know and have used all of them and usually employ them quite naturally. When reworking your final draft, though, be sure you have provided transitions. If you haven't, work these words in to alert your readers to what's coming next.

ALTERNATE TRANSITIONAL DEVICES.   Other common devices that signal transitions include subheadings, lines, alternate typefaces, and white spaces. The first two are more common in textbooks and technical reports, the latter two may appear in any text, including literary-style essays. When you edit your final draft, consider if using any of these techniques would make your ideas clearer.

SUBHEADS.   To call extra attention to material or to indicate logical divisions of ideas, some writers use subheads. They are more common in long research papers, technical reports, and laboratory analyses and less common in narrative essays. They are essential in textbooks, such as this one, for indicating divisions of complex material.

LINES.   Blocks of text can be separated by either continuous or broken dashes (-------) or asterisks (*****), which signify material clearly to be set off from other material. In technical writing, for example, material may even be boxed in by continuous lines to call special attention to itself. In a *New Yorker* research essay or short story, a broken line of asterisks may suggest a switch in time, place, or point of view.

ALTERNATE TYPEFACES. Writers who use computers can change fonts with ease. When they use alternate typefaces, they are indicating a transition or a change. In a narrative or essay, *italics* may suggest someone talking or the narrator thinking aloud. A switch to a smaller or larger typeface may signal information of less or more importance.

WHITE SPACE. You can indicate a sharp break in thought between one paragraph and the next by leaving an extra line of space between them (although the space break does not tell the reader what to expect next). When I use a space break, I am almost always suggesting a change in direction more substantial than a mere paragraph indentation; I want readers to notice the break and be prepared to make a larger jump than a paragraph break signals. In a narrative essay, I may use the space to suggest a jump in time (the next day, week, or year); in argumentative writing, to begin a presentation of an opposing point of view; in any essay, to introduce another voice. White space, in other words, substitutes for clear transition words and subheadings but does not explicitly explain the shift.

When I work on early drafts, I may use some of these transition or separation devices to help me keep straight the different parts of what I'm writing. In final drafts, I decide which devices will help my readers as much as they have helped me, and I eliminate those that no longer work. In other words, paragraphs and transitions are as useful for me when I'm drafting as they will be later for my readers.

WRITING 3

When you edit a final draft, look carefully at your use of transitional devices. Identify those that are doing their work well; add new ones where appropriate.

PARAGRAPHS AND THE ESSAY EXAM

Paragraph breaks, topic sentences, and transition and separation devices can have a marked impact on the readability of your answers on essay exams. Make an indentation each time you make a new point, so your reader will be sure to see each point. Use white space to emphasize a shift in topic or direction. (See Reference 3 for more information on essay examinations.)

Chapter 26

Opening and Closing

I could start this essay just about anywhere at all,
by telling you about the background, by stating the thesis, by telling
a funny story, or even by rambling, which is what I usually do.
Where do you think I should start?

— WENDY

M Y ADVICE, WENDY, is to lead with your best punch. Make your opening so strong your reader feels compelled to continue. Make your closing so memorable that your reader can't forget it.

Readers pay special attention to openings and closings, so make them work for you. Start with titles and lead paragraphs that grab readers' attention and alert them to what is to come; end with closings that sum up and reinforce where they've been. This chapter looks closely at how these special paragraphs function and how you can make these paragraphs stronger through skillful editing.

OPENINGS

Openings are first impressions. Your first paragraph — in fact, your whole first page — sets readers up for the rest of the paper. Here you provide the first clues about your subject, purpose, and voice and invite your audience to keep reading.

Good opening paragraphs are seldom written in first drafts. Often, it's not until you've finished a draft or two that you know exactly what your paper says and does. So when your paper is nearly finished, return to your first page, read it again, and edit carefully. The following examples of effective openings are taken from the student papers reproduced earlier in this textbook; all of them were rewritten at the editing stage.

Open with the Thesis Statement

Traditional college papers often open with a clear thesis statement that the rest of the paper will demonstrate. The following first paragraph from Heather's interpretive essay was edited extensively until it summarized the paper precisely and concluded with the thesis that the rest of the paper illustrates.

> "Angelique's Letter" tells a story about how a Puerto Rican college student named Angel decides to see his nine-year-old sister Angelique grow up having pride in herself and her culture, despite the disadvantages she will have to face throughout her life because of her race and economic background. Understanding the importance of education and achievement, Angel sets out to instill in his sister a sense of value towards these things, hoping that he will help her become all that she is capable of being.

Summary and thesis writing are among the most difficult of all writing tasks and for that reason are best written only when you are thoroughly familiar with your subject, which is seldom the case with early drafts. Hone your thesis statement to the sharpest possible sentence — this work will take a fair amount of effort — and then use it to conclude your opening paragraph.

Open with a Story

Most readers enjoy stories. Professional writers often open articles with anecdotes to catch readers' attention. The following first paragraph is from Judith's reflective essay about finding a safe place to study in the library. Only in her last draft did she decide to start at the door, in present tense, locking up. Then she edited carefully to bring readers with her as she developed her theme about the importance of personal safety.

> It is already afternoon. I fiddle with the key to lock the apartment door after me. I am not accustomed to locking doors. Except for the six months I spent in Boston, I have never lived in a place where I did not trust my neighbors. When I was little, we couldn't lock our farmhouse door; the wood had swollen, and the bolt no longer lined up properly with the hole, and nobody ever bothered to fix it. I still remember the time our babysitter, Rosie, hammered the bolt closed and we had to take the bolt off the hinges to get it open.

Open with a Specific Detail

Specific details appeal to readers' visual sense and help them see situations and settings. In early drafts, Beth opened her profile of Becky with Becky speaking; only in this latest version did she decide to set the physical scene first, letting Becky's manner and surroundings characterize her right from the start.

> Becky sits cross-legged at the foot of the bottom bunk on her pink and green homemade quilt. She leans up against the wall and runs her fingers through her brown shoulder-length hair. The sound of James Taylor's "Carolina on my Mind" softly fills the room. Posters of John Lennon, James Dean, and Cher look down on us from her walls. Becky stares at the floor and scrunches her face as if she were thinking hard.

Open with a Quotation

Although Beth decided not to open with her subject talking, an opening quotation can be an effective hook. Readers enjoy hearing the voices of people on the subject of the piece.

The following paragraph was Beth's original opening; she moved it to the second paragraph, adding the transitional first sentence to link the two paragraphs. (It would work equally well as her opening, since it introduces the reader to Becky's lively and interesting human voice, after which we expect more talk about her early years growing up "forever" with her mother and sister.)

> Finally, after minutes of silence [Becky] says, "I don't ever remember my father ever living in my house, really. He left when I was three and my sister was just a baby, about a year old. My mom took care of us all. Forever, it was just Mom, Kate, and me. I loved it, you know. Just the three of us together."

Sometimes it's just a matter of personal preference in deciding where to start. That, of course, is what editing is all about: trying one thing, then another, looking at options, in the end selecting the one that you think is best.

Open with an Interesting Statistic

Statistics that tell a clear story are another form of opening that suggests immediately that the writer has done his or her homework. The following sentences open the coauthored paper about the rise of the microbrewing industry in Vermont.

> The beer industry in the United States grosses forty billion dollars a year. Ninety-nine percent of those profits have been made by giant corporations such as Anheuser-Busch, Miller, and Coors (Mares, 1984, p. 112). But today, even though dollars are tight and industries are struggling to hold their ground, several microbreweries have gained a foothold in Vermont and they are fighting for their share of the profits (Shaw, 1990). This paper examines the options available to the Vermont beer drinker and explains what distinguishes these locally produced beers from their national competitors.

The more dramatic your statistics are, the more you should consider giving them prominence in your paper. In the preceding examples, the writers might have added one more sentence (always, more choices!) saying something like, "However, the new microbreweries, which today account for the 1 percent, are out to change that."

Open with a Question

Questions alert readers to the writer's subject and imply that the answer will be forthcoming in the paper. In the following example, Zoe leads with a simple question for readers to consider — and a question she intends to answer by becoming a professional photographer.

What makes a good advertising photograph?

Most writers ask unstated questions as the basis for their writing. For example, the microbrewery paper implicitly asks, "Why are microbreweries popular?" Beth's profile asks, "What is Becky like?" and Judith asks, "What has scholarship to do with safety?"

WRITING 1

Recast the opening of a paper you are currently working on using one or more of the suggestions in this section: a thesis, story, specific detail, quotation, interesting statistic, or provocative question. For your final draft, use the opening that pleases you most.

CLOSINGS

Closings are final impressions. Your concluding sentences, paragraphs, or the entire last page are your final chance to make the point of your paper stick in readers' minds. The closing can summarize your main point, draw a logical conclusion, speculate about the issues you've raised, make a recommendation for some further action, or leave your reader with yet another question to ponder.

After writing and revising your paper, attend once more to the conclusion, and consider if the final impression is the one you want. You may discover an earlier paragraph makes a more suitable ending, or you may need to write a new one to conclude what you've started. The following examples of effective closings are from student papers reproduced earlier in this textbook.

Close with a Summary Statement

The end of your paper is a good place to summarize the point of your paper. The following paragraph concludes Keith's investigation into the high cost of compact discs.

> So the next time you walk into Record Land, you know what you
> are paying for. A CD may be twice as expensive as a record, but the
> sound is twice as clear and the disc will last forever.

This conclusion closes a frame for Keith's paper, since his first paragraph invited readers to consider why CDs cost so much. Writers often develop such frames, a setting or idea in which the main part of the story takes place, in the final stages of writing to attract audience attention, and conclude by returning the essay to the place from which it started.

Close with a Logical Conclusion

Many argumentative papers present first one side of an issue and then the other side, ending by drawing conclusions that reasonable readers could be expected to believe. The final paragraph of Brendan's position paper draws the conclusion that wolves should be reintroduced into Yellowstone National Park.

> The reintroduction of wolves into Yellowstone National Park is
> both an important and reasonable proposal. In this age of environmen-
> tal abuse and excessive development by human beings, it seems only
> appropriate to set aside areas for the complete preservation of nature.
> Our National Parks are the ideal place for this. The wolf was once an
> integral part of the Yellowstone environment. Its reintroduction would
> complete the ecosystem and improve the natural situation. The argu-
> ments posed by farmers and hunters are insubstantial. An act of
> Congress requires government agencies to return the wolf to its original
> habitat. Why, then, are there still no wolves in Yellowstone?

In argumentative papers, with two reasonable sides to an issue, use your most careful and precise language when you draw conclusions. For this reason, it's especially important to edit carefully at the very end of your paper, assessing the impact of your final words on your audience.

Close with a Real or a Rhetorical Question

When you close a paper with a question, you invite readers to give the answer you've led them to. The final sentence of Brendan's wolf paper asks a rhetorical question, which he expects readers to answer in a predictable manner.

> Why, then, are there still no wolves in Yellowstone?

Another effective way to end is to pose unanswered questions that you have not investigated, in this way inviting readers to take the issue further. For example, Brendan might have asked similar questions about the disappearance of other large predators, such as mountain lions, from other national parks or about the disappearance of wolves from parks in the eastern United States.

Close with a Speculation

In papers relating personal experience, reflection, or speculation, the issues you raise have no clear-cut conclusions or demonstrated theses. In these papers, then, the most effective conclusion is often one in which you admit some uncertainty, as Zoe does at the end of her investigation of about becoming a photographer's assistant.

> So I'll keep sitting around hoping for a break. I can't guarantee that this research method for landing an internship will work; it still remains to be tried and tested. To my knowledge, there is no foolproof formula for a successful start. Like everybody else before me, I'm creating my own method as I go along.

The casualness in such a paragraph, as if it were written off the cuff, is often deceptive. While that is the effect Zoe wanted to create, this paragraph emerged only late in her drafting process, and when it did, she edited and reedited it to achieve just the effect she wanted.

Close with a Recommendation

Sometimes writers conclude by inviting their readers to do something — to support some cause, for example, or take some action. For example, the Yellowstone wolf paper could have ended by urging readers to petition their legislator to support a bill on behalf of the wolves. The end of the research essay on Ben and Jerry's ice cream makes a subtle recommendation for the kind of business the writers hope will characterize the next century.

> Ben and Jerry's is a growing enterprise which shows promising signs of worldwide expansion, not only for its excellent ice cream, but for its responsibility as well. Through caring capitalism Ben and Jerry have gained the support of both environmentalists and the business community. We believe Ben and Jerry's provides a good model of corporate responsibility as America enters the twenty-first century.

Close by Completing a Frame

An effective way to end some papers is to return to the issue or situation with which you began — to frame the body of your paper with an opening and a closing that mirror each other. Keith's CD paper used as a frame a customer considering the cost of a CD. Judith uses a frame in her paper about personal safety, returning in the closing to the setting of the opening — her front door.

> Hours later--my paper started, my exam studied for, my eyes tired--I retrace the path to my apartment. It is dark now, and I listen closely when I hear footsteps behind, stepping to the sidewalk's edge to let a man walk briskly past. At my door, I again fumble for the now familiar key, insert it in the lock, open the door, turn on the hall light, and step inside. Here, too, I am safe, ready to eat, read a bit, and finish my reflective essay.

WRITING 2

Recast the closing of a current draft using one or more of the suggestions in this section: a summary, a logical conclusion, a real or a rhetorical question, a speculation, a recommendation, or the completion of a frame. In the final draft, use the closing that pleases you most.

FINDING THE TITLE

Finally, after revising and editing to your satisfaction, return to your title and ask, Does it work? You want to make sure it sets up the essay to follow in the best possible way, both catching readers' attention and providing a clue for the content to follow.

One good strategy for deciding on a title is to create a list of five or ten possibilities and then select the most suitable one. Play with words, arranging and rearranging them until they strike you as just right. Many writers spend a great deal of concentrated time on this task because titles are so important. Following are seven tips:

1. Use one good sentence from your paper that captures the essence of your subject.
2. Ask a question that your paper answers.
3. Use a strong sense word or image from your paper.
4. Locate a famous line or saying that relates to your paper.
5. Write a one-word title (a two-word, a three-word title, and so on).
6. Make a title from a gerund (an *-ing* word, such as *brainstorming*).
7. Make a title starting with the word *on* and the name of your topic.

When I was casting about for a title for this book, I happened to be riding my motorcycle late one chilly October night on the interstate highway between Binghamton and Albany, New York. I was cold and knew I had a good hour before arriving at my destination, so to distract myself from my discomfort I set about brainstorming titles and came up with "Writing to Discover" or "The Discovering Writer." As I thought about them, I decided to keep the word *writing* but to move away from *discover* toward *work*, and so played with "The Writer Working," "Working Writers," "The Writer at Work," "Work and the Writer." You know the result. Work hard to find the words that seem about right, and play with them until they form a construction that pleases you.

WRITING 3

Using some of the strategies described in this section, write five titles for a paper you are currently working on. For the final draft, use the title that pleases you most.

Chapter 27

Working Sentences

Teachers are always nitpicking about little things, but I think
writing is for communicating, not nitpicking. I mean, if you
can read it and it makes sense, what else do you want?

– OMAR

OMAR, EDITING IS ABOUT NITPICKING. It's about making your text read well, with the most possible sense. After the ideas are in order and well supported, your job is to polish the paragraphs, sentences, and individual words so that they shine. Then you correct to get rid of all the "nitpicky" errors in punctuation, spelling, and grammar. In other words, you attend to editing *after* your ideas are conceptually sound, carefully supported, skillfully organized, and fairly well aimed at your readers. (Even now, it doesn't hurt to review it once more to make sure it represents your voice and ideas in the best way possible.)

In editing sentences, as in editing paragraphs, there is no one best way to go about this work. You edit in such a way that you remain, as much as possible, in control of your text. (As you probably know by now, texts have a way of getting away from all of us at times. Editing is how we try to get control back!) At the same time you're wrestling for final control of a text for yourself, you're also anticipating reader needs. In this sense, sentence editing is your final balancing act, as you work to please yourself and your readers.

EDITING FOR CLARITY, STYLE, AND GRACE

To effect maximum communication, you should edit your sentences first for clarity, making sure each sentence clearly reflects your purpose. You also must edit to convey an appropriate style for the occasion, that is, the formality or informality of the language. And at perhaps the highest level, you must edit to convey grace — some sense that this text is not only clearly written, by you, but that it is also particularly well written — what we might call elegant or graceful.

While I can explain this loose hierarchy as if these several levels are easily distinguished, in fact, they are not, and they mix and overlap easily. For instance, in writing the chapters for this text I have tried to edit each chapter, paragraph, and sentence with all three goals in mind, demanding that all my language is clear, hoping that my style is friendly and that my sentences are also graceful — knowing that, in many cases, grace has proved beyond my reach. The remainder of this chapter will examine the fine tuning of words and phrases that make clear, stylistically appropriate, and sometimes graceful sentences.

WRITING 1

Reread a near-final draft of one of your papers, and draw a straight vertical line next to places where your text seems especially clear. Draw a wavy line next to passages where the style sounds especially like you. And put an asterisk next to any passages that you think are especially graceful. Exchange drafts with a classmate and see if you agree with each other's assessment.

THE WORK OF SENTENCES

Sentences are written in relation to other sentences, so most of our attention thus far has been on larger units of composition, from whole texts on down to individual paragraphs. This chapter focuses on strategies for strengthening sentences. In editing, you should first look at the effect of particular words within sentences, especially nouns, verbs, and modifiers. Second, you should consider the importance of rhythm and emphasis in whole sentences. And finally, you should learn to identify and avoid the common problems of wordiness, clichés, jargon, passive constructions, and biased language.

Write with Concrete Nouns

Nouns label or identify persons (*man, Gregory*), animals (*dog, golden retriever*), places (*city, Boston*), things (*book, The Working Writer*), or ideas (*conservation, Greater Yellowstone Coalition*). General nouns name general classes or categories of things (*man, dog, city*); concrete nouns refer to particular things (*Gregory, golden retriever, Boston*). Notice that concrete nouns (not just any dog, but a golden retriever) appeal more strongly to a reader's senses (I can see the dog!) than abstract nouns do and create a more vivid and lively reading experience.

Here is an example of a paragraph composed primarily of general nouns (underlined in the passage).

> Approaching the library I see lots of people and dogs milling about, but
> no subjects to write about. I'm tired from my walk and go inside.

When Judith described a similar scene for her essay on personal safety, she used specific nouns (which are underlined) to let us see her story sharply.

> Approaching the library, I see skateboarders and bikers weaving
> through students who talk in clusters on the library steps. A friendly
> black dog is tied to a bench watching for its master to return. Subjects
> to write about? Nothing strikes me as especially interesting and, be-
> sides, my heart is still pounding from the walk up the hill. I wipe my
> damp forehead and go inside.

Judith could have gone even further (writers always can) in using concrete nouns. She could have named the library, described some individual students, identified the dog, and described the bench. None of these modifications would have changed the essential meaning of the sentences, but each would have added a dimension of specific reality — one of the key ways writers convince readers that what they are writing about is true or really happened.

Write with Action Verbs

Action verbs *do* something in your sentences; they make something happen. *Walk, stride, run, jump, fly, hum, sing, sail, swim, lean, fall, stop, look, listen, sit, state, decide, choose,* and *conclude* — all these words and hundreds more are action verbs. Static verbs, in contrast, simply *appear* to describe how something *is* — like the verb *is* in this sentence. Action verbs, like concrete nouns, appeal to the senses, letting readers see, hear, touch, taste, or smell what is happening. They create more vivid images for readers, drawing them more deeply into the essay.

In the following passage, the conclusion to Judith's reflective essay, notice how action verbs (underlined) help you see clearly what is going on.

> Hours later--my paper started, my exam studied for, my eyes
> tired--I retrace the path to my apartment. It is dark now, and I listen
> closely when I hear footsteps behind, stepping to the sidewalk's edge to
> let a man walk briskly past. At my door, I again fumble for the now
> familiar key, insert it in the lock, open the door, turn on the hall light,
> and step inside. Here, too, I am safe, ready to eat, read a bit, and fin-
> ish my reflective essay.

Judith also uses several static verbs (*is, am*) in other places; these verbs describe necessary states of being, carrying a different kind of weight. When they are used among action verbs, they do good work. But the paragraph gets its life and strength from the verbs that show action.

Editing for action verbs is one of the chief ways to cut unneeded words, thus increasing readability and vitality. Whenever you find one of the following noun phrases (in the first column) consider substituting an action verb (in the second column):

reach a decision	decide
make a choice	choose
hold a meeting	meet
formulate a plan	plan
arrive at a conclusion	conclude
have a discussion	discuss
go for a run	run

Use Modifiers Carefully and Selectively

Well-chosen modifiers can make both nouns and verbs more concrete and appealing to readers' senses. Words that modify — describe, identify, or limit — nouns are called *adjectives* (*damp* forehead); words that amplify verbs are called *adverbs* (listen *closely*). Modifiers convey useful clarifying information and make sentences vivid and realistic.

In the previous example paragraph, Judith could have added several more modifiers to nouns such as *man* (*tall, thin, sinister*) and *door* (*red, heavy wooden*). And she could have used modifiers with verbs such as *retrace* (*wearily, slowly*) and *fumble* (*nervously, expectantly*). Judith's writing would not necessarily benefit by these additions, but they are further possibilities for her to examine as she edits her near-final sentences. Sometimes adding modifiers to sentences distracts from rather than enhances a paragraph's purpose. And that's what editing is all about: looking carefully, trying out new possibilities, settling for the effect that pleases you most.

Not all modifiers are created equal. Specific modifiers that add descriptive information about size, shape, color, texture, speed, and so on appeal to the senses and usually make writing more realistic and vivid. General modifiers such as the adjectives *pretty, beautiful, good, bad, ugly, young,* or *old* can weaken sentences by adding extra words that do not convey specific or vital information. And the adverbs *very, really,* and *truly* can have the same weakening effect because they provide no specific clarifying information.

WRITING 2

Review a near-final draft, and mark all concrete nouns (underline once), action verbs (underline twice), and modifiers (circle). Then place parentheses around the general nouns, static verbs, and general modifiers. Reconsider these words, and edit appropriately.

Find a Pleasing Rhythm

Rhythm is the pattern of sound sentences make when you read them out loud. Some rhythms sound natural — like a person in a conversation. Such sentences are easy to follow and understand and are usually pleasing to the ear. Others sound awkward and forced, make comprehension difficult, and offend the ear. It pays to read your sentences out loud and see if they sound like a real human being talking. To make sentence clusters sound better, use varied sentence patterns and parallel construction.

Varied sentence patterns make sentence clusters clear and enjoyable for readers. Judith effectively varied her sentences — some long, some short, some simple, some complex. For example, note the dramatic effect of following a lengthy compound sentence with a short simple sentence (made up of short words) to end the paragraph on page 353: "Nothing strikes me as especially interesting and, besides, my heart is still pounding from the walk up the hill. I wipe my damp forehead and go inside."

Parallelism, the repetition of a word or grammatical construction within a sentence, creates symmetry and balance, makes an idea easier to remember, and is pleasing to the ear. The following sentence from Brendan's essay demonstrates the pleasing rhythmic effect of parallel construction:

> A battle is being waged between environmental conservationists, <u>who</u> <u>support</u> the reintroduction of wolves, and sheep and cattle farmers and western hunters, <u>who oppose</u> it.

The parallelism is established by repetition of the word *who* plus a verb — and the verbs, opposite in meaning, provide additional dramatic effect.

In the following example, the repetition of the word *twice* establishes a rhythm and contributes as well to the writer's point about costs.

> A CD may <u>be twice</u> as expensive as a record, but the sound <u>is twice as</u> clear and the disc will last forever.

Place the Most Important Point Last

As in paragraphs so in sentences, the most emphatic place is last. You achieve the best effect by placing information that is contextual, introductory, or less essential earlier in the sentence and end with the idea you most want readers to remember. Sometimes you write first-draft sentences with emphatic endings, but often such emphasis needs to be edited in.

Notice the difference in emphasis in the following version of the same idea:

> Angel needs to start now if he wants to have an impact on his sister's life.

> If Angel wants to have an impact on his sister's life, he has to start now.

The second sentence is much more dramatic, emphasizing the need for action on Angel's part.

The next two sentences also illustrate the power of placing what you consider important at the end of the sentence:

> Becky stares at the floor and scrunches her face as if she were thinking hard.

> As if she is thinking hard, Becky stares at the floor and scrunches up her face.

The first sentence emphasizes Becky's concentration. To end with Becky's scrunching up her face diminishes the emphasis on her thinking.

In the following sentence, Judith uses end-of-sentence emphasis for a transitional purpose.

> I wipe my damp forehead and go inside.

The ending forecasts the next paragraph — in which Judith goes inside the library. To reverse the actions would emphasize the damp forehead instead of Judith's entrance into the library.

One more example from Judith's essay suggests how emphasis at the end can increase and then resolve suspense.

> It is dark now, and I listen closely when I hear footsteps behind, stepping to the sidewalk's edge to let a man walk briskly past.

At first we are alarmed that footsteps are coming up behind the writer — as Judith wants us to be. Then we are relieved that a man passes harmlessly by — as Judith also wants us to be. The end of the sentence relieves the tension and resolves the suspense.

WRITING 3

Examine the sentences in a recent draft for rhythm and end-of-sentence emphasis by reading the draft out loud, listening for awkward or weak spots. Edit for sentence variety and emphasis as necessary.

Edit Wordy Sentences

Cut out words that do not pull their weight or add meaning, rhythm, or emphasis. Sentences clogged with unnecessary words cause readers to lose interest, patience, and comprehension. Editing sentences for concrete nouns, action verbs, and well-chosen modifiers will help you weed out unnecessary words. Writing varied and emphatic sentences helps with this task too. Look at the following sentences, which all say essentially the same thing:

> In almost every situation that I can think of, with few exceptions, it will make good sense for you to look for as many places as possible to cut out needless, redundant, and repetitive words from the papers and reports, paragraphs and sentences you write for college assignments. [48 words]

> In most situations it makes good sense to cut out needless words from your college papers. [16 words]

> Whenever possible, omit needless words from your writing. [8 words]

> Omit needless words. [3 words]

The forty-eight-word-long first sentence is full of early-draft language; you can almost see the writer finding his or her way while writing. The sixteen-word sentence says much the same thing, with only one-third the number of words. Most of this editing simply cut out unnecessary words. Only at the end were several wordy phrases condensed: "from the papers and reports, paragraphs and sentences you write for college assignments" was reduced to "from your college papers."

That sixteen-word sentence was reduced by half by rephrasing and dropping the emphasis on college writing. And that sentence was whittled down by nearly two-thirds, to arrive at the core three-word sentence, "Omit needless words."

The first sentence was long-winded by any standard or in any context; each of the next three might serve well in different situations. Thus, when you edit to make language more concise, you need to think about the overall effect you intend to create. Sometimes the briefest construction is not the best one for your purpose. For example, the three-word sentence is more suited to a brief list than to a sentence of advice for this book. To fit the purposes of this book, in fact, I might write a fifth version on needless words, one including more of my own voice.

> I prefer to read carefully edited papers, where every word works purposefully and pretty much pulls its own weight. [19 words]

In this sentence, I chose to include *I* to emphasize my own preference as a teacher and reader and to add the qualifying phrase *pretty much* to impart a conversational tone to the sentence.

In the following example, one of Judith's effective paragraphs has been deliberately padded with extra words, some of which might have existed in earlier drafts.

> It is now several hours later, almost midnight, in fact. I have finally managed to get my paper started and probably overstudied for my exam. My eyes are very tired. I get up and leave my comfortable chair and walk out of the library, through the glass doors again, and retrace the path to my apartment. Since it is midnight, it is dark, and I nervously listen to footsteps coming up behind me. When they get too close for comfort, I step to the sidewalk's edge, scared out of my wits, to let a man walk briskly past. When I am finally at my door, I again fumble for the now familiar key, insert it in the lock, open the door, turn on the hall light, and step inside. Here, too, I am safe, ready to eat leftover pizza, study some more for my exam, and finish my reflective essay.

Now compare this with Judith's final version for simplicity, brevity, smoothness, and power.

> Hours later--my paper started, my exam studied for, my eyes tired--I retrace the path to my apartment. It is dark now, and I listen closely when I hear footsteps behind, stepping to the sidewalk's edge to let a man walk briskly past. At my door, I again fumble for the now familiar key, insert it in the lock, open the door, turn on the hall light, and step inside. Here, too, I am safe, ready to eat, read a bit, and finish my reflective essay.

The best test of whether words are pulling their own weight and providing rhythm, balance, and emphasis is to read the passage out loud and let your ear tell you what is sharp and clear and what could be sharper and clearer.

Edit Clichés

Clichés are phrases we've heard so often before that they no longer convey an original or individual thought. In the wordy paragraph above, the phrase "scared out of my wits" is a cliché. As you edit, note whether you remember hearing the same exact words before, especially more than once. If so, look for fresher language that is your own. Common clichés to avoid include the following:

> throwing the baby out with the bath water
>
> a needle in a haystack
>
> the last straw
>
> better late than never
>
> without further ado
>
> the handwriting on the wall
>
> tried and true
>
> last but not least
>
> lay the cards on the table
>
> jump start the economy
>
> winning isn't everything

Each of these phrases was once new and original and attracted attention when it was used; now when we read or hear these phrases, we pay them no conscious mind and may even note that the writer or speaker using them is not very thoughtful or original.

Edit Passive Constructions

A construction is passive when something is done to the subject rather than the subject's doing something. *The ball was hit by John* is passive. *John hit the ball* is active. Not only is the first sentence needlessly longer by two words, it takes readers a second or two longer to understand since it is a roundabout way to make an assertion. Writing that is larded up with such passive constructions lacks vitality and is tiresome to read.

Most of the example paragraphs in this book contain good examples of active constructions: *I retrace . . . I get up . . . Becky sits . . . Greg attributes . . . He said . . .*

Edit Biased Language

Your writing should not hurt people. As you edit, make sure your language doesn't discriminate against categories of people based on gender, race, ethnicity, or social class.

ELIMINATE SEXISM.   Language is sexist when it includes only one gender. The most common occurrence of sexist language is the use of the word *man* or *men* to stand for *human being* or *people* — which seems to omit *women* from participation in the species. Americans have been sensitized to the not-so-subtle bias against woman embedded in our use of language.

It is important to remember that many thoughtful and powerful English-language works from the past took masculine words for granted, using *man, men, he, him,* and *his* to stand for all members of the human race. Consider Thomas Jefferson's "All men are created equal" and Tom Paine's "These are the times that try men's souls." Today we would write "All people are created equal" or "These are the times that try our souls" — two of several possible fixes for this gender nearsightedness. When you read older texts, recognize that the composing rules were different then and the writers no more at fault than the culture in which they lived.

As you edit to avoid sexist language, you will notice that the English language does not have a gender-neutral third-person singular pronoun to match the gender-neutral third-person plural (*they, their, them*). We use *he* (*him, his*) for men and *she* (*her, hers*) for women. In the sentence, "Everybody has his own opinion," the indefinite pronoun *everybody* needs a singular pronoun to refer to it. While it is grammatically correct to say "Everybody has his own opinion," the sentence seems to exclude women. But it is grammatically incorrect to write "Everybody has *their* own opinion," although *their* is gender neutral. In editing, be alert to such constructions and consider several ways to fix them:

- Make the sentence a plural so it reads: "*People* have *their* own opinions."
- Include both pronouns: "Everybody has *his or her* own opinion."
- Eliminate the pronoun: "Everybody has *an* opinion."
- Alternate masculine and feminine pronouns throughout your sentences or paragraphs, using *she* in one paragraph and *he* in the next.

In my own writing, I have used all of these solutions at one time or another. The rule I most commonly follow is to use the strategy that makes for the clearest, most graceful writing.

AVOID STEREOTYPES.   Stereotypes lump individuals into oversimplified and usually negative categories based on race, ethnicity, class, gender, sexual preference, religion, or age. You know many of these terms. The kindest are perhaps "Get out of the way old man" and "Don't behave like a baby." I am willing to set these down in this book since we've all been babies and we're all growing older. The other terms offend me too much to write.

The mission of all institutions of higher learning is to teach you to read, write, speak, and think critically, which means treating each situation, case, problem, or person individually on its own merits and not prejudging it by rumor, innuendo, or hearsay unsupported by evidence or reason. To use stereotypes in academic writing will label you as someone who has yet to learn critical literacy. To write with stereotypes in any setting not only reveals your ignorance but hurts people.

Proofread

The last act of editing is proofreading, the process of reading your manuscript word for word to make sure it is correct in every way. Here are some tips to help you in this process:

- Proofread for typing and spelling errors first by using a spelling checker on your computer, if you have one. But be aware that computers will *not* catch certain errors, such as omitted words or mistyping (e.g., *if* for *of*). So you must also proofread the old-fashioned way — by reading slowly, line by line, word by word.
- Proofread for punctuation by reading your essay out loud and looking for places where your voice pauses, comes to a full stop, questions, or exclaims. Let your verbal inflections suggest appropriate punctuation (commas, periods, question marks, and exclamation points, respectively). Also review the punctuation reference at the end of this book, paying special attention to the use of commas, the most common source of punctuation errors.
- Proofread the work of others, and ask others to proofread for you. It's easy when reading your own writing to fill in missing words and read through small errors; you're much more likely to catch such errors in someone else's writing. We are all our own worst proofreaders; ask somebody you trust to help you.
- Proofread as a whole class: Tape final drafts on the wall, and roam the class with pencils reading one another's final drafts, for both pleasure and correctness.

WRITING 4

Examine a recent draft for wordiness, clichés, passive constructions, and biased language. Edit as necessary according to the suggestions in this section. Proofread before you hand in or publish the paper.

WRITER'S REFERENCES

Reference 1

Writing Portfolios

A WRITING PORTFOLIO IS SIMPLY a collection of your writing. It may be the writing you've done over a number of weeks, months, or even years. It may be a private folder that you keep for yourself, containing writing you think worth keeping, or it may contain work to share with another audience — an instructor, a prospective employer — to demonstrate the range or quality of your writing. A portfolio prepared for a writing class usually contains a cumulative record of your work over a semester and is used to assign a grade. A portfolio prepared for employment interviews may contain samples of your best work over several years, and it may help determine whether or not you are offered a job. While private portfolios can be whatever you want them to be, those for a wider audience need to be more carefully considered.

MAKE YOUR PORTFOLIO SPEAK FOR YOU. If your portfolio is neatly prepared, complete, and carefully organized, you will be judged accordingly. If it's unique, colorful, creative, and imaginative as well, all the better. But if you present a messy, incomplete, and haphazardly assembled portfolio, you will be judged on that basis. Before giving your portfolio to someone for evaluation, consider if it presents you in the best possible light, in the way you want to be presented.

INCLUDE WHAT IS ASKED FOR. If an instructor wants three finished papers and a dozen sample journal entries, your portfolio should contain those items, at a minimum. If an employer wants to see five samples of different kinds of writing, be sure to include those five samples. You may include more than asked for, but do not include less than asked for.

ADD SUPPLEMENTAL MATERIAL JUDICIOUSLY.   Portfolios are among the most flexible means of presenting yourself. If you believe that extra samples of writing will present you in a better light, include them, but only after the required material and accompanied by an explanation of why they are there. Include samples of journals, letters, sketches, or diagrams when they suggest interesting, relevant dimensions of your thinking.

MAKE YOUR FINAL DRAFTS PERFECT.   Or as close to perfect as you can manage. In your portfolio show that your own standard for finished work is high. Each final draft should be typed double-spaced, on one side only of high-quality paper; carefully proofread each one, and follow the style conventions required by a particular discipline or appropriate to the particular piece of writing, unless otherwise requested.

DEMONSTRATE EVOLUTION AND GROWTH.   Portfolios, unlike most other instruments of assessment, can demonstrate that you and your writing have matured over a certain span of time. The signal value of portfolios in writing classes is that they allow you to show your instructor how a finished product evolved. Instructors commonly ask for early drafts to be attached to final drafts, most recent on top — an order that shows how you followed revision suggestions, how many drafts you wrote, and how often you experimented. To create such a record of your work, date all drafts and keep them in a safe place.

DEMONSTRATE WORK IN PROGRESS.   Portfolios allow writers to present partially finished work to suggest future direction and intention. Both instructors and future employers may find such preliminary drafts or outlines as valuable as some of your finished work. When you include an unfinished draft, be sure to attach a note explaining why you have included it and where you plan to take it next.

INCLUDE A COVER LETTER AND TABLE OF CONTENTS.   A cover letter is your chance to introduce your portfolio: your rationale for putting it together, its organization, your criteria for selection, the evolution of the major works, and any items of special interest. For portfolios containing many samples of work, prepare a table of contents. For those containing only a few papers, you can embed your table of contents in the cover letter.

ATTEND TO THE MECHANICS OF THE PORTFOLIO.   Make sure the folder containing your writing is the kind specified and that it is clean and attractive. If you have no specifications, use a pocket folder, which is an inexpensive way to keep the contents organized and secure. Put your name and address on the outside cover. Organize the material inside as requested. And turn it in on time.

Reference 2

Publishing Your Writing

Iᴏ ʏᴏᴜ'ᴠᴇ ᴛᴀᴋᴇɴ ᴛɪᴍᴇ ᴛᴏ ᴄᴀʀᴇꜰᴜʟʟʏ ʀᴇᴠɪꜱᴇ ᴀɴᴅ ᴇᴅɪᴛ your writing, it's time to think about publishing it for the world.

- Publish it for your instructor, which you do, in fact, every time you hand in a final draft or submit a writing portfolio for review. Prepare your manuscript exactly as requested, keeping in mind that it stands in for you and will speak for you. If your writing is included in a portfolio, arrange the writing carefully and include everything your instructor asked for in the best final form possible.
- Publish it for your classmates in a student-edited anthology for the whole class to read at the end of the term. With your instructor's permission or help, ask classmates to each submit a best piece. Then get help with editing and designing a cover; and distribute your class anthology the last week of class.
- Publish your more interesting papers in the school newspaper, literary review, or English Department magazine to share your writing with a broader community than even your writing class. Whichever publication you submit to, study it carefully to see what kinds of papers it publishes, on what topics, and in what forms or genres. Notice the format it asks for and the deadlines it requires.
- Publish your writing for your family. Papers written about personal experience are especially appropriate to share with your parents, grandparents, brother, and sisters. Consider presenting your story in a nicely bound edition to your family as a holiday or birthday gift. In addition, many families have a relative who collects family

memorabilia and stories — perhaps your writing could be included in this collection.

- Publish selected pieces in local newspapers, especially if you have written research essays about local subjects or profiles of local people. Select those publications that seem to publish works similar to yours. Before mailing your manuscript, send a letter of inquiry, called a query letter, to the editor and ask about his or her interest in your topic. This will save you both some time: if the editor wants to see your piece, it will now be expected rather than arriving uninvited; the editor won't have to read a piece he or she has no interest in, and you won't write an article that has no chance of being published.

- Think also about sending your writing out into the larger world, to journals, magazines, and small presses that publish work of like subject or form to your own. Consult *Writer's Marketplace* or *The International Directory of Little Magazines and Small Presses* or ask your reference librarian for other listings. Again, match your subject, topic, and genre to the publication, and pay close attention to instructions for submitting manuscripts (usually found in the front of the publication).

Reference 3

Writing Essay Examinations

Essay examinations are common writing assignments in the humanities, but they are important in the social and physical sciences as well. Such exams require students to sit and compose responses to instructors' questions about information, issues, and ideas covered in the course. Instructors assign essay exams instead of "objective" tests (multiple choice, matching, true/false) because they want students to go beyond identifying facts and to demonstrate, in their own language, mastery of concepts covered in the course.

The best preparation for taking an essay exam is a thorough knowledge of the course subject matter. If you have attended all classes, done all assignments, and read all texts, you should be in good shape for such writing. If you have also kept journals, annotated textbooks, discussed course material with other students, and posed (and answered) possible essay exam questions, you should be in even better shape. Equally important is your strategic thinking about the course and its syllabus. If the course has been divided into different topics or themes, anticipate a general question on each one covered; if it has been arranged chronologically, expect questions focusing on comparisons or cause-and-effect relations within a particular period or across periods. Consider, too, the amount of class time spent on each topic or work, and pay proportionately greater attention to emphasized areas.

To score well on an essay examination, there is simply no substitute for careful preparation. However, using writing strategies will enhance your presentation of information in an exam. The following guidelines will help you write these high-pressure exams.

Before answering a single question, read over the whole exam to assess its scope and focus. Answering three of four questions in 50 minutes requires a different approach than answering, say, five of eight questions. If you have a choice, plan to answer those questions that provide a good demonstration of your knowledge of the whole course rather than those that might result in repetitious writing. Finally, decide which questions you are best prepared to answer, and respond to those first (but remember to budget your time to allow you to deal fully with the others later). Starting with the questions you know best warms you up intellectually and often triggers knowledge about the others in the process.

Understand the Requirements of Each Question

Once you decide which questions to answer, analyze each one carefully before you begin to write. Read the question two or three times, making sure you understand its scope and emphasis. Underline the direction words in the question, those that identify the task you are to carry out.

The direction *define* or *identify* asks for the distinguishing traits of a term, subject, or event but does not require an interpretation or judgment. In answering, use appropriate terminology learned in the course. For example, "Define John Locke's concept of *tabula rasa*" is best answered using some of Locke's own terminology along with your own.

Describe may ask for a physical description ("Describe a typical performance in ancient Greek theater"), or it may be used more loosely to request an explanation of a process, phenomenon, or event ("Describe the culture and practices of the mound builders"). Such questions generally do not ask for interpretation or judgment but require abundant details and examples.

Summarize asks for an overview or a synthesis of the main points. Keep in mind that "Summarize the impact of the Battle of Gettysburg on the future conduct of the war" asks only that you hit the highlights; avoid getting bogged down in too much detail. Focus on the main point — to summarize not the battle itself but its "impact . . . on the future conduct of the war."

Compare and contrast suggests that you point out both similarities and differences, generally between two subjects but sometimes among three or more. Other direction words may also ask for comparison or contrast: "Describe the differences between the paintings of Monet and Manet."

Analyze asks that you write about a subject in terms of its component parts. The subject may be concrete ("Analyze the typical seating plan of a symphony orchestra") or abstract ("Analyze the ethical ramifications of Kant's categorical imperative"). In general, your response should look at one part at a time.

Interpret asks for a definition or analysis of a subject based on internal evidence and your own viewpoint: "Interpret Flannery O'Connor's short story 'Revelation' in terms of your understanding of her central religious and moral themes."

Explain asks what causes something or how something operates. Such questions may ask for an interpretation and an evaluation. "Explain the function of color in the work of Picasso," for example, clearly asks for interpretation of the artist's use of color; although it does not explicitly ask for a judgment, some judgment might be appropriate.

Evaluate or *critique* asks for a judgment based on clearly articulated analysis and reasoning. "Evaluate Plato's concept of the ideal state" and "Critique the methodology of this experiment," for example, ask for your opinions on these topics. In responding to these kinds of questions, be analytical as you lead up to your judgmental verdict, and don't feel that your verdict must be completely one-sided. In many cases, you will want to cite more experienced judgments to back up your own.

Discuss or *comment on* is a general request that allows considerable latitude. Your answers to questions such as "Discuss the effects of monetarist economic theories on current third world development" often let you demonstrate what you know especially well. Use terms and ideas as they have been discussed in the course, and add your own insights with care and thoughtfulness.

Plan and Outline

Take one or two minutes per question to make a few notes and a quick outline of your answer. If asked, for example, to compare and contrast three impressionist painters, decide in advance which three you will write about and in what order. (And if asked to compare their treatment of nature, don't spend too much time on other areas of their work.) Granted, as you start writing, other ideas will come to you, and you should use those. But starting with an organizational plan often allows you to write more effectively: you can alert your instructor to your intention to discuss "three reasons" or "four main differences" and thereby suggest a broad command of the subject. An outline also allows you to plan to build up to your most important points rather than discussing them randomly.

Write with Specific Detail, Examples, and Illustrations

Remember, most good writing contains specific information that lets readers see for themselves the evidence for your position. Be prepared to use as many supportive specifics as you can; memorize them as you prepare for the exam so you can recall them accurately as needed. Dates, names, titles, and statistics alone may not be worth much, but when embedded as evidence in an essay that also contains strong reasoning, such specifics often make the difference between good and mediocre answers.

Provide Context

In answering a question posed by an instructor who is an expert in the field, you may be tempted to assume that your instructor does not need a full explanation and to answer too briefly. However, on an essay exam you are seldom being asked to teach your instructor something new, but rather to demonstrate how much *you* understand. Briefly explain any concepts or terms that are central to your answer. Take the time to fit any details into the larger scheme of the subject. View each question as an opportunity to show how much you know about the subject.

Use the Technical Terminology of the Discipline

Be careful not to drop in names or terms randomly, but if names and terms have been an integral part of your work in the course or if they provide supportive details or add context, use them in your answer. Make sure you define them, use them appropriately, and spell them correctly. Essay exams also test your facility with the language and concepts used in a particular discipline. For example, you should know that terms such as *perspective* and *foreground* have technical meanings in the visual arts but more general or metaphoric meanings in history.

Write to Persuade

No matter what the question asks, write as though you are trying to convince a skeptic. See your answer as a deliberate act of persuasion in which you need to marshal evidence to make your reader believe what you write. Even when responding to questions that ask you to describe, define, or discuss, formulate your answer to be as convincing as possible. At the same time, remember that there are few absolutes in the humanities and in some areas of the social and physical sciences — many situations and issues are not black or white. When you answer a question, alert your reader that you are aware of the gray areas. In fact, one of the marks of sophisticated learners is their understanding that every issue has two, if not more, sides to it. You need to be assertive and knowledgeable, but neither arrogant nor wishy-washy.

Budget Your Time

Ideally, you should allow yourself a few minutes at the end of the exam period to reread and proofread your answers. In reality, this is not always possible. If you find yourself running out of time, outline answers to questions you do not have time to finish; you may be given partial credit.

Other Strategies for Taking Essay Examinations

Below are some other conventions to remember when you are writing essay examinations.

1. Avoid the first person (*I, my*) unless asked otherwise or unless you need to make a personal distinction or judgment.

2. Start a new paragraph for each new point.
3. Spell, punctuate, and use grammar conventionally.
4. Write in complete sentences rather than fragments or phrases.
5. Underline titles of published works; use quotation marks for stories, poems, and chapters within works.
6. Double-space or print your answers if your handwriting is hard to read.
7. Skip several spaces between answers or start each answer on a new page.
8. Make any changes as neatly and legibly as possible.

Reference 4

A Brief Guide to Punctuation

THE FOLLOWING GUIDE EXPLAINS the most common uses of the most common punctuation marks. If you have further questions or need more detail, consult a grammar handbook or a dictionary.

Period Stops Sentences and Abbreviates Words

1. Use a period to end a sentence that is a statement, a mild command, or an indirect question.

   The administration has canceled classes.

   Do not attempt to drive to school this morning.

   We wondered who had canceled classes.

2. Use a period for certain abbreviations.

   Dr. Joan Sharp

   Ms. Amy Bowen

   6:30 A.M.

3. Do not use periods to abbreviate most words in formal writing or in acronyms.

   He made $200 per week [*not* wk.].

   He worked for the FBI [*not* F.B.I.].

Question Mark Ends a Direct Question and Indicates Uncertainty in Dates

1. Use a question mark to end a direct question.

   Where is Times Square?

   She asked, "What time is it?"

2. Use a question mark to indicate uncertainty in a date.

   The plays of Francis Beaumont (1584?–1616) were as popular as Shakespeare's plays.

Exclamation Point Ends an Emphatic or Emotional Sentence

1. Use an exclamation point to end a sentence that is emphatic or conveys strong emotion.

   What a mess!

   "Ouch! That hurts !" he screamed.

Comma Alerts Readers to Brief Pauses within Sentences

1. Use a comma before a coordinating conjunction joining independent clauses.

   We must act quickly, or the problem will continue.

2. Use a comma after an introductory element.

   After we attend class, we'll eat lunch.

   Whistling, he waited for his train.

3. Use a comma around nonrestrictive modifiers (modifiers that are not essential to the meaning of the sentence).

   Cats, which are nocturnal animals, hunt small rodents.

4. Use a comma between items in a series.

   He studied all of the notes, memos, letters, and reports.

5. Use a comma to set off parenthetical elements or transitional expressions.

   Surprisingly enough, none of the bicycles was stolen.

6. Use a comma to set off attributory words with direct quotations.

   "Time will prove us right," he said.

7. Use a comma with numbers, dates, titles with names, and addresses.

    The sign gave the city's population as 79,087.

    She was born on June 19, 1976.

    Joyce B. Wong, M.D., supervised the CPR training.

    His new address is 169 Elm Street, Boston, Massachusetts 02116.

Semicolon Joins Independent Clauses and Connects Items in a Complex Series

1. Use a semicolon between independent clauses not joined with a coordinating conjunction.

    The storm raged all night; most of us slept fitfully, if at all.

2. Use semicolons between items in a series that contain internal commas.

    The candidates for the award are Maria, who won the essay competition; Elaine, the top debater; and Shelby, who directed several student productions.

Colon Introduces Lists, Summaries, and Quotations, and Separates Titles and Subtitles

1. Use a colon to introduce a list.

    Writers need three conditions to write well: time, ownership, and response.

2. Use a colon before a summary or explanation.

    He had only one goal left: to win the race.

3. Use a colon to formally introduce a quotation in text or to introduce a long indented quotation.

    He quoted Puck's final lines from *A Midsummer Night's Dream*: "Give me your hands, if we be friends, / And Robin shall restore amends."

4. Use a colon to separate a title and subtitle.

    Blue Highways: A Journey into America

Apostrophe Indicates Possession, Forms Certain Plurals, Forms Contractions

1. Use an apostrophe to indicate possession in a noun or indefinite pronoun.

Jack's brother

anyone's guess

2. Use an apostrophe to form the plural of a word used as a word and the plural of letters.

She wouldn't accept any *if*'s, *and*'s, or *but*'s.

The word *occurrence* is spelled with two *r*'s.

3. Use an apostrophe to replace missing letters in contractions.

I can't means I won't.

Quotation Mark Indicates Direct Quotations and Certain Titles

1. Use quotation marks around words quoted directly from a written or spoken source.

She said, "It really doesn't matter anymore."

Who wrote, "Fourscore and seven years ago"?

2. Use quotation marks for titles of stories, short poems, book chapters, magazine articles, and songs.

"Barn Burning" (short story)

"To an Athlete Dying Young" (poem)

"Finding Your Voice" (book chapter)

"Symbolism in Shakespeare's Tragedies" (magazine article)

"A Day in the Life" (song)

3. Place periods and commas inside closed quotation marks. Place semicolons and colons outside closed quotation marks. Place question marks and exclamation points inside or outside quotation marks depending on the meaning of the sentence.

After Gina finished singing "Memories," Joe began to hum "The Way We Were."

The sign read "Closed": there would be no cold soda for us today.

"Would you like some fruit?" Phil asked.

I can't believe you've never read "The Lottery"!

Parentheses Enclose Nonessential or Digressive but Useful Information

1. Use parentheses to enclose nonessential information: explanations, examples, asides.

In 1929 (the year the stock market crashed) he proposed to his first wife.

He graduated with high honors (or so he said) and found a job immediately.

Dashes **Enclose Nonessential Information and Indicate Abrupt Changes of Direction**

1. Use dashes to enclose nonessential information and to indicate contrast or a pause or change of direction.

    At first we did not notice the rain -- it began so softly -- but soon we were soaked.

    Nothing is as exciting as seeing an eagle -- except maybe seeing two eagles.

Ellipsis Points **Indicate the Omission of Words in a Direct Quotation**

1. Use ellipsis points (three dots) to indicate where you have omitted words in a direct quotation from a written or spoken source.

    "We the People of the United States, in Order to form a more perfect Union . . . do ordain and establish this Constitution for the United States of America."

Brackets **Indicate Changes to or Comments on a Direct Quotation**

1. Use brackets when you make changes to or comments on a direct quotation.

    E. B. White describes a sparrow on a spring day: "Any noon, in Madison Square [in New York City], you may see one pick up a straw in his beak."

Index